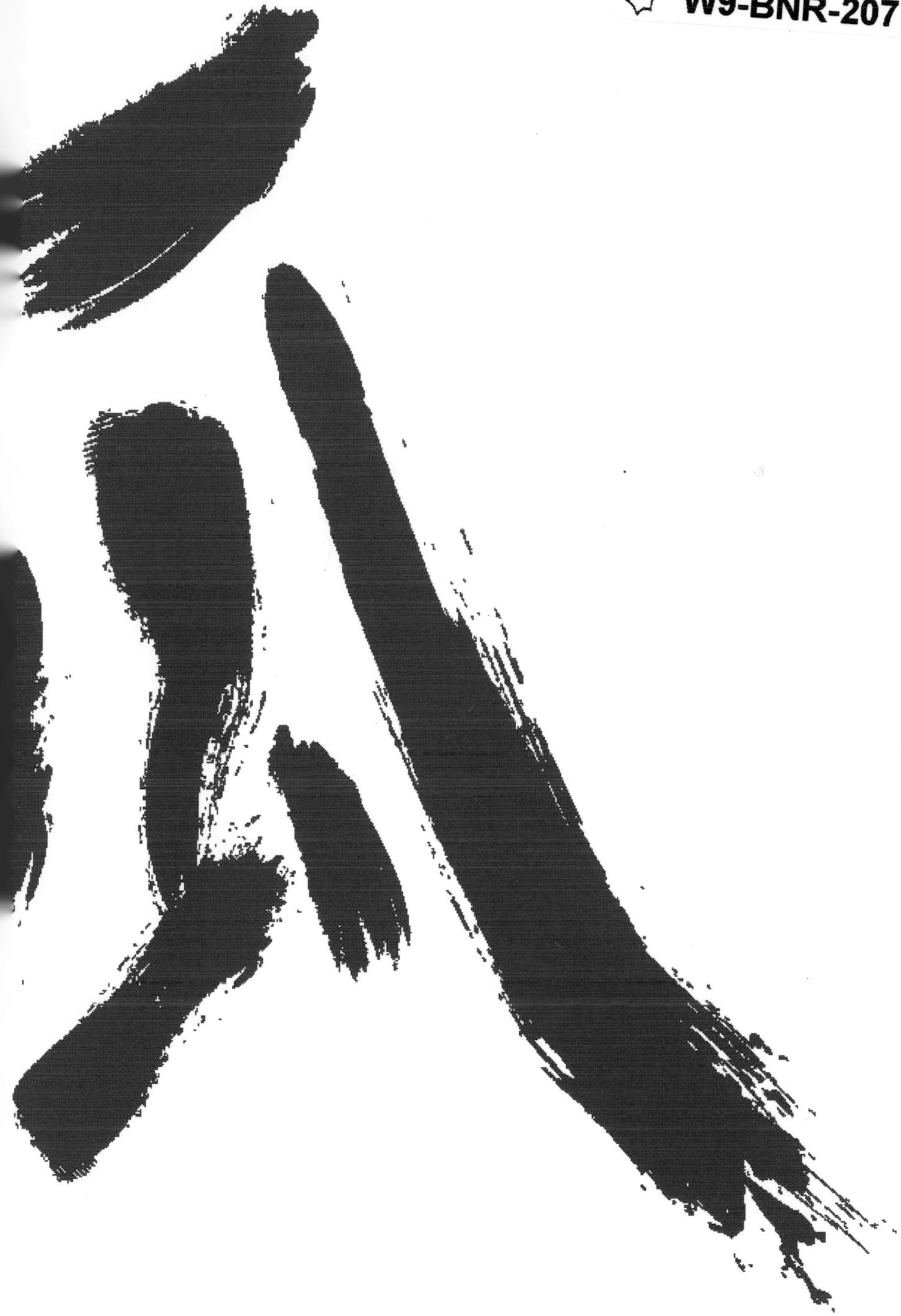

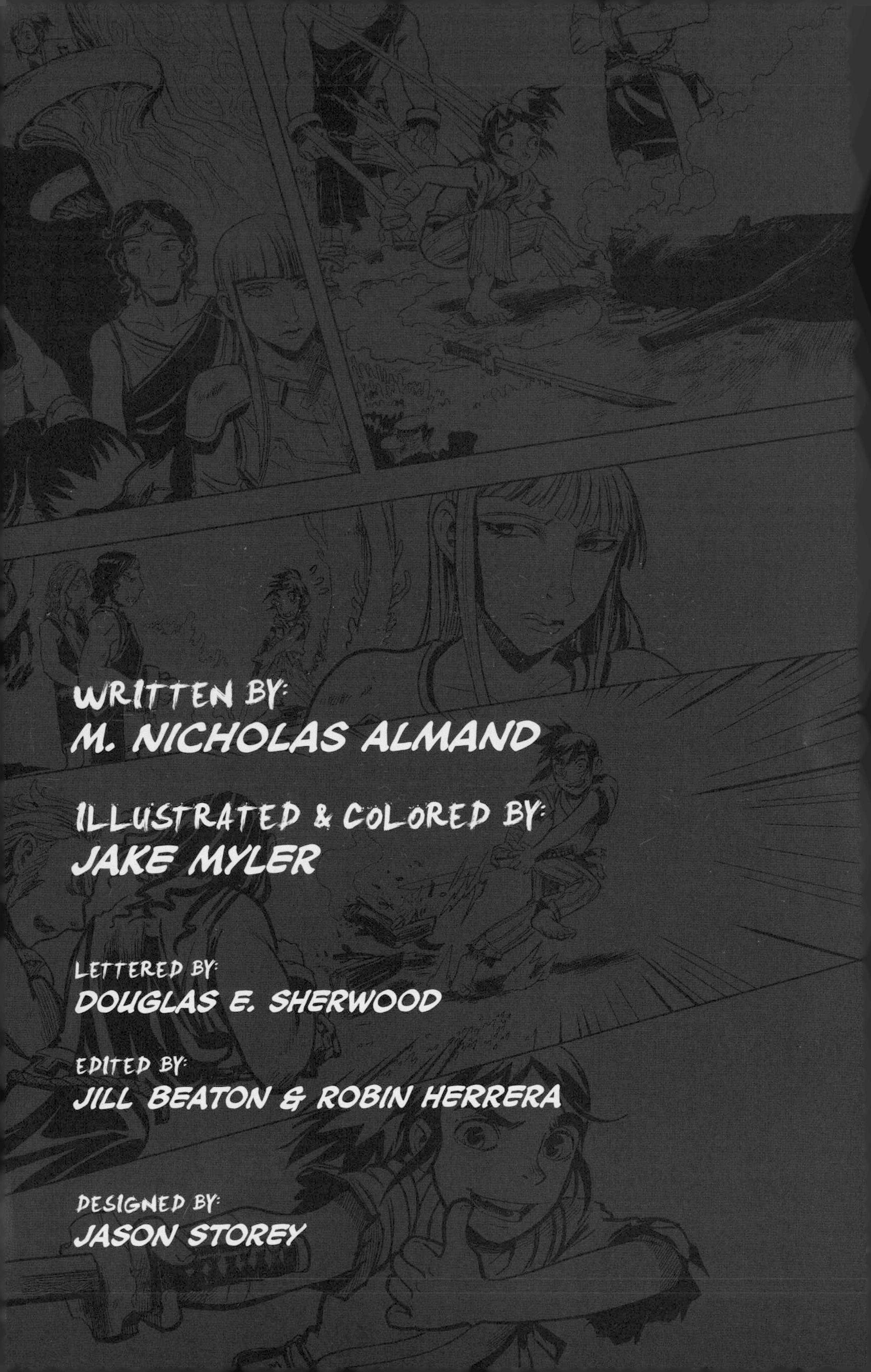

WRITTEN BY:
M. NICHOLAS ALMAND

ILLUSTRATED & COLORED BY:
JAKE MYLER

LETTERED BY:
DOUGLAS E. SHERWOOD

EDITED BY:
JILL BEATON & ROBIN HERRERA

DESIGNED BY:
JASON STOREY

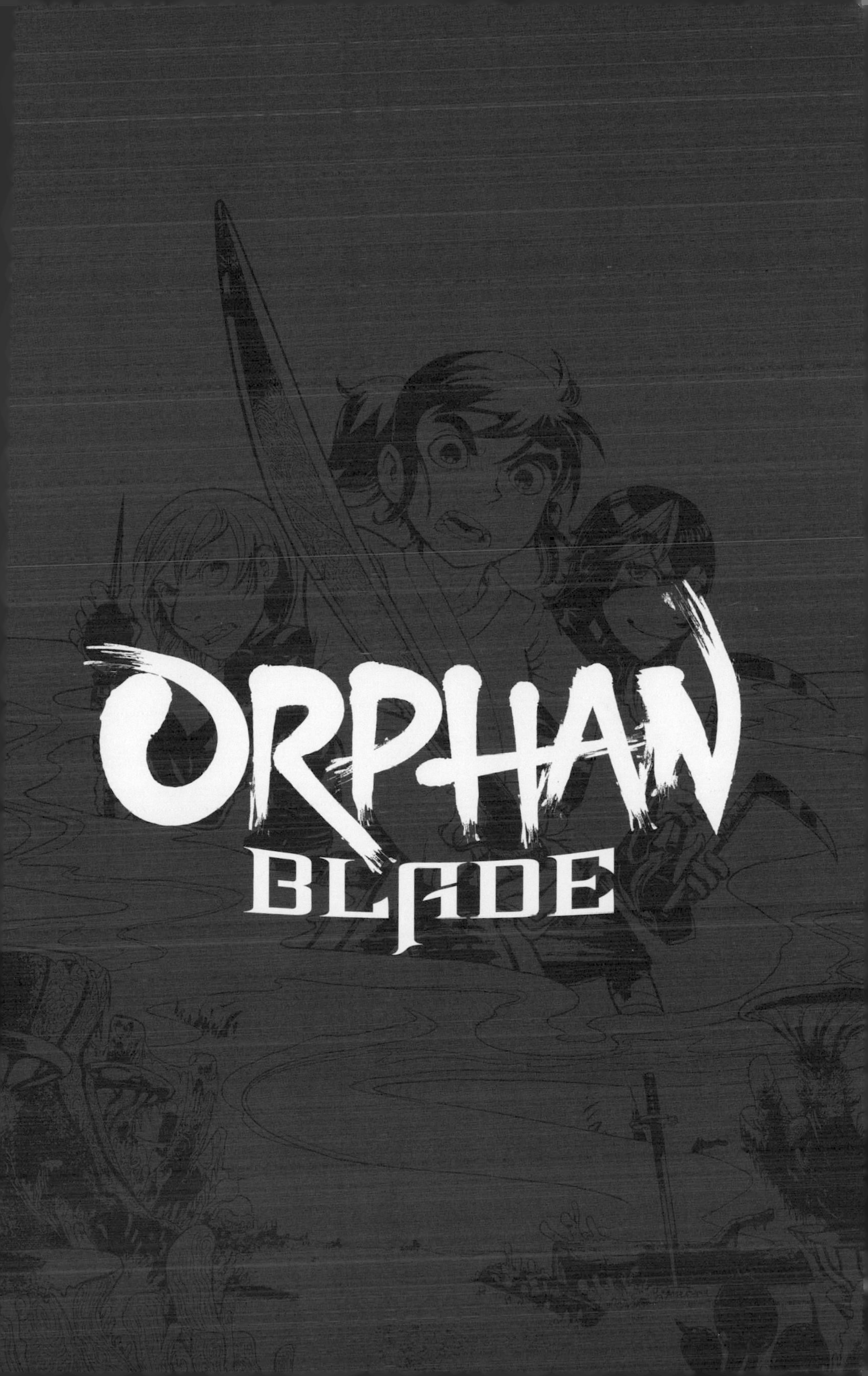
ORPHAN
BLADE

PUBLISHED BY ONI PRESS, INC.

JOE NOZEMACK, PUBLISHER
JAMES LUCAS JONES, EDITOR IN CHIEF
TIM WIESCH, VP OF BUSINESS DEVELOPMENT
CHEYENNE ALLOTT, DIRECTOR OF SALES
JOHN SCHORK, DIRECTOR OF PUBLICITY
CHARLIE CHU, EDITOR
ROBIN HERRERA, ASSOCIATE EDITOR
TROY LOOK, PRODUCTION MANAGER
JASON STOREY, SENIOR DESIGNER
ARI YARWOOD, ADMINISTRATIVE ASSISTANT
BRAD ROOKS, INVENTORY COORDINATOR
JUNG LEE, OFFICE ASSISTANT
JARED JONES, PRODUCTION ASSISTANT

ONI PRESS, INC.
1305 SE MARTIN LUTHER KING JR. BLVD
SUITE A
PORTLAND, OR 97214

ONIPRESS.COM
FACEBOOK.COM/ONIPRESS
TWITTER.COM/ONIPRESS
ONIPRESS.TUMBLR.COM

JAKEMYLER.COM / @LAZESUMMERSTONE

FIRST EDITION: DECEMBER 2014

ISBN 978-1-62010-120-9 / EISBN 978-1-62010-150-6

ORPHAN BLADE, DECEMBER 2014. PUBLISHED BY ONI PRESS, INC. 1305 SE MARTIN
LUTHER KING JR. BLVD., SUITE A, PORTLAND, OR 97214. ORPHAN BLADE IS ™ & © 2014 M.
NICHOLAS ALMAND. ALL RIGHTS RESERVED. ONI PRESS LOGO AND ICON ™ & © 2014 ONI
PRESS, INC. ALL RIGHTS RESERVED. ONI PRESS LOGO AND ICON ARTWORK CREATED BY
KEITH A. WOOD. THE EVENTS, INSTITUTIONS, AND CHARACTERS PRESENTED IN THIS BOOK
ARE FICTIONAL. ANY RESEMBLANCE TO ACTUAL PERSONS, LIVING OR DEAD, IS PURELY
COINCIDENTAL. NO PORTION OF THIS PUBLICATION MAY BE REPRODUCED, BY ANY MEANS,
WITHOUT THE EXPRESS WRITTEN PERMISSION OF THE COPYRIGHT HOLDERS.

LIBRARY OF CONGRESS CONTROL NUMBER: 2014938499

10 9 8 7 6 5 4 3 2 1

PRINTED IN CHINA

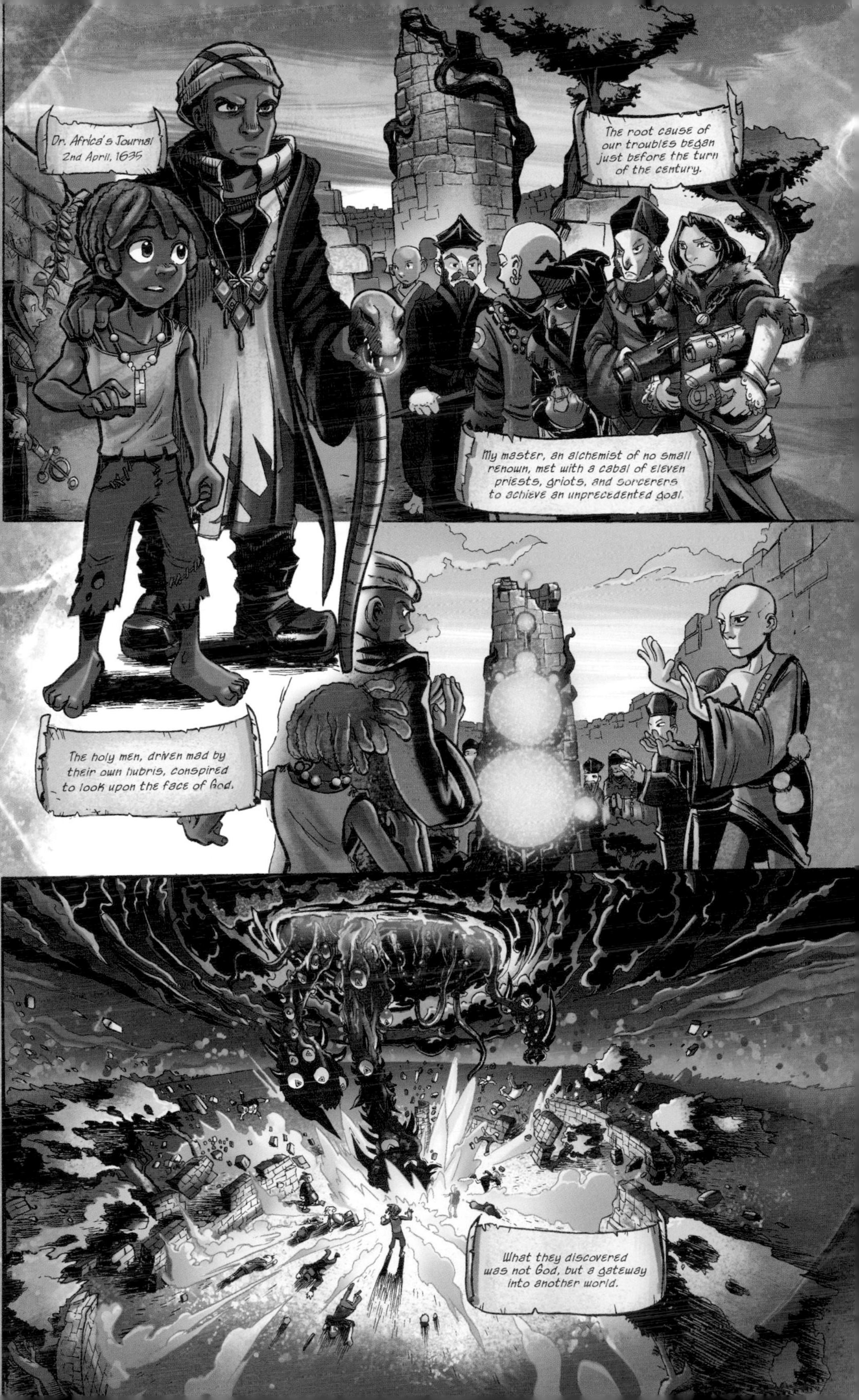
Dr. Africa's Journal
2nd April, 1635
The root cause of our troubles began just before the turn of the century.
My master, an alchemist of no small renown, met with a cabal of eleven priests, griots, and sorcerers to achieve an unprecedented goal.
The holy men, driven mad by their own hubris, conspired to look upon the face of God.
What they discovered was not God, but a gateway into another world.

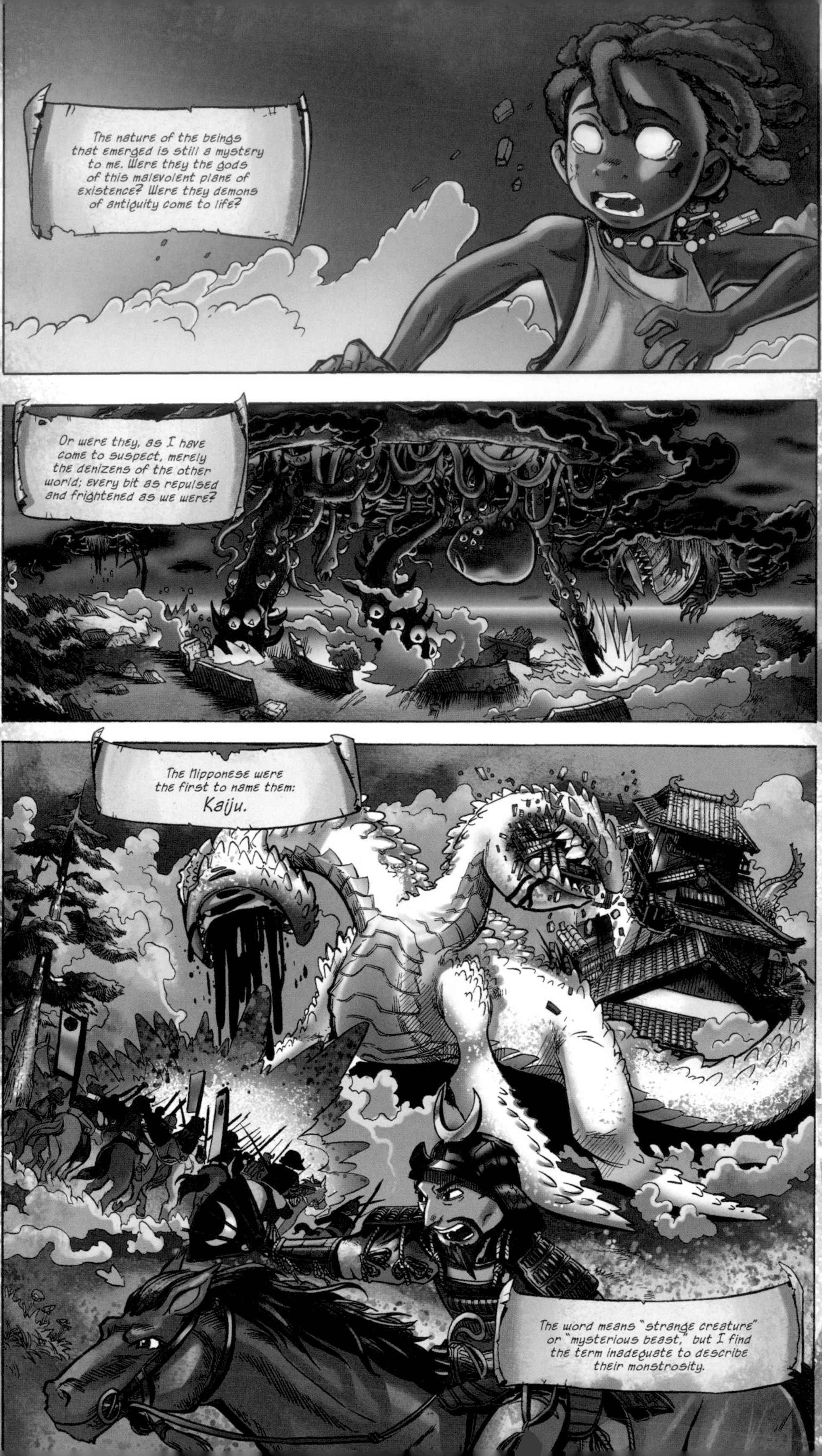

The nature of the beings that emerged is still a mystery to me. Were they the gods of this malevolent plane of existence? Were they demons of antiquity come to life?
Or were they, as I have come to suspect, merely the denizens of the other world; every bit as repulsed and frightened as we were?
The Nipponese were the first to name them:
Kaiju.
The word means "strange creature" or "mysterious beast," but I find the term inadequate to describe their monstrosity.

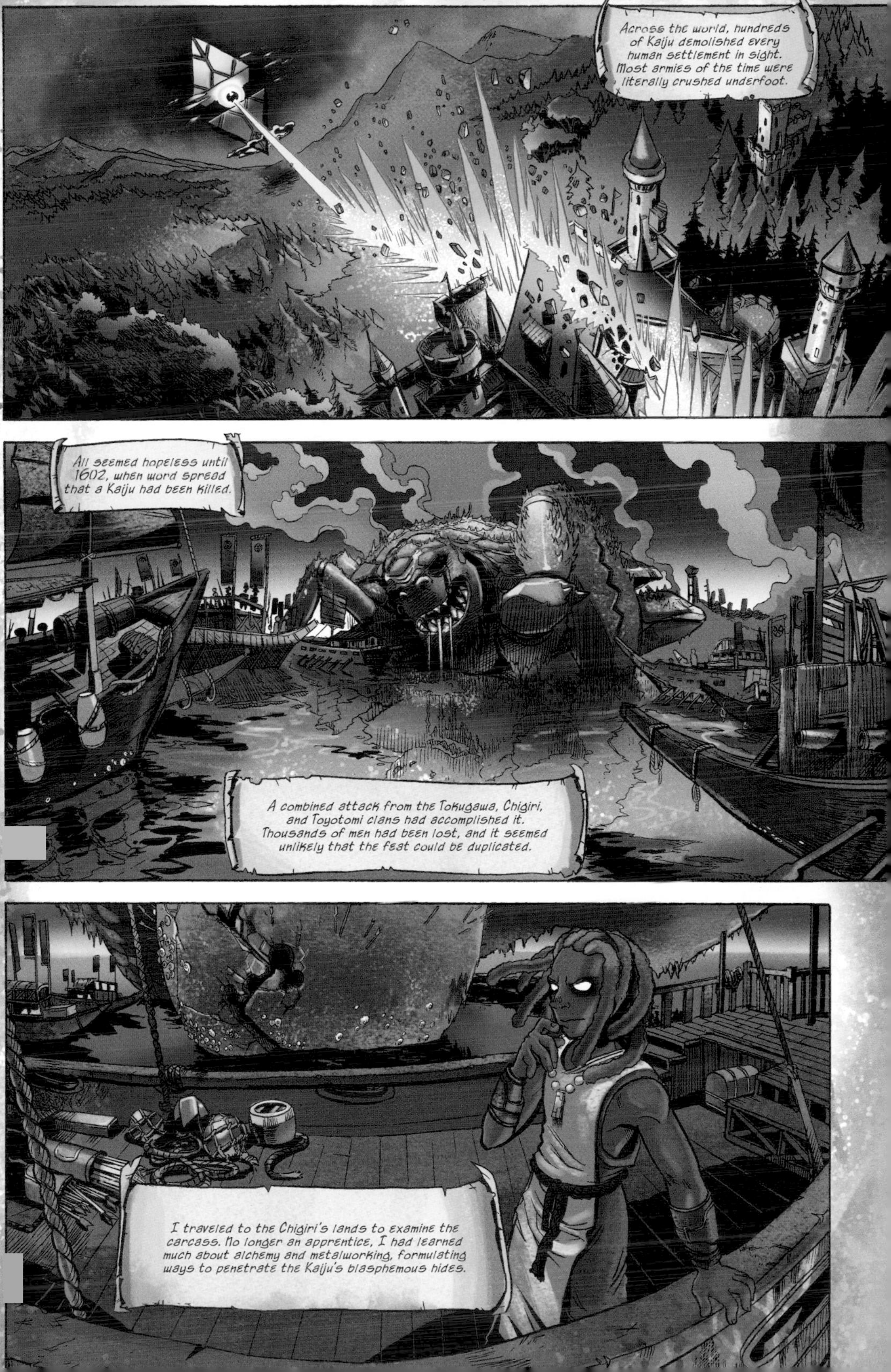
Across the world, hundreds of Kaiju demolished every human settlement in sight. Most armies of the time were literally crushed underfoot.
All seemed hopeless until 1602, when word spread that a Kaiju had been killed.
A combined attack from the Tokugawa, Chigiri, and Toyotomi clans had accomplished it. Thousands of men had been lost, and it seemed unlikely that the feat could be duplicated.
I traveled to the Chigiri's lands to examine the carcass. No longer an apprentice, I had learned much about alchemy and metalworking, formulating ways to penetrate the Kaiju's blasphemous hides.

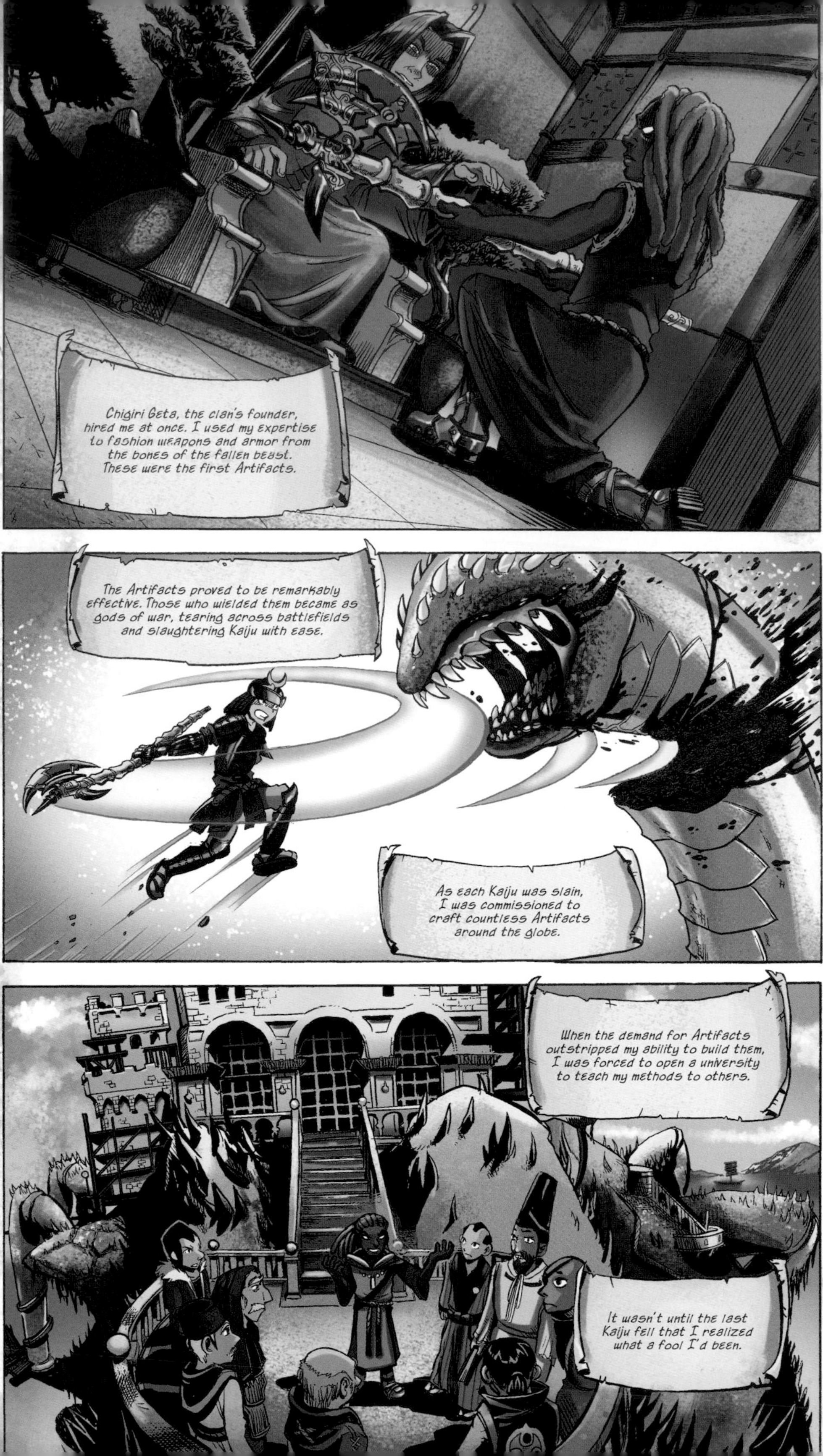
Chigiri Geta, the clan's founder, hired me at once. I used my expertise to fashion weapons and armor from the bones of the fallen beast. These were the first Artifacts.
The Artifacts proved to be remarkably effective. Those who wielded them became as gods of war, tearing across battlefields and slaughtering Kaiju with ease.
As each Kaiju was slain, I was commissioned to craft countless Artifacts around the globe.
When the demand for Artifacts outstripped my ability to build them, I was forced to open a university to teach my methods to others.
It wasn't until the last Kaiju fell that I realized what a fool I'd been.

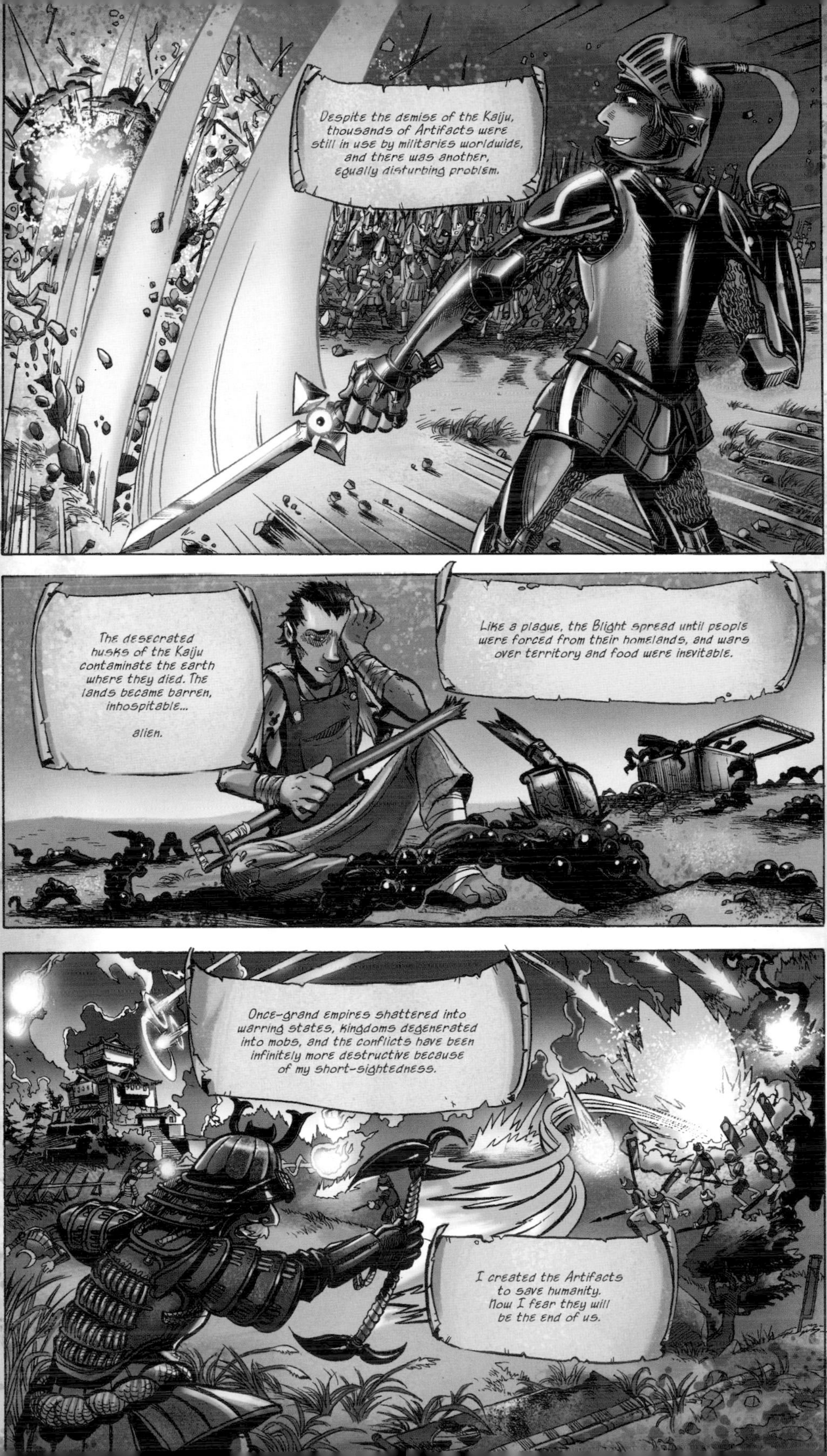
Despite the demise of the Kaiju, thousands of Artifacts were still in use by militaries worldwide, and there was another, equally disturbing problem.
The desecrated husks of the Kaiju contaminate the earth where they died. The lands became barren, inhospitable...
alien.
Like a plague, the Blight spread until people were forced from their homelands, and wars over territory and food were inevitable.
Once-grand empires shattered into warring states, kingdoms degenerated into mobs, and the conflicts have been infinitely more destructive because of my short-sightedness.
I created the Artifacts to save humanity. Now I fear they will be the end of us.

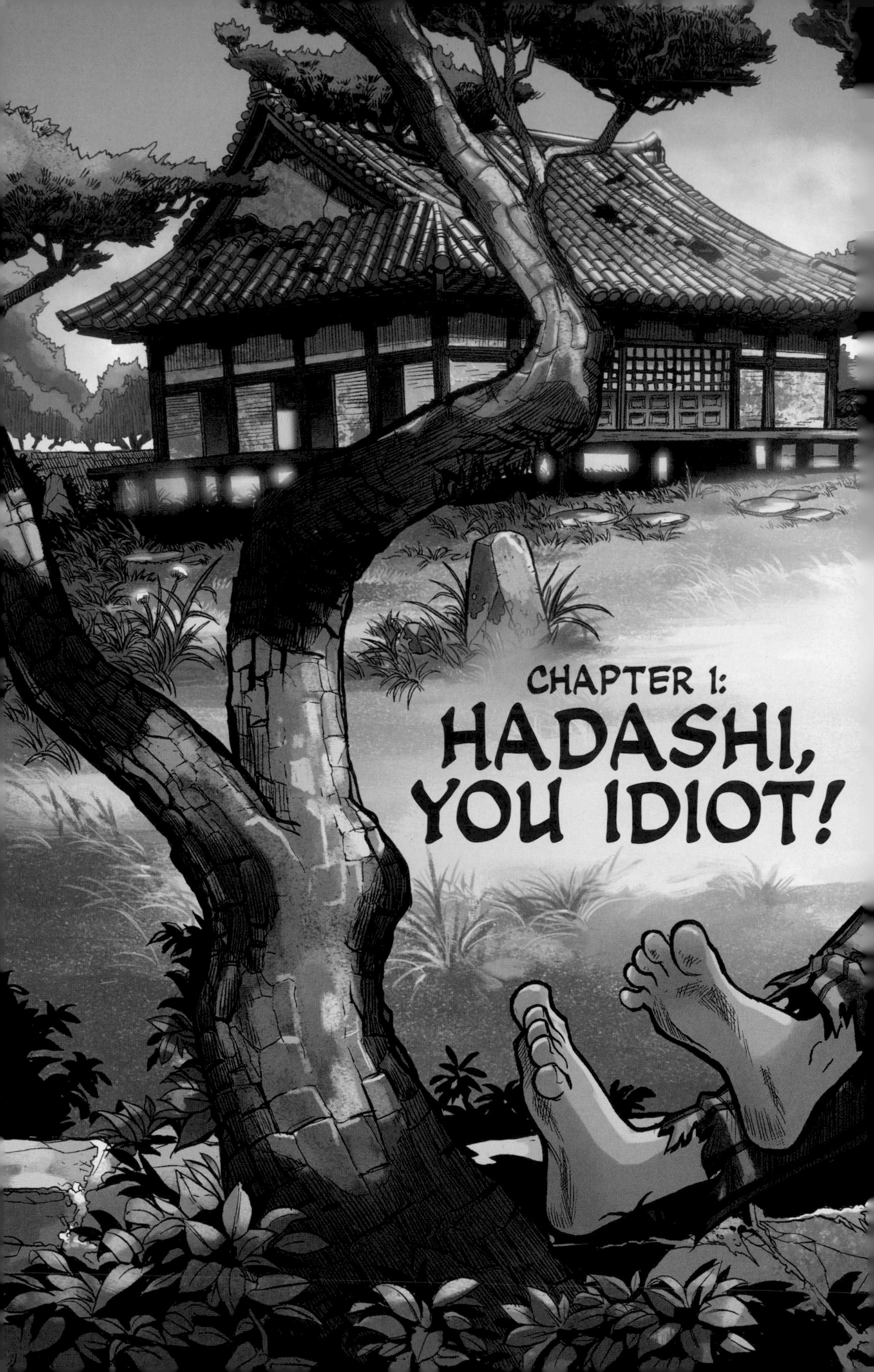
CHAPTER 1:
HADASHI, YOU IDIOT!

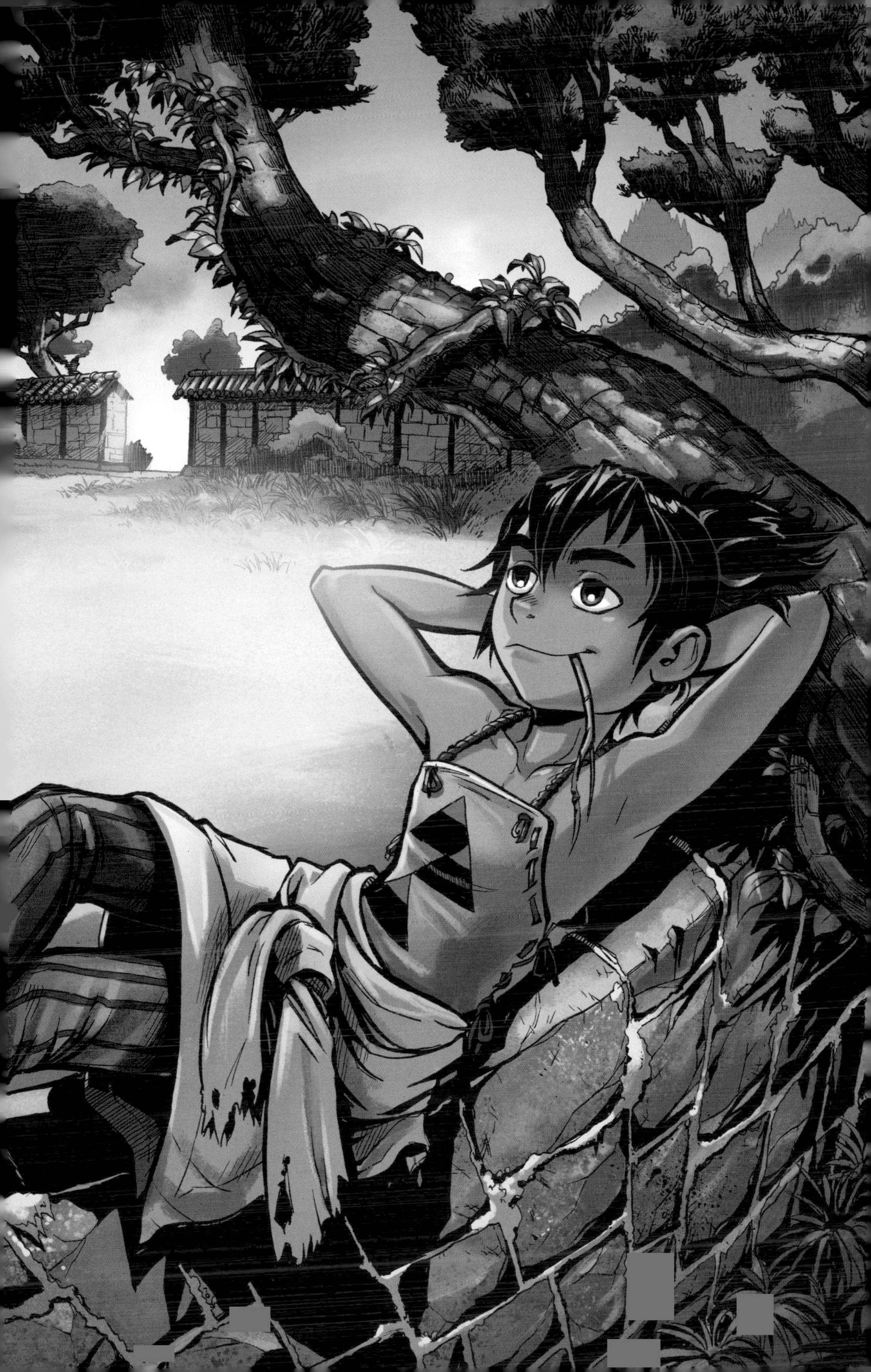

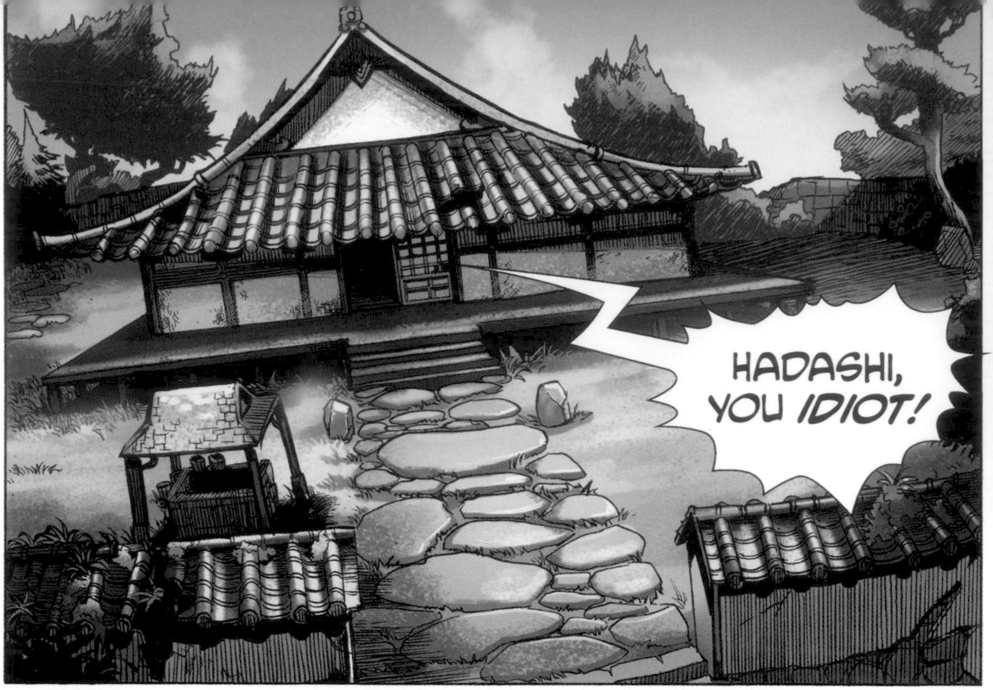
HADASHI, YOU *IDIOT!*

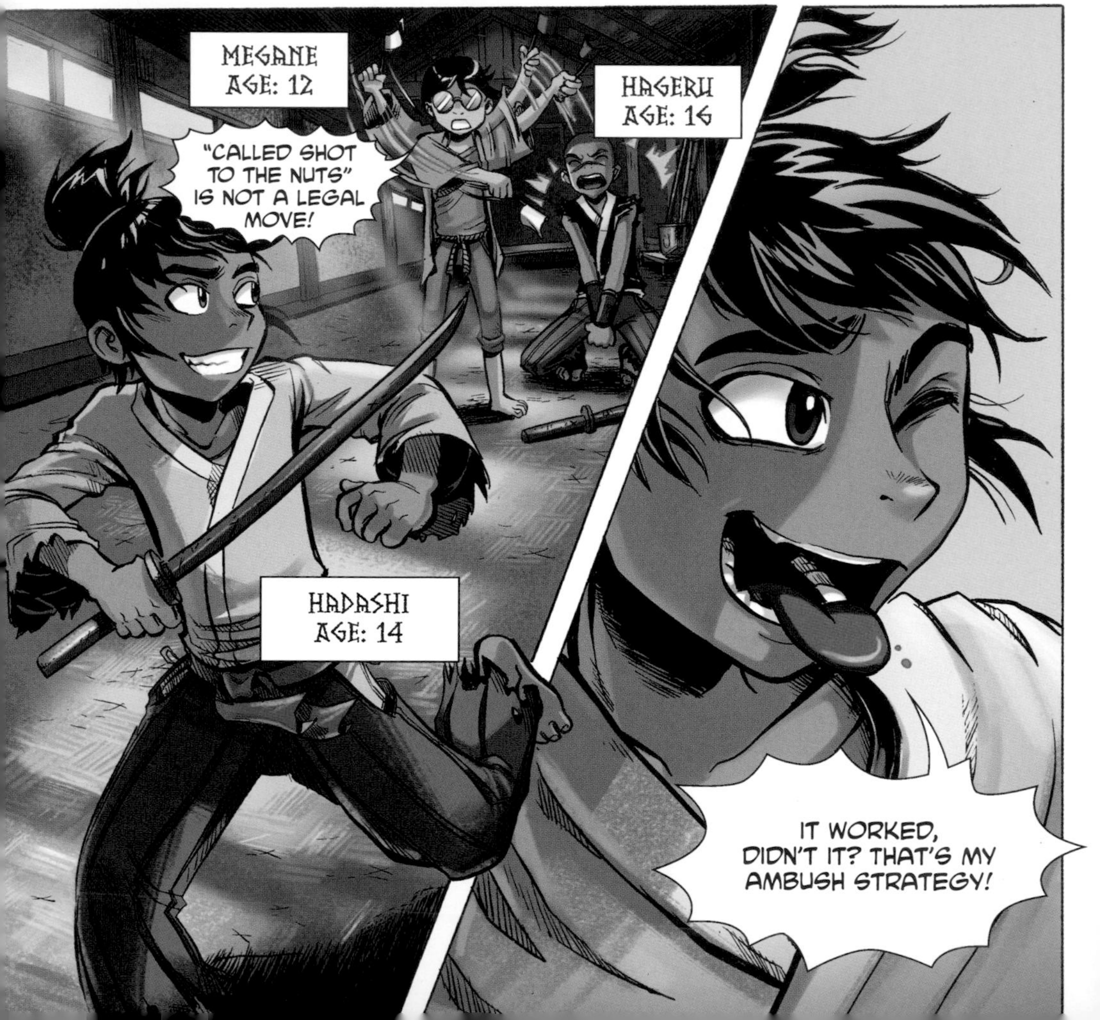
MEGANE
AGE: 12
HAGERU
AGE: 16
"CALLED SHOT TO THE NUTS" IS NOT A LEGAL MOVE!
HADASHI
AGE: 14
IT WORKED, DIDN'T IT? THAT'S MY AMBUSH STRATEGY!

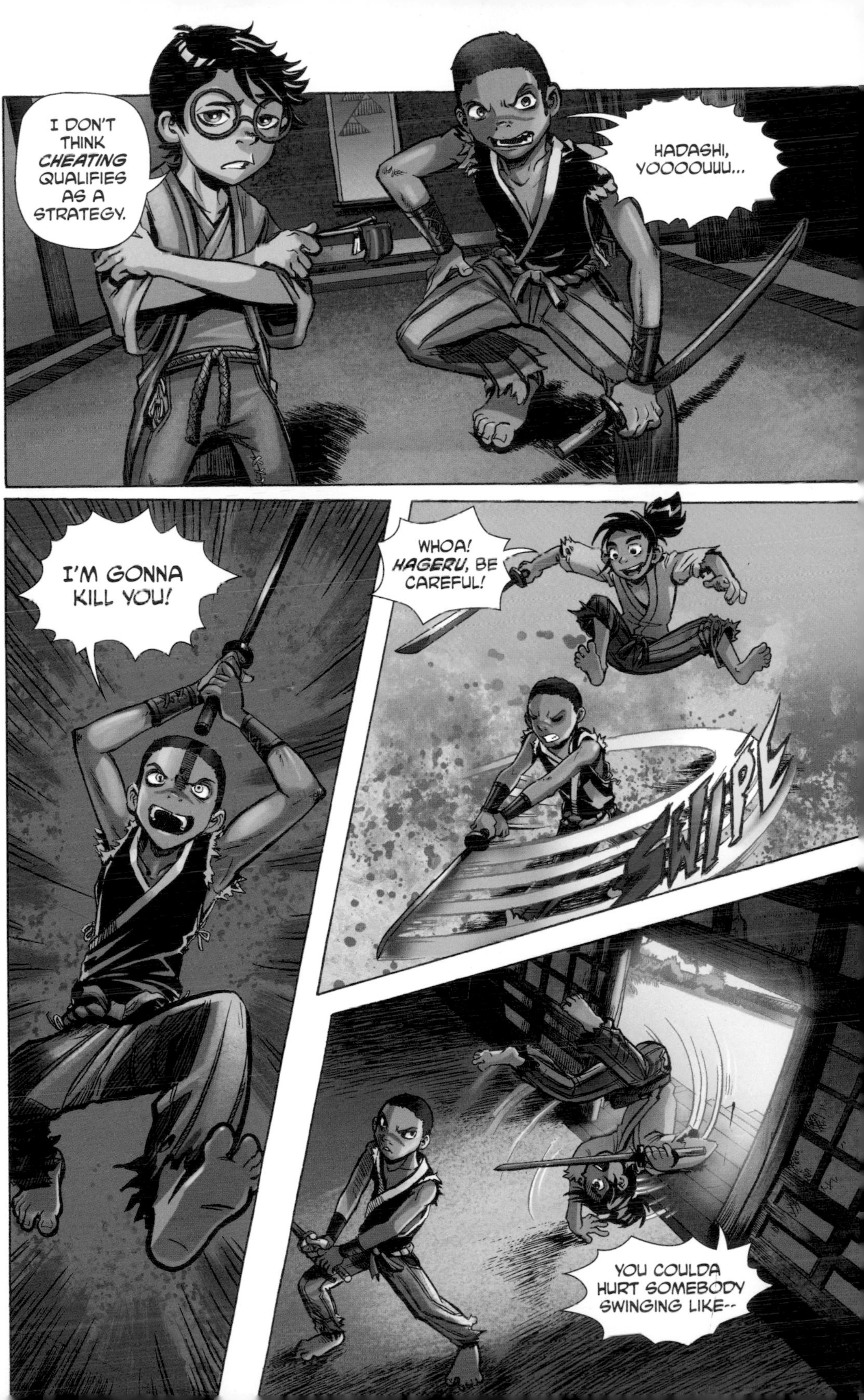
I DON'T THINK *CHEATING* QUALIFIES AS A STRATEGY.
HADASHI, YOOOOUUU...
I'M GONNA KILL YOU!
WHOA! *HAGERU*, BE CAREFUL!
SWIPE
YOU COULDA HURT SOMEBODY SWINGING LIKE--

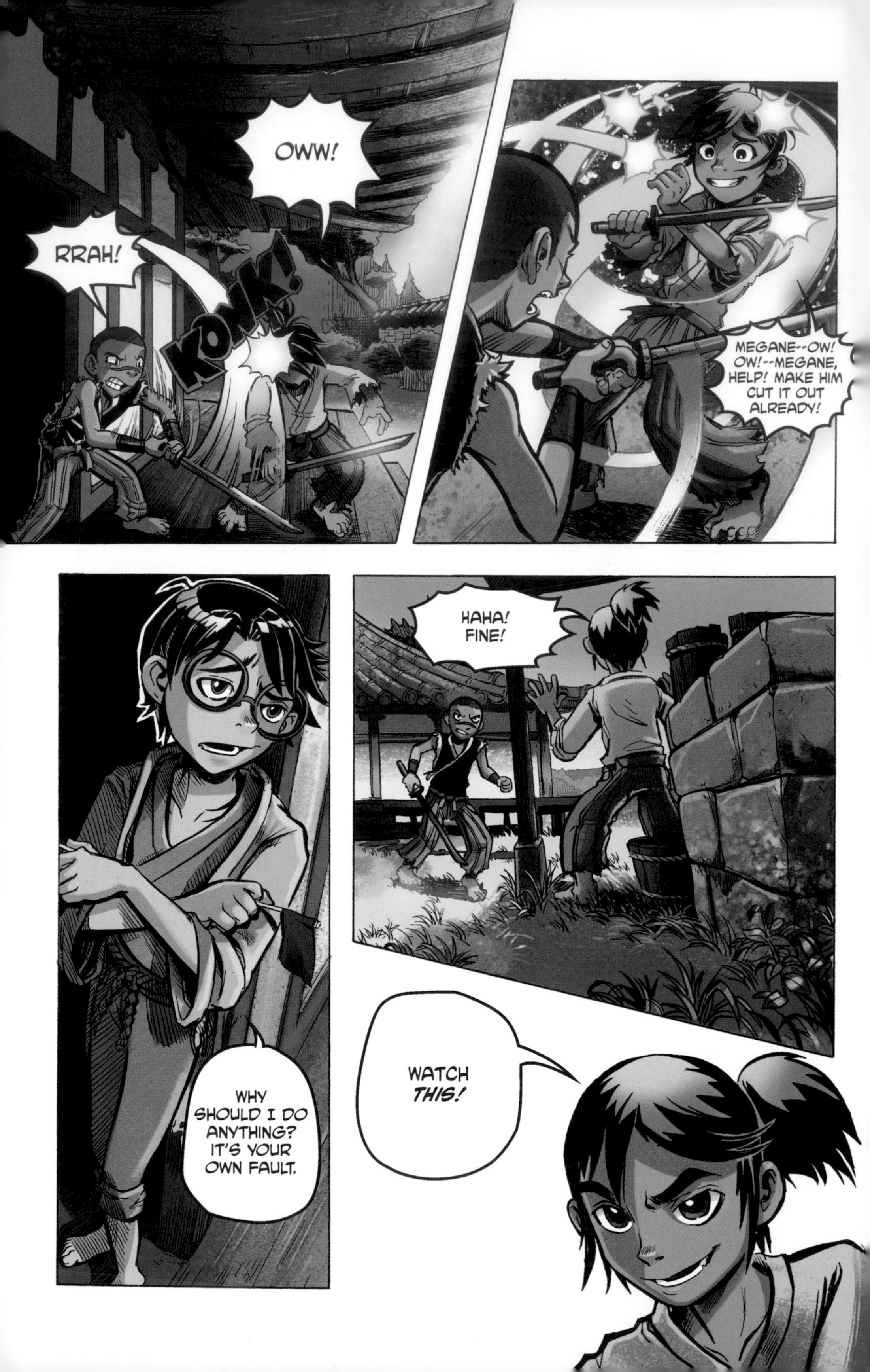
RRAH!
KONK!
OWW!
MEGANE--OW! OW!--MEGANE, HELP! MAKE HIM CUT IT OUT ALREADY!
WHY SHOULD I DO ANYTHING? IT'S YOUR OWN FAULT.
HAHA! FINE!
WATCH *THIS!*

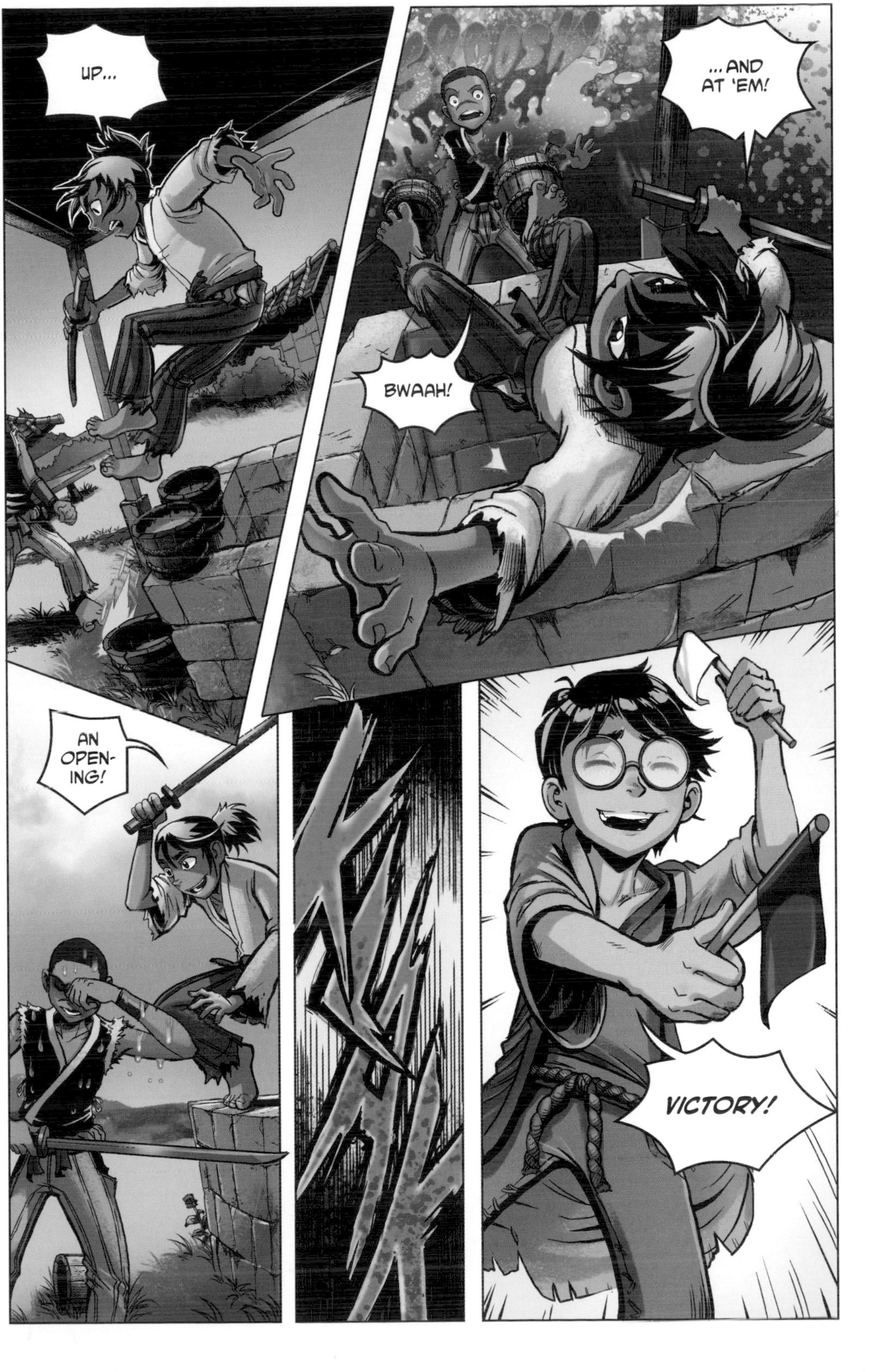
UP...
...AND AT 'EM!
BWAAH!
AN OPEN-ING!
VICTORY!

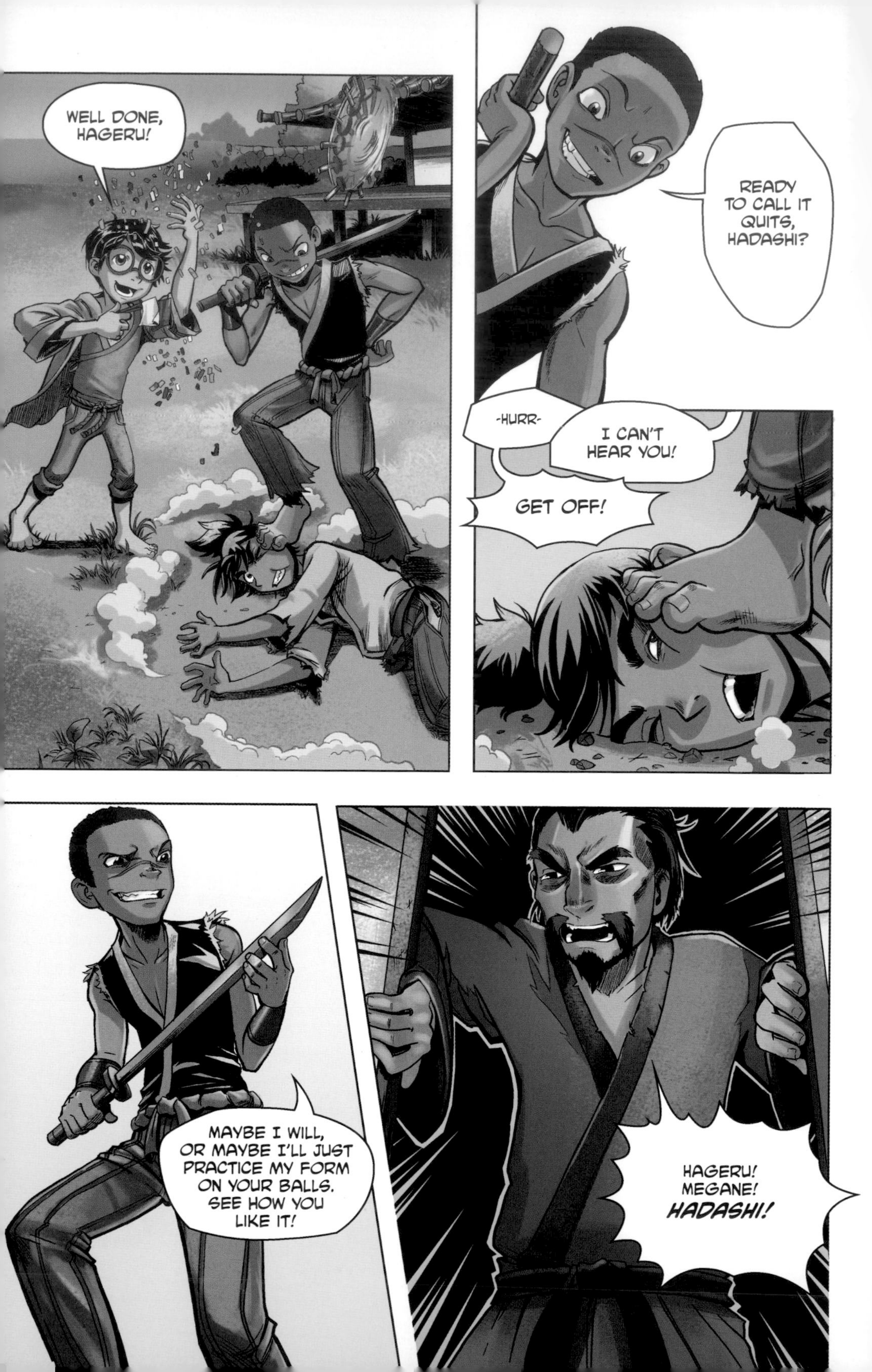
WELL DONE, HAGERU!
READY TO CALL IT QUITS, HADASHI?
-HURR-
I CAN'T HEAR YOU!
GET OFF!
MAYBE I WILL, OR MAYBE I'LL JUST PRACTICE MY FORM ON YOUR BALLS. SEE HOW YOU LIKE IT!
HAGERU! MEGANE! *HADASHI!*

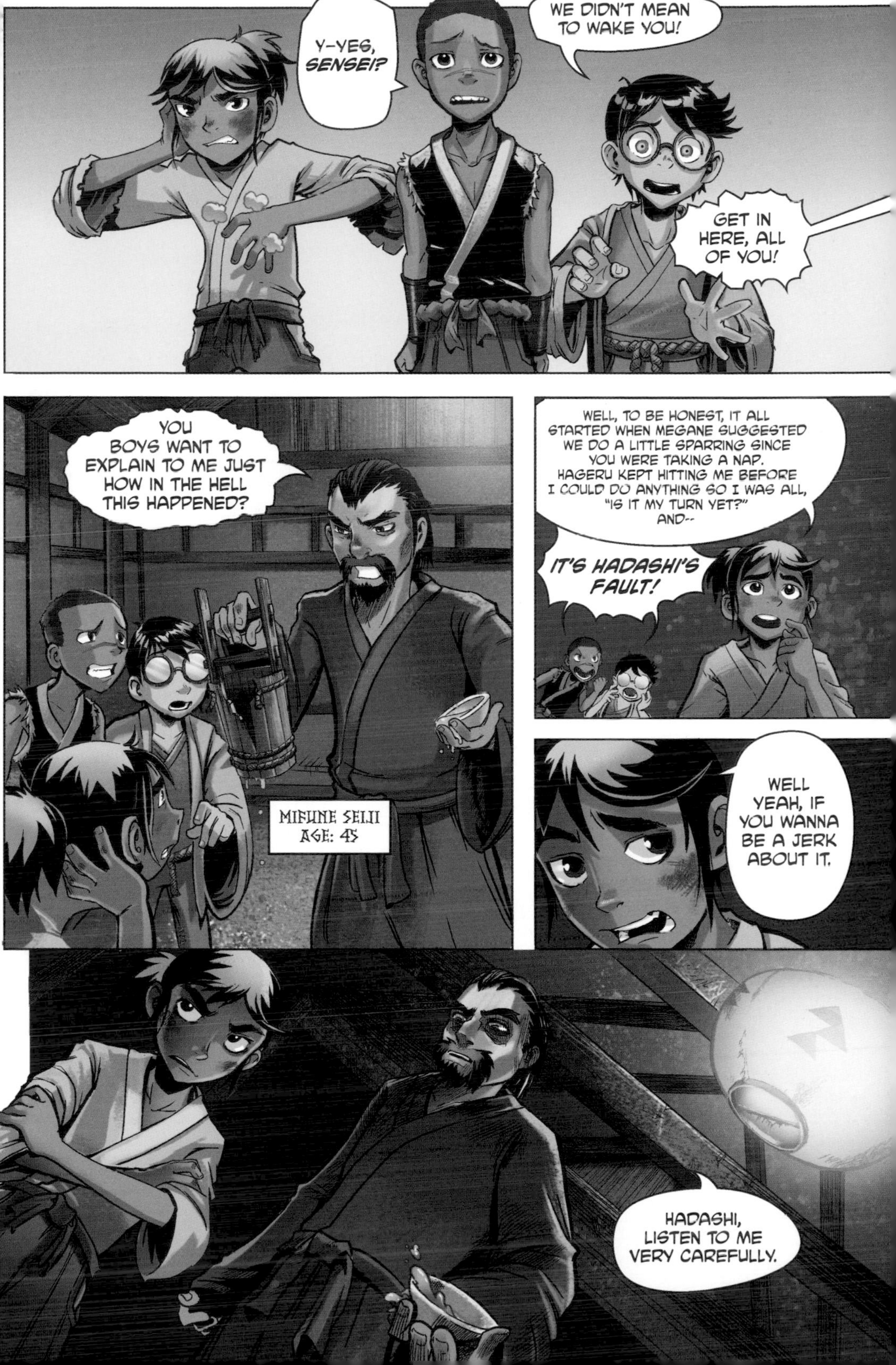
Y-YES, SENSEI?
WE DIDN'T MEAN TO WAKE YOU!
GET IN HERE, ALL OF YOU!
YOU BOYS WANT TO EXPLAIN TO ME JUST HOW IN THE HELL THIS HAPPENED?
MIFUNE SEIJI
AGE: 45
WELL, TO BE HONEST, IT ALL STARTED WHEN MEGANE SUGGESTED WE DO A LITTLE SPARRING SINCE YOU WERE TAKING A NAP. HAGERU KEPT HITTING ME BEFORE I COULD DO ANYTHING SO I WAS ALL, "IS IT MY TURN YET?" AND--
IT'S HADASHI'S FAULT!
WELL YEAH, IF YOU WANNA BE A JERK ABOUT IT.
HADASHI, LISTEN TO ME VERY CAREFULLY.

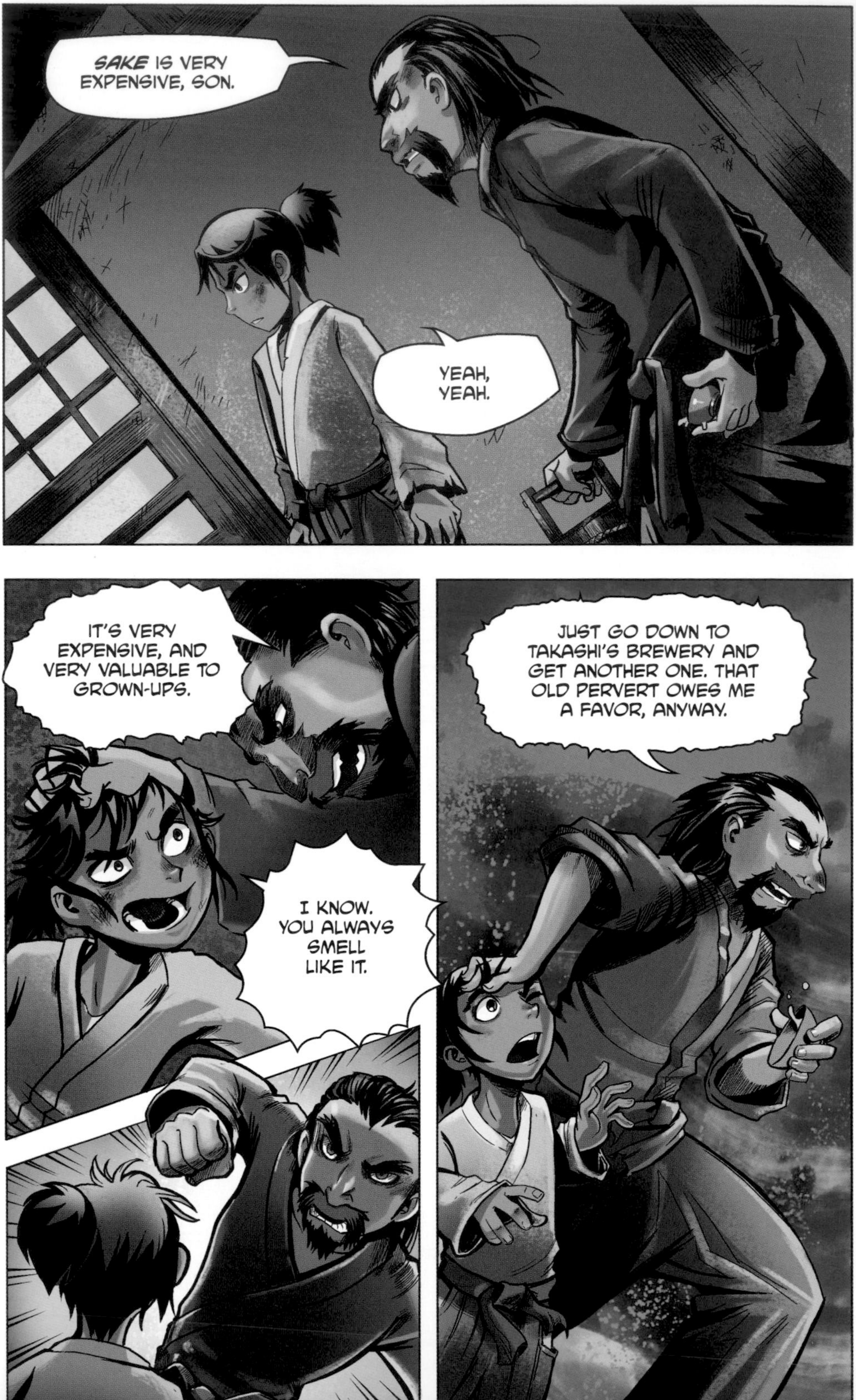
SAKE IS VERY EXPENSIVE, SON.
YEAH, YEAH.
IT'S VERY EXPENSIVE, AND VERY VALUABLE TO GROWN-UPS.
I KNOW. YOU ALWAYS SMELL LIKE IT.
JUST GO DOWN TO TAKASHI'S BREWERY AND GET ANOTHER ONE. THAT OLD PERVERT OWES ME A FAVOR, ANYWAY.

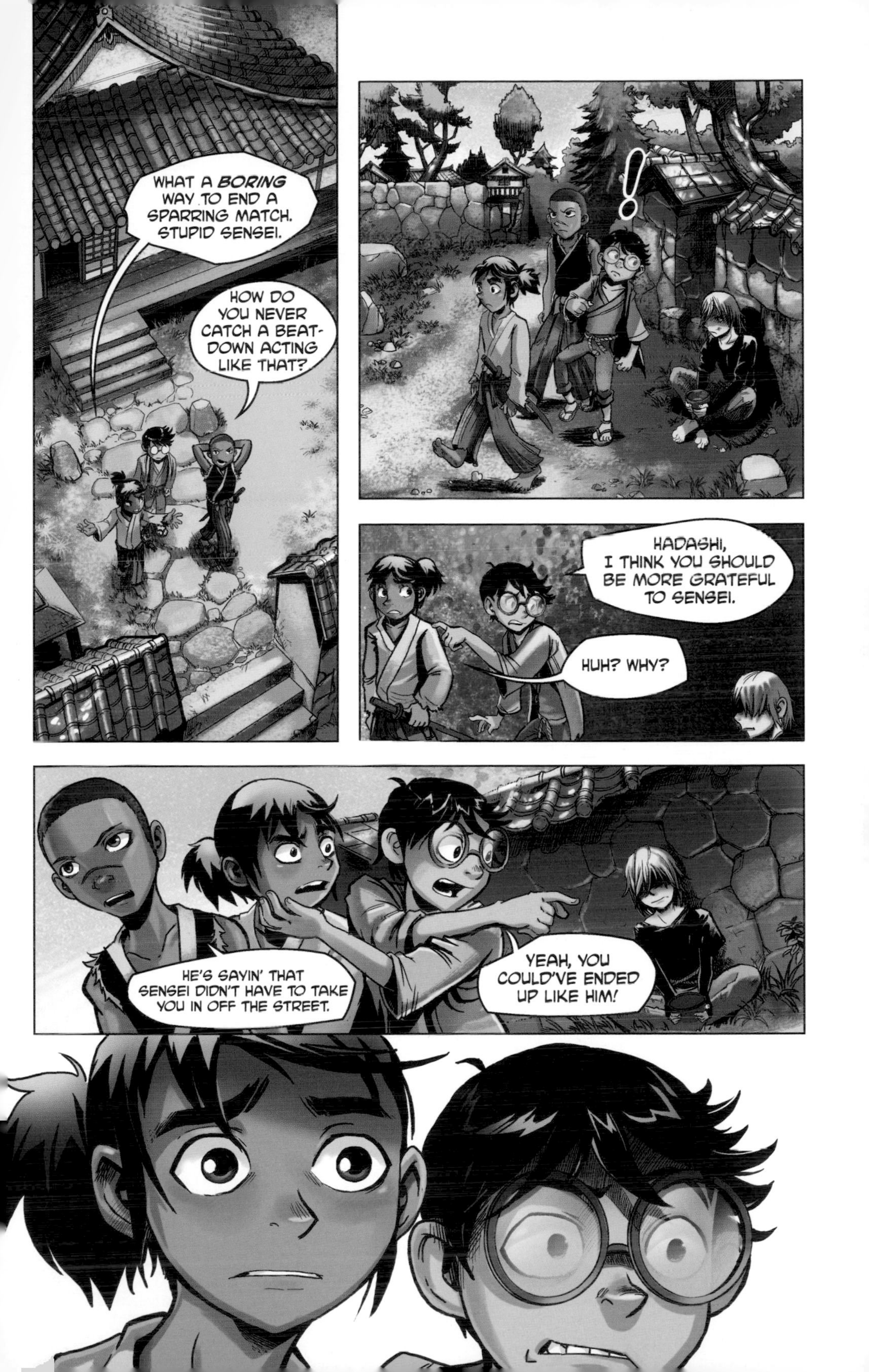
WHAT A *BORING* WAY TO END A SPARRING MATCH. STUPID SENSEI.
HOW DO YOU NEVER CATCH A BEAT-DOWN ACTING LIKE THAT?
!
HADASHI, I THINK YOU SHOULD BE MORE GRATEFUL TO SENSEI.
HUH? WHY?
HE'S SAYIN' THAT SENSEI DIDN'T HAVE TO TAKE YOU IN OFF THE STREET.
YEAH, YOU COULD'VE ENDED UP LIKE HIM!

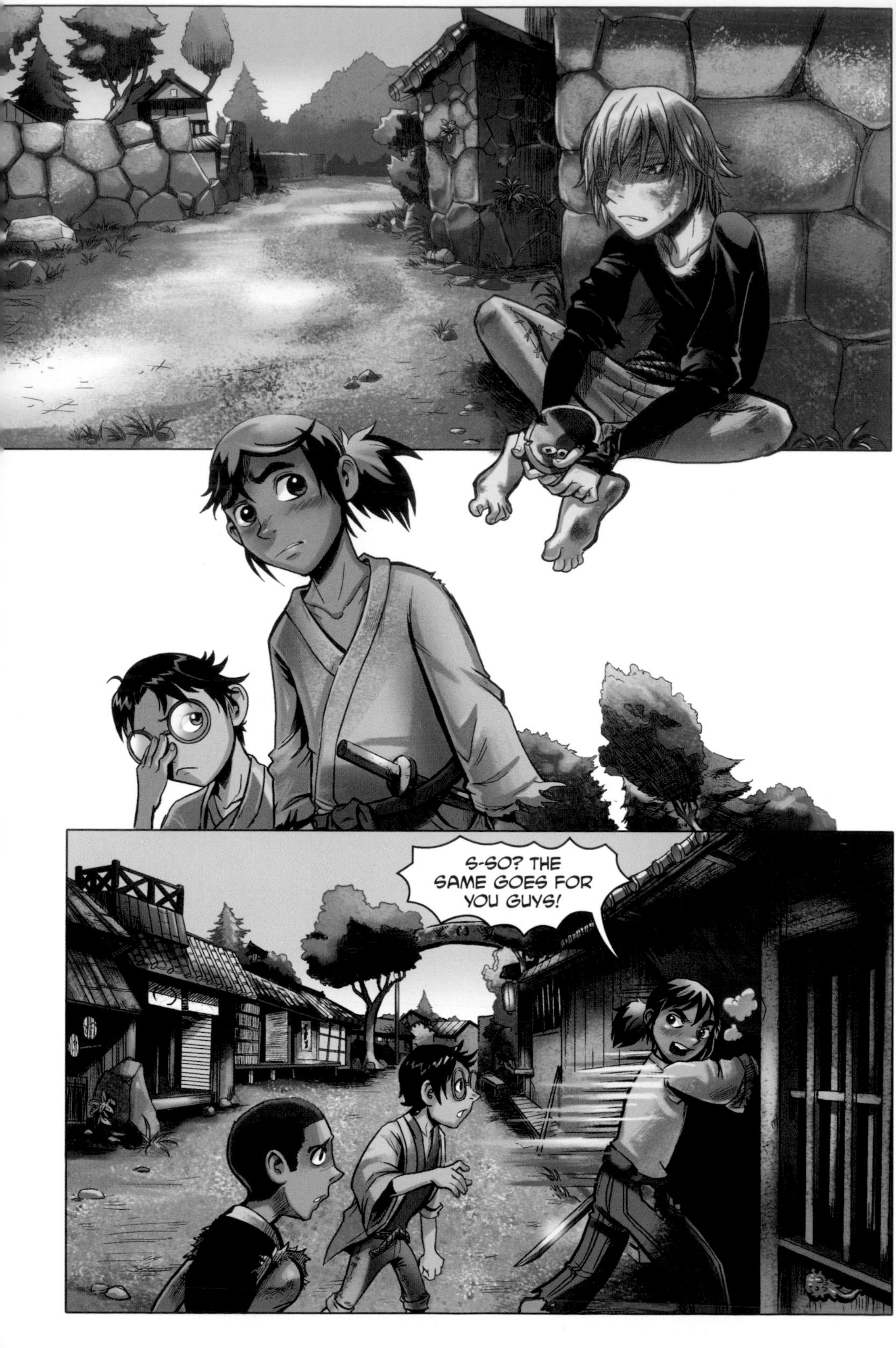
S-SO? THE SAME GOES FOR YOU GUYS!

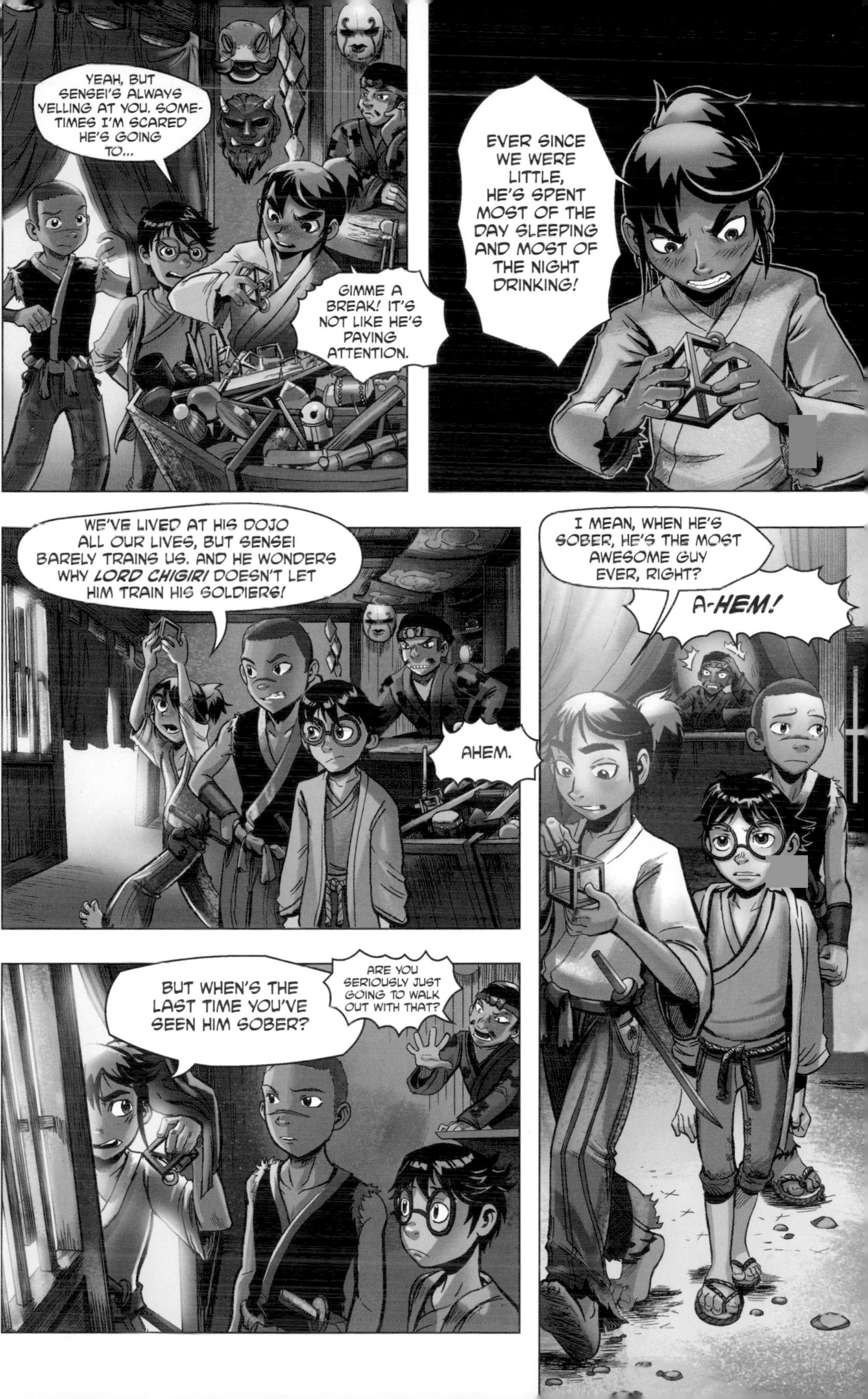
YEAH, BUT SENSEI'S ALWAYS YELLING AT YOU. SOMETIMES I'M SCARED HE'S GOING TO...
GIMME A BREAK! IT'S NOT LIKE HE'S PAYING ATTENTION.
EVER SINCE WE WERE LITTLE, HE'S SPENT MOST OF THE DAY SLEEPING AND MOST OF THE NIGHT DRINKING!
WE'VE LIVED AT HIS DOJO ALL OUR LIVES, BUT SENSEI BARELY TRAINS US. AND HE WONDERS WHY LORD CHIGIRI DOESN'T LET HIM TRAIN HIS SOLDIERS!
AHEM.
BUT WHEN'S THE LAST TIME YOU'VE SEEN HIM SOBER?
ARE YOU SERIOUSLY JUST GOING TO WALK OUT WITH THAT?
I MEAN, WHEN HE'S SOBER, HE'S THE MOST AWESOME GUY EVER, RIGHT?
A-HEM!

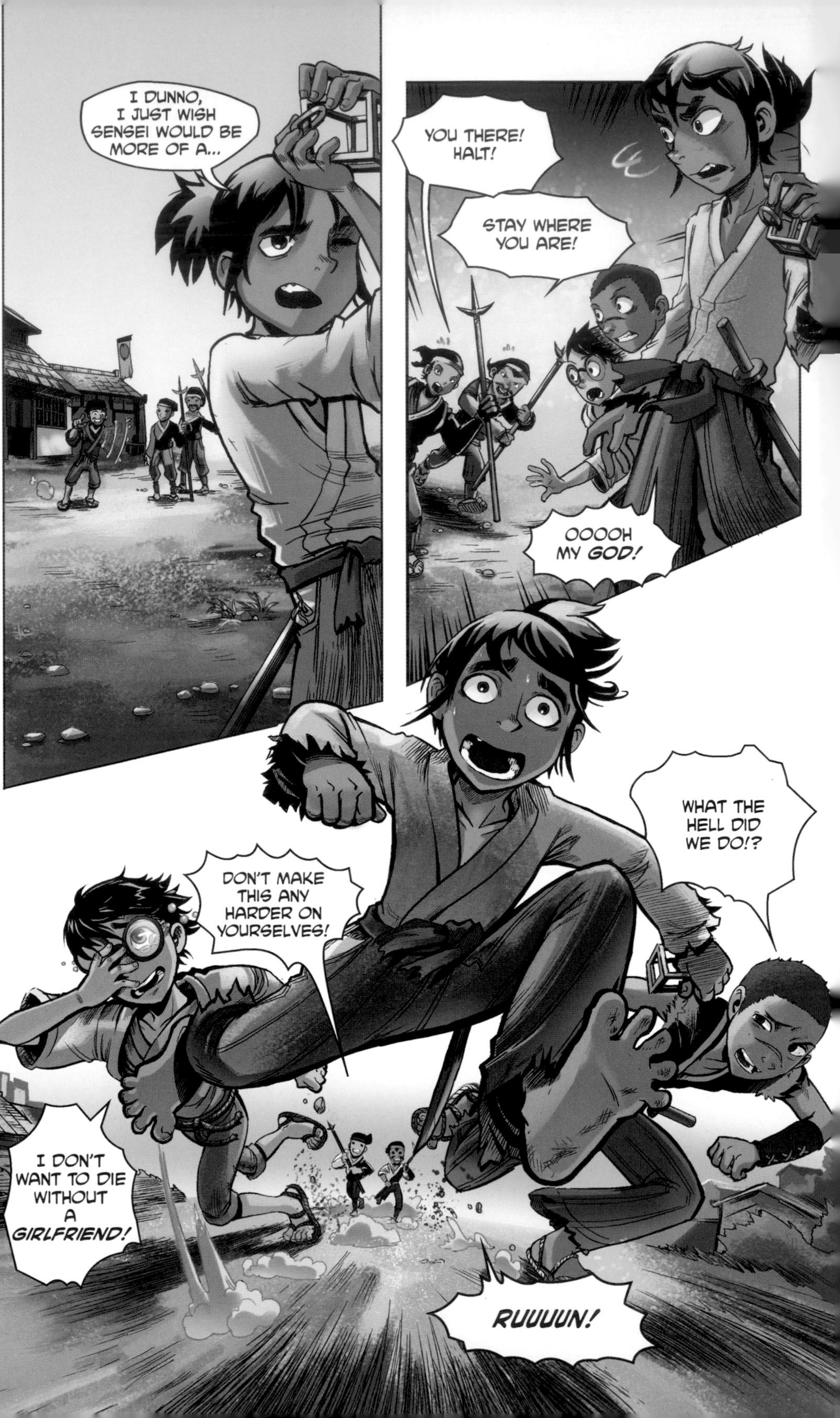
I DUNNO, I JUST WISH SENSEI WOULD BE MORE OF A...
YOU THERE! HALT!
STAY WHERE YOU ARE!
OOOOH MY GOD!
DON'T MAKE THIS ANY HARDER ON YOURSELVES!
WHAT THE HELL DID WE DO!?
I DON'T WANT TO DIE WITHOUT A GIRLFRIEND!
RUUUUN!

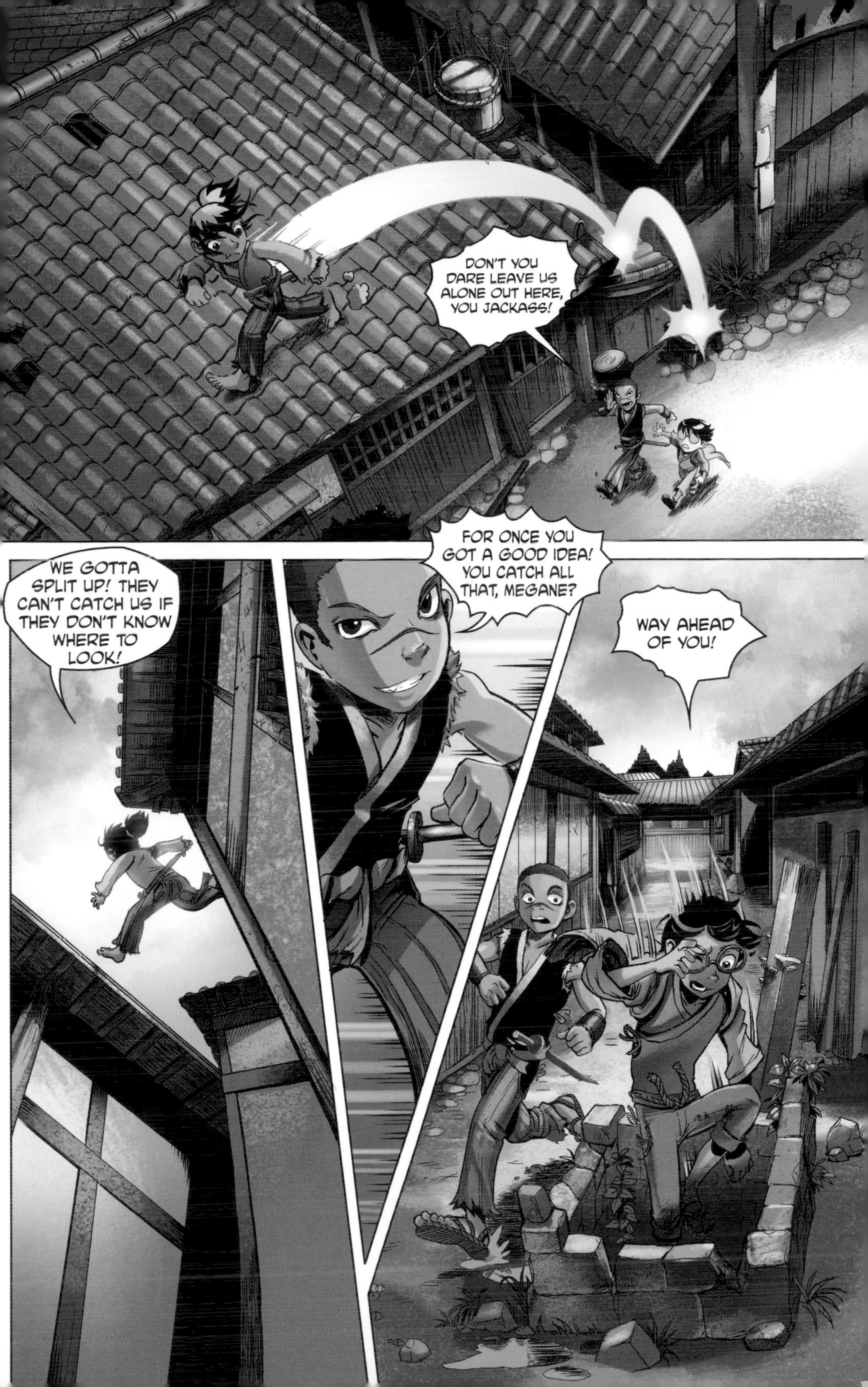
DON'T YOU DARE LEAVE US ALONE OUT HERE, YOU JACKASS!
WE GOTTA SPLIT UP! THEY CAN'T CATCH US IF THEY DON'T KNOW WHERE TO LOOK!
FOR ONCE YOU GOT A GOOD IDEA! YOU CATCH ALL THAT, MEGANE?
WAY AHEAD OF YOU!

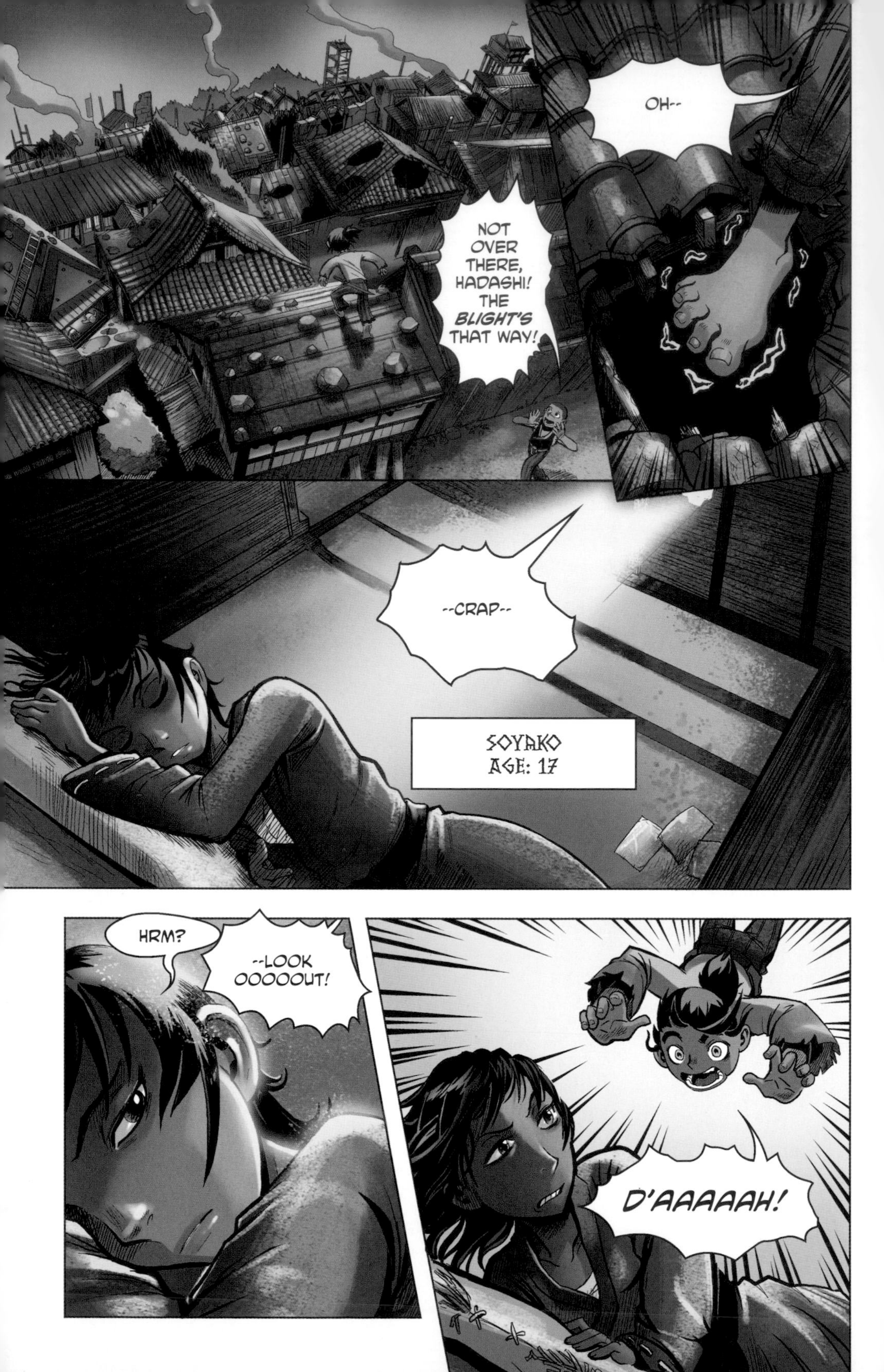
OH--
NOT OVER THERE, HADASHI! THE *BLIGHT'S* THAT WAY!
--CRAP--
SOYAKO
AGE: 17
HRM?
--LOOK OOOOOUT!
D'AAAAAH!

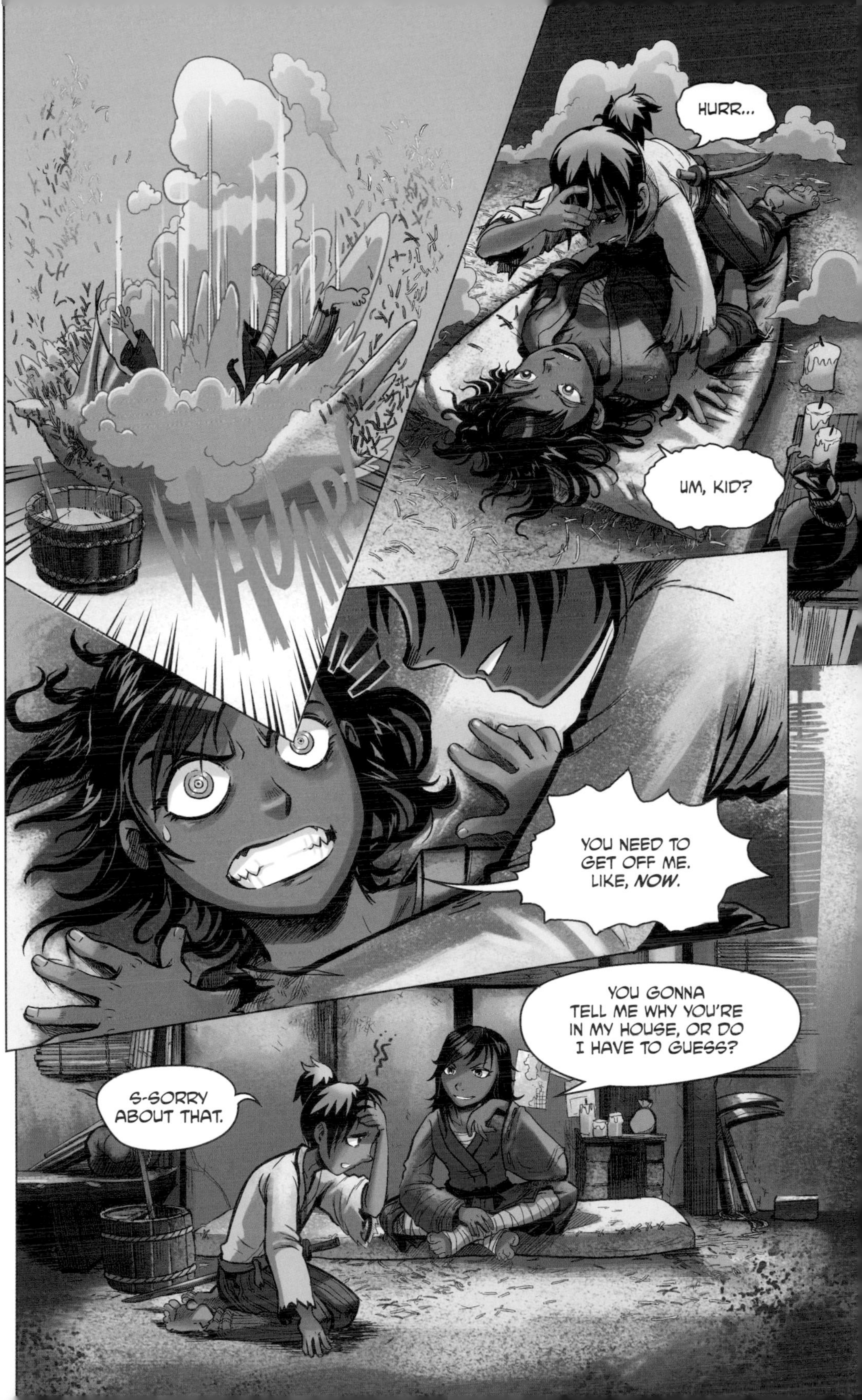
WHUMP!
HURR...
UM, KID?
YOU NEED TO GET OFF ME. LIKE, *NOW*.
S-SORRY ABOUT THAT.
YOU GONNA TELL ME WHY YOU'RE IN MY HOUSE, OR DO I HAVE TO GUESS?

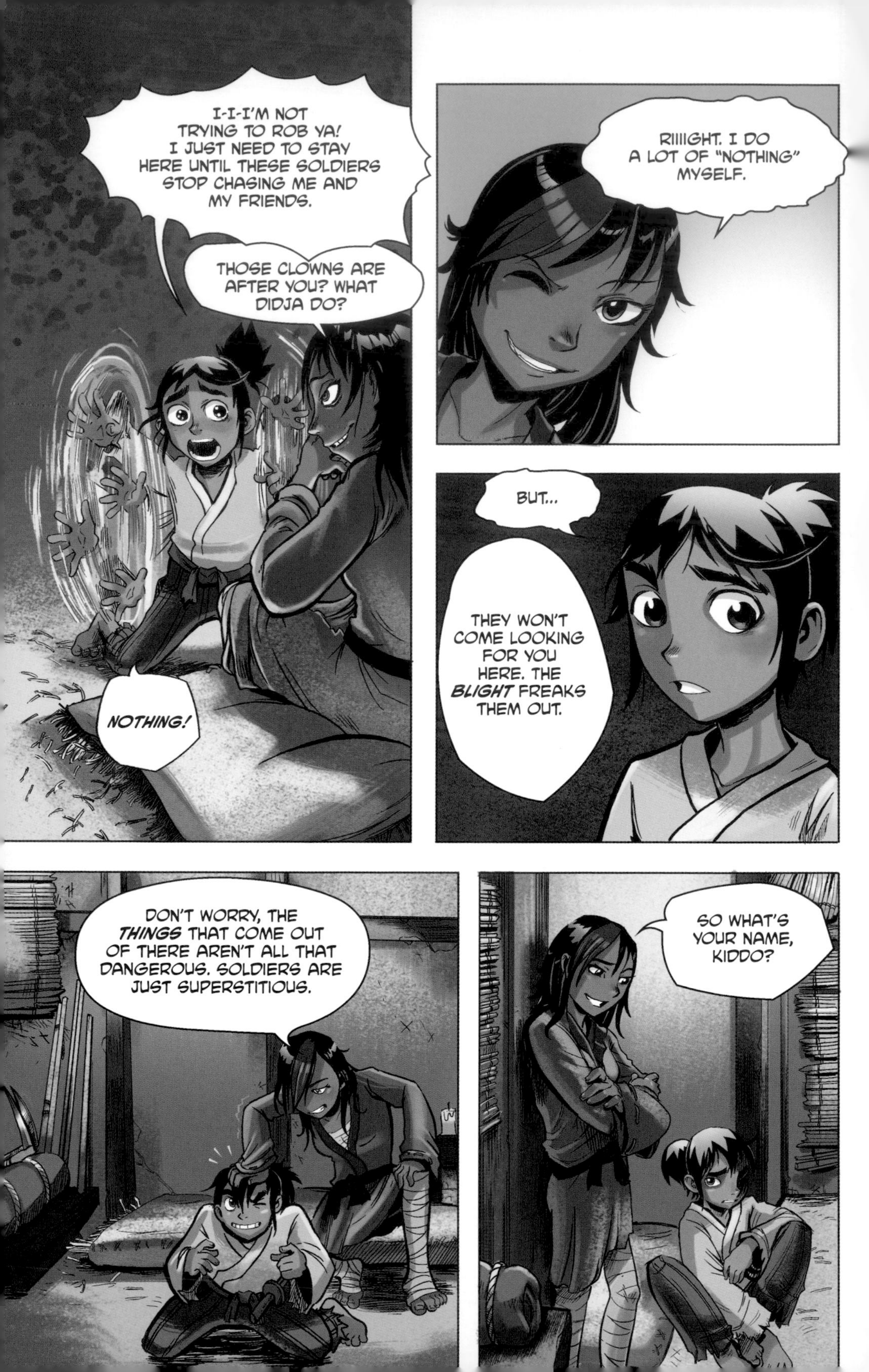
I-I-I'M NOT TRYING TO ROB YA! I JUST NEED TO STAY HERE UNTIL THESE SOLDIERS STOP CHASING ME AND MY FRIENDS.
THOSE CLOWNS ARE AFTER YOU? WHAT DIDJA DO?
NOTHING!
RIIIIGHT. I DO A LOT OF "NOTHING" MYSELF.
BUT...
THEY WON'T COME LOOKING FOR YOU HERE. THE BLIGHT FREAKS THEM OUT.
DON'T WORRY, THE THINGS THAT COME OUT OF THERE AREN'T ALL THAT DANGEROUS. SOLDIERS ARE JUST SUPERSTITIOUS.
SO WHAT'S YOUR NAME, KIDDO?

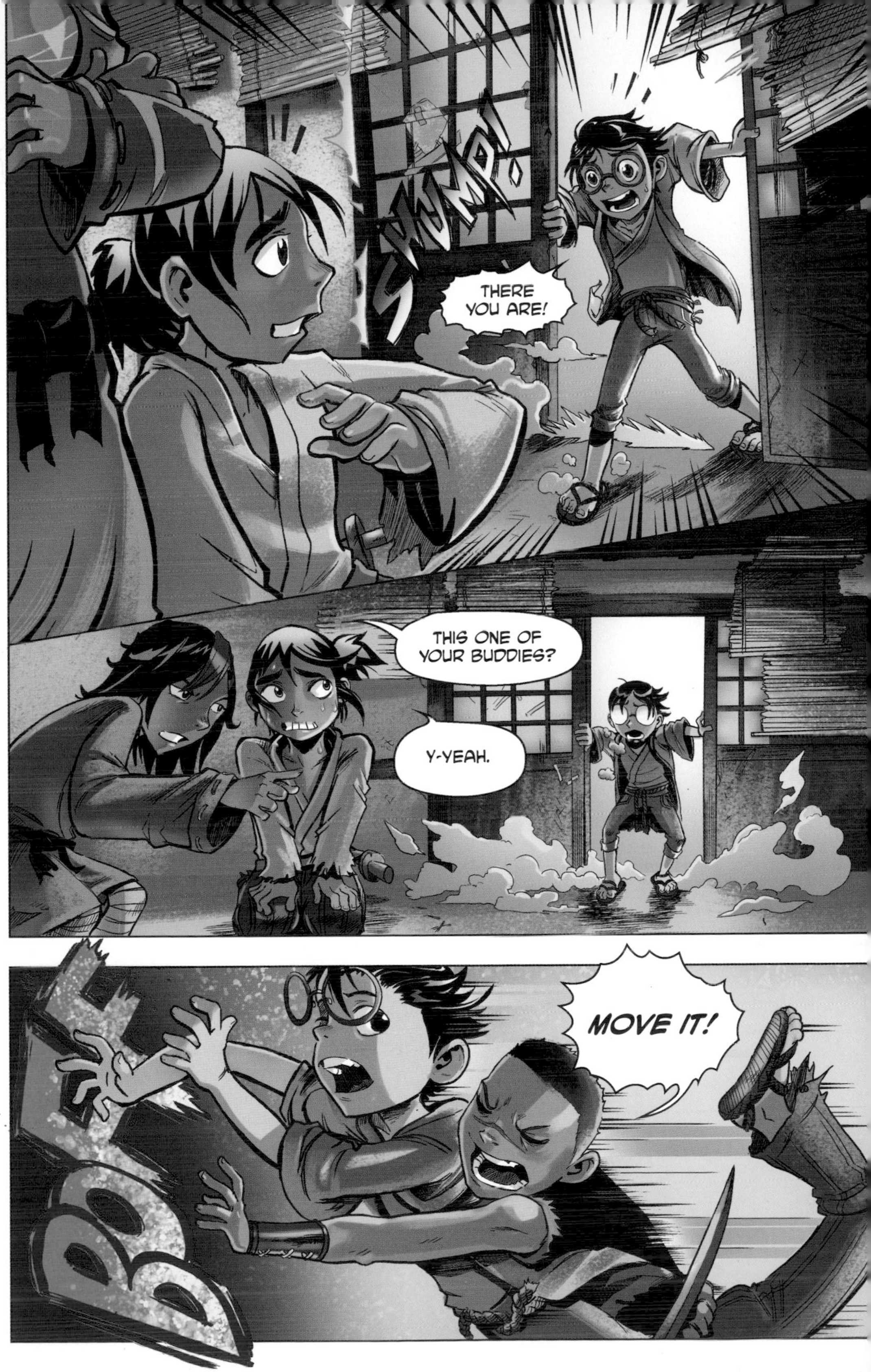
SHUMP!
THERE YOU ARE!
THIS ONE OF YOUR BUDDIES?
Y-YEAH.
MOVE IT!
BOF

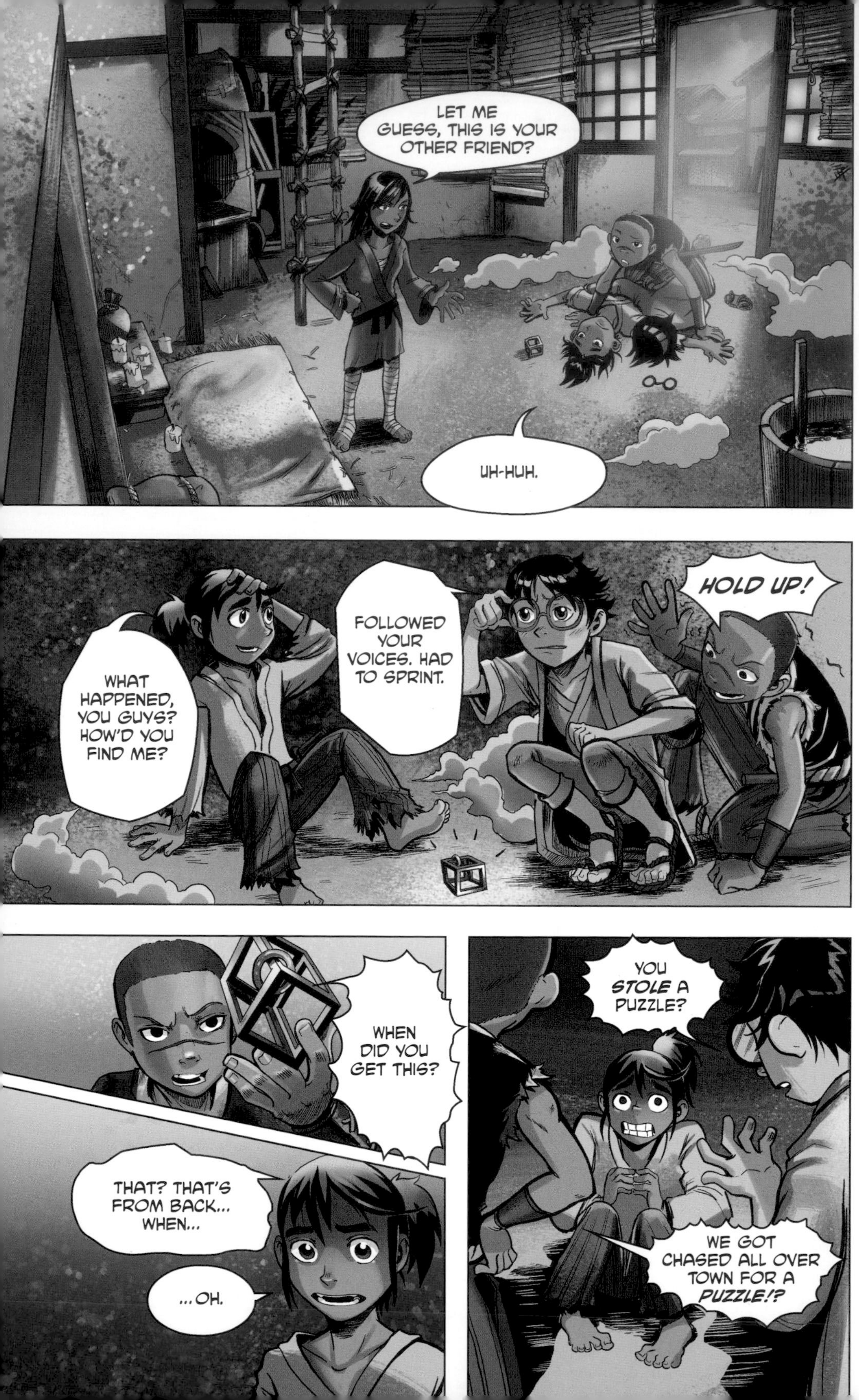
LET ME GUESS, THIS IS YOUR OTHER FRIEND?
UH-HUH.
WHAT HAPPENED, YOU GUYS? HOW'D YOU FIND ME?
FOLLOWED YOUR VOICES. HAD TO SPRINT.
HOLD UP!
WHEN DID YOU GET THIS?
THAT? THAT'S FROM BACK... WHEN...
...OH.
YOU STOLE A PUZZLE?
WE GOT CHASED ALL OVER TOWN FOR A PUZZLE!?

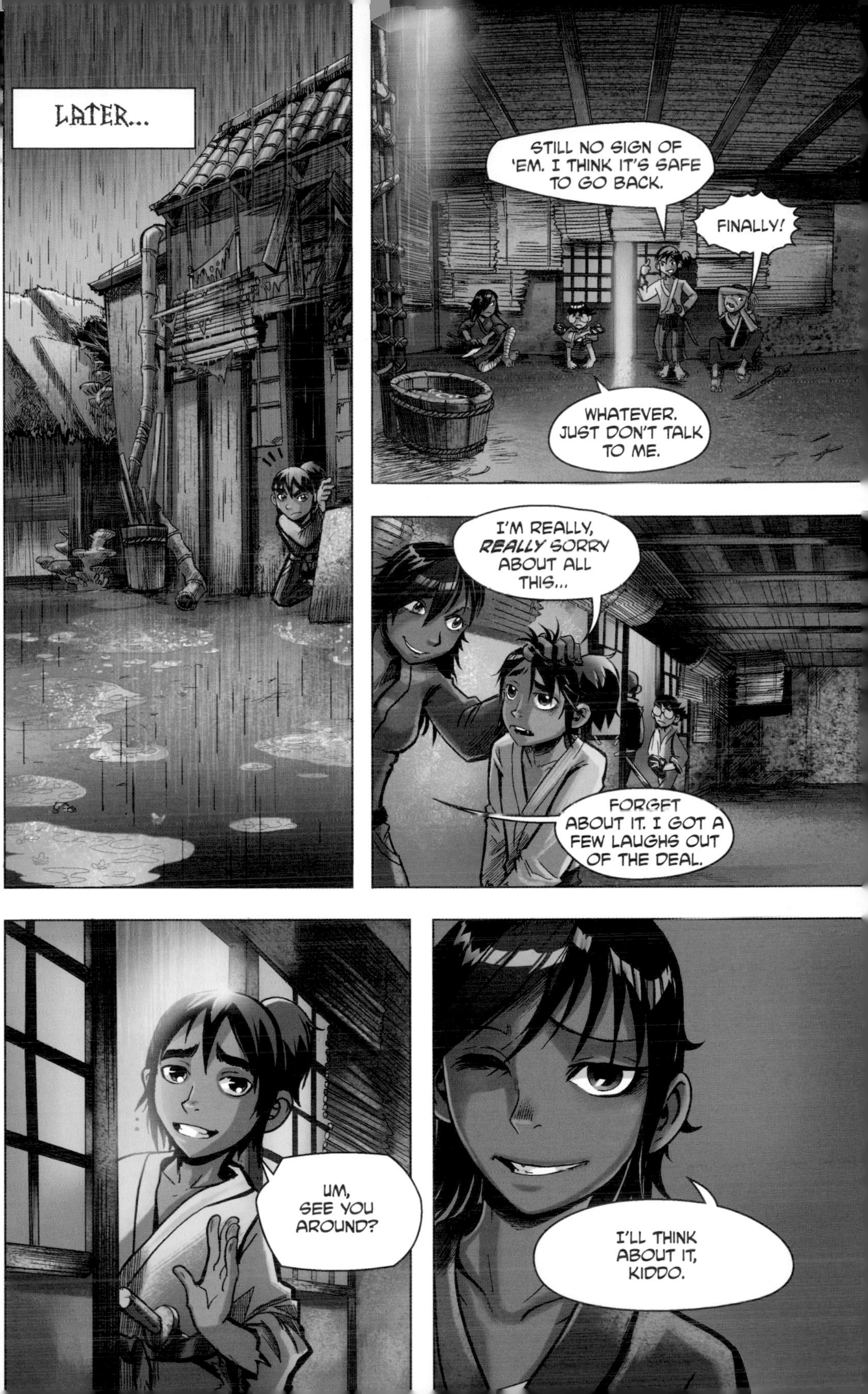
LATER...
STILL NO SIGN OF 'EM. I THINK IT'S SAFE TO GO BACK.
FINALLY!
WHATEVER. JUST DON'T TALK TO ME.
I'M REALLY, *REALLY* SORRY ABOUT ALL THIS...
FORGET ABOUT IT. I GOT A FEW LAUGHS OUT OF THE DEAL.
UM, SEE YOU AROUND?
I'LL THINK ABOUT IT, KIDDO.

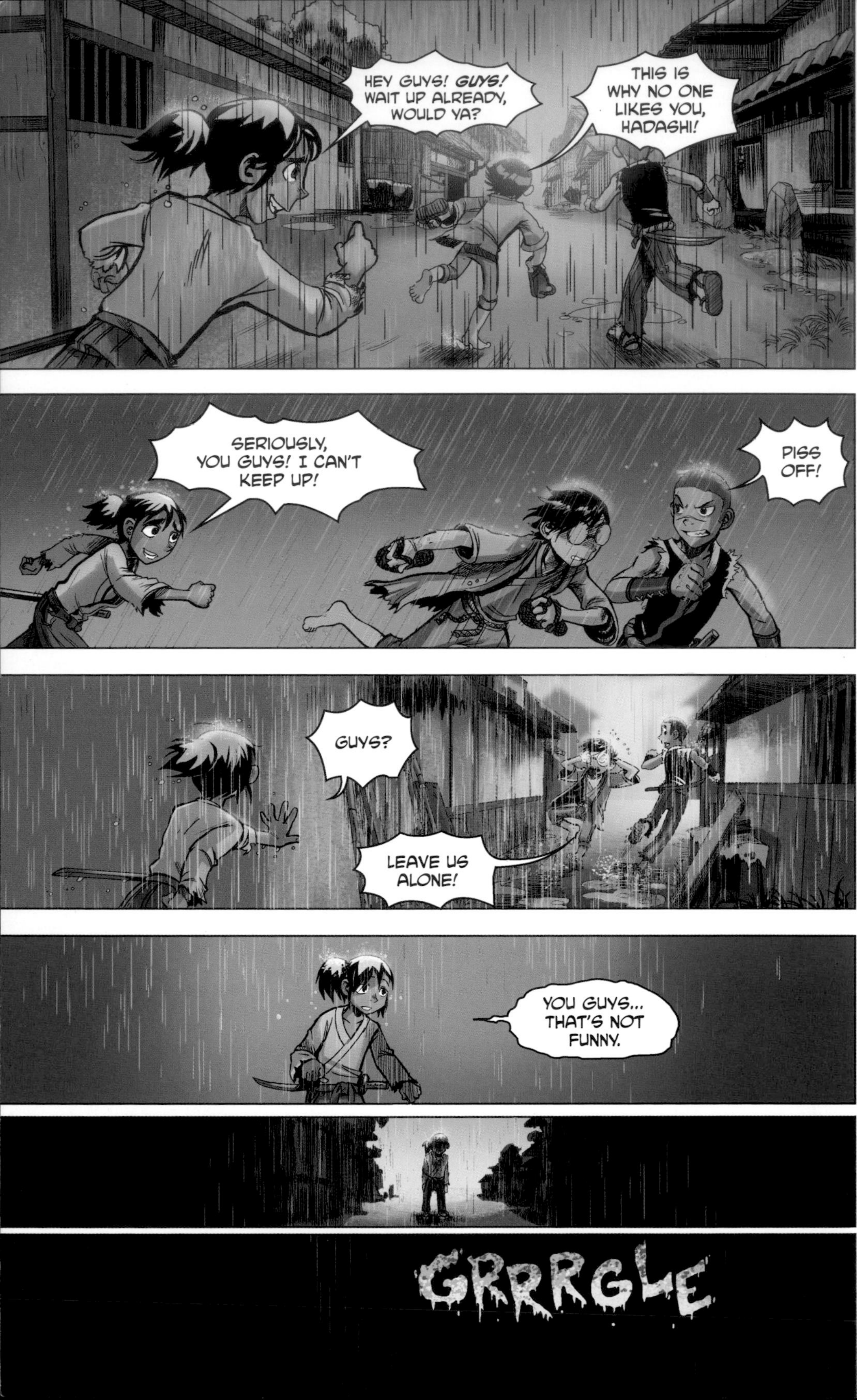
HEY GUYS! *GUYS!* WAIT UP ALREADY, WOULD YA?
THIS IS WHY NO ONE LIKES YOU, HADASHI!
SERIOUSLY, YOU GUYS! I CAN'T KEEP UP!
PISS OFF!
GUYS?
LEAVE US ALONE!
YOU GUYS... THAT'S NOT FUNNY.
GRRRGLE

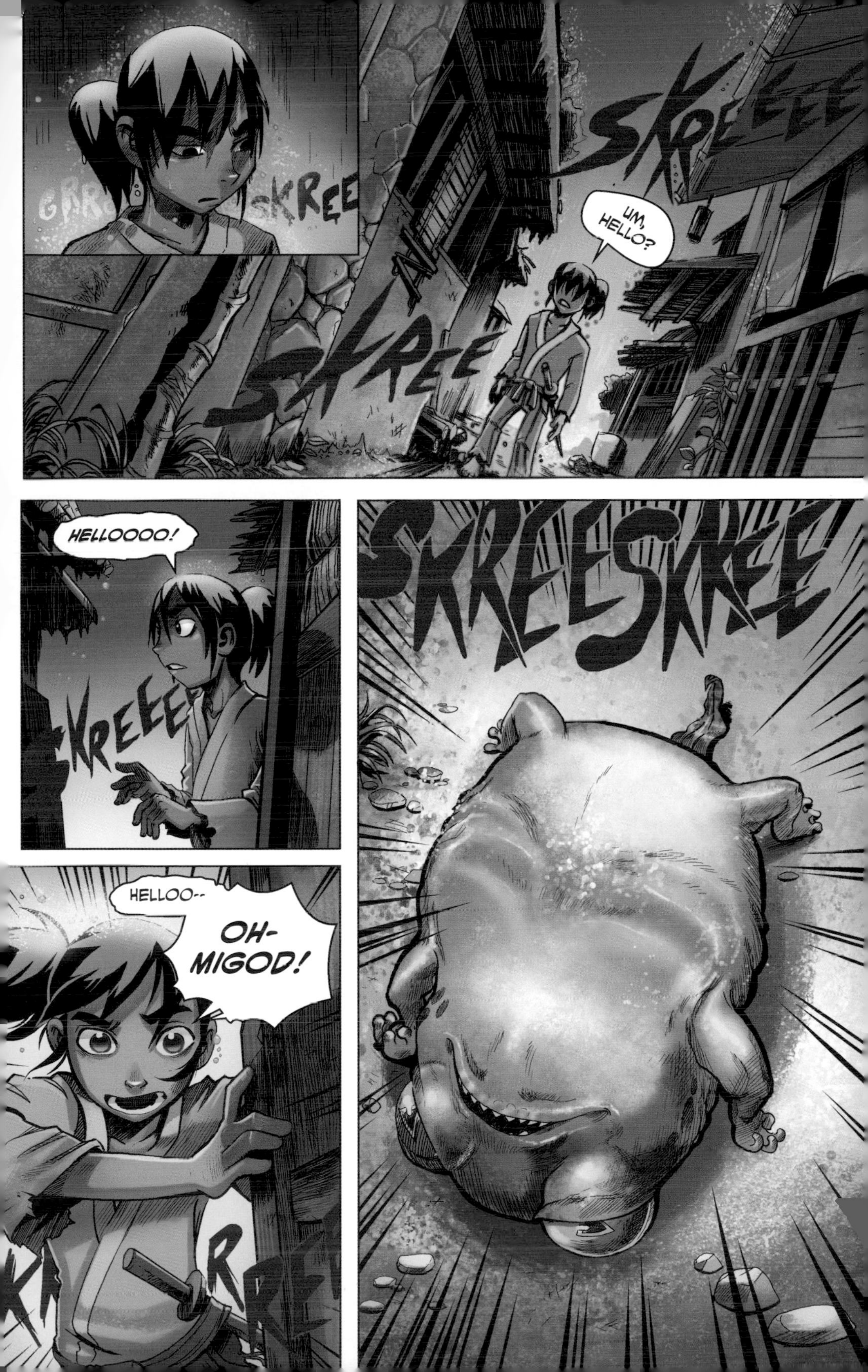
GRRR
SKREE
SKREEEE
UM, HELLO?
SKREE
HELLOOOO!
SKREEEE
SKREESKREE
HELLOO--
OH-MIGOD!
KRRRR

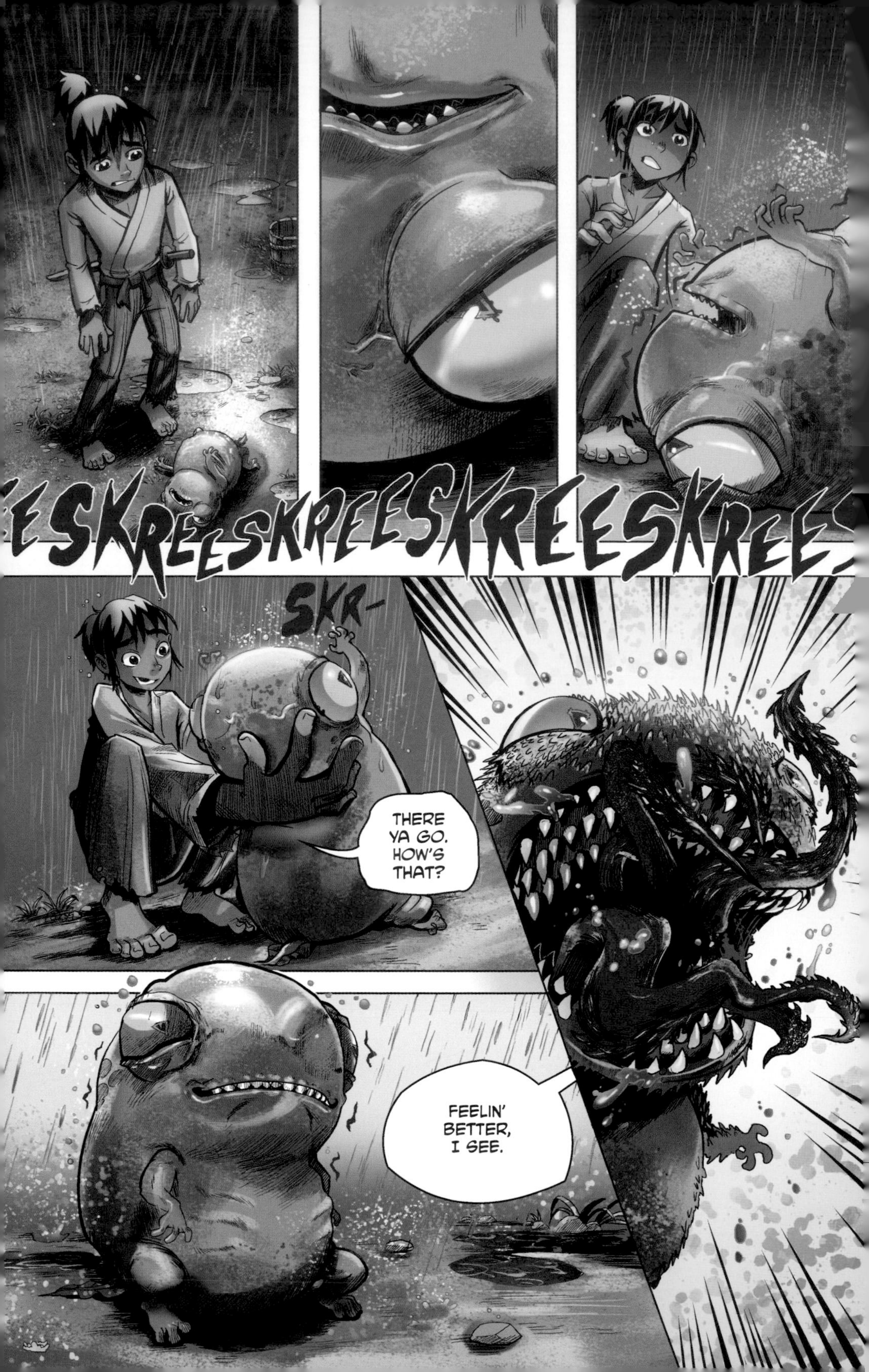
ESKREESKREESKREESKREES
SKR-
THERE YA GO. HOW'S THAT?
FEELIN' BETTER, I SEE.

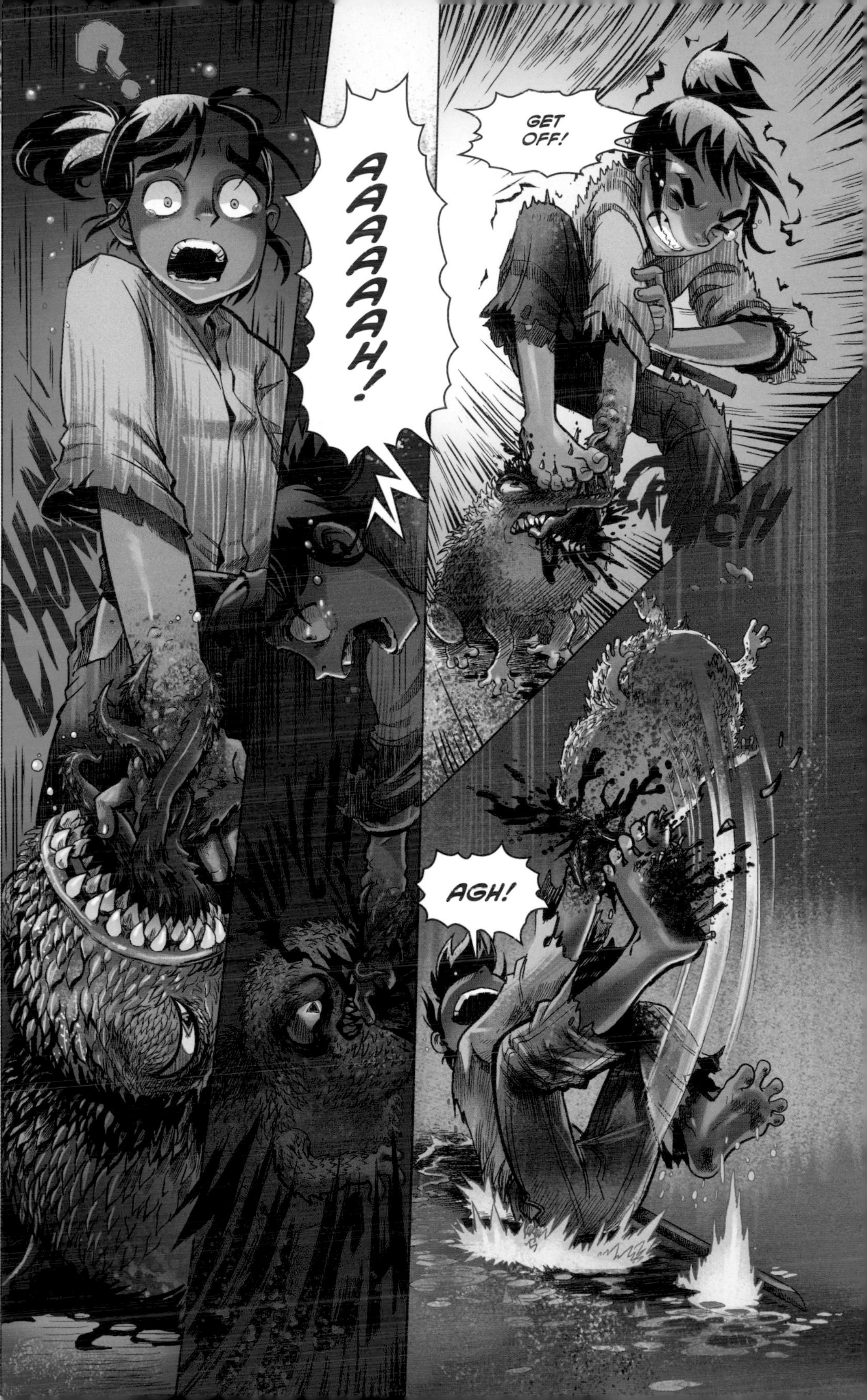
?
AAAAAAH!
GET OFF!
AGH!

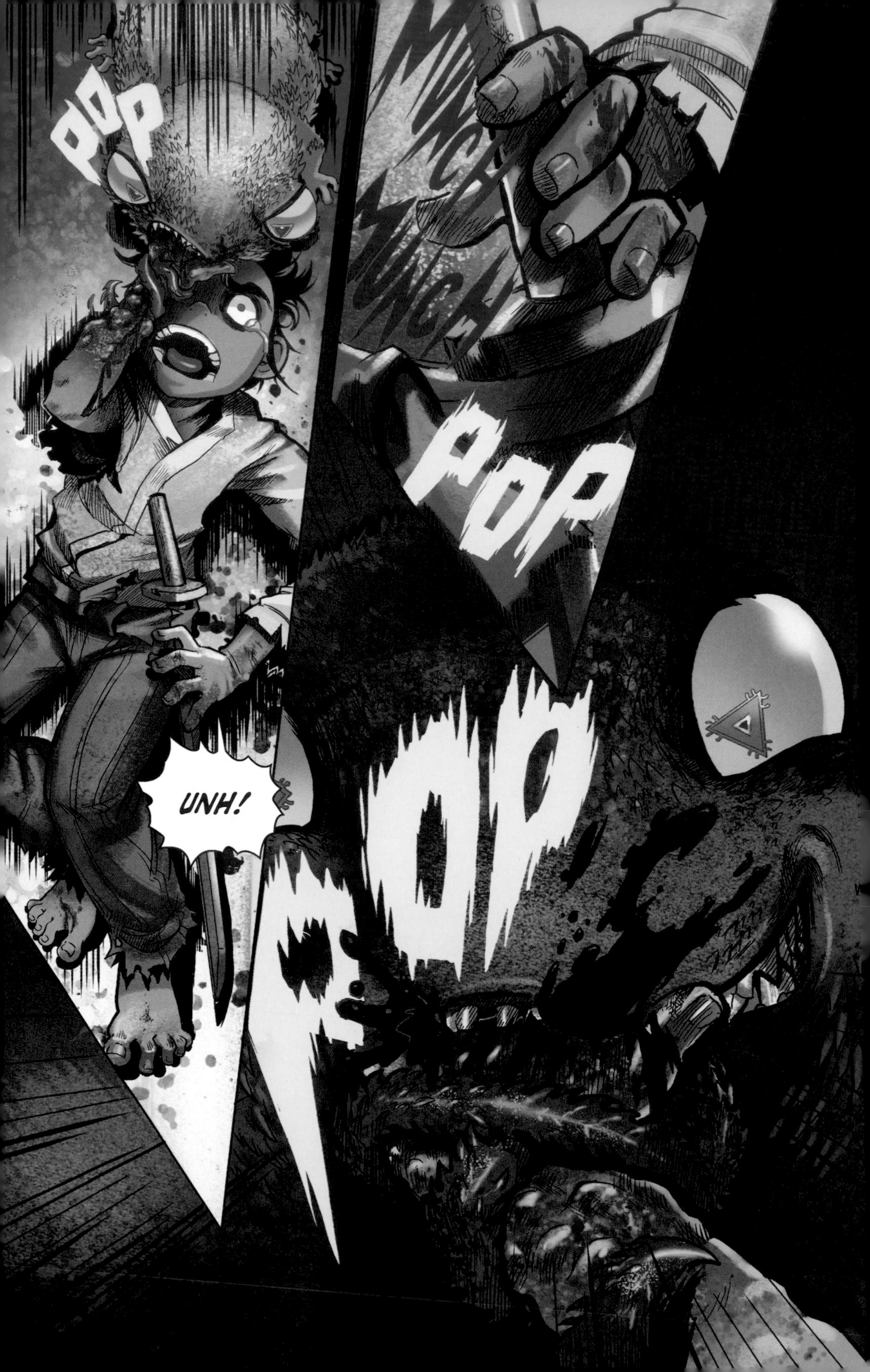
POP
MUNCH
MUNCH
MUNCH
POP
UNH!
POP

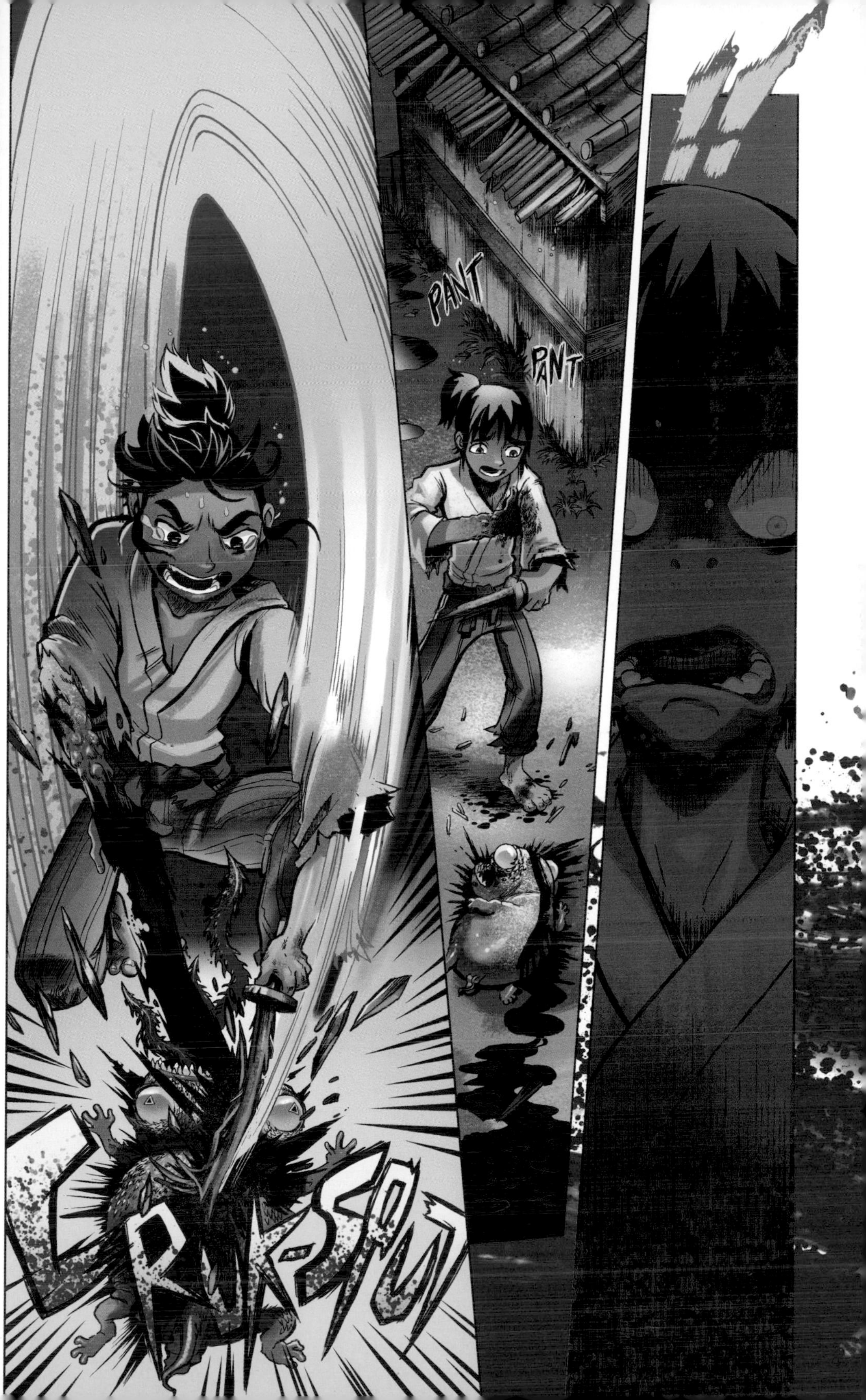

CRUNCH-SPLUT
PANT
PANT
!!

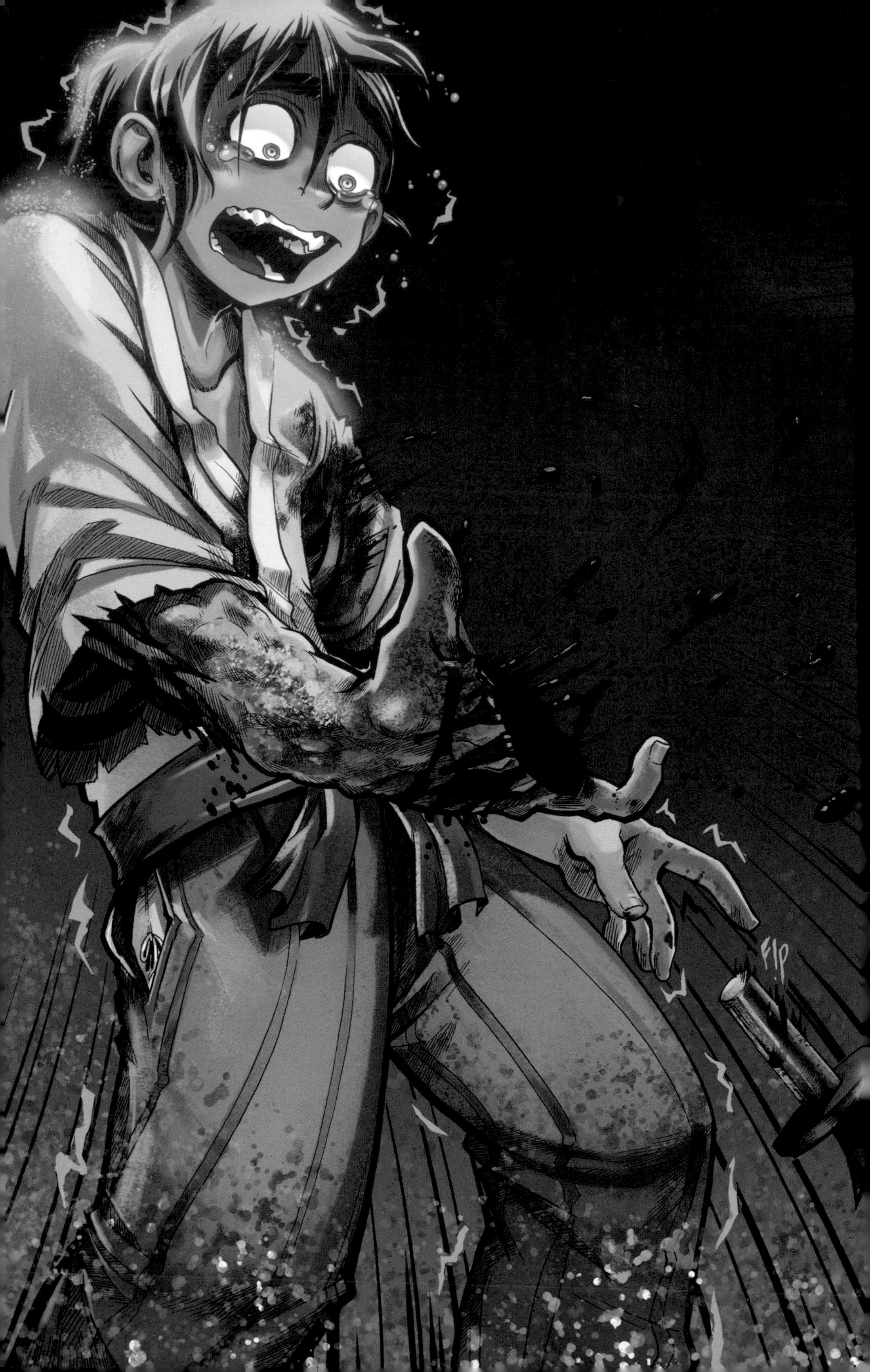
FIP

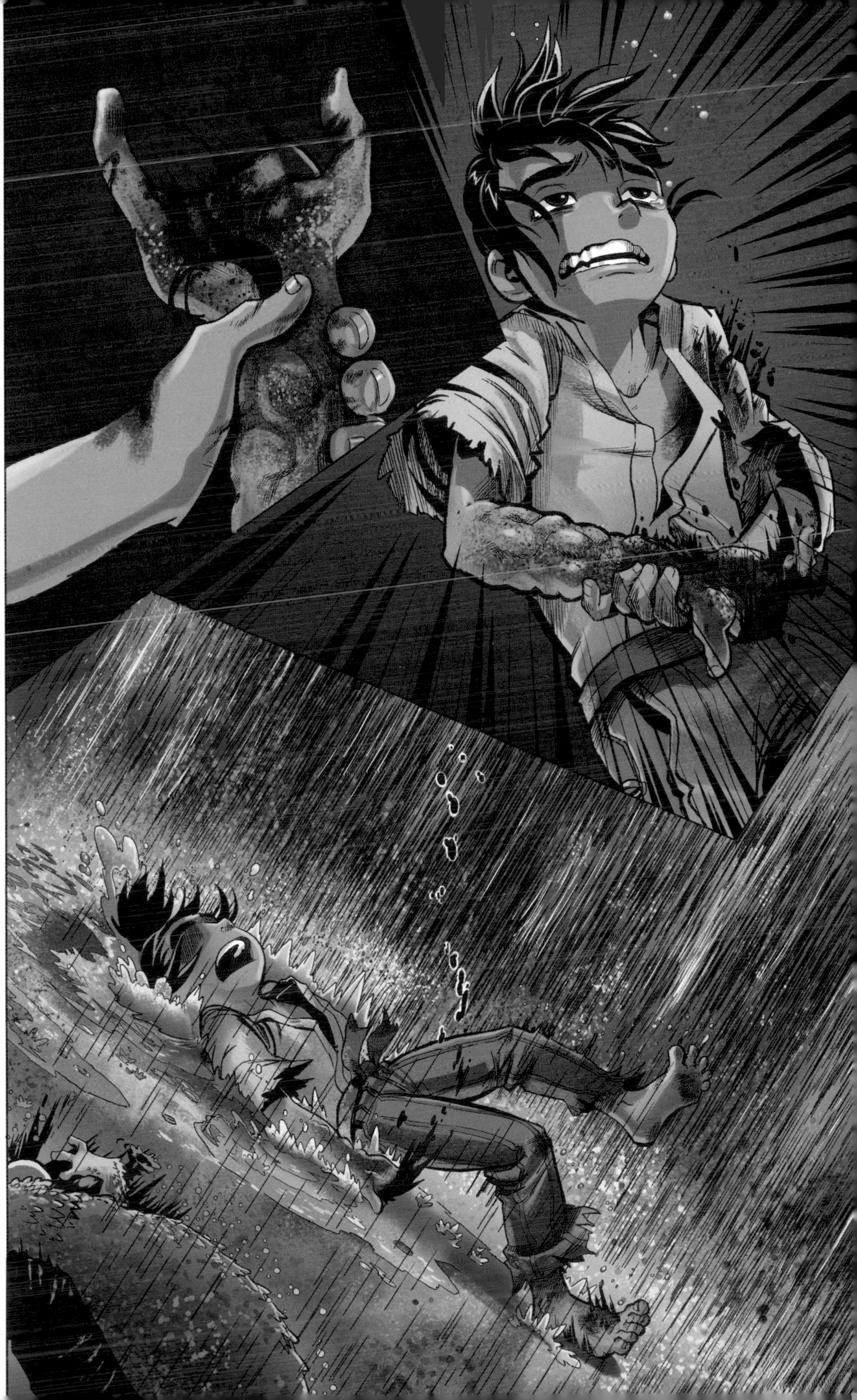

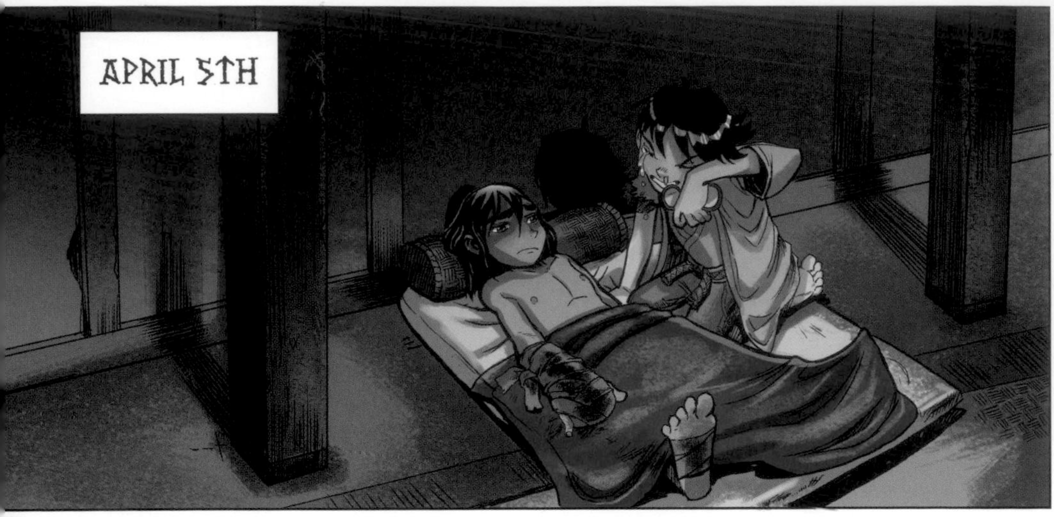
APRIL 5TH

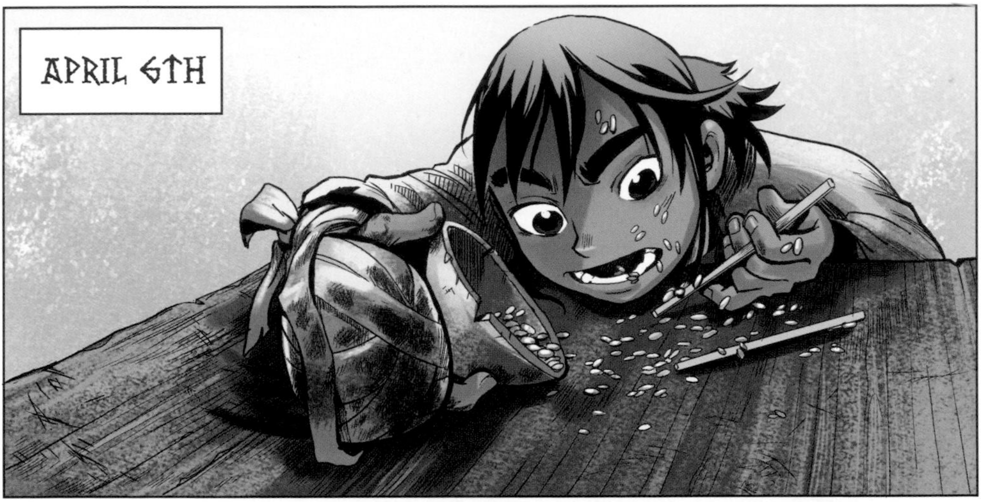
APRIL 6TH

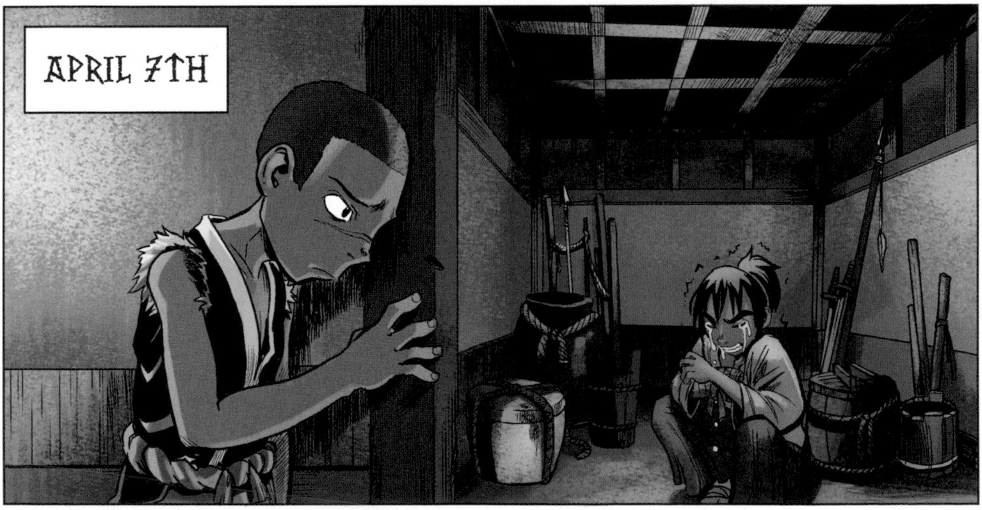
APRIL 7TH

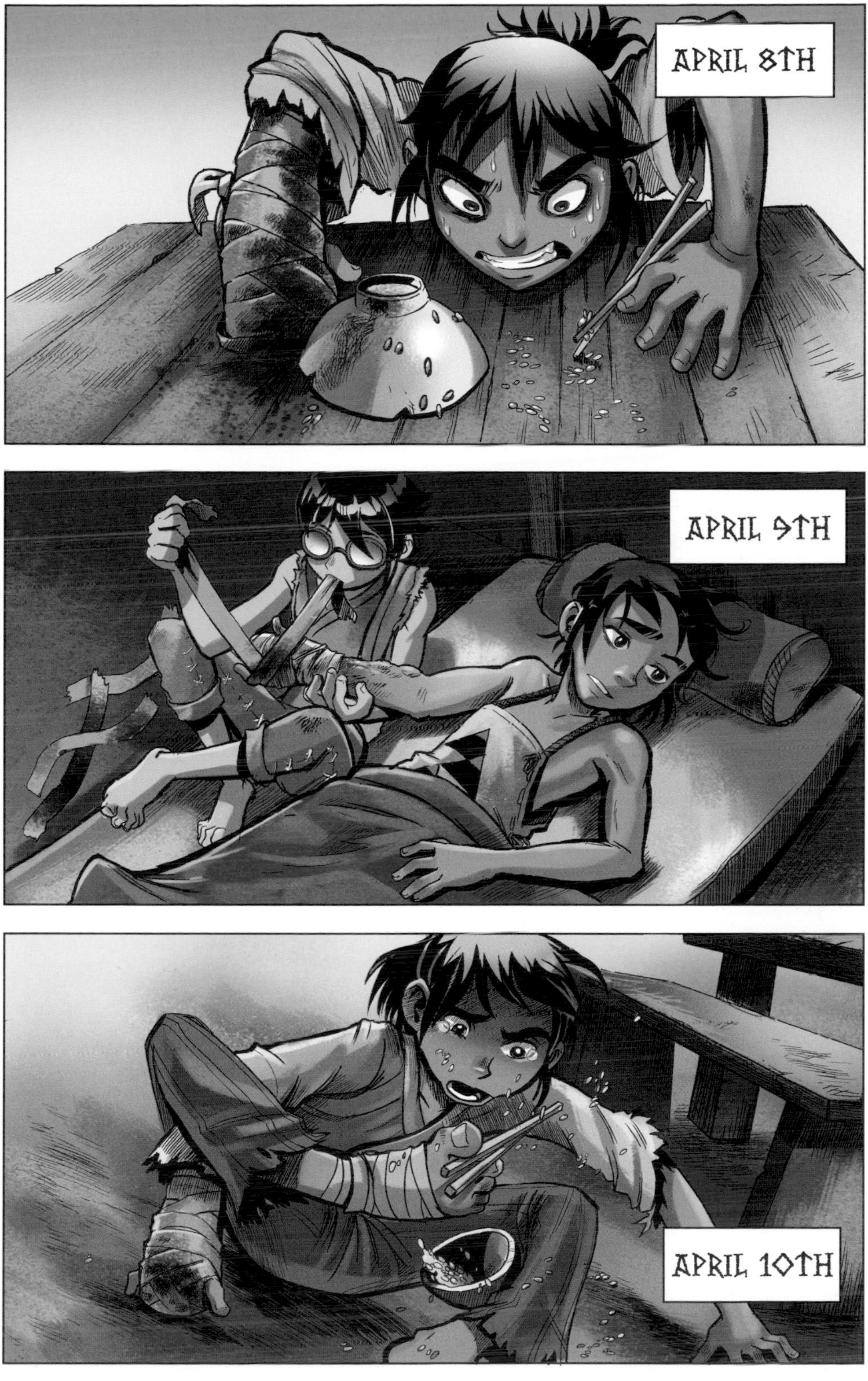
APRIL 8TH
APRIL 9TH
APRIL 10TH

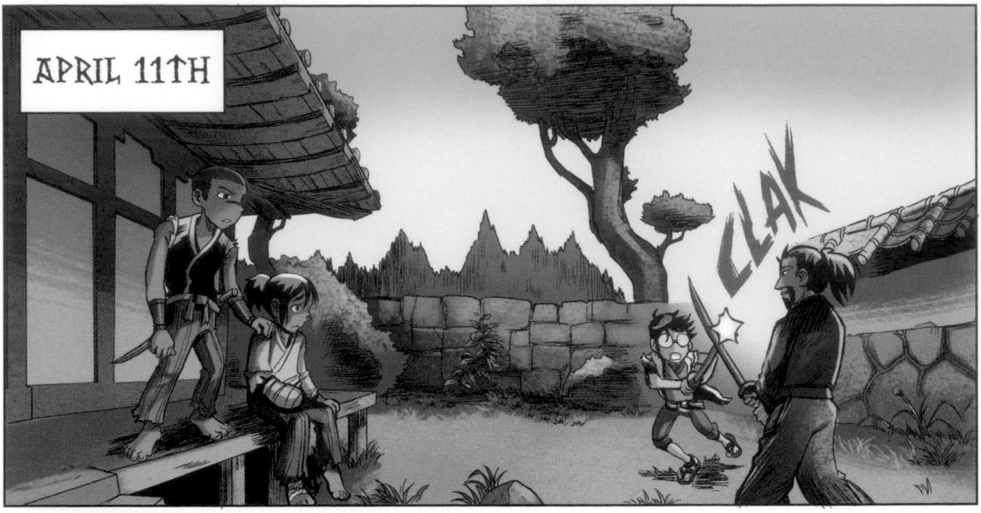
APRIL 11TH
CLAK

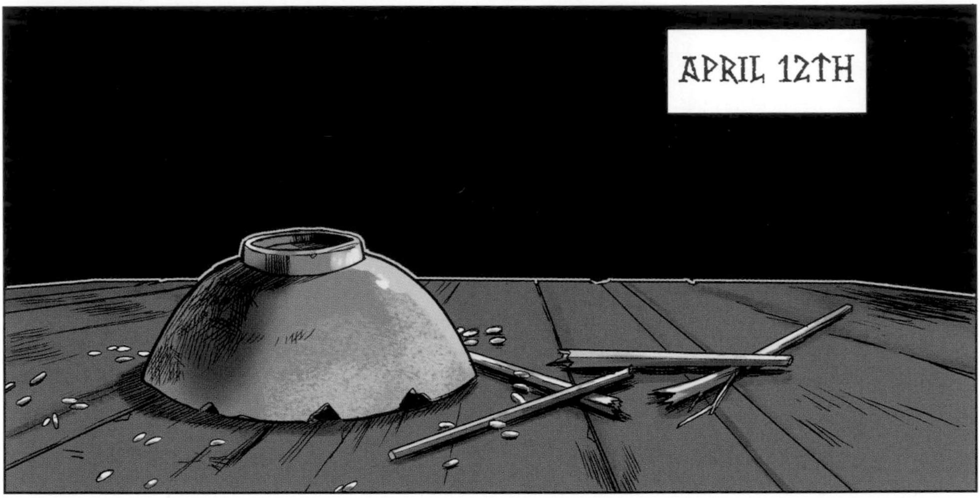
APRIL 12TH

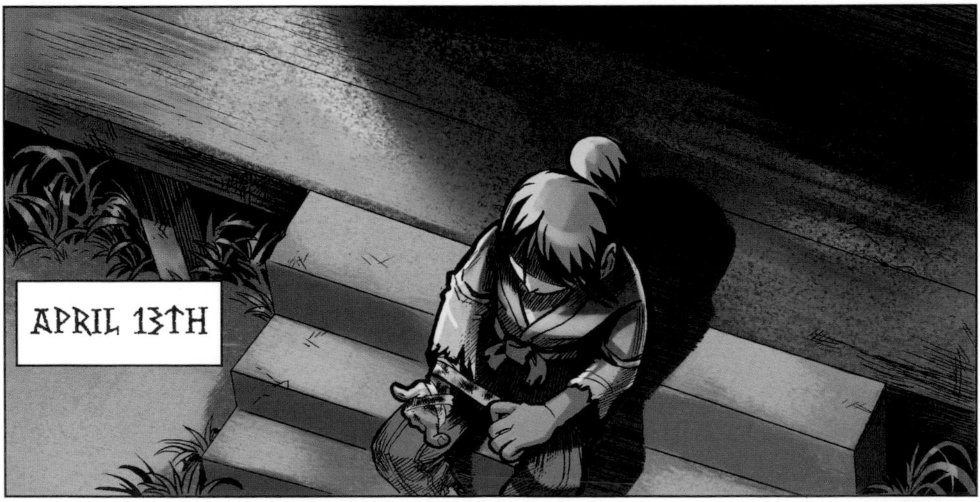
APRIL 13TH

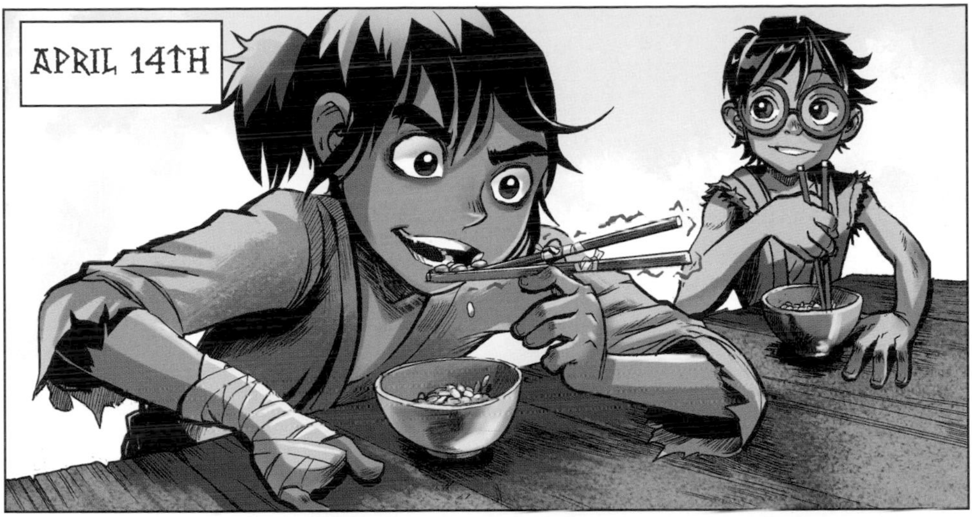
APRIL 14TH

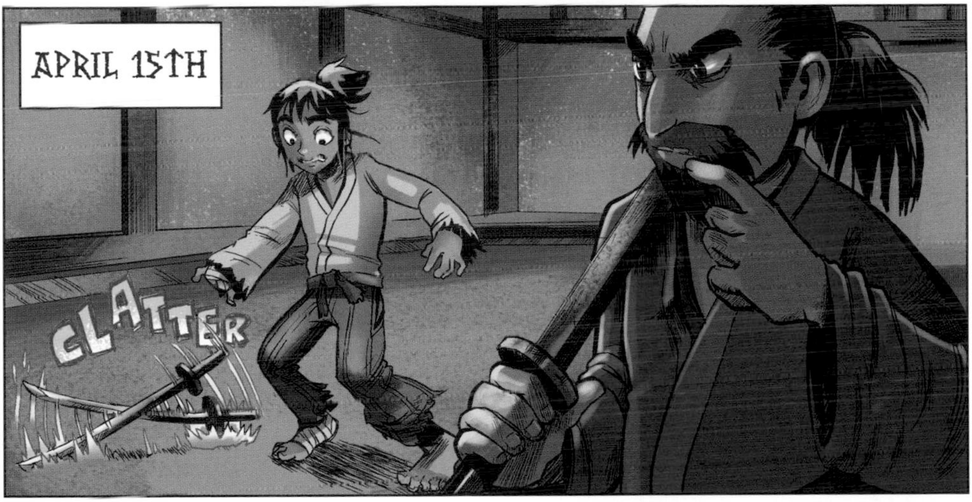
APRIL 15TH
CLATTER

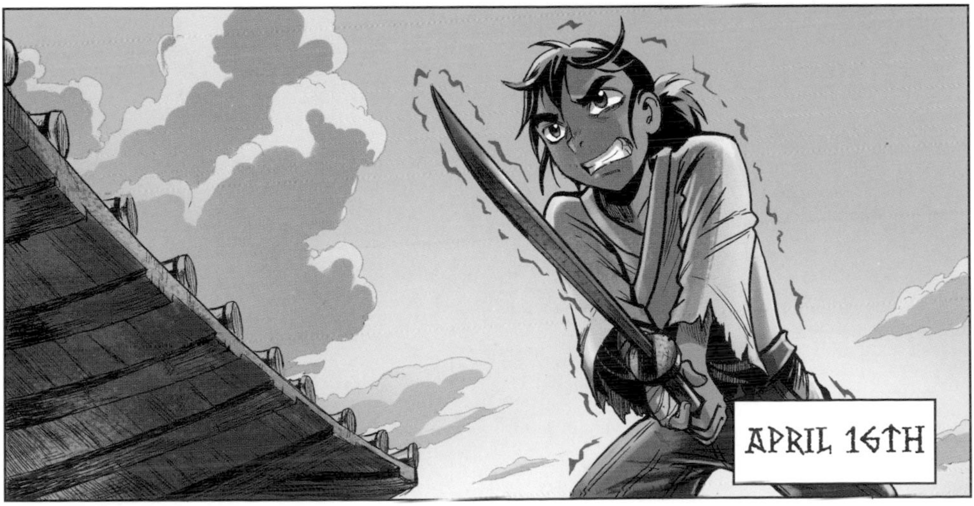
APRIL 16TH

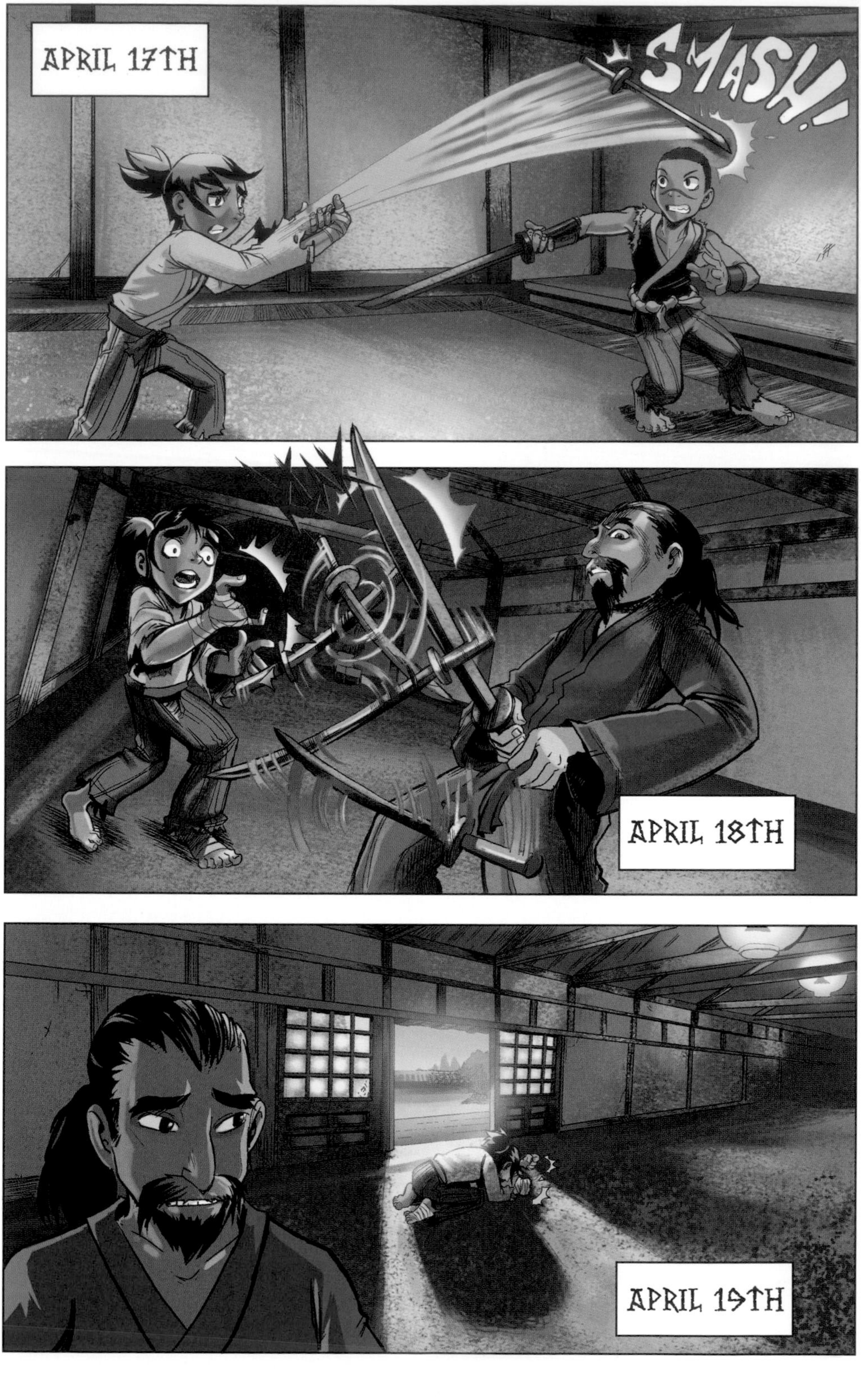
APRIL 17TH
SMASH!
APRIL 18TH
APRIL 19TH

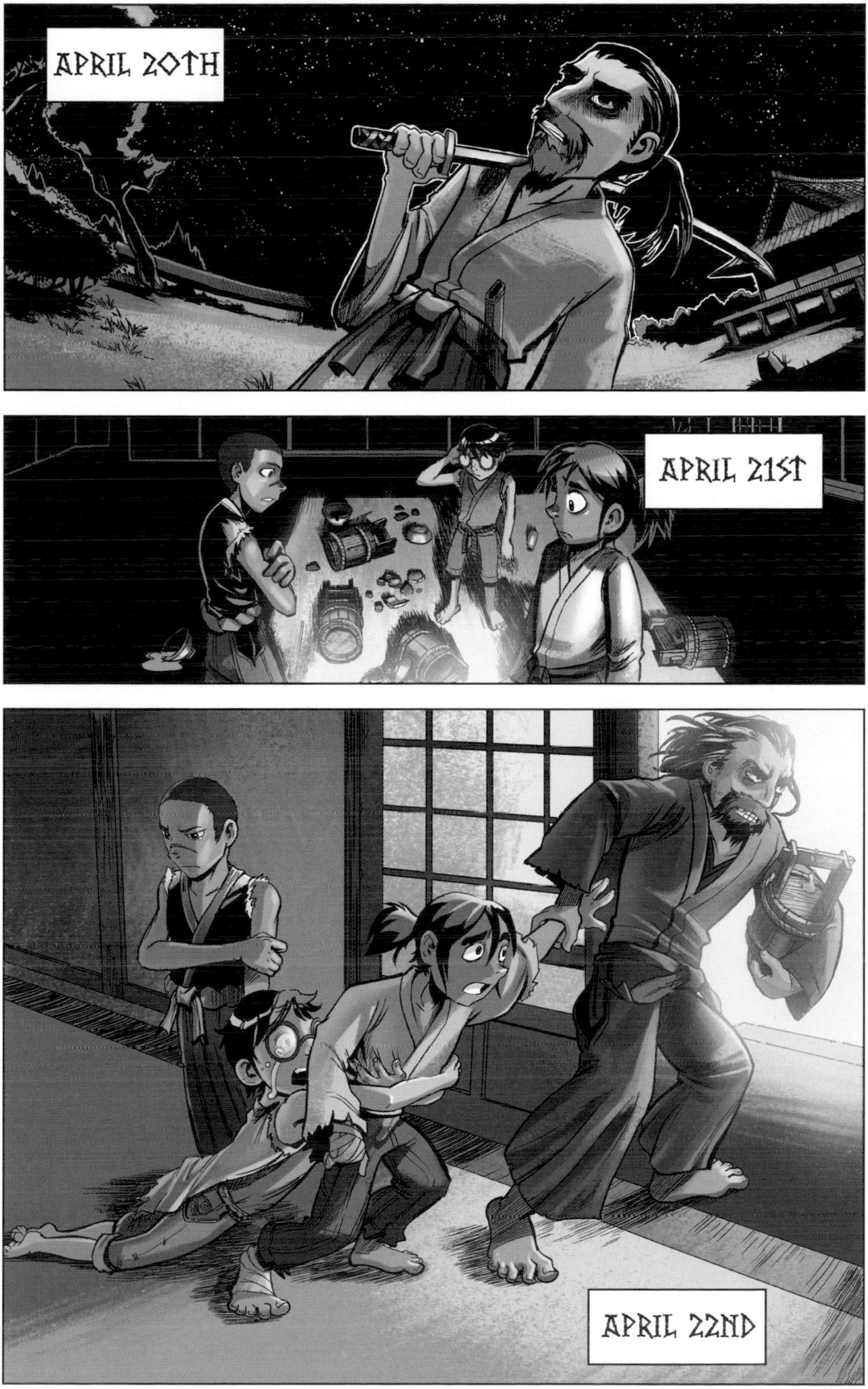
APRIL 20TH
APRIL 21ST
APRIL 22ND

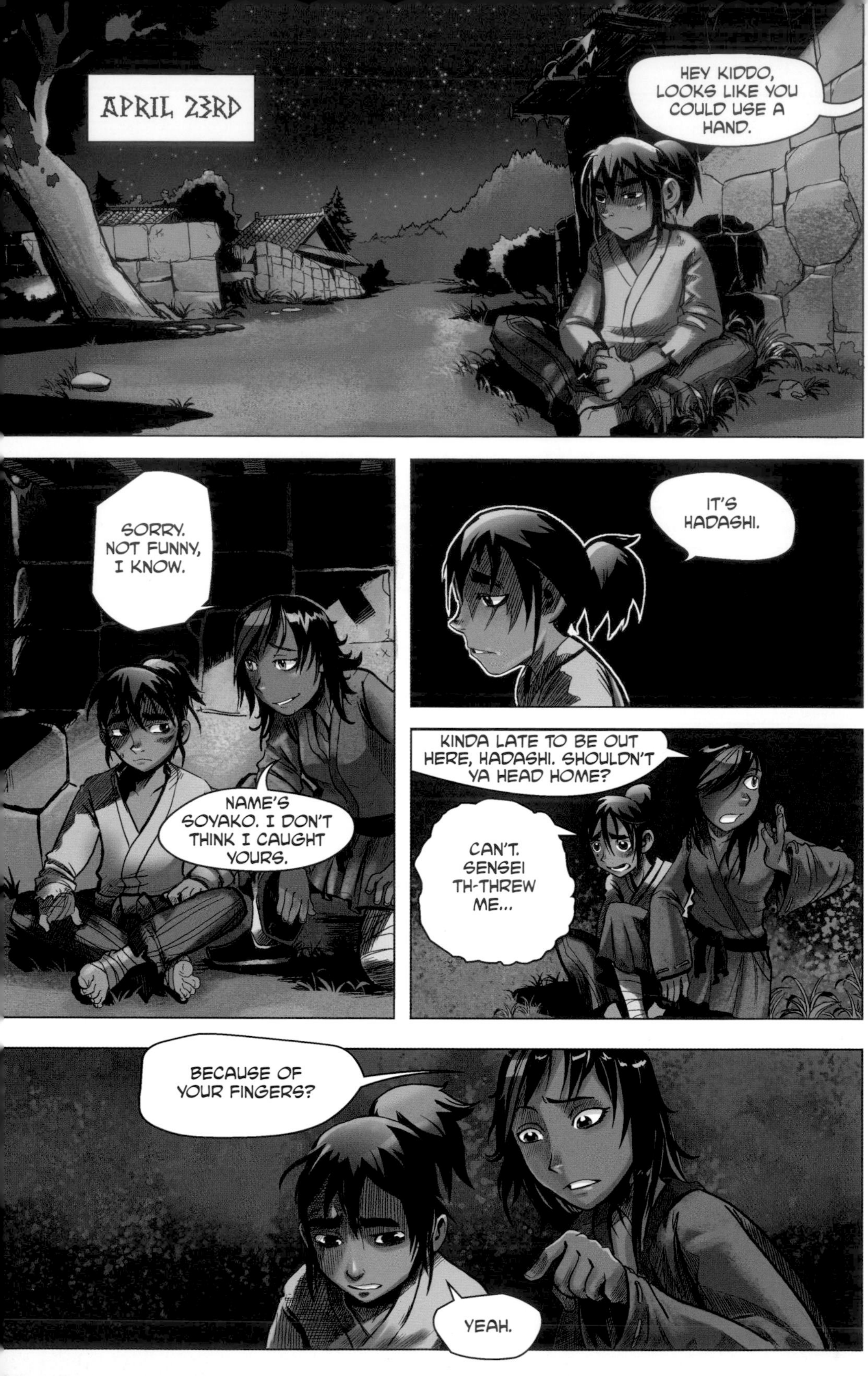
APRIL 23RD
HEY KIDDO, LOOKS LIKE YOU COULD USE A HAND.
SORRY. NOT FUNNY, I KNOW.
NAME'S SOYAKO. I DON'T THINK I CAUGHT YOURS.
IT'S HADASHI.
KINDA LATE TO BE OUT HERE, HADASHI. SHOULDN'T YA HEAD HOME?
CAN'T. SENSEI TH-THREW ME...
BECAUSE OF YOUR FINGERS?
YEAH.

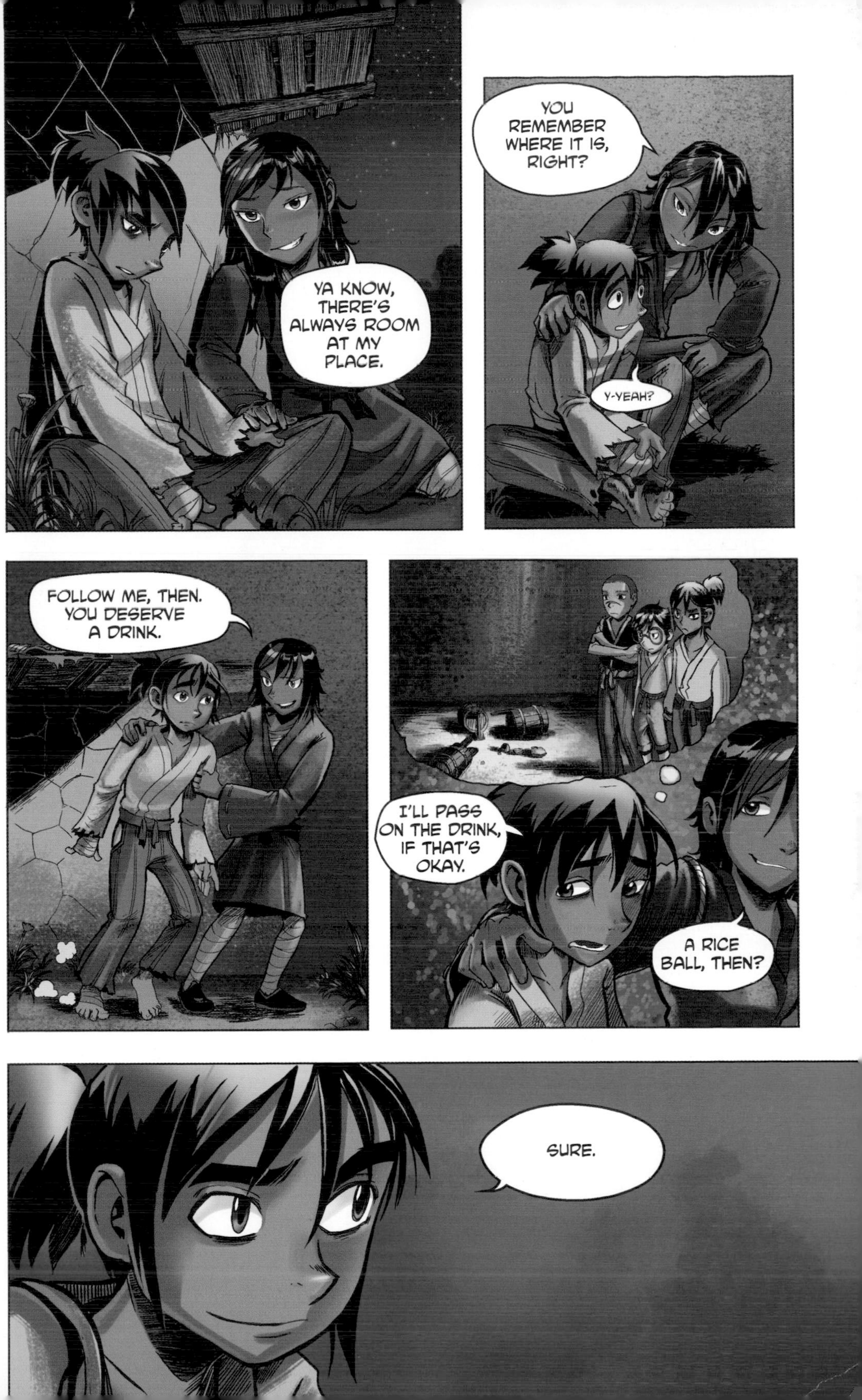
YA KNOW, THERE'S ALWAYS ROOM AT MY PLACE.
YOU REMEMBER WHERE IT IS, RIGHT?
Y-YEAH?
FOLLOW ME, THEN. YOU DESERVE A DRINK.
I'LL PASS ON THE DRINK, IF THAT'S OKAY.
A RICE BALL, THEN?
SURE.

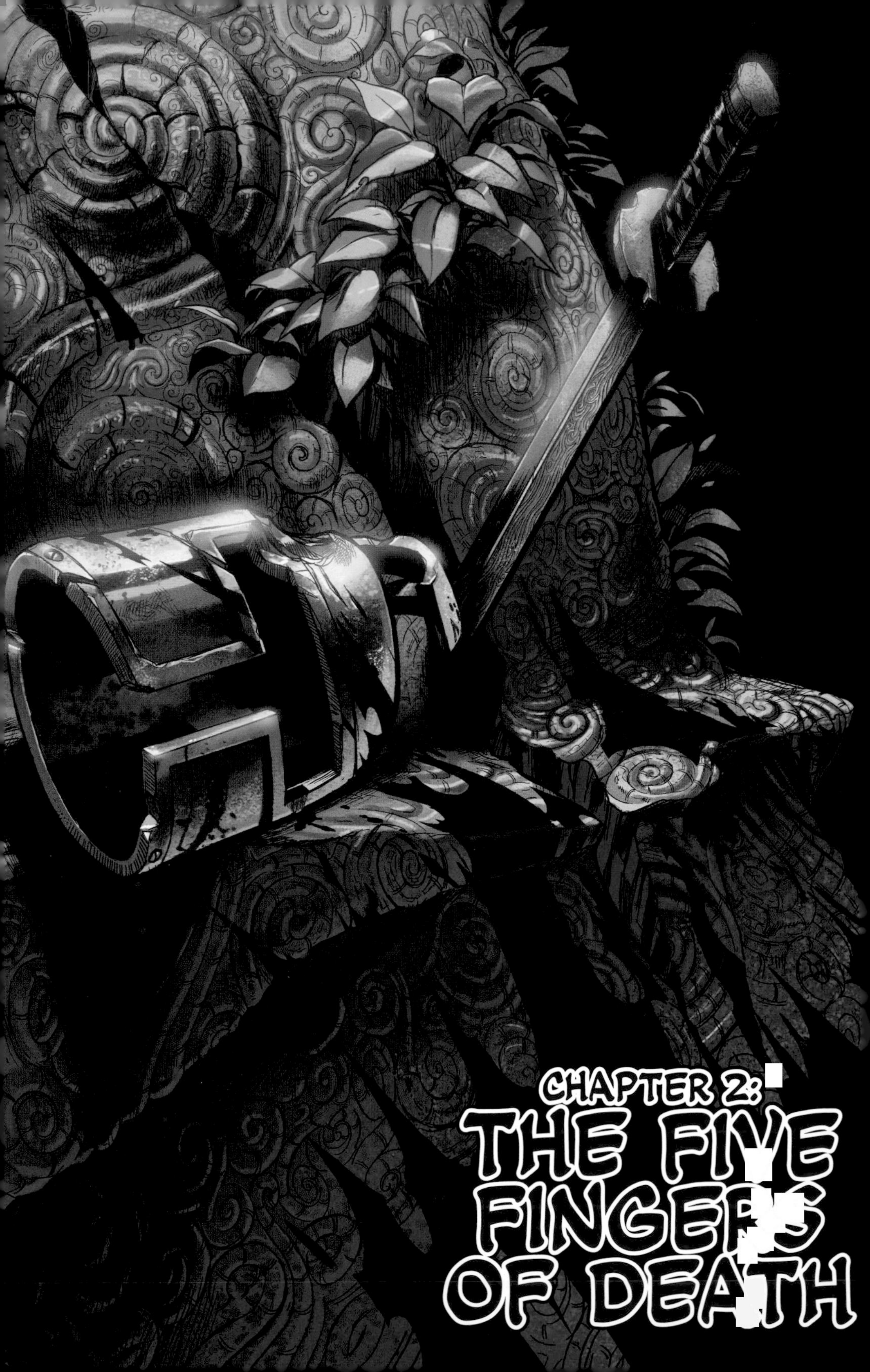
CHAPTER 2:
THE FIVE FINGERS OF DEATH

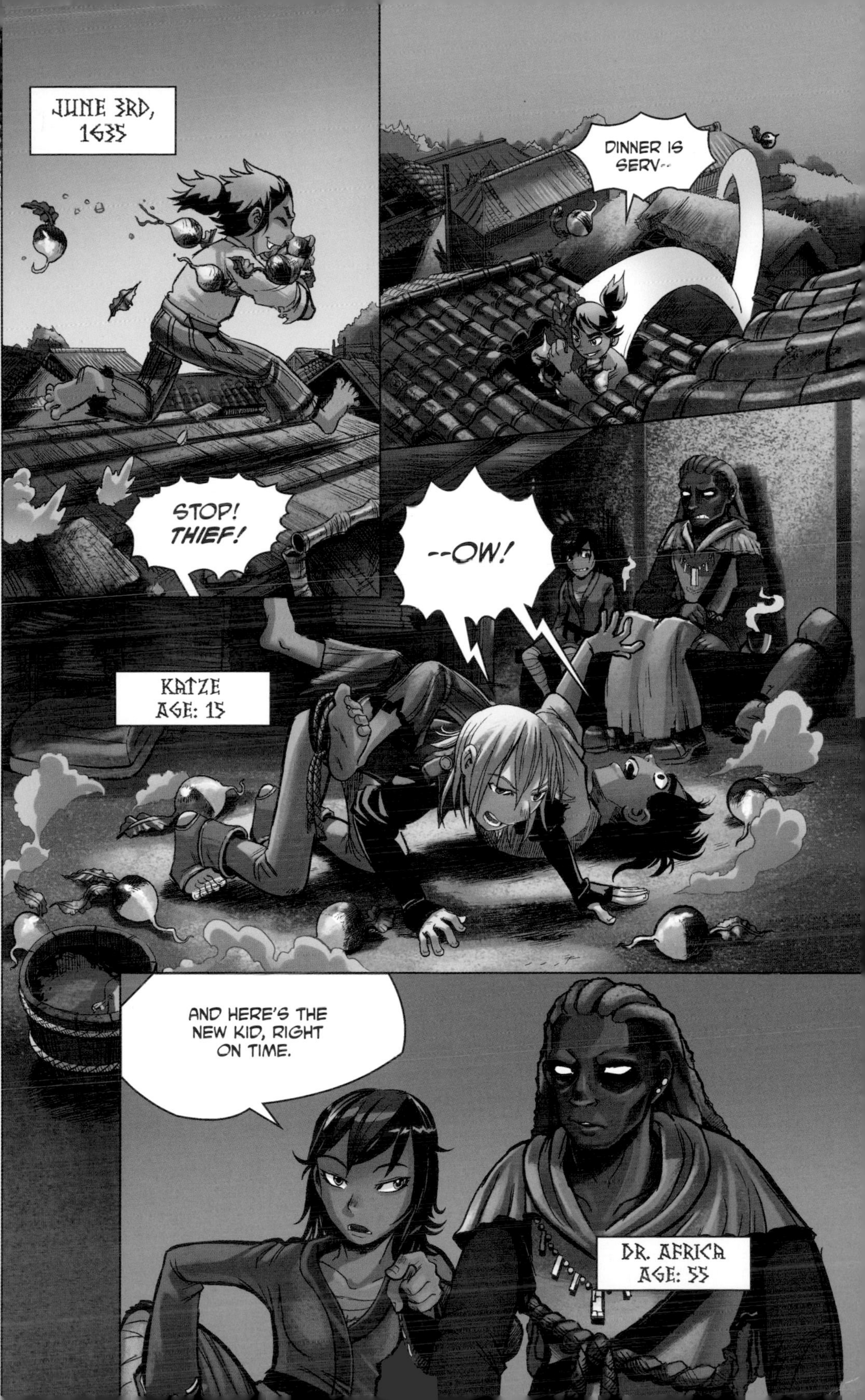
JUNE 3RD, 1635
DINNER IS SERV--
STOP! THIEF!
--OW!
KATZE AGE: 15
AND HERE'S THE NEW KID, RIGHT ON TIME.
DR. AFRICA AGE: 55

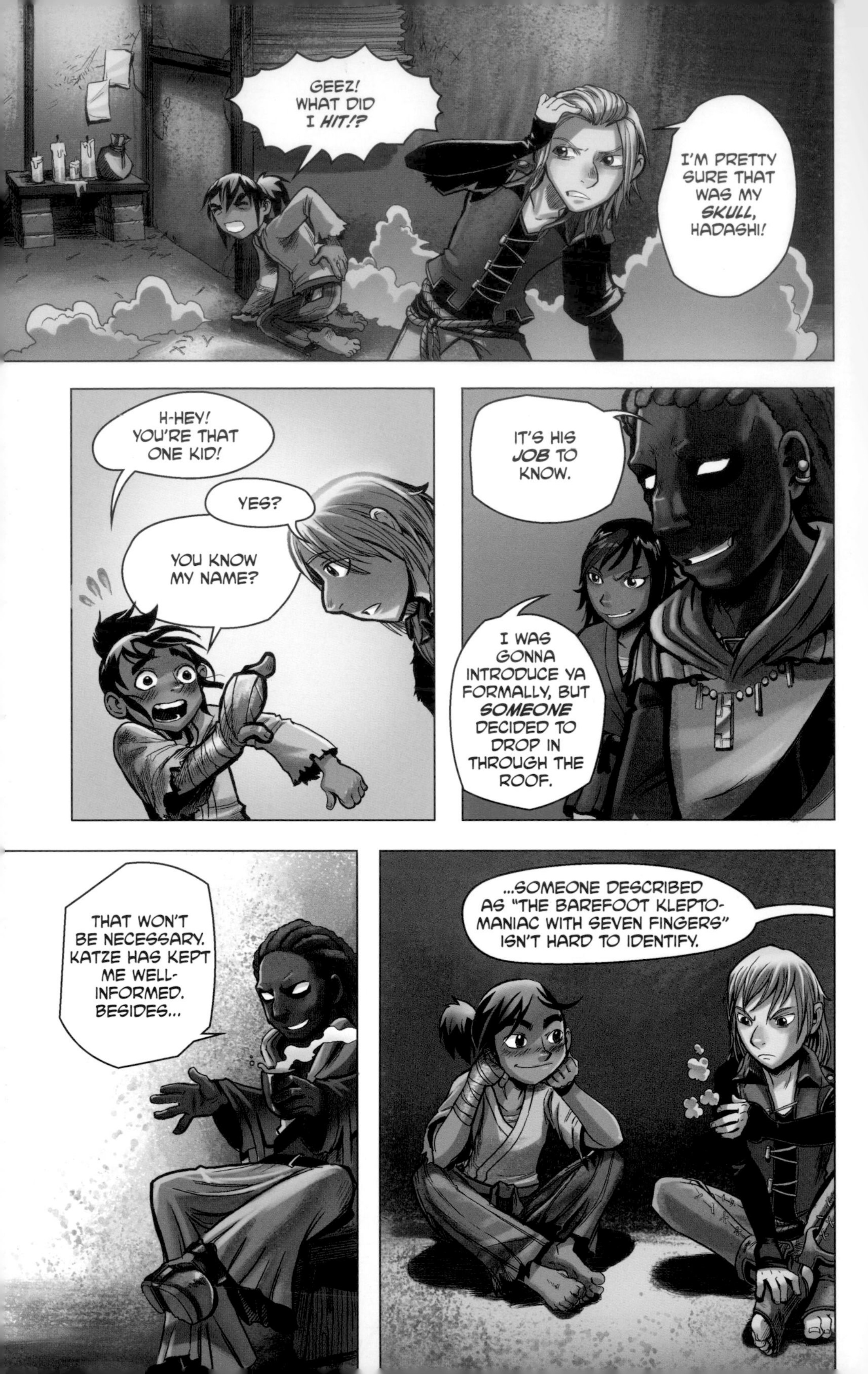
GEEZ! WHAT DID I HIT!?
I'M PRETTY SURE THAT WAS MY SKULL, HADASHI!
H-HEY! YOU'RE THAT ONE KID!
YES?
YOU KNOW MY NAME?
IT'S HIS JOB TO KNOW.
I WAS GONNA INTRODUCE YA FORMALLY, BUT SOMEONE DECIDED TO DROP IN THROUGH THE ROOF.
THAT WON'T BE NECESSARY. KATZE HAS KEPT ME WELL-INFORMED. BESIDES...
...SOMEONE DESCRIBED AS "THE BAREFOOT KLEPTO-MANIAC WITH SEVEN FINGERS" ISN'T HARD TO IDENTIFY.

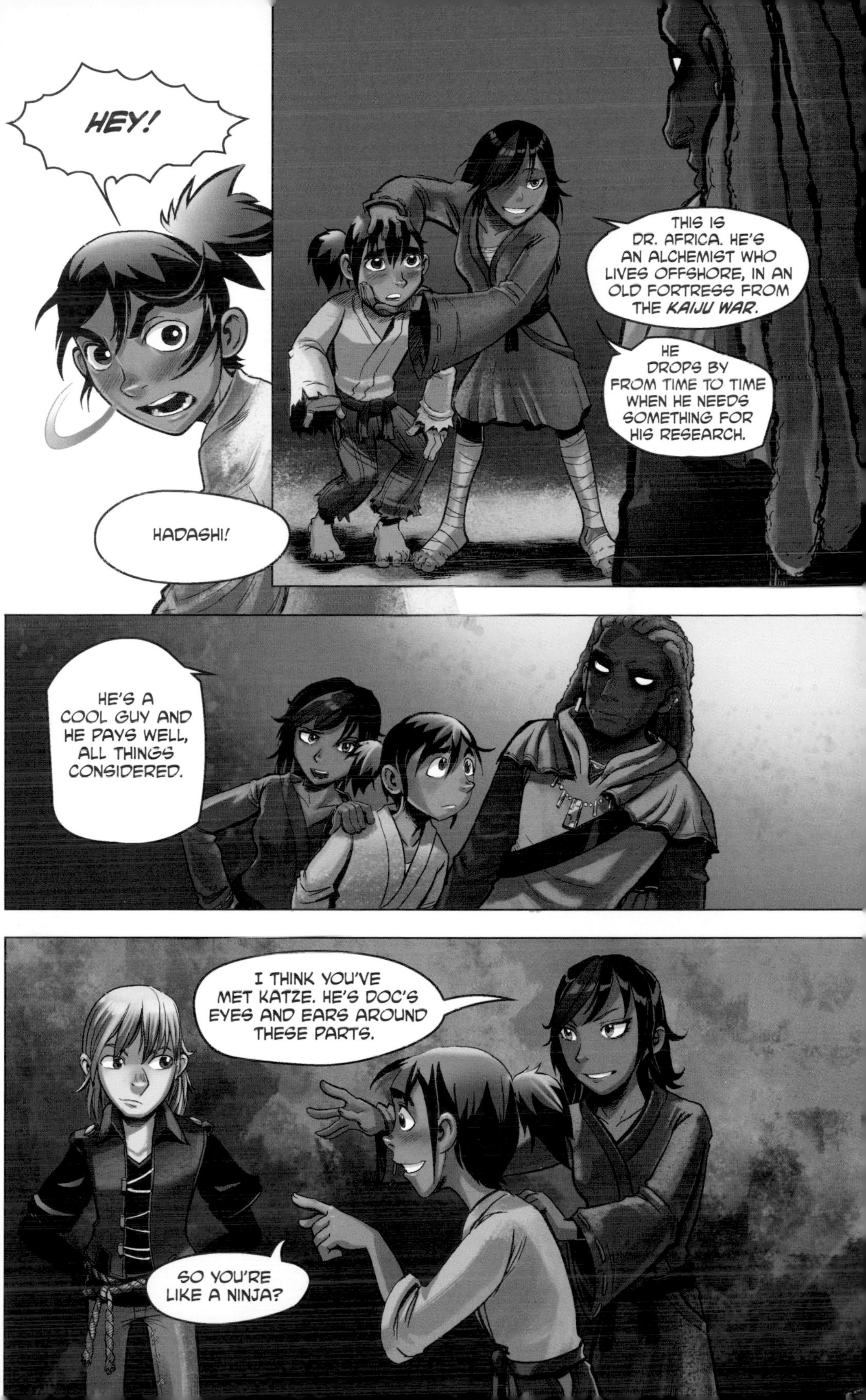
HEY!
HADASHI!
THIS IS DR. AFRICA. HE'S AN ALCHEMIST WHO LIVES OFFSHORE, IN AN OLD FORTRESS FROM THE *KAIJU WAR*.
HE DROPS BY FROM TIME TO TIME WHEN HE NEEDS SOMETHING FOR HIS RESEARCH.
HE'S A COOL GUY AND HE PAYS WELL, ALL THINGS CONSIDERED.
I THINK YOU'VE MET KATZE. HE'S DOC'S EYES AND EARS AROUND THESE PARTS.
SO YOU'RE LIKE A NINJA?

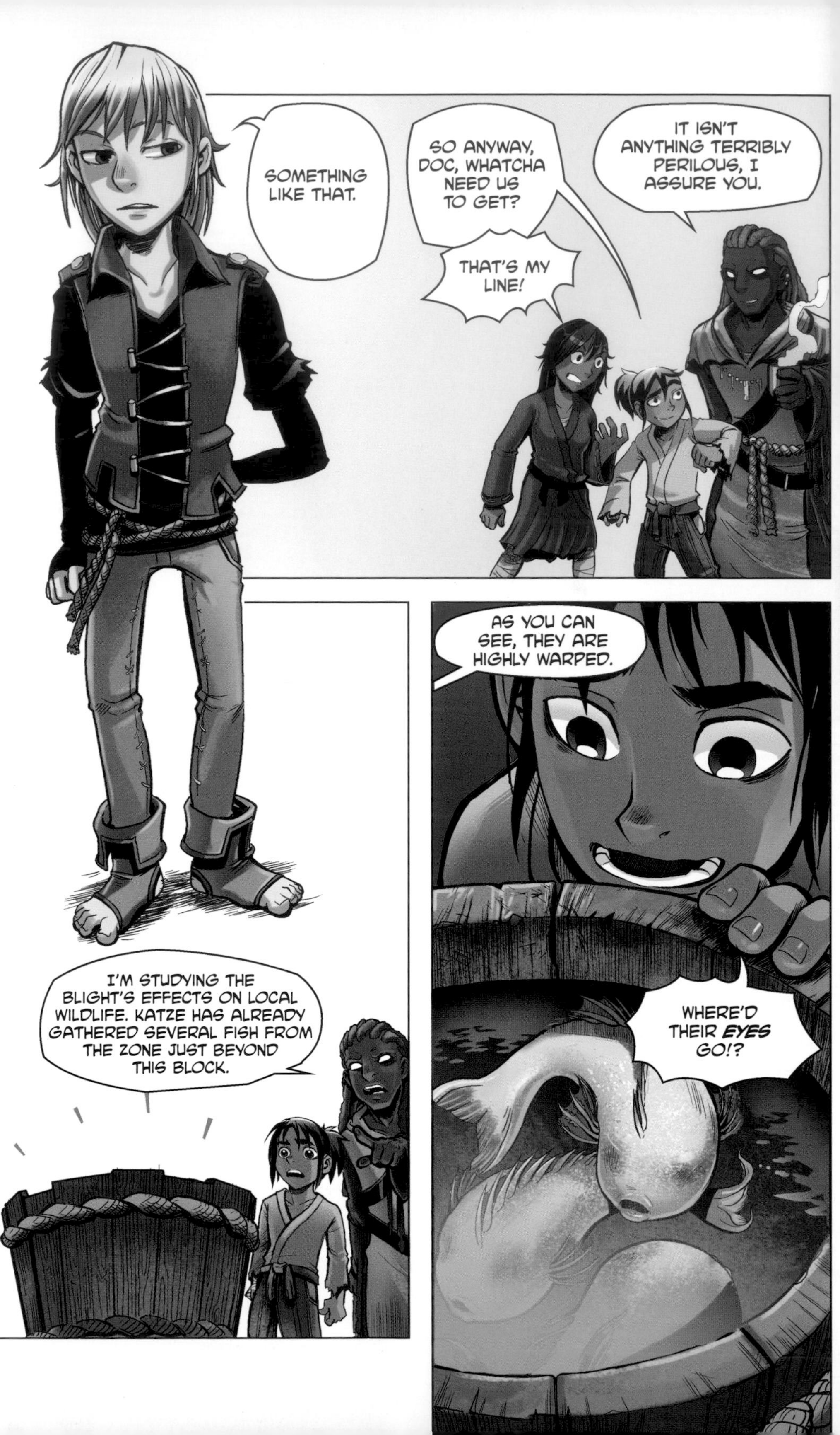
SOMETHING LIKE THAT.
SO ANYWAY, DOC, WHATCHA NEED US TO GET?
THAT'S MY LINE!
IT ISN'T ANYTHING TERRIBLY PERILOUS, I ASSURE YOU.
I'M STUDYING THE BLIGHT'S EFFECTS ON LOCAL WILDLIFE. KATZE HAS ALREADY GATHERED SEVERAL FISH FROM THE ZONE JUST BEYOND THIS BLOCK.
AS YOU CAN SEE, THEY ARE HIGHLY WARPED.
WHERE'D THEIR ***EYES*** GO!?

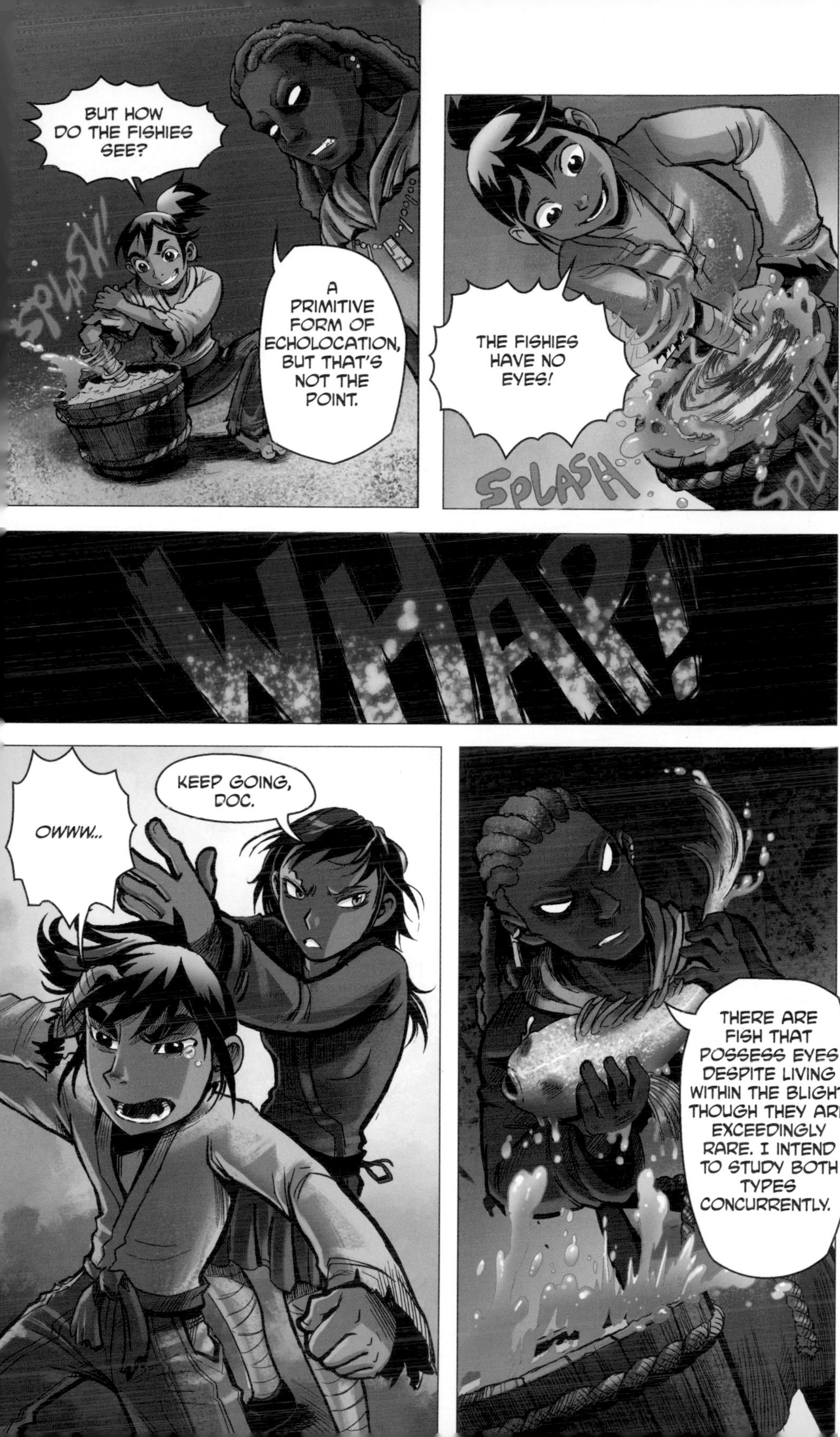
BUT HOW DO THE FISHIES SEE?
SPLASH!
A PRIMITIVE FORM OF ECHOLOCATION, BUT THAT'S NOT THE POINT.
THE FISHIES HAVE NO EYES!
SPLASH
SPLASH
WHAP!
OWWW...
KEEP GOING, DOC.
THERE ARE FISH THAT POSSESS EYES DESPITE LIVING WITHIN THE BLIGHT, THOUGH THEY ARE EXCEEDINGLY RARE. I INTEND TO STUDY BOTH TYPES CONCURRENTLY.

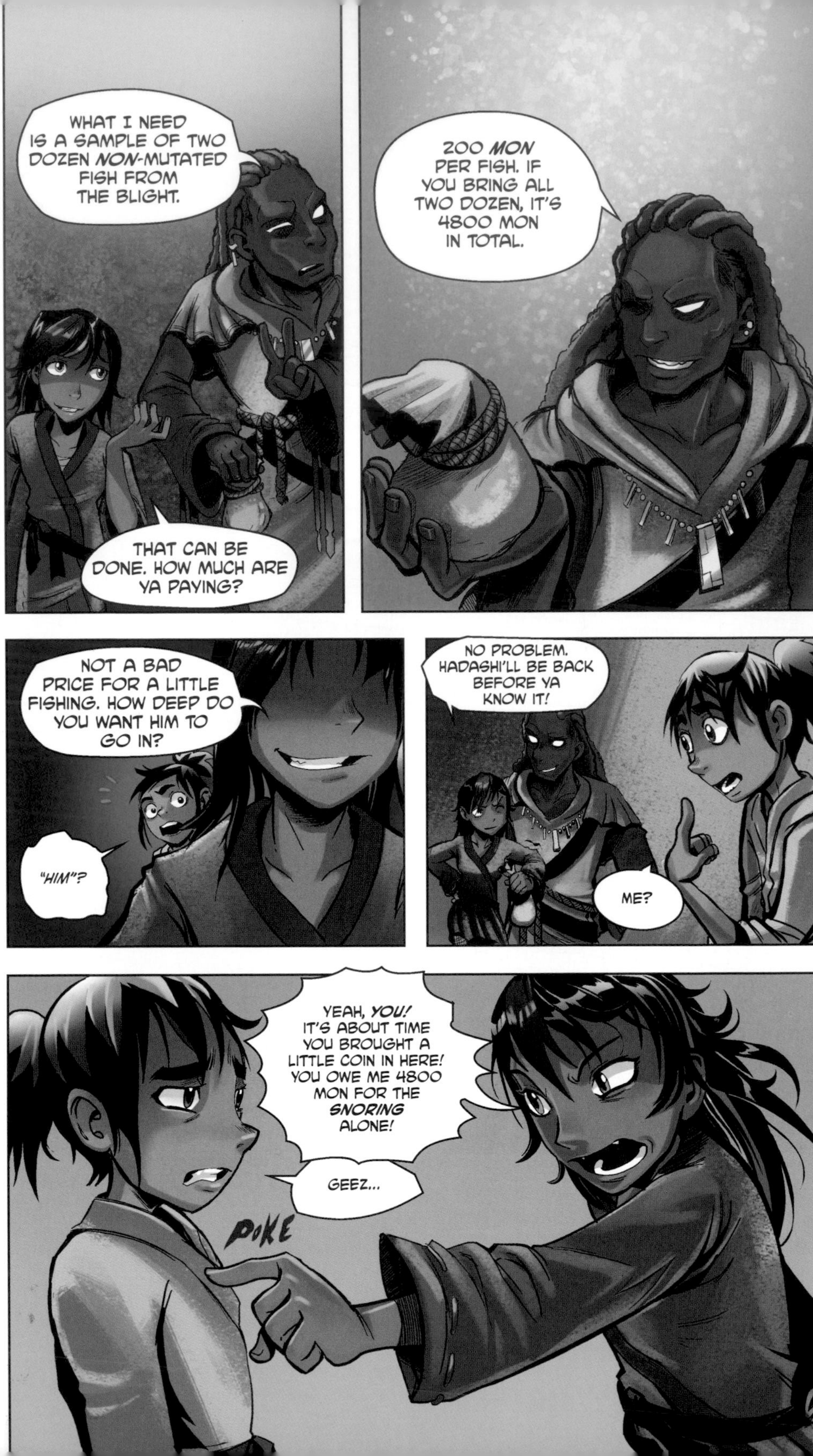

WHAT I NEED IS A SAMPLE OF TWO DOZEN *NON*-MUTATED FISH FROM THE BLIGHT.
THAT CAN BE DONE. HOW MUCH ARE YA PAYING?
200 *MON* PER FISH. IF YOU BRING ALL TWO DOZEN, IT'S 4800 MON IN TOTAL.
NOT A BAD PRICE FOR A LITTLE FISHING. HOW DEEP DO YOU WANT HIM TO GO IN?
"HIM"?
NO PROBLEM. HADASHI'LL BE BACK BEFORE YA KNOW IT!
ME?
YEAH, *YOU!* IT'S ABOUT TIME YOU BROUGHT A LITTLE COIN IN HERE! YOU OWE ME 4800 MON FOR THE *SNORING* ALONE!
GEEZ...
POKE

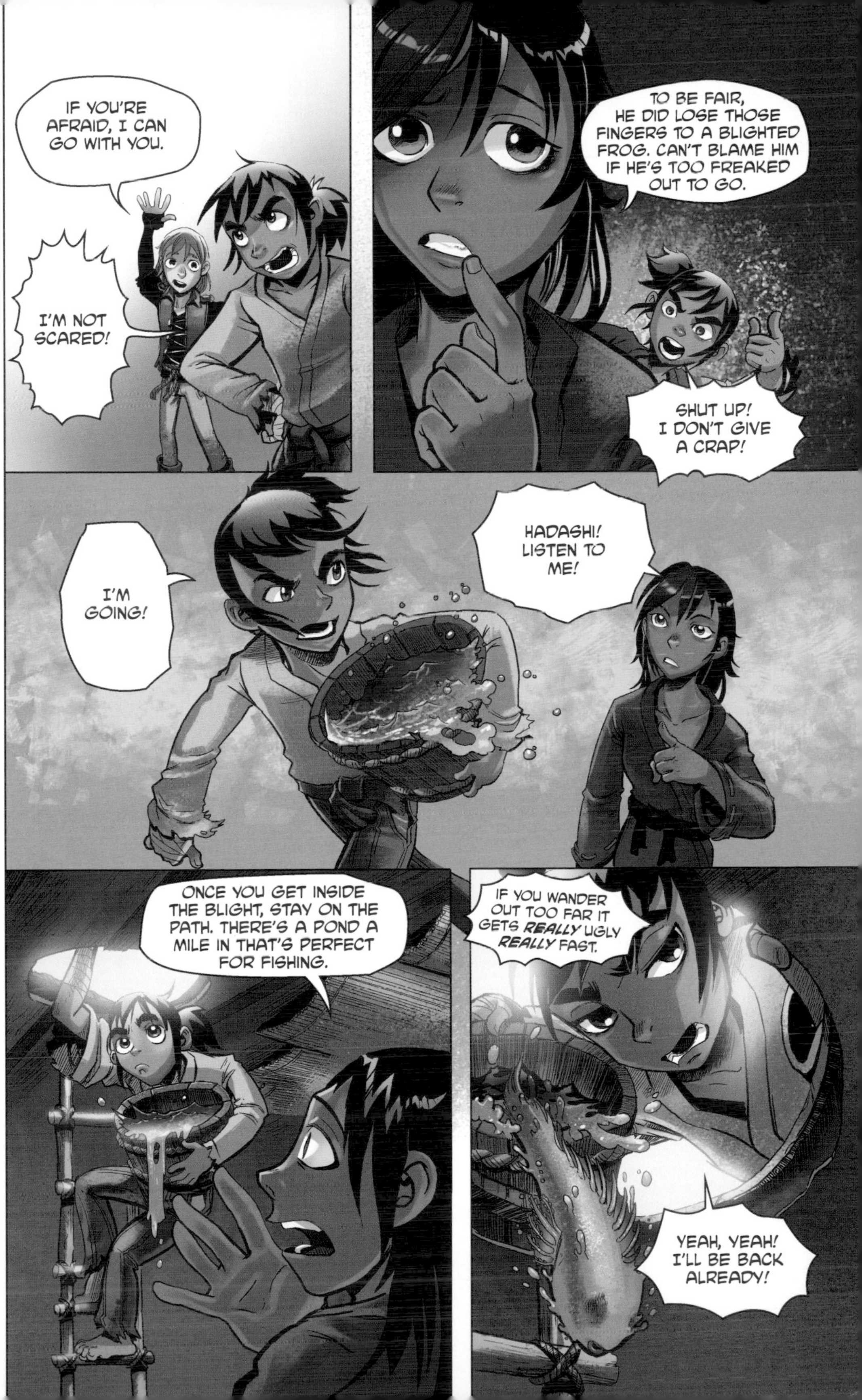
IF YOU'RE AFRAID, I CAN GO WITH YOU.
I'M NOT SCARED!
TO BE FAIR, HE DID LOSE THOSE FINGERS TO A BLIGHTED FROG. CAN'T BLAME HIM IF HE'S TOO FREAKED OUT TO GO.
SHUT UP! I DON'T GIVE A CRAP!
I'M GOING!
HADASHI! LISTEN TO ME!
ONCE YOU GET INSIDE THE BLIGHT, STAY ON THE PATH. THERE'S A POND A MILE IN THAT'S PERFECT FOR FISHING.
IF YOU WANDER OUT TOO FAR IT GETS REALLY UGLY REALLY FAST.
YEAH, YEAH! I'LL BE BACK ALREADY!

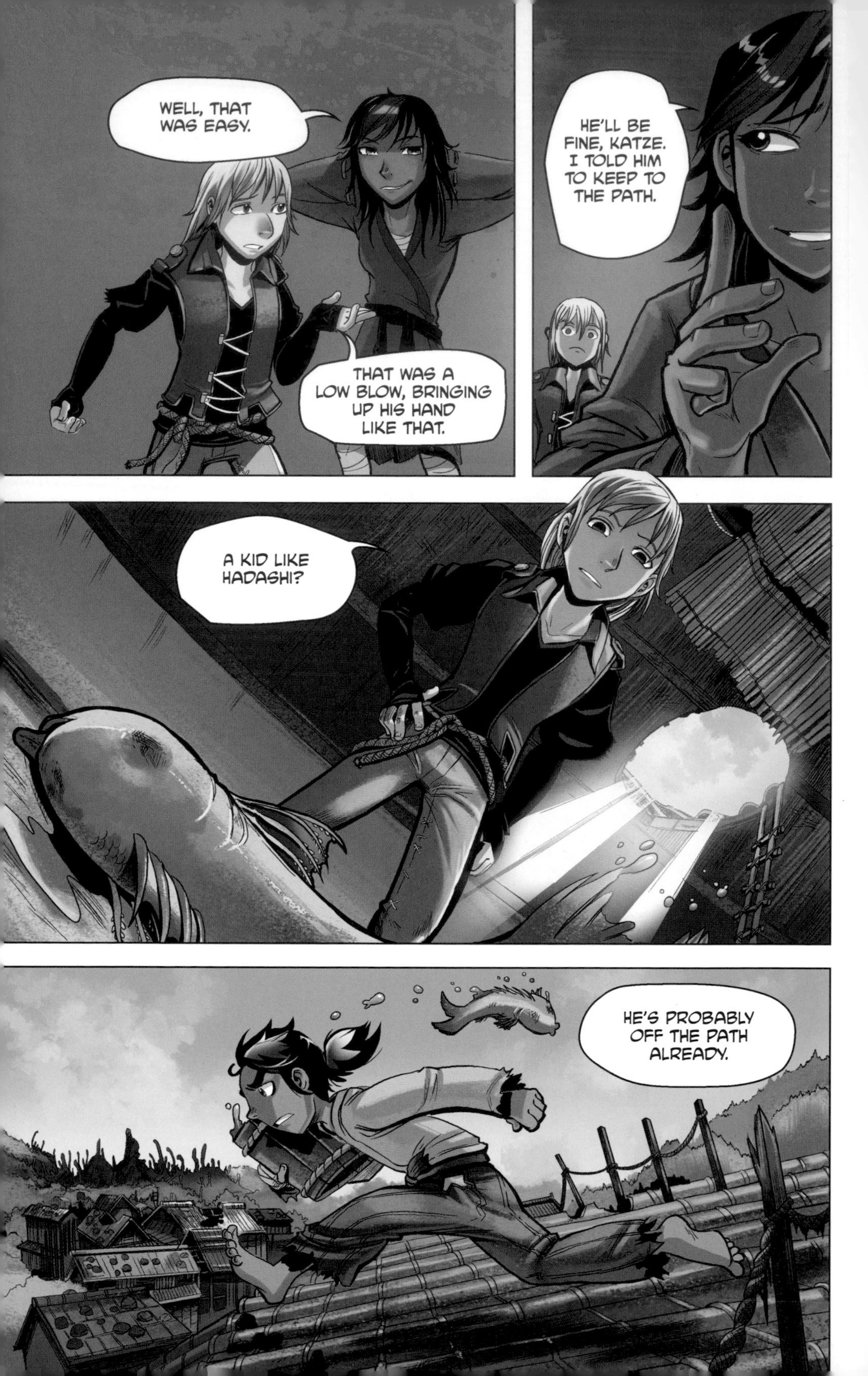
WELL, THAT WAS EASY.
THAT WAS A LOW BLOW, BRINGING UP HIS HAND LIKE THAT.
HE'LL BE FINE, KATZE. I TOLD HIM TO KEEP TO THE PATH.
A KID LIKE HADASHI?
HE'S PROBABLY OFF THE PATH ALREADY.

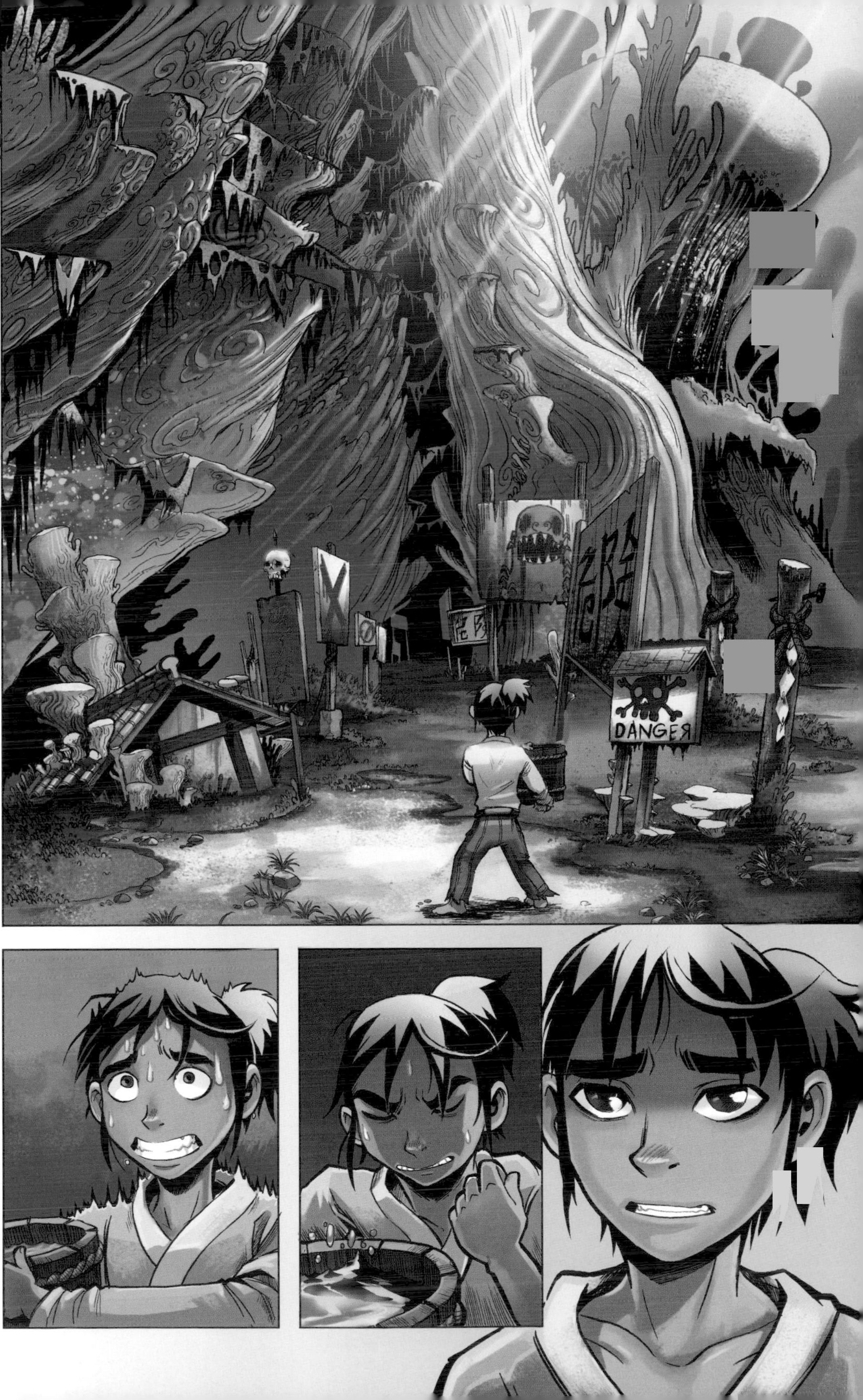
DANGEЯ

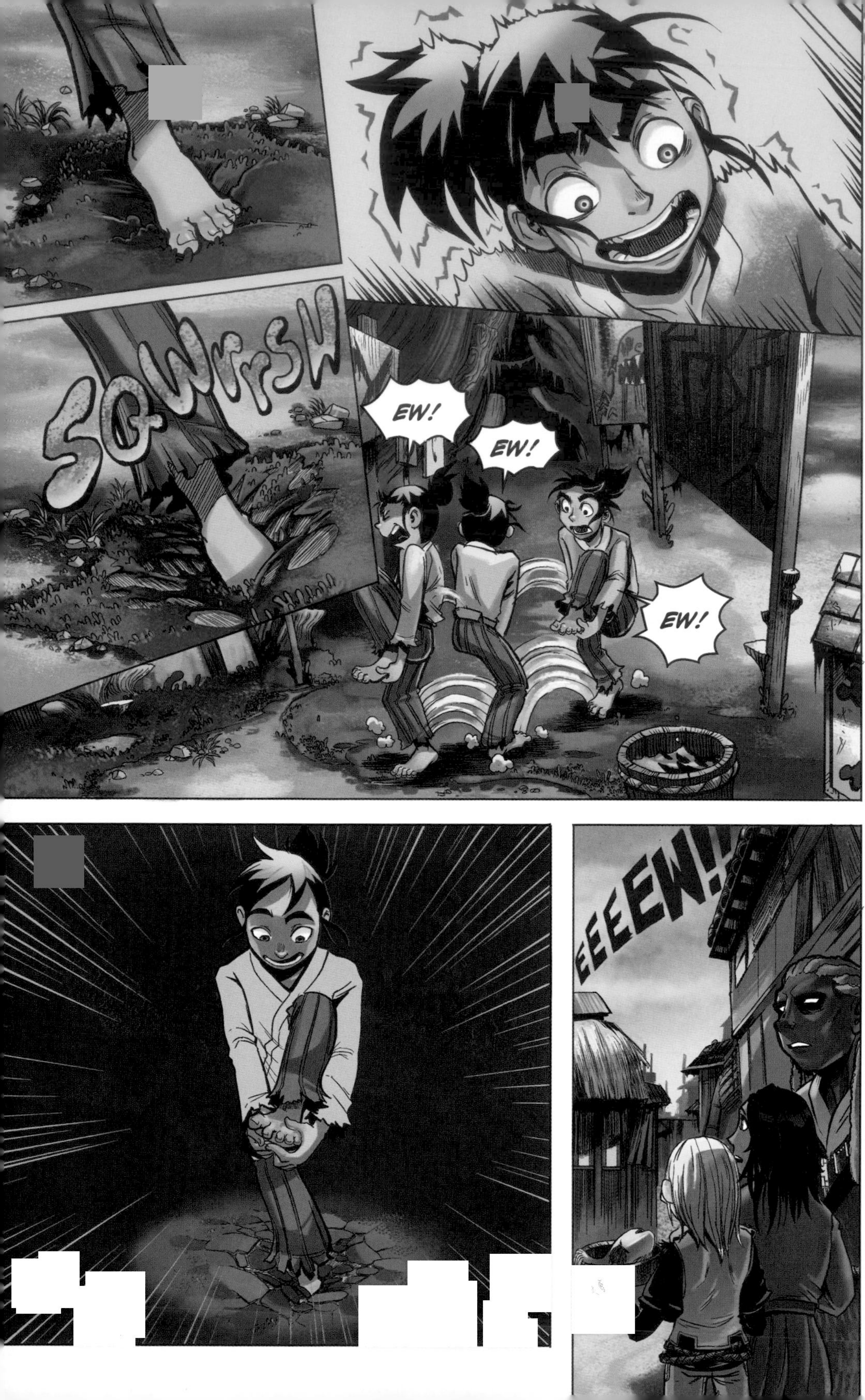
SQWRRSH
EW!
EW!
EW!
EEEEW!!

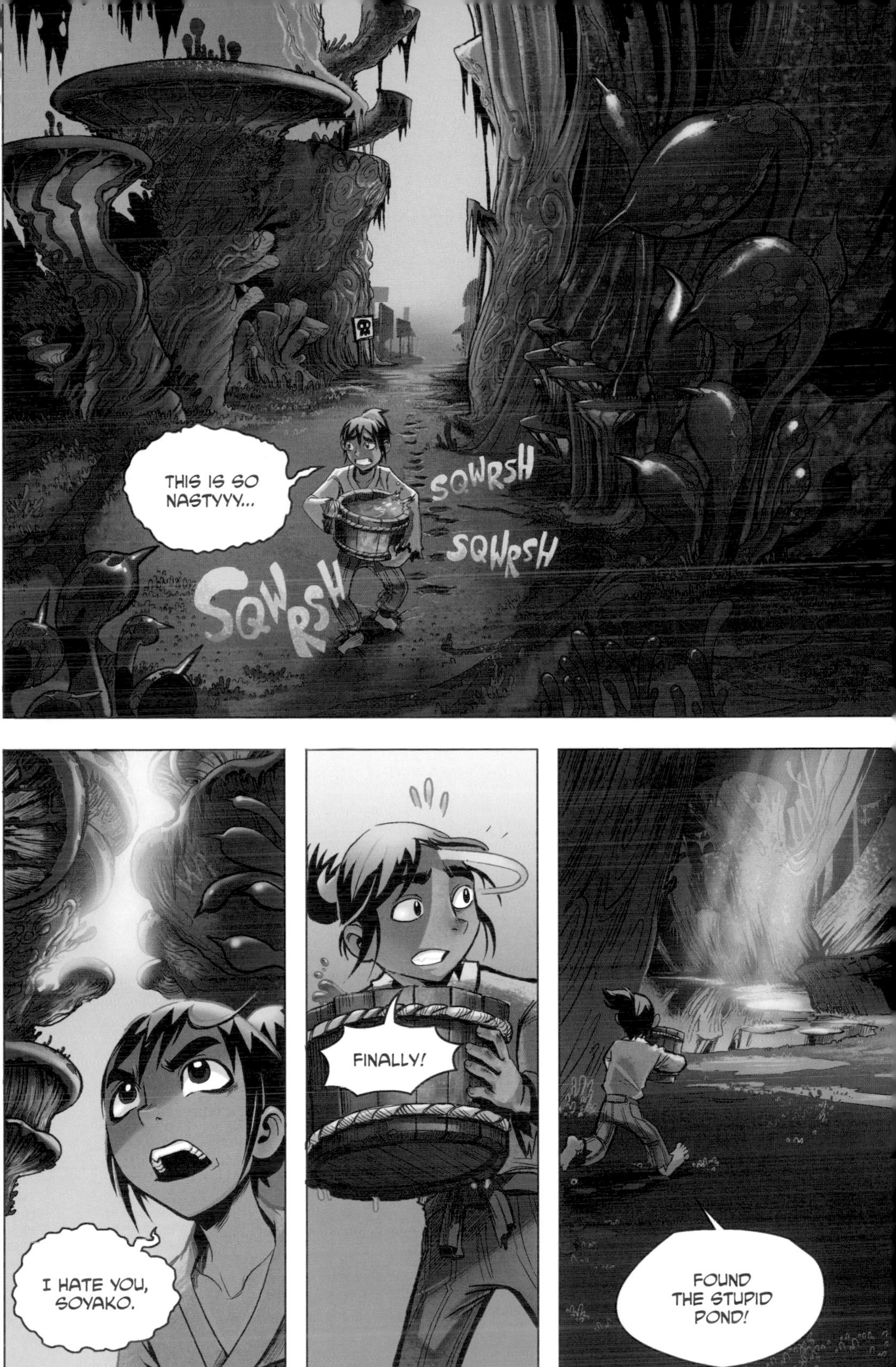
THIS IS SO NASTYYY...
SQWRSH
SQWRSH
SQWRSH
I HATE YOU, SOYAKO.
FINALLY!
FOUND THE STUPID POND!

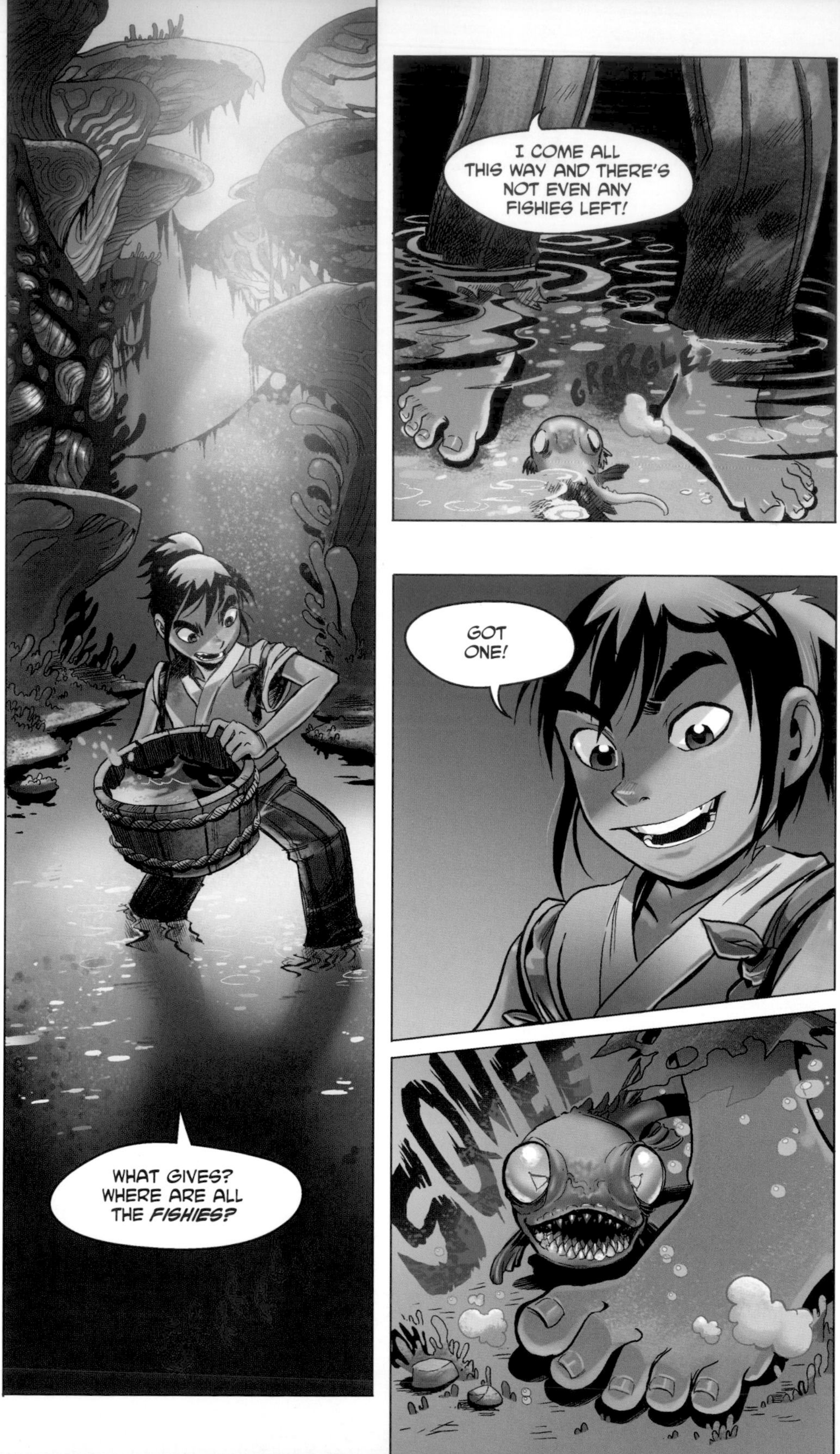
WHAT GIVES? WHERE ARE ALL THE *FISHIES?*
I COME ALL THIS WAY AND THERE'S NOT EVEN ANY FISHIES LEFT!
GRRRGLE
GOT ONE!

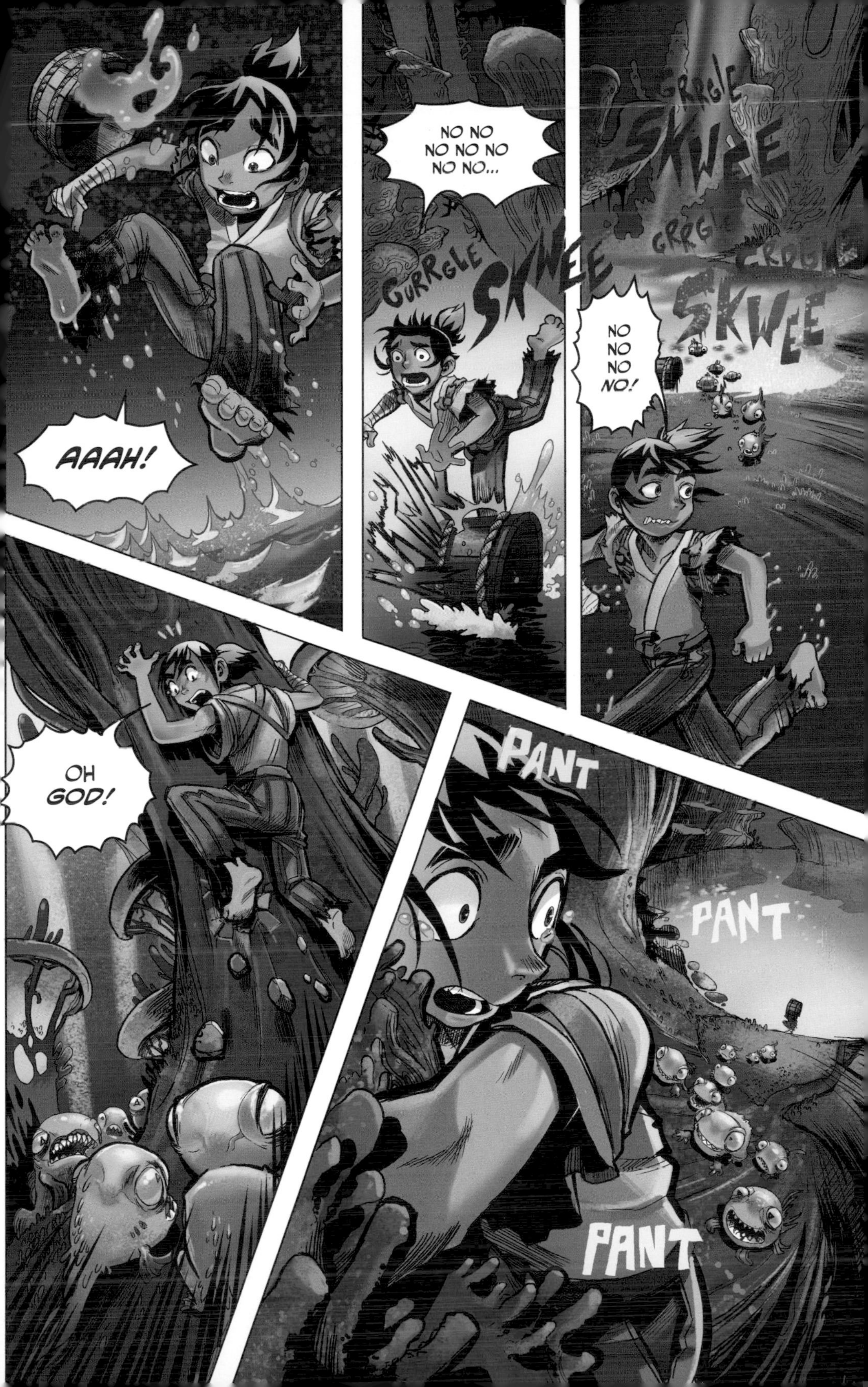
AAAH!
NO NO
NO NO NO
NO NO...
GURRGLE
SKWEE
GRRGLE
SKWEE
GRRGLE
GRRGLE
SKWEE
NO
NO
NO
NO!
OH
GOD!
PANT
PANT
PANT

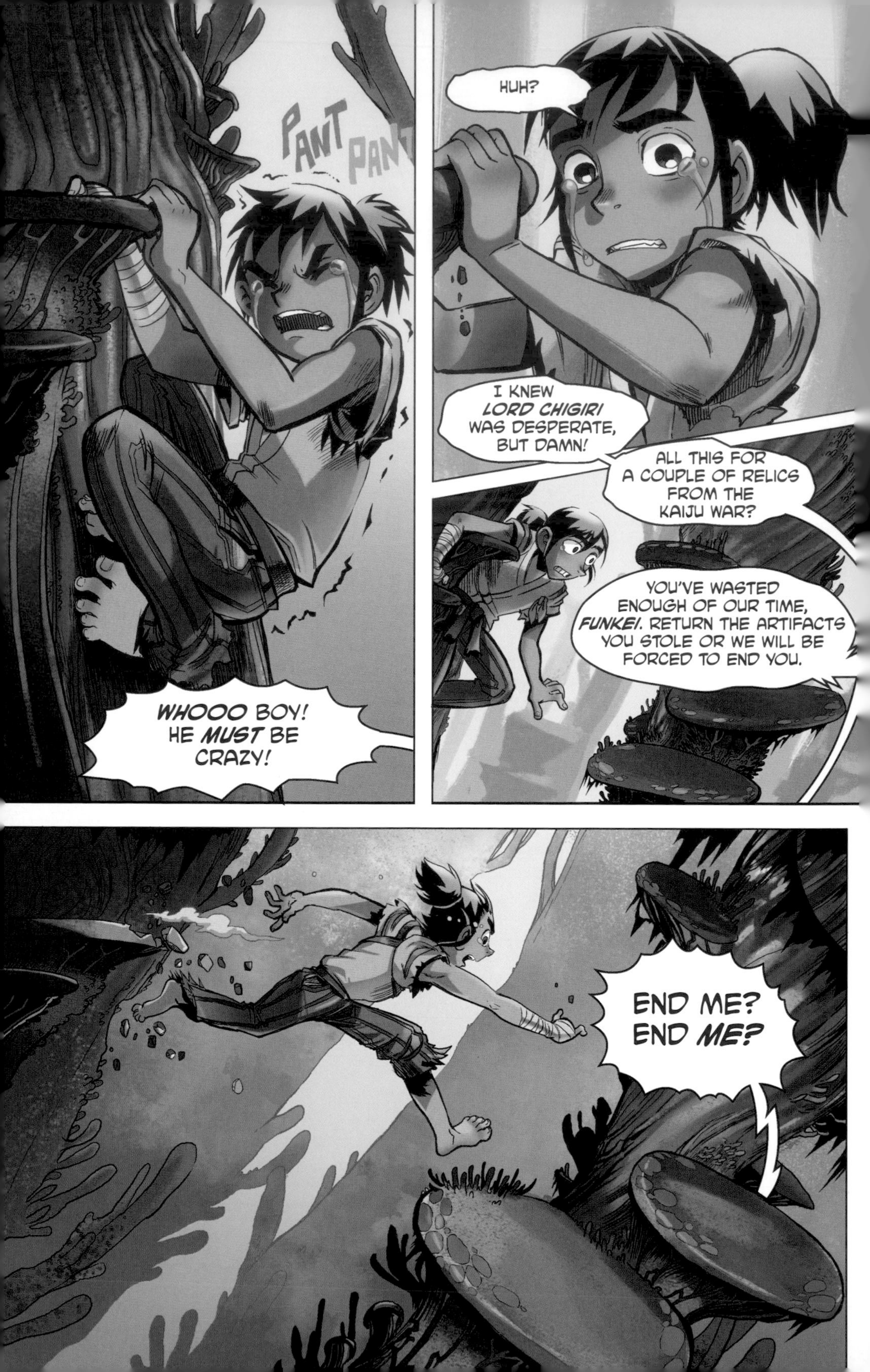
PANT PANT
WHOOO BOY! HE MUST BE CRAZY!
HUH?
I KNEW LORD CHIGIRI WAS DESPERATE, BUT DAMN!
ALL THIS FOR A COUPLE OF RELICS FROM THE KAIJU WAR?
YOU'VE WASTED ENOUGH OF OUR TIME, FUNKEI. RETURN THE ARTIFACTS YOU STOLE OR WE WILL BE FORCED TO END YOU.
END ME? END ME?

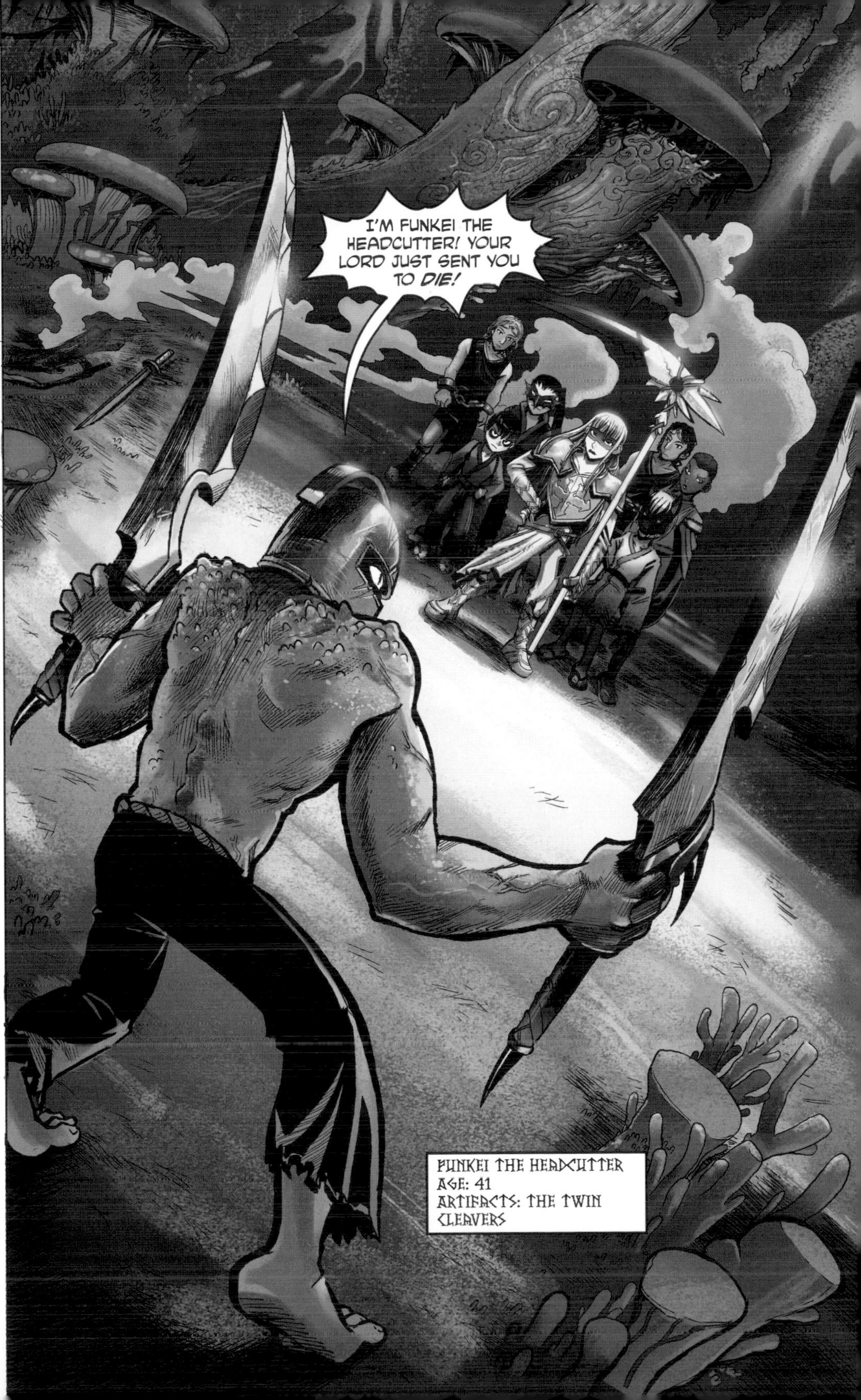
I'M FUNKEI THE HEADCUTTER! YOUR LORD JUST SENT YOU TO *DIE!*
FUNKEI THE HEADCUTTER
AGE: 41
ARTIFACTS: THE TWIN CLEAVERS

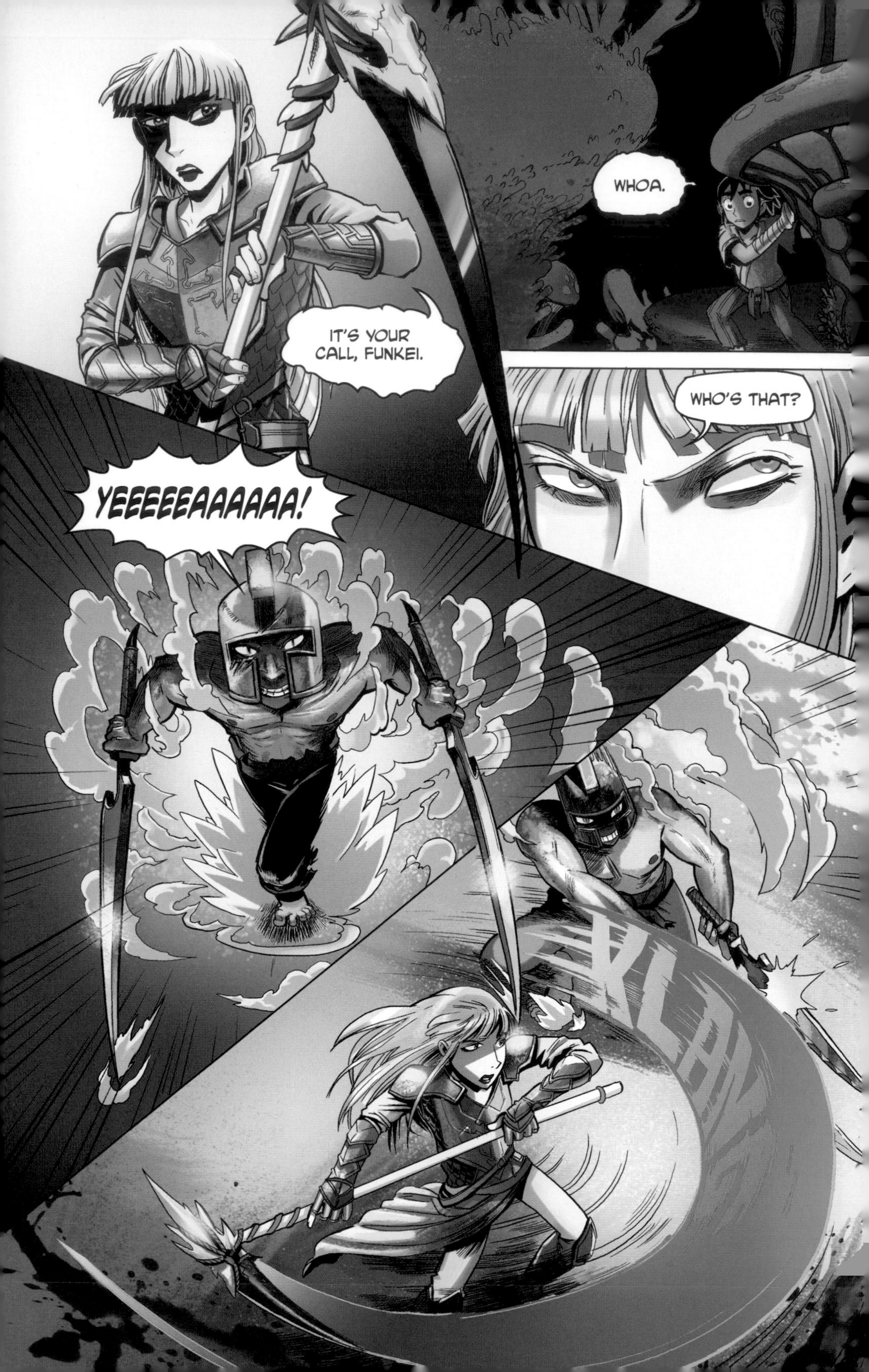
WHOA.
IT'S YOUR CALL, FUNKEI.
WHO'S THAT?
YEEEEEAAAAAA!

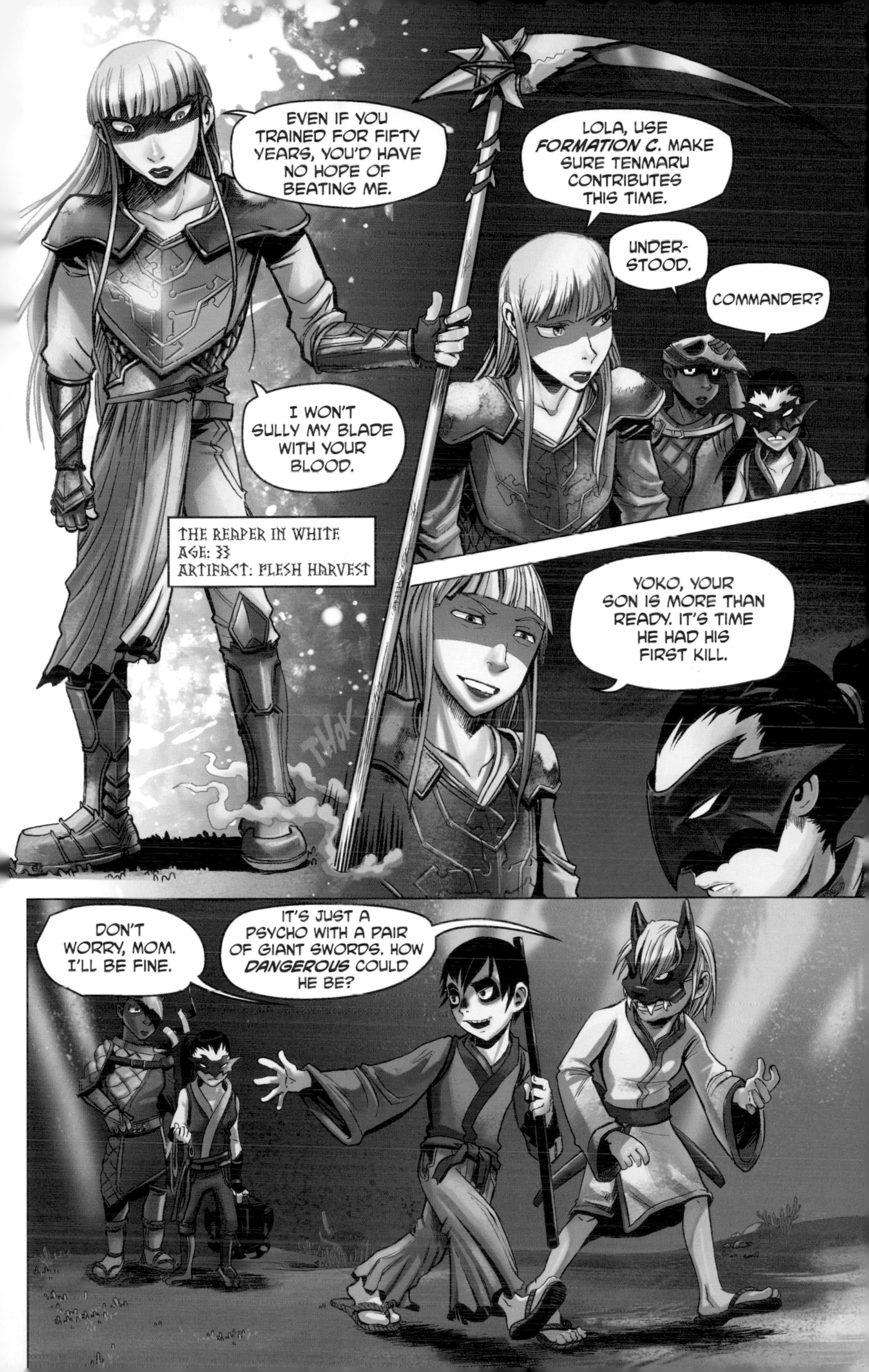
EVEN IF YOU TRAINED FOR FIFTY YEARS, YOU'D HAVE NO HOPE OF BEATING ME.
I WON'T SULLY MY BLADE WITH YOUR BLOOD.
THE REAPER IN WHITE
AGE: 33
ARTIFACT: FLESH HARVEST
LOLA, USE *FORMATION C*. MAKE SURE TENMARU CONTRIBUTES THIS TIME.
UNDER-STOOD.
COMMANDER?
YOKO, YOUR SON IS MORE THAN READY. IT'S TIME HE HAD HIS FIRST KILL.
THOK
DON'T WORRY, MOM. I'LL BE FINE.
IT'S JUST A PSYCHO WITH A PAIR OF GIANT SWORDS. HOW *DANGEROUS* COULD HE BE?

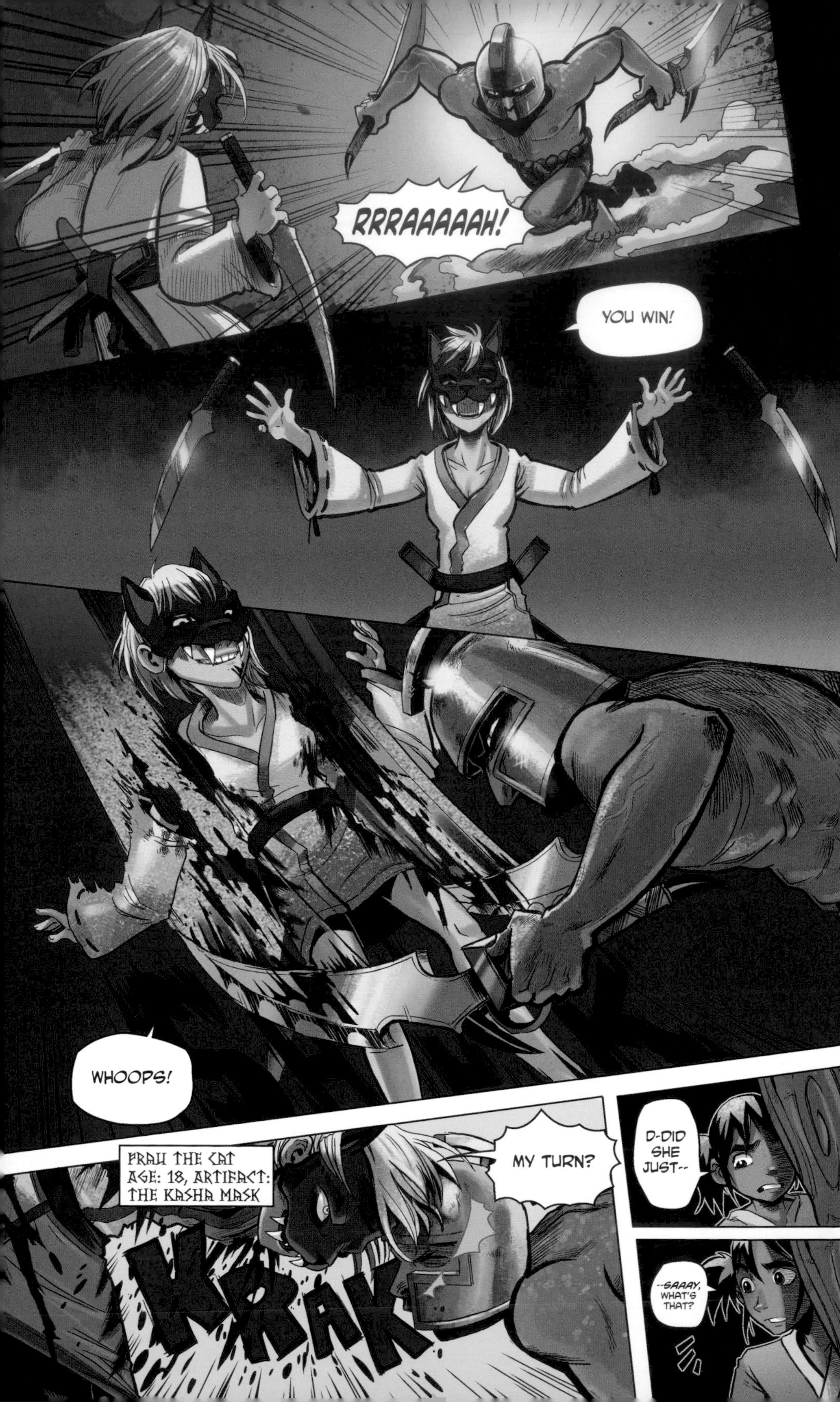

RRRAAAAAH!
YOU WIN!
WHOOPS!
FRAU THE CAT
AGE: 18, ARTIFACT:
THE KASHA MASK
MY TURN?
KRAK
D-DID SHE JUST--
--SAAAY, WHAT'S THAT?

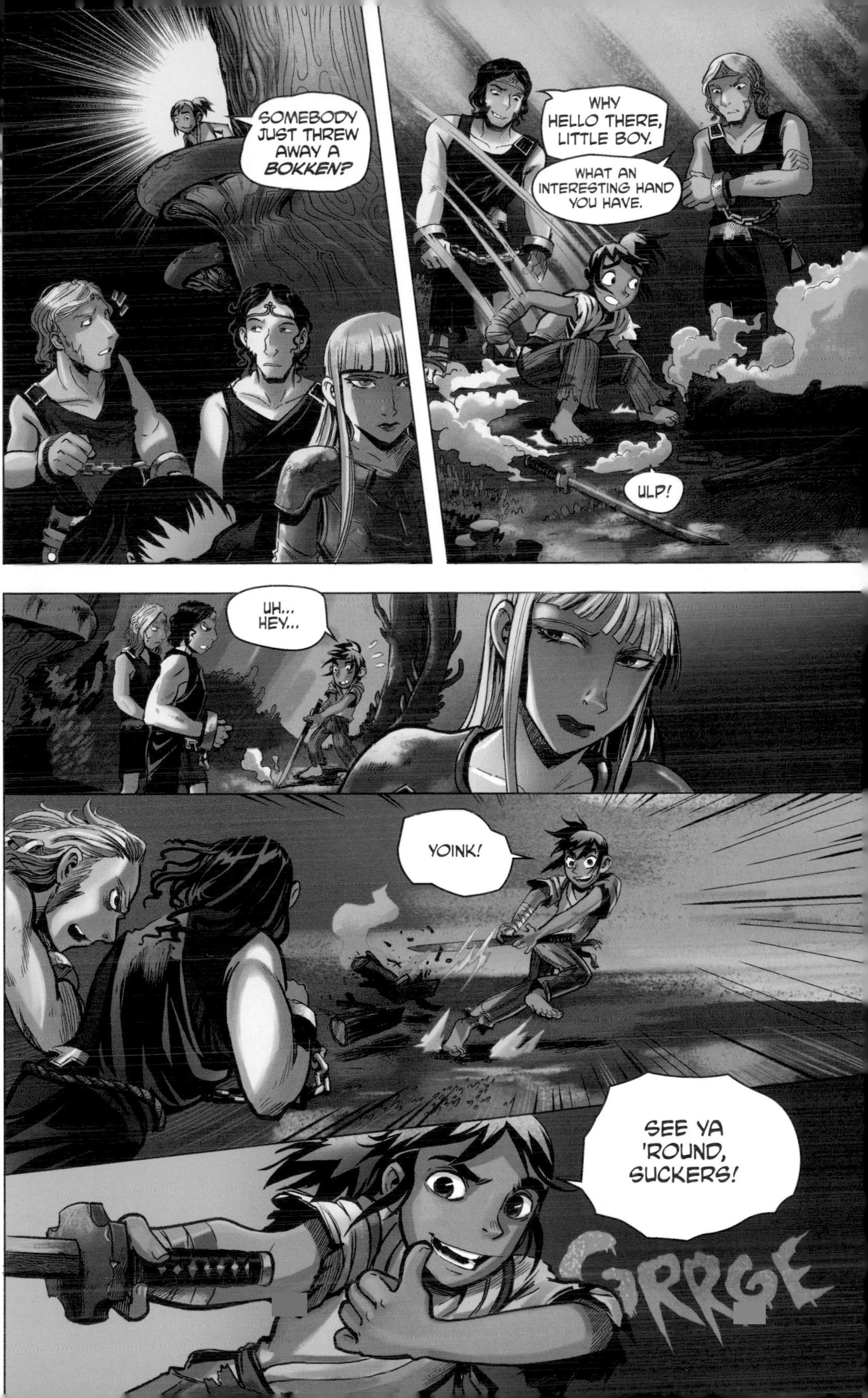
SOMEBODY JUST THREW AWAY A *BOKKEN?*
WHY HELLO THERE, LITTLE BOY.
WHAT AN INTERESTING HAND YOU HAVE.
ULP!
UH... HEY...
YOINK!
SEE YA 'ROUND, SUCKERS!
GRRGE

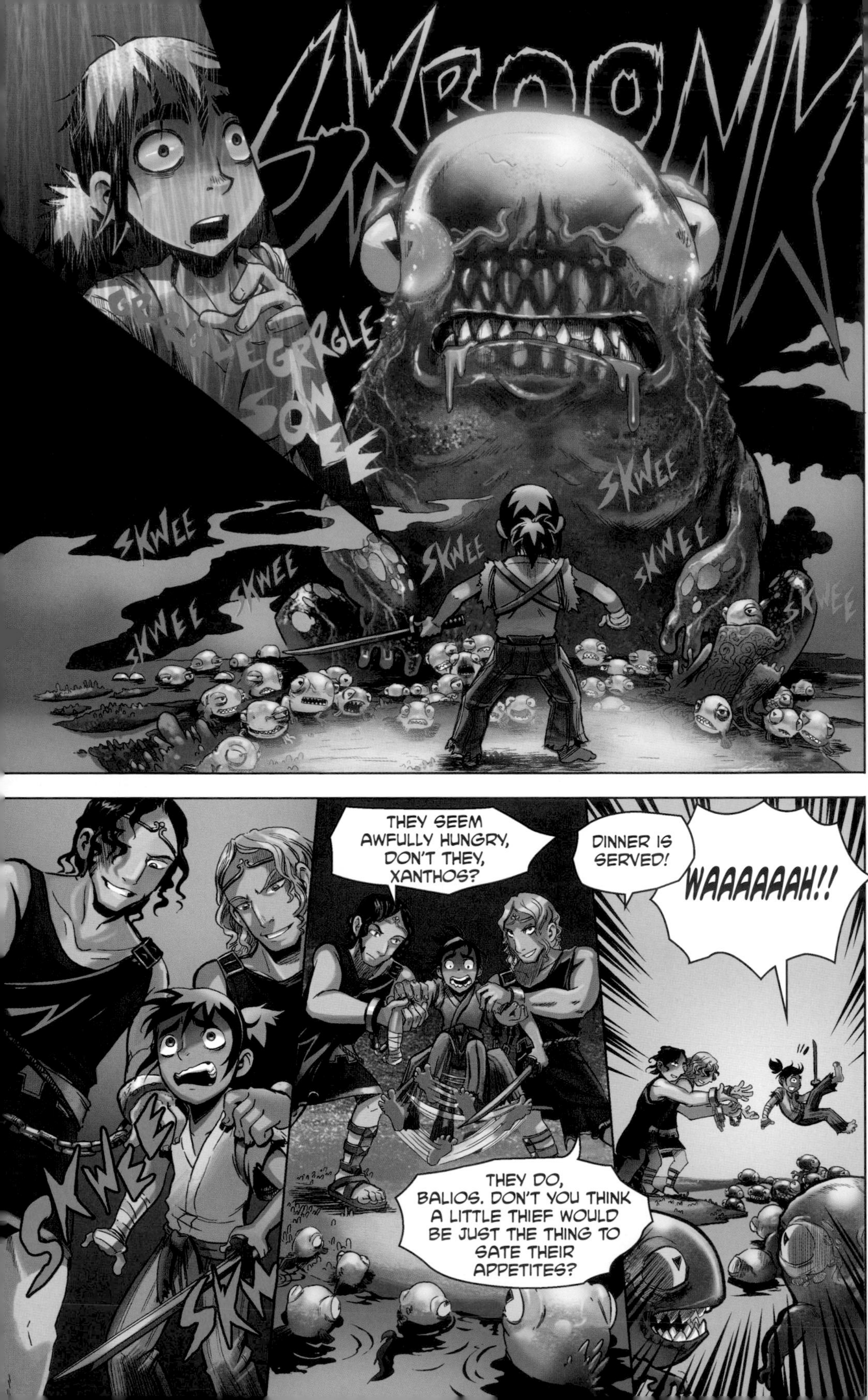
SKROOMK
GRRGLE
GRRGLE
SQWEE
SKWEE
SKWEE
SKWEE
SKWEE
SKWEE
SKWEE
SKWEE
THEY SEEM AWFULLY HUNGRY, DON'T THEY, XANTHOS?
THEY DO, BALIOS. DON'T YOU THINK A LITTLE THIEF WOULD BE JUST THE THING TO SATE THEIR APPETITES?
DINNER IS SERVED!
WAAAAAAH!!

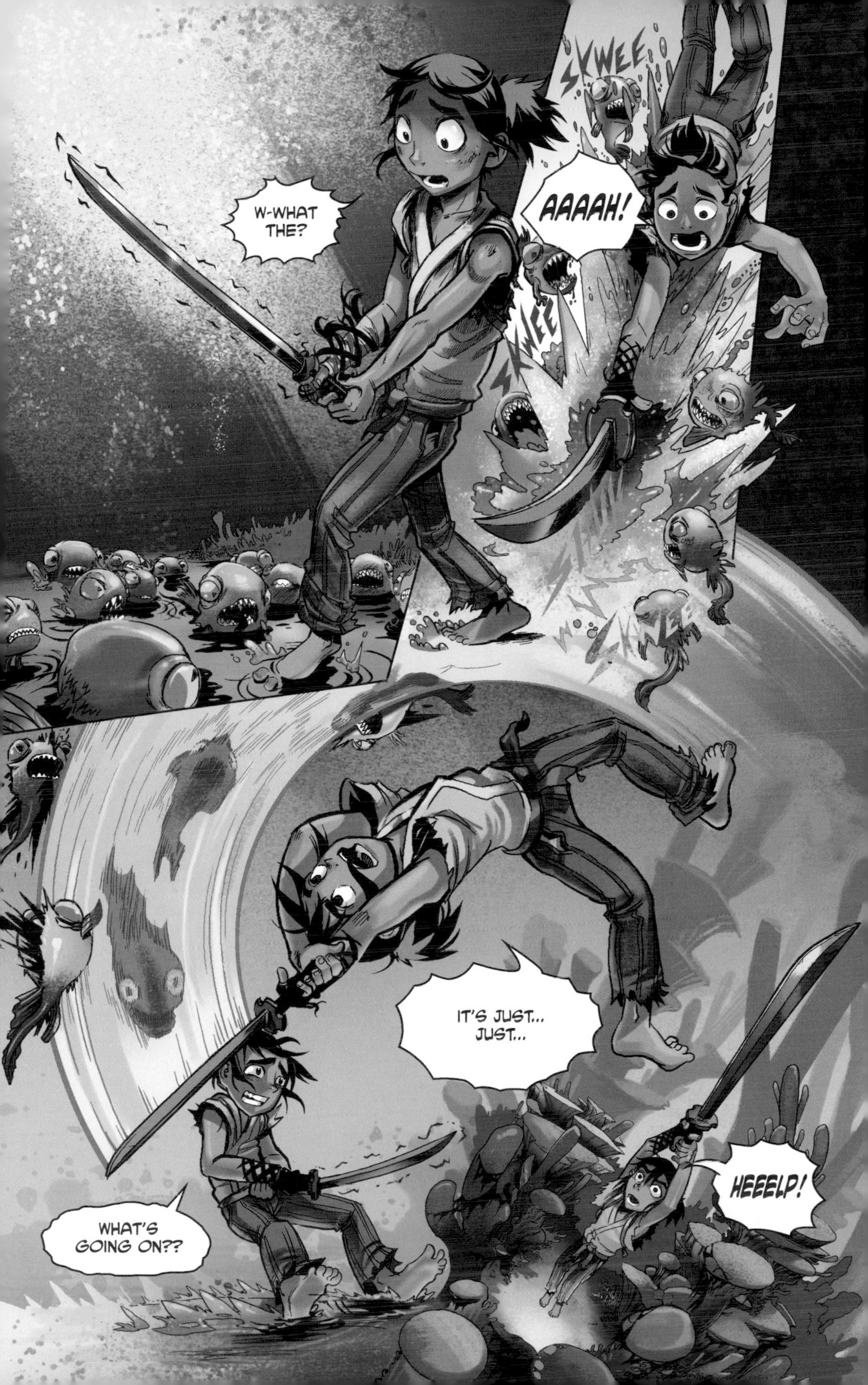
W-WHAT THE?
SKWEE
AAAAH!
SKWEE
SKWEE
IT'S JUST... JUST...
WHAT'S GOING ON??
HEEELP!

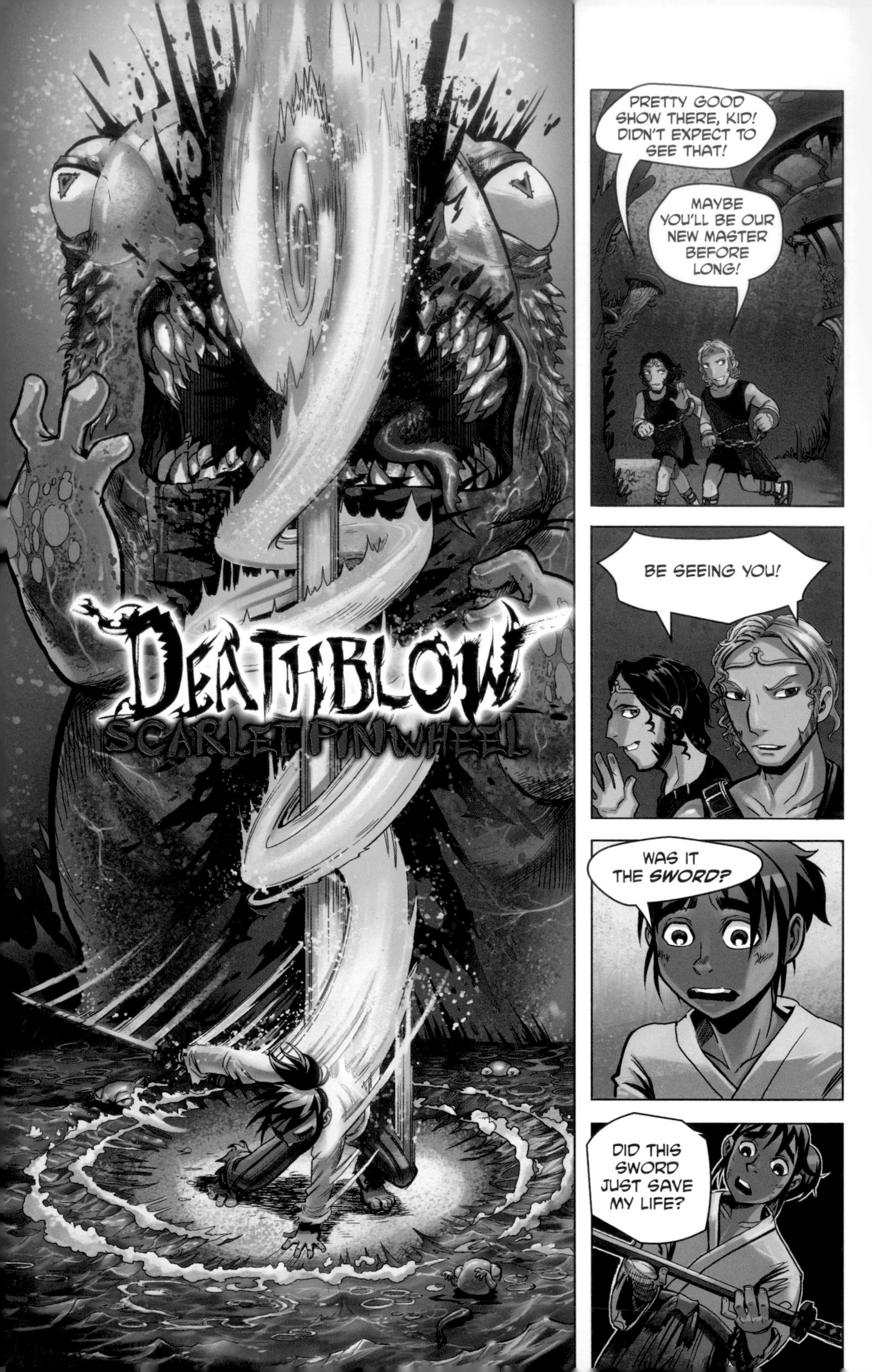
DEATHBLOW
SCARLET PINWHEEL
PRETTY GOOD SHOW THERE, KID! DIDN'T EXPECT TO SEE THAT!
MAYBE YOU'LL BE OUR NEW MASTER BEFORE LONG!
BE SEEING YOU!
WAS IT THE *SWORD?*
DID THIS SWORD JUST SAVE MY LIFE?

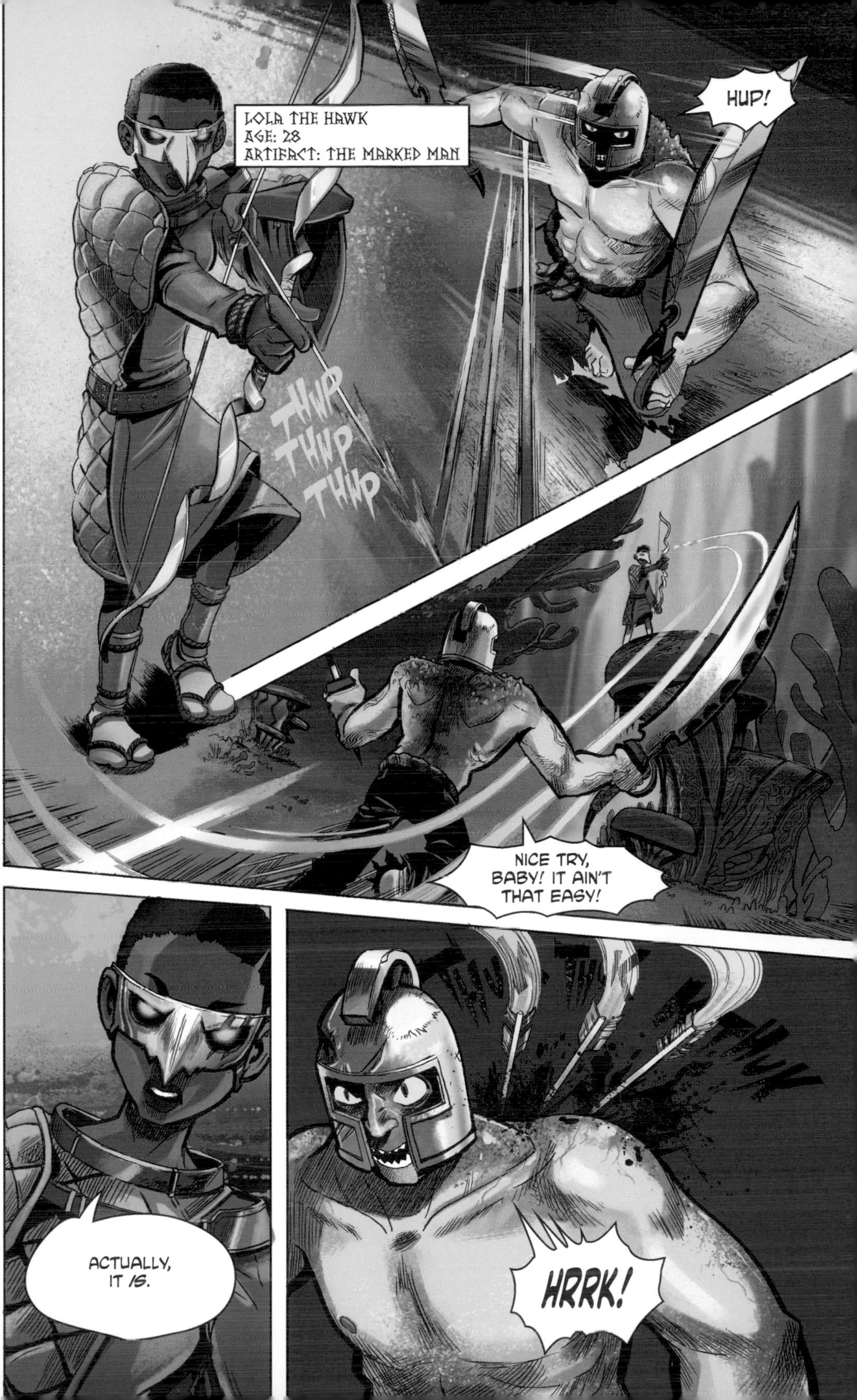
LOLA THE HAWK
AGE: 28
ARTIFACT: THE MARKED MAN
HUP!
THWP THWP THWP
NICE TRY, BABY! IT AIN'T THAT EASY!
ACTUALLY, IT IS.
HRRK!

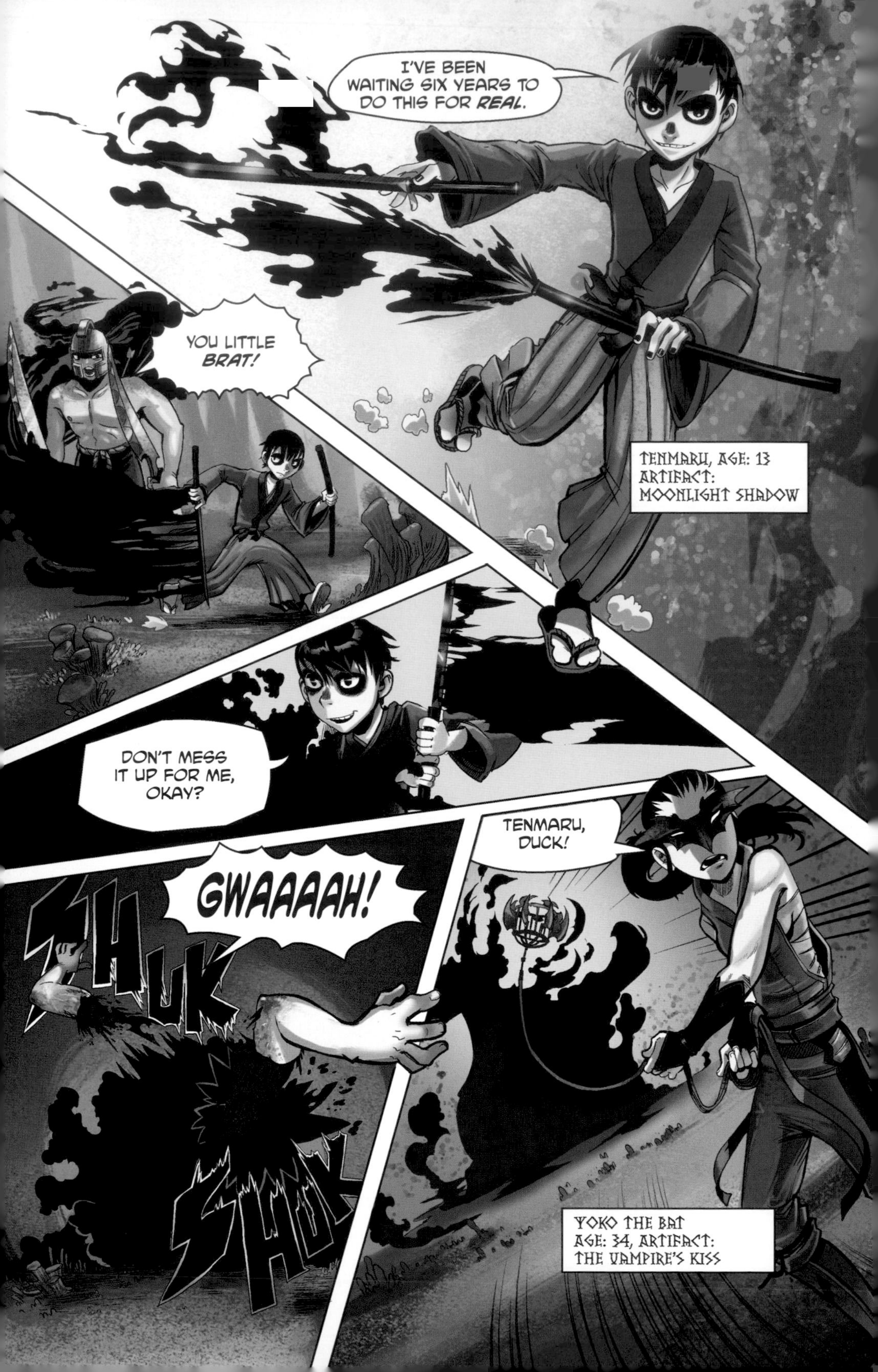
I'VE BEEN WAITING SIX YEARS TO DO THIS FOR REAL.
TENMARU, AGE: 13 ARTIFACT: MOONLIGHT SHADOW
YOU LITTLE BRAT!
DON'T MESS IT UP FOR ME, OKAY?
GWAAAAH!
TENMARU, DUCK!
YOKO THE BAT AGE: 34, ARTIFACT: THE VAMPIRE'S KISS

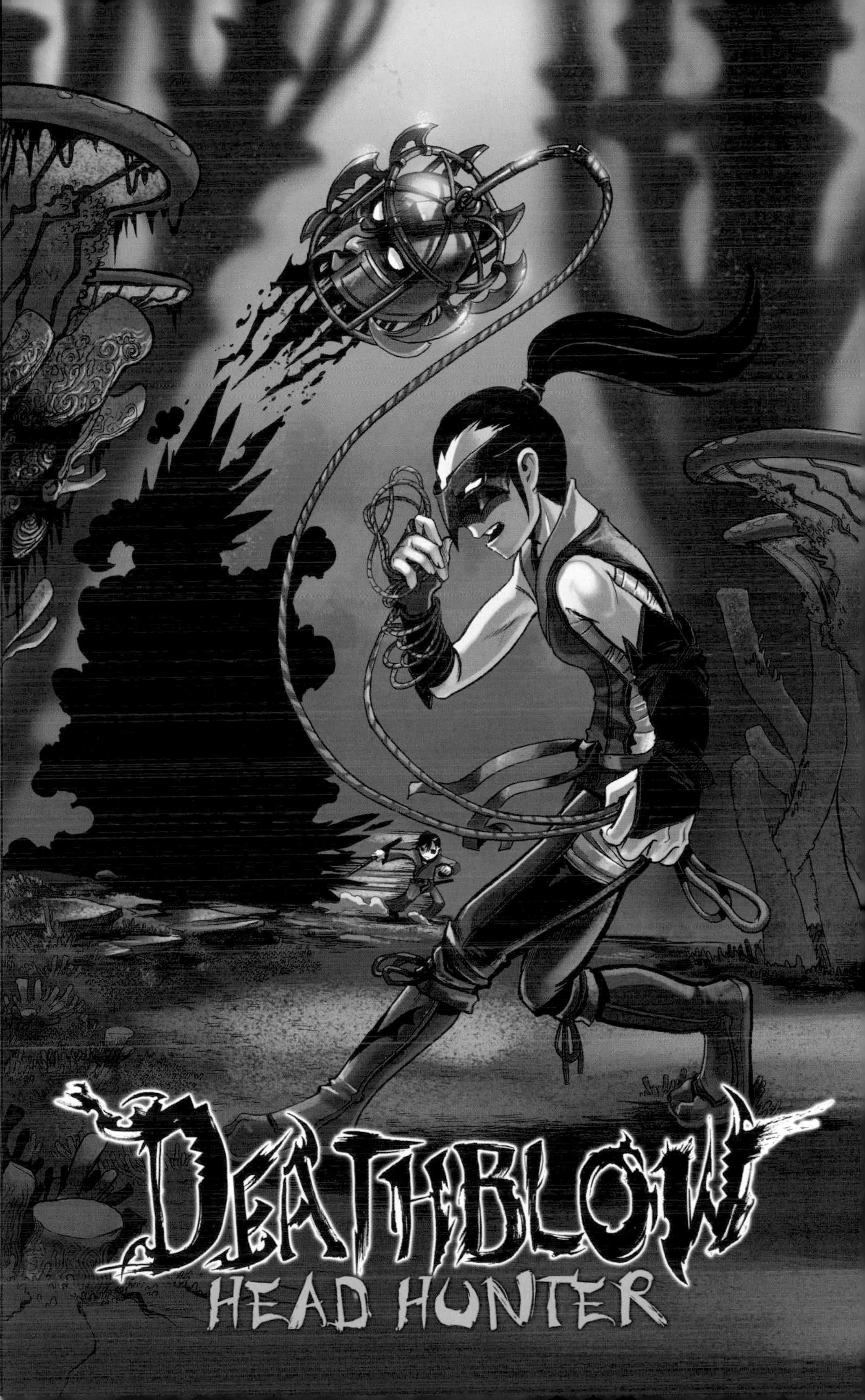
DEATHBLOW
HEAD HUNTER

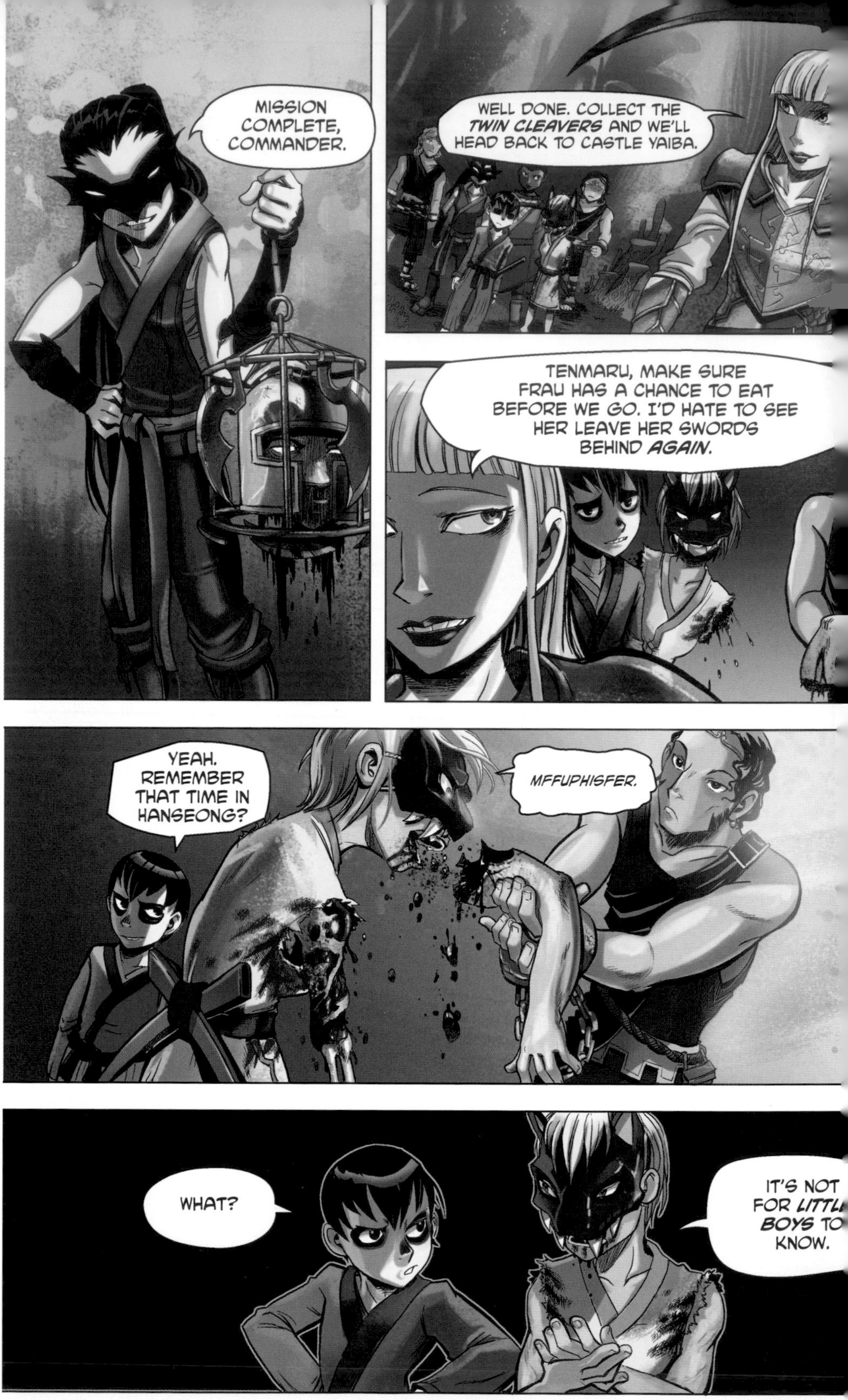
MISSION COMPLETE, COMMANDER.
WELL DONE. COLLECT THE *TWIN CLEAVERS* AND WE'LL HEAD BACK TO CASTLE YAIBA.
TENMARU, MAKE SURE FRAU HAS A CHANCE TO EAT BEFORE WE GO. I'D HATE TO SEE HER LEAVE HER SWORDS BEHIND *AGAIN*.
YEAH. REMEMBER THAT TIME IN HANSEONG?
MFFUPHISFER.
WHAT?
IT'S NOT FOR *LITTL* *BOYS* TO KNOW.

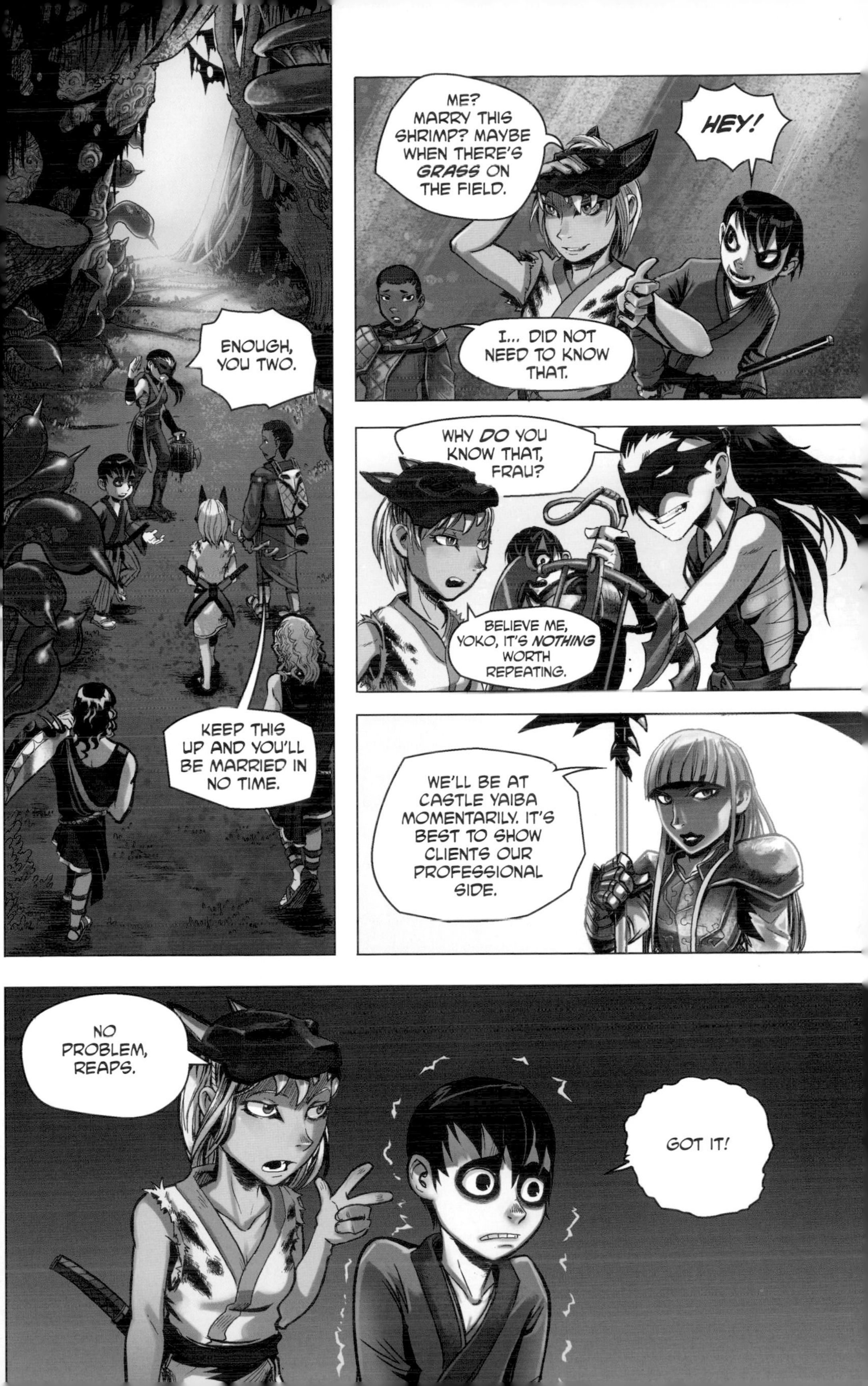
ENOUGH, YOU TWO.
KEEP THIS UP AND YOU'LL BE MARRIED IN NO TIME.
ME? MARRY THIS SHRIMP? MAYBE WHEN THERE'S GRASS ON THE FIELD.
HEY!
I... DID NOT NEED TO KNOW THAT.
WHY DO YOU KNOW THAT, FRAU?
BELIEVE ME, YOKO, IT'S NOTHING WORTH REPEATING.
WE'LL BE AT CASTLE YAIBA MOMENTARILY. IT'S BEST TO SHOW CLIENTS OUR PROFESSIONAL SIDE.
NO PROBLEM, REAPS.
GOT IT!

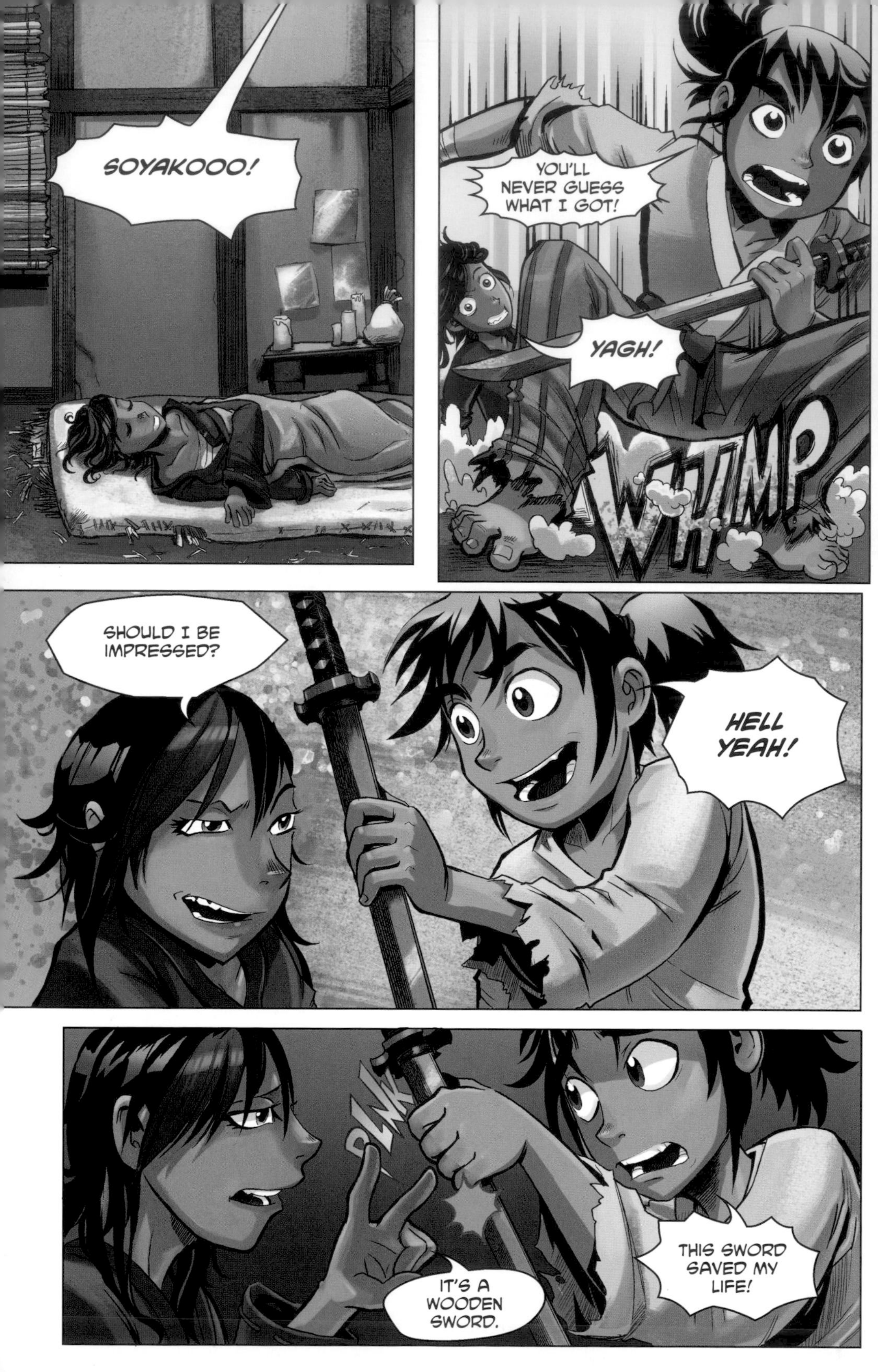
SOYAKOOO!
YOU'LL NEVER GUESS WHAT I GOT!
YAGH!
WHUMP
SHOULD I BE IMPRESSED?
HELL YEAH!
BLNK
IT'S A WOODEN SWORD.
THIS SWORD SAVED MY LIFE!

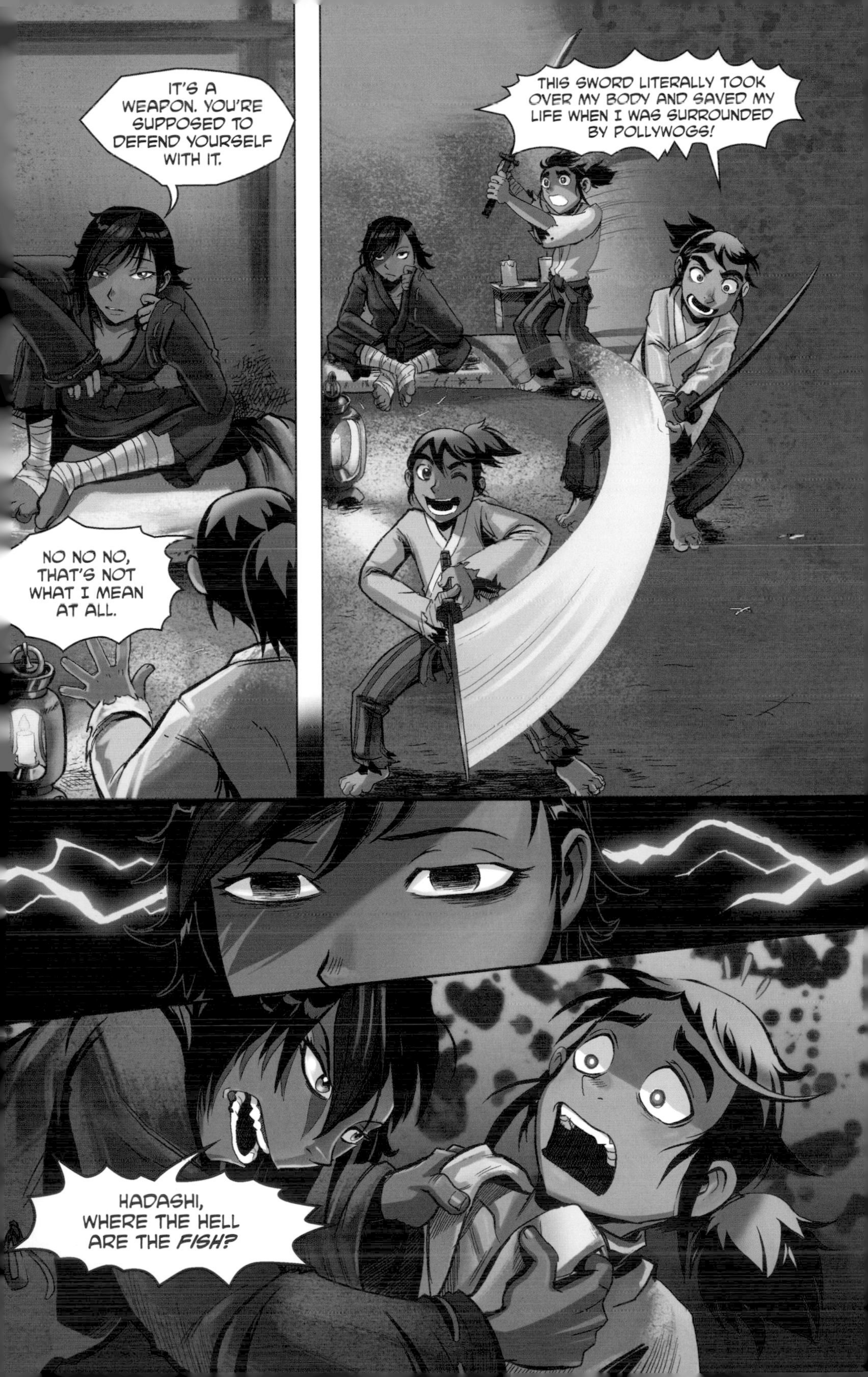
IT'S A WEAPON. YOU'RE SUPPOSED TO DEFEND YOURSELF WITH IT.
NO NO NO, THAT'S NOT WHAT I MEAN AT ALL.
THIS SWORD LITERALLY TOOK OVER MY BODY AND SAVED MY LIFE WHEN I WAS SURROUNDED BY POLLYWOGS!
HADASHI, WHERE THE HELL ARE THE *FISH*?

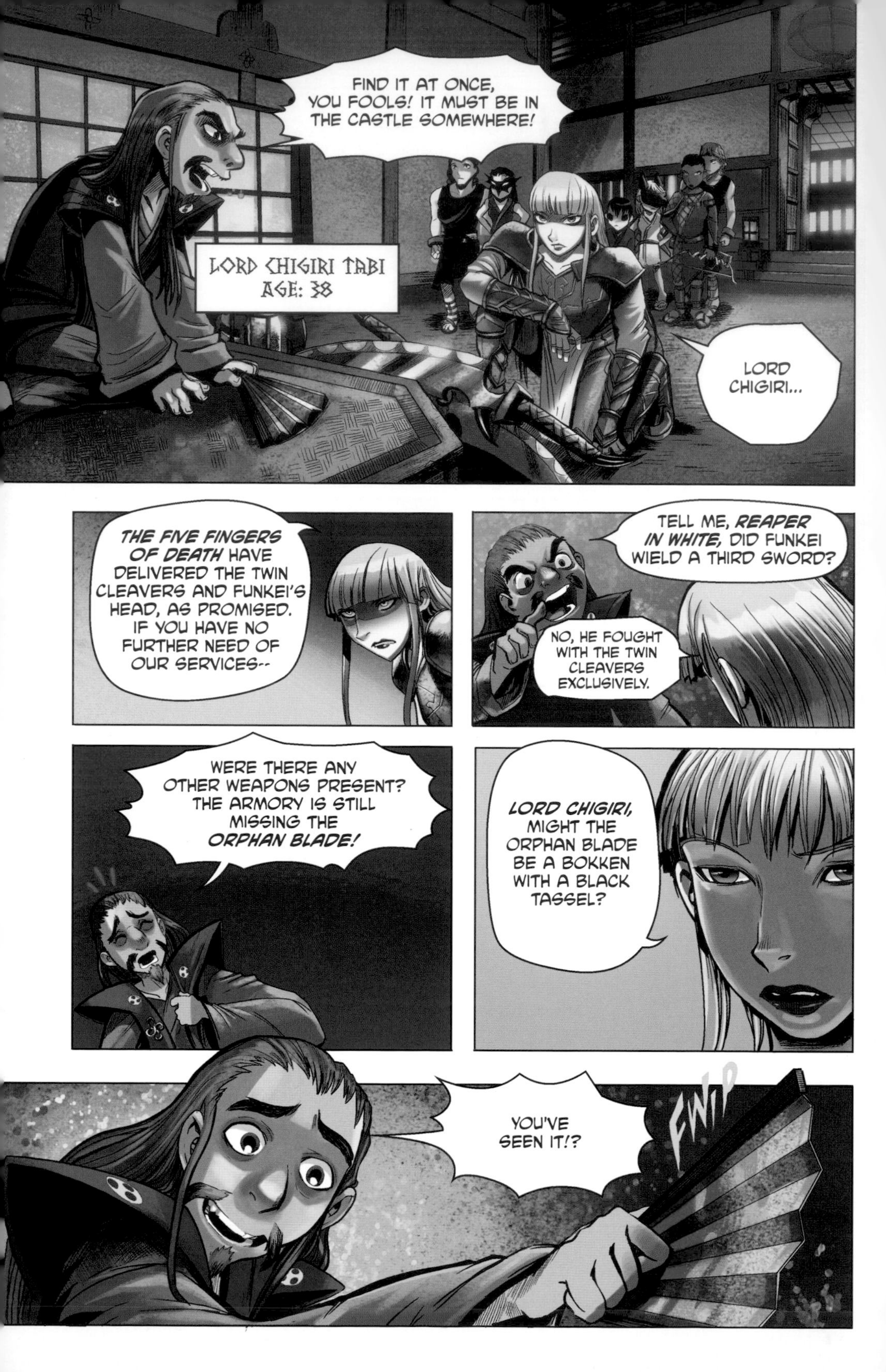
FIND IT AT ONCE, YOU FOOLS! IT MUST BE IN THE CASTLE SOMEWHERE!
LORD CHIGIRI TABI
AGE: 38
LORD CHIGIRI...
THE FIVE FINGERS OF DEATH HAVE DELIVERED THE TWIN CLEAVERS AND FUNKEI'S HEAD, AS PROMISED. IF YOU HAVE NO FURTHER NEED OF OUR SERVICES--
TELL ME, REAPER IN WHITE, DID FUNKEI WIELD A THIRD SWORD?
NO, HE FOUGHT WITH THE TWIN CLEAVERS EXCLUSIVELY.
WERE THERE ANY OTHER WEAPONS PRESENT? THE ARMORY IS STILL MISSING THE ORPHAN BLADE!
LORD CHIGIRI, MIGHT THE ORPHAN BLADE BE A BOKKEN WITH A BLACK TASSEL?
YOU'VE SEEN IT!?
FWIP

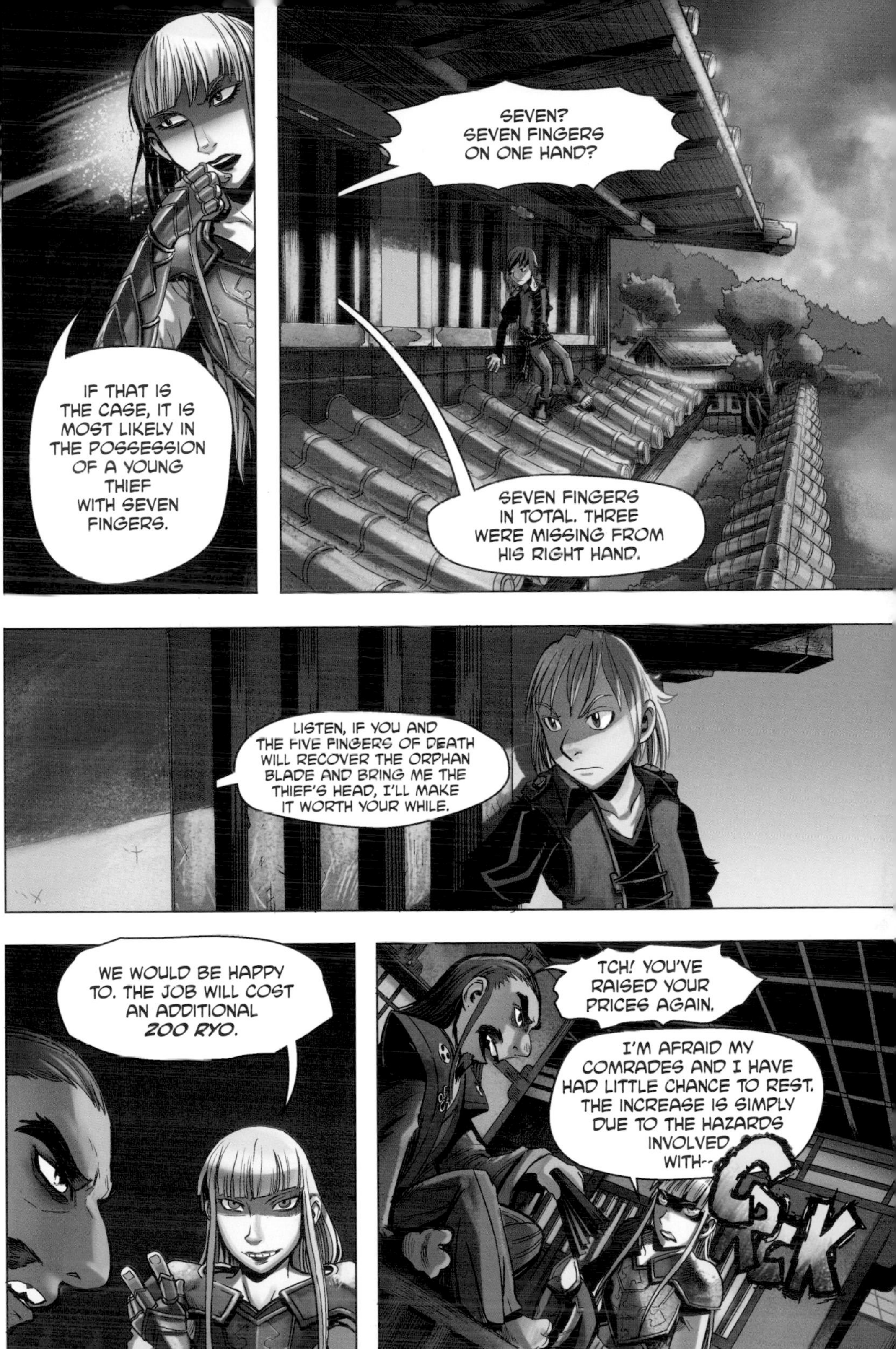

SEVEN? SEVEN FINGERS ON ONE HAND?
IF THAT IS THE CASE, IT IS MOST LIKELY IN THE POSSESSION OF A YOUNG THIEF WITH SEVEN FINGERS.
SEVEN FINGERS IN TOTAL. THREE WERE MISSING FROM HIS RIGHT HAND.
LISTEN, IF YOU AND THE FIVE FINGERS OF DEATH WILL RECOVER THE ORPHAN BLADE AND BRING ME THE THIEF'S HEAD, I'LL MAKE IT WORTH YOUR WHILE.
WE WOULD BE HAPPY TO. THE JOB WILL COST AN ADDITIONAL *200 RYO*.
TCH! YOU'VE RAISED YOUR PRICES AGAIN.
I'M AFRAID MY COMRADES AND I HAVE HAD LITTLE CHANCE TO REST. THE INCREASE IS SIMPLY DUE TO THE HAZARDS INVOLVED WITH--
GAK

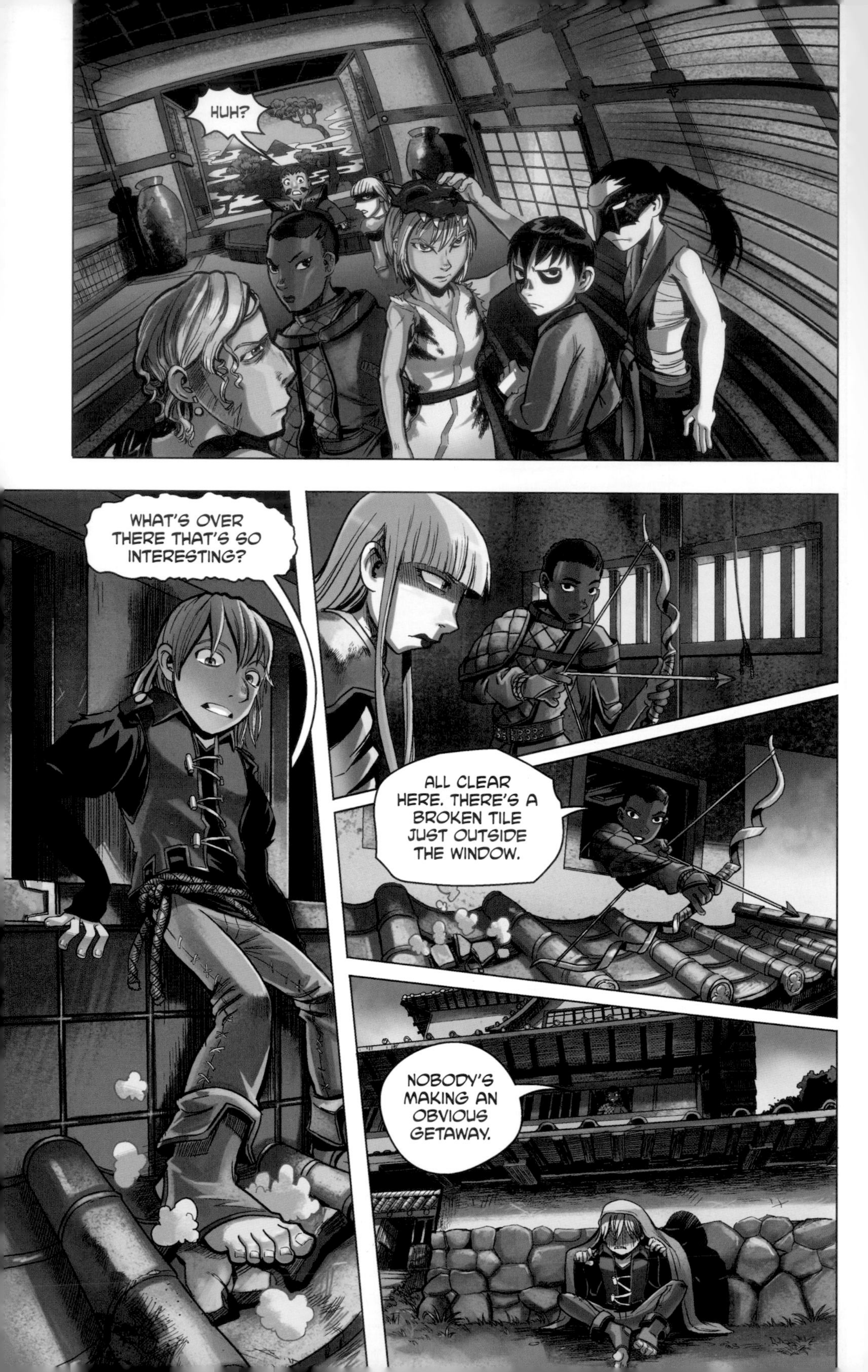
HUH?
WHAT'S OVER THERE THAT'S SO INTERESTING?
ALL CLEAR HERE. THERE'S A BROKEN TILE JUST OUTSIDE THE WINDOW.
NOBODY'S MAKING AN OBVIOUS GETAWAY.

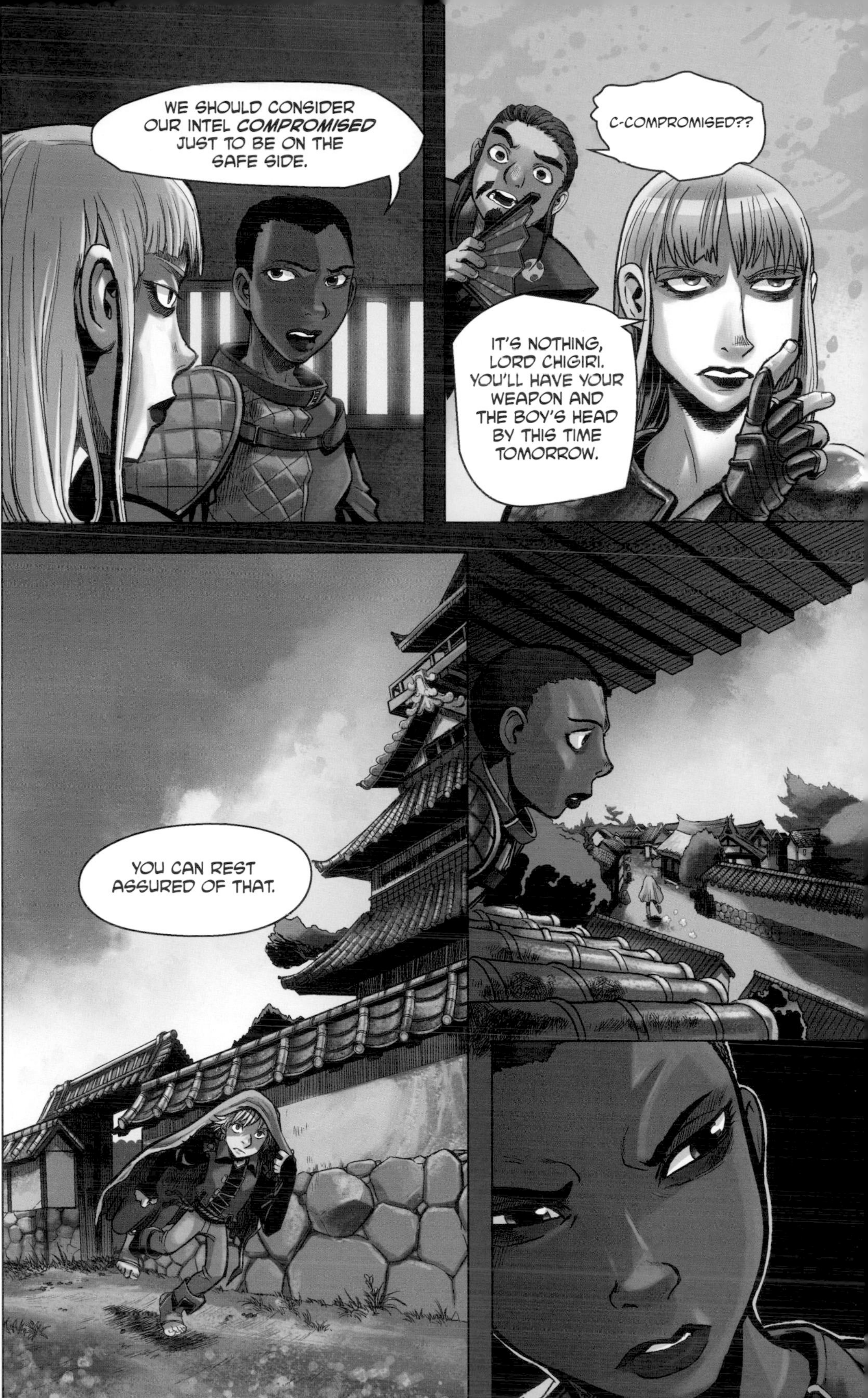
WE SHOULD CONSIDER OUR INTEL *COMPROMISED* JUST TO BE ON THE SAFE SIDE.
C-COMPROMISED??
IT'S NOTHING, LORD CHIGIRI. YOU'LL HAVE YOUR WEAPON AND THE BOY'S HEAD BY THIS TIME TOMORROW.
YOU CAN REST ASSURED OF THAT.

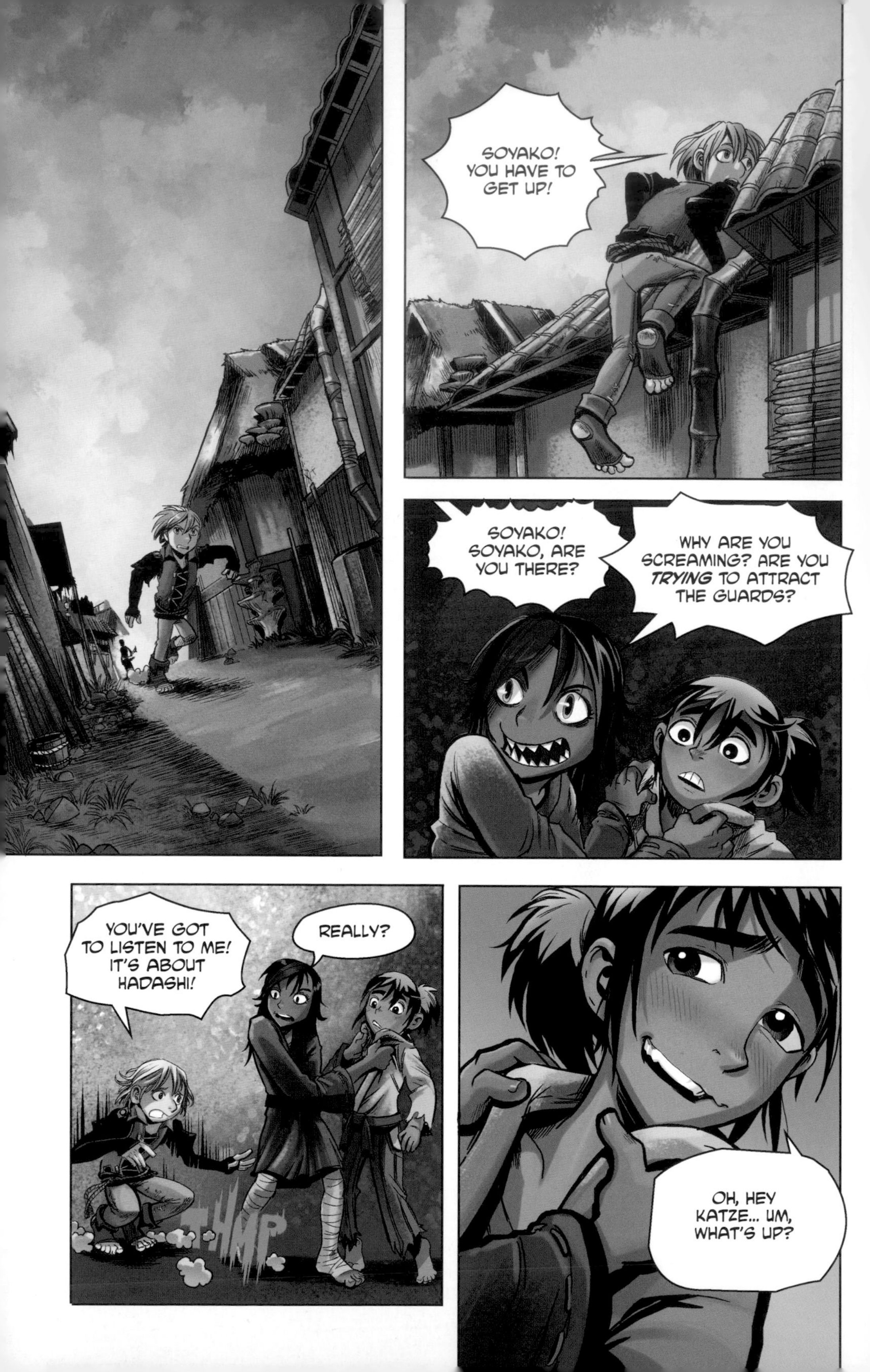
SOYAKO! YOU HAVE TO GET UP!
SOYAKO! SOYAKO, ARE YOU THERE?
WHY ARE YOU SCREAMING? ARE YOU *TRYING* TO ATTRACT THE GUARDS?
YOU'VE GOT TO LISTEN TO ME! IT'S ABOUT HADASHI!
REALLY?
THMP
OH, HEY KATZE... UM, WHAT'S UP?

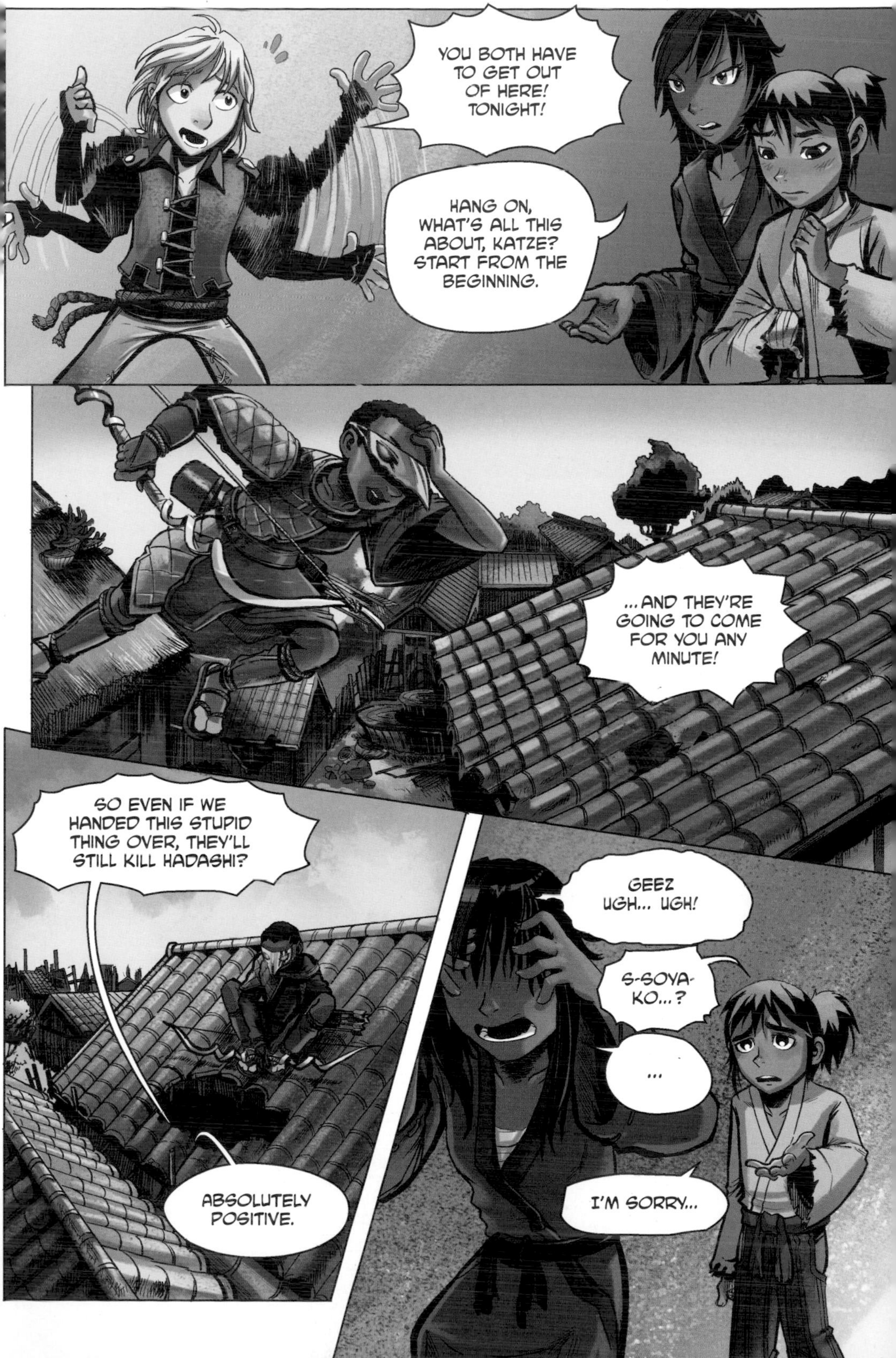
YOU BOTH HAVE TO GET OUT OF HERE! TONIGHT!
HANG ON, WHAT'S ALL THIS ABOUT, KATZE? START FROM THE BEGINNING.
...AND THEY'RE GOING TO COME FOR YOU ANY MINUTE!
SO EVEN IF WE HANDED THIS STUPID THING OVER, THEY'LL STILL KILL HADASHI?
ABSOLUTELY POSITIVE.
GEEZ UGH... UGH!
S-SOYA-KO...?
...
I'M SORRY...

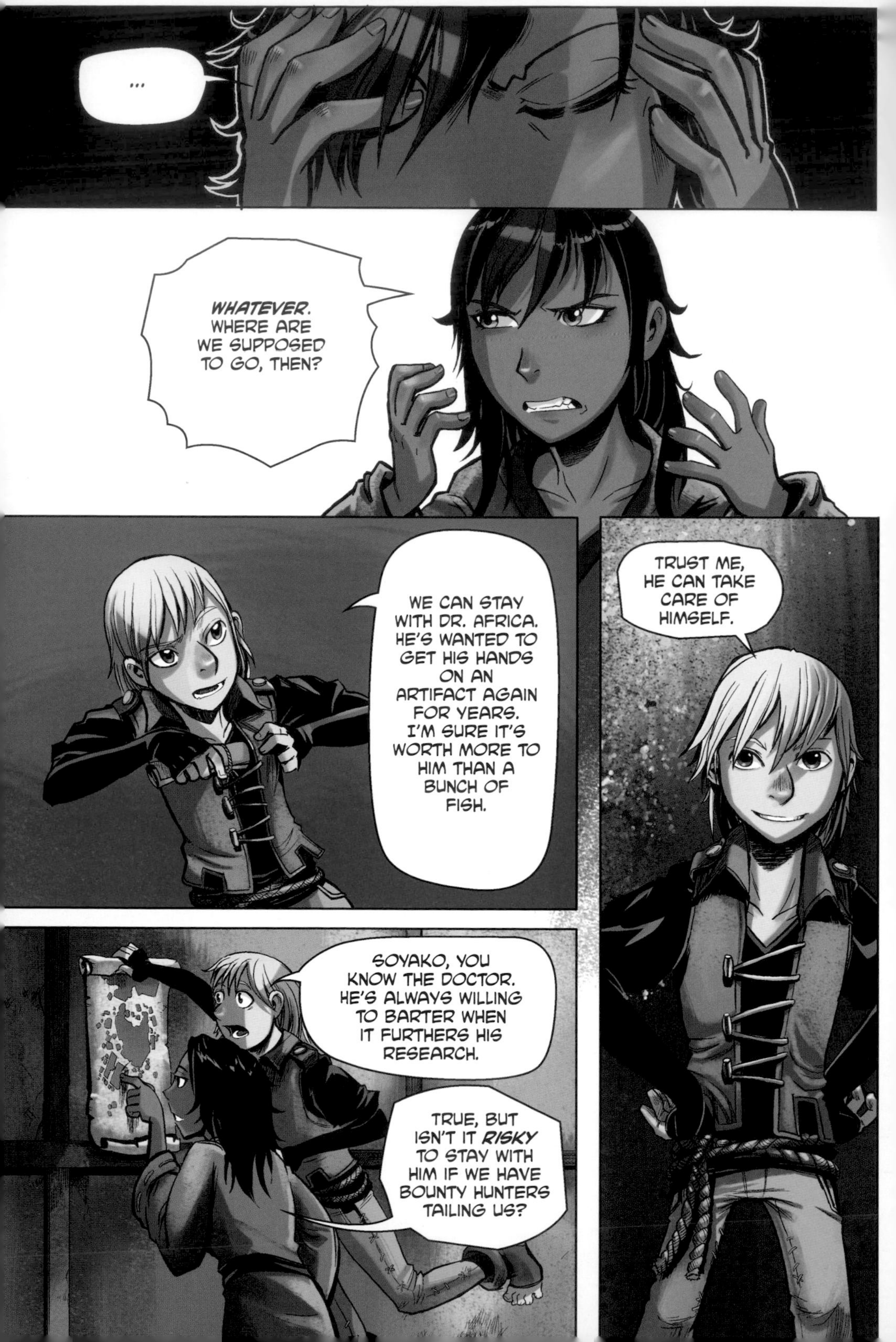
...
WHATEVER. WHERE ARE WE SUPPOSED TO GO, THEN?
WE CAN STAY WITH DR. AFRICA. HE'S WANTED TO GET HIS HANDS ON AN ARTIFACT AGAIN FOR YEARS. I'M SURE IT'S WORTH MORE TO HIM THAN A BUNCH OF FISH.
TRUST ME, HE CAN TAKE CARE OF HIMSELF.
SOYAKO, YOU KNOW THE DOCTOR. HE'S ALWAYS WILLING TO BARTER WHEN IT FURTHERS HIS RESEARCH.
TRUE, BUT ISN'T IT *RISKY* TO STAY WITH HIM IF WE HAVE BOUNTY HUNTERS TAILING US?

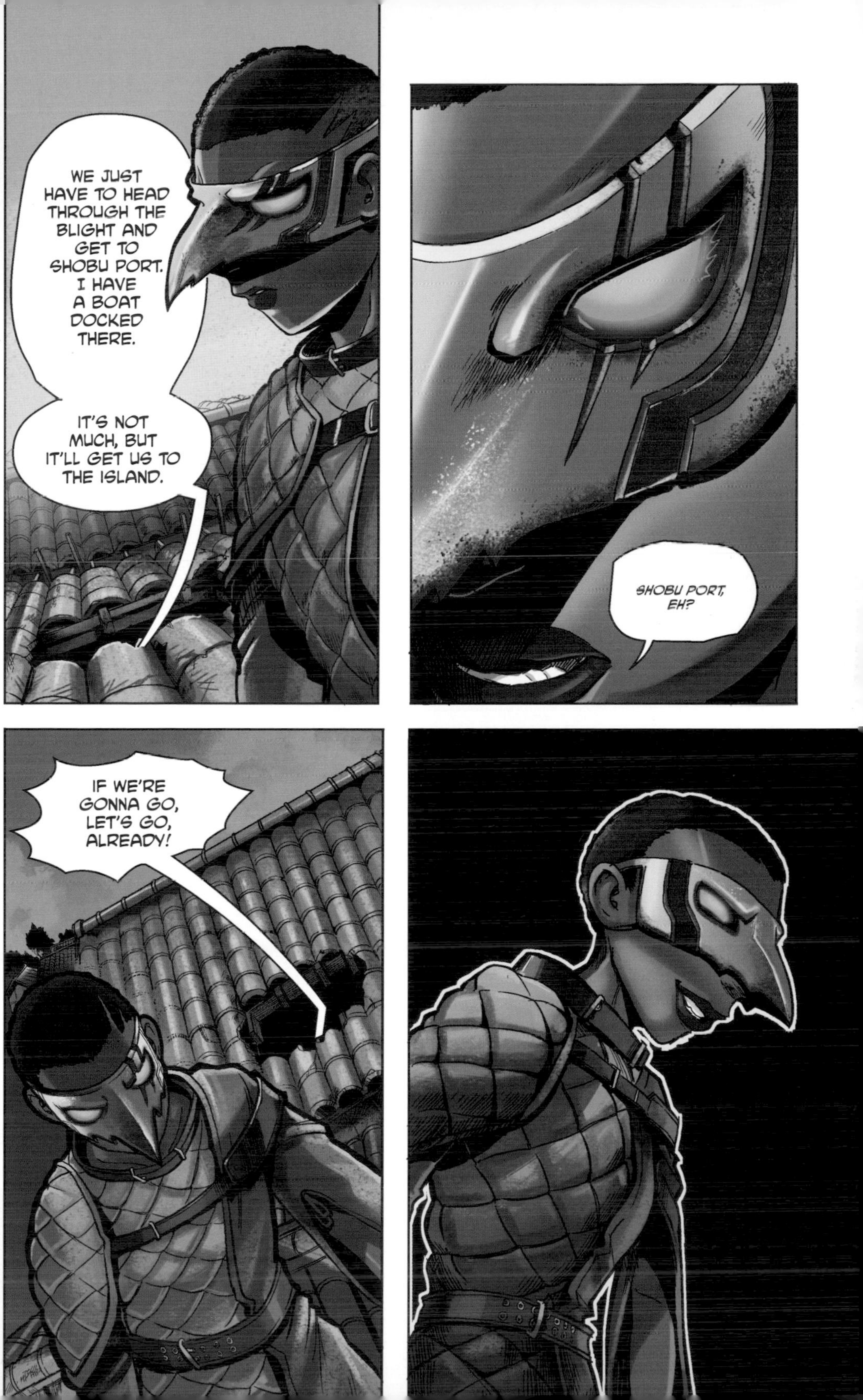
WE JUST HAVE TO HEAD THROUGH THE BLIGHT AND GET TO SHOBU PORT. I HAVE A BOAT DOCKED THERE.
IT'S NOT MUCH, BUT IT'LL GET US TO THE ISLAND.
SHOBU PORT, EH?
IF WE'RE GONNA GO, LET'S GO, ALREADY!

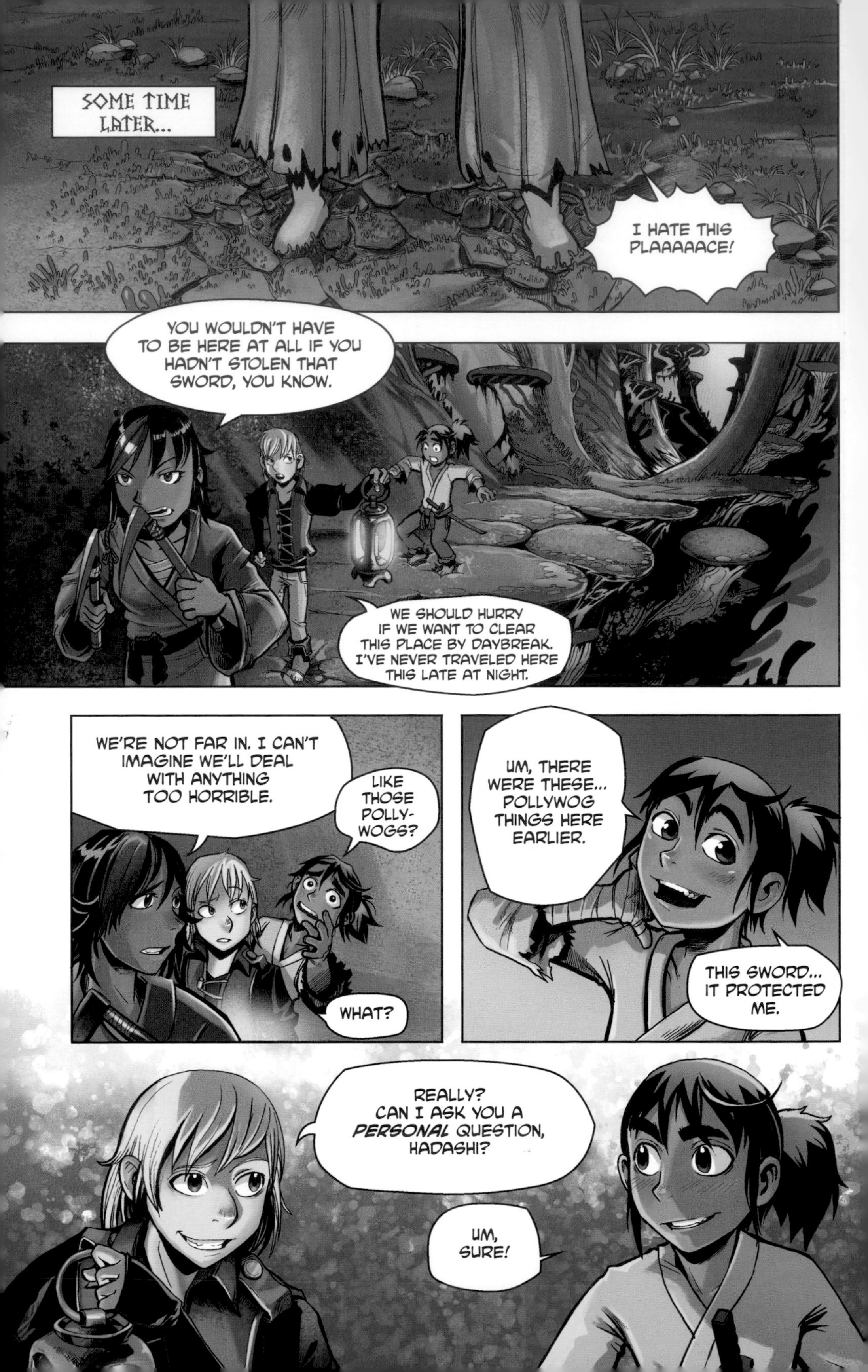
SOME TIME LATER...
I HATE THIS PLAAAAACE!
YOU WOULDN'T HAVE TO BE HERE AT ALL IF YOU HADN'T STOLEN THAT SWORD, YOU KNOW.
WE SHOULD HURRY IF WE WANT TO CLEAR THIS PLACE BY DAYBREAK. I'VE NEVER TRAVELED HERE THIS LATE AT NIGHT.
WE'RE NOT FAR IN. I CAN'T IMAGINE WE'LL DEAL WITH ANYTHING TOO HORRIBLE.
LIKE THOSE POLLY-WOGS?
WHAT?
UM, THERE WERE THESE... POLLYWOG THINGS HERE EARLIER.
THIS SWORD... IT PROTECTED ME.
REALLY? CAN I ASK YOU A *PERSONAL* QUESTION, HADASHI?
UM, SURE!

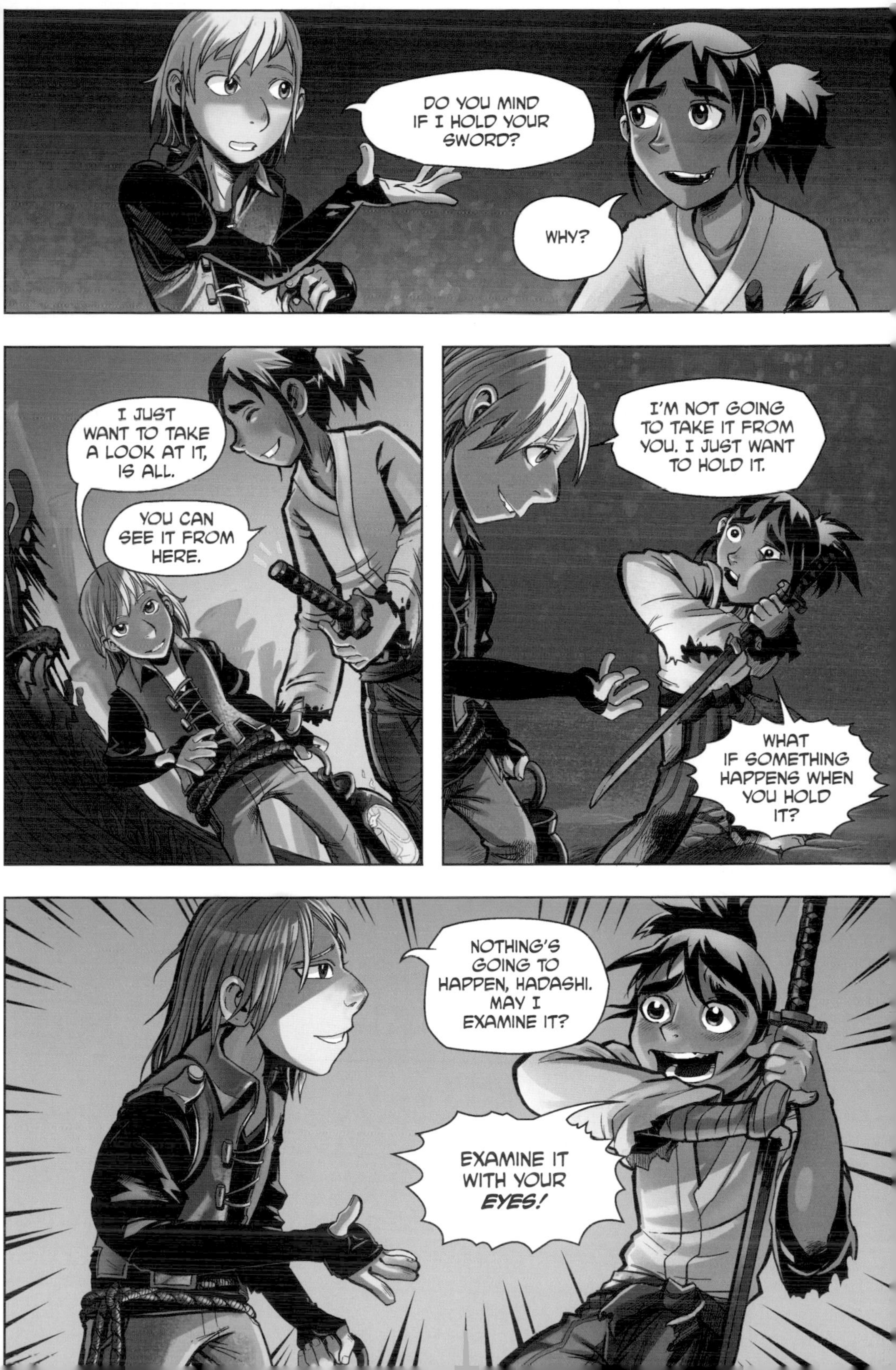
DO YOU MIND IF I HOLD YOUR SWORD?
WHY?
I JUST WANT TO TAKE A LOOK AT IT, IS ALL.
YOU CAN SEE IT FROM HERE.
I'M NOT GOING TO TAKE IT FROM YOU. I JUST WANT TO HOLD IT.
WHAT IF SOMETHING HAPPENS WHEN YOU HOLD IT?
NOTHING'S GOING TO HAPPEN, HADASHI. MAY I EXAMINE IT?
EXAMINE IT WITH YOUR *EYES!*

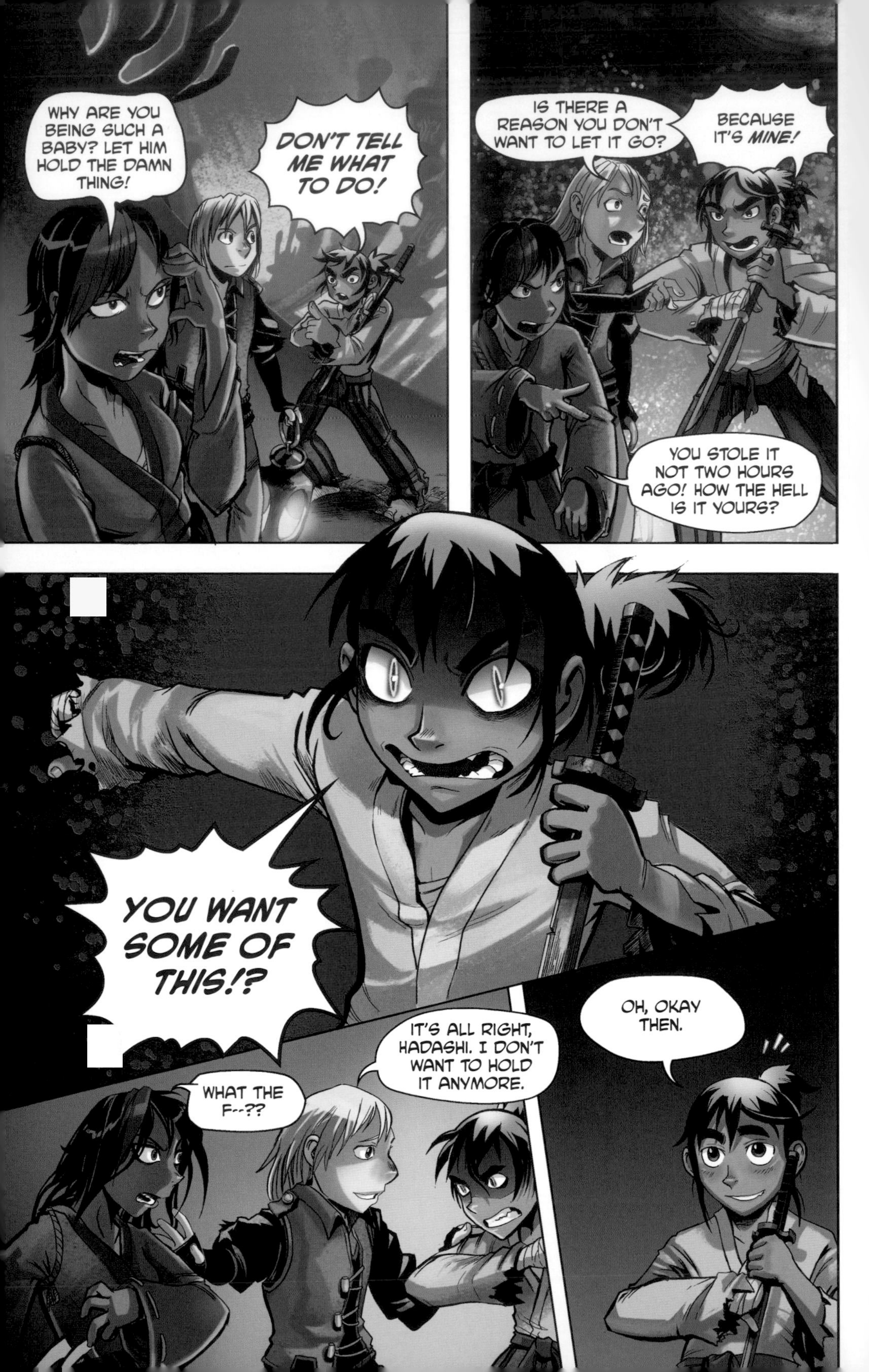
WHY ARE YOU BEING SUCH A BABY? LET HIM HOLD THE DAMN THING!
DON'T TELL ME WHAT TO DO!
IS THERE A REASON YOU DON'T WANT TO LET IT GO?
BECAUSE IT'S MINE!
YOU STOLE IT NOT TWO HOURS AGO! HOW THE HELL IS IT YOURS?
YOU WANT SOME OF THIS!?
WHAT THE F--??
IT'S ALL RIGHT, HADASHI. I DON'T WANT TO HOLD IT ANYMORE.
OH, OKAY THEN.

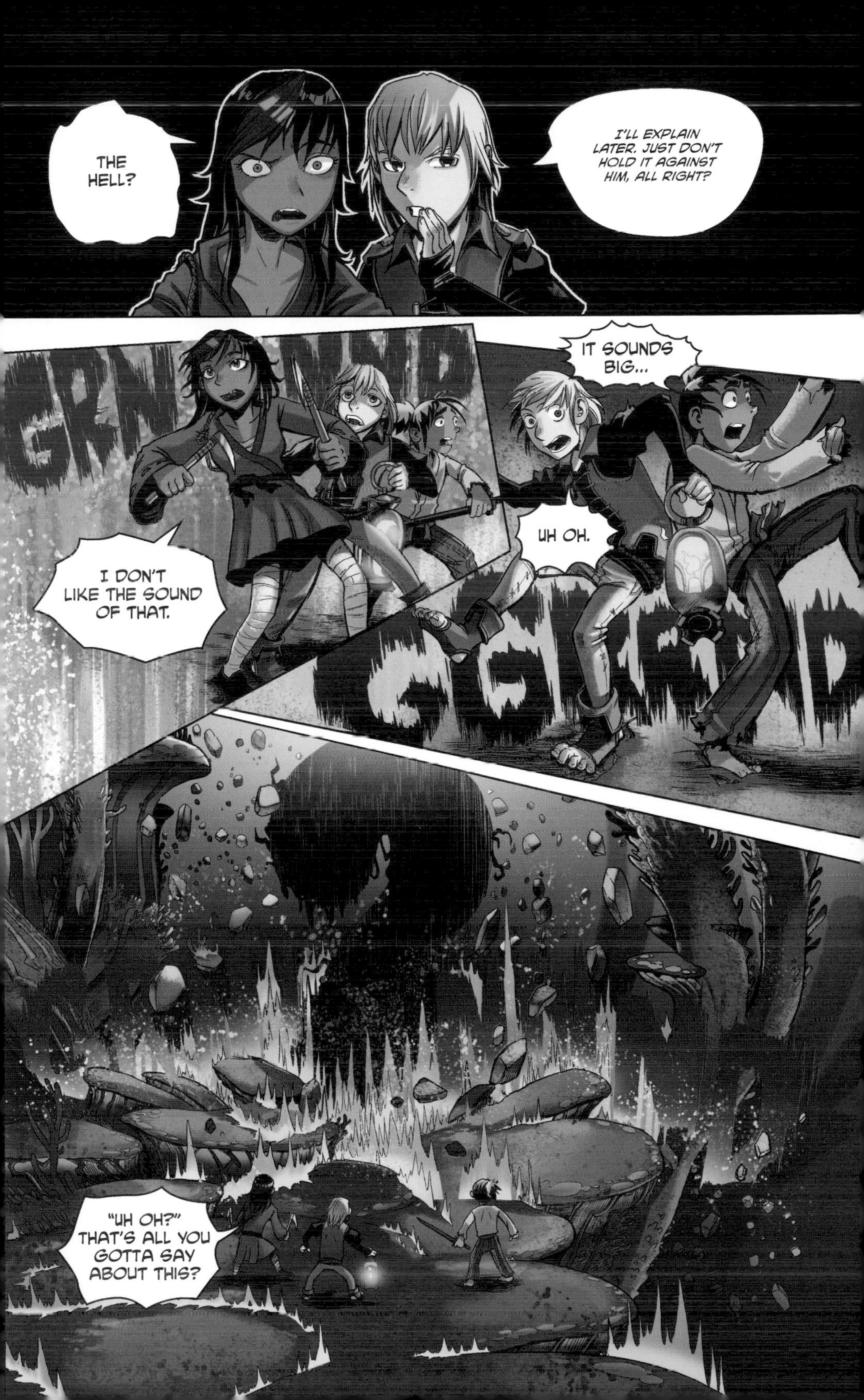
THE HELL?
I'LL EXPLAIN LATER. JUST DON'T HOLD IT AGAINST HIM, ALL RIGHT?
GRNNND
I DON'T LIKE THE SOUND OF THAT.
IT SOUNDS BIG...
UH OH.
"UH OH?" THAT'S ALL YOU GOTTA SAY ABOUT THIS?

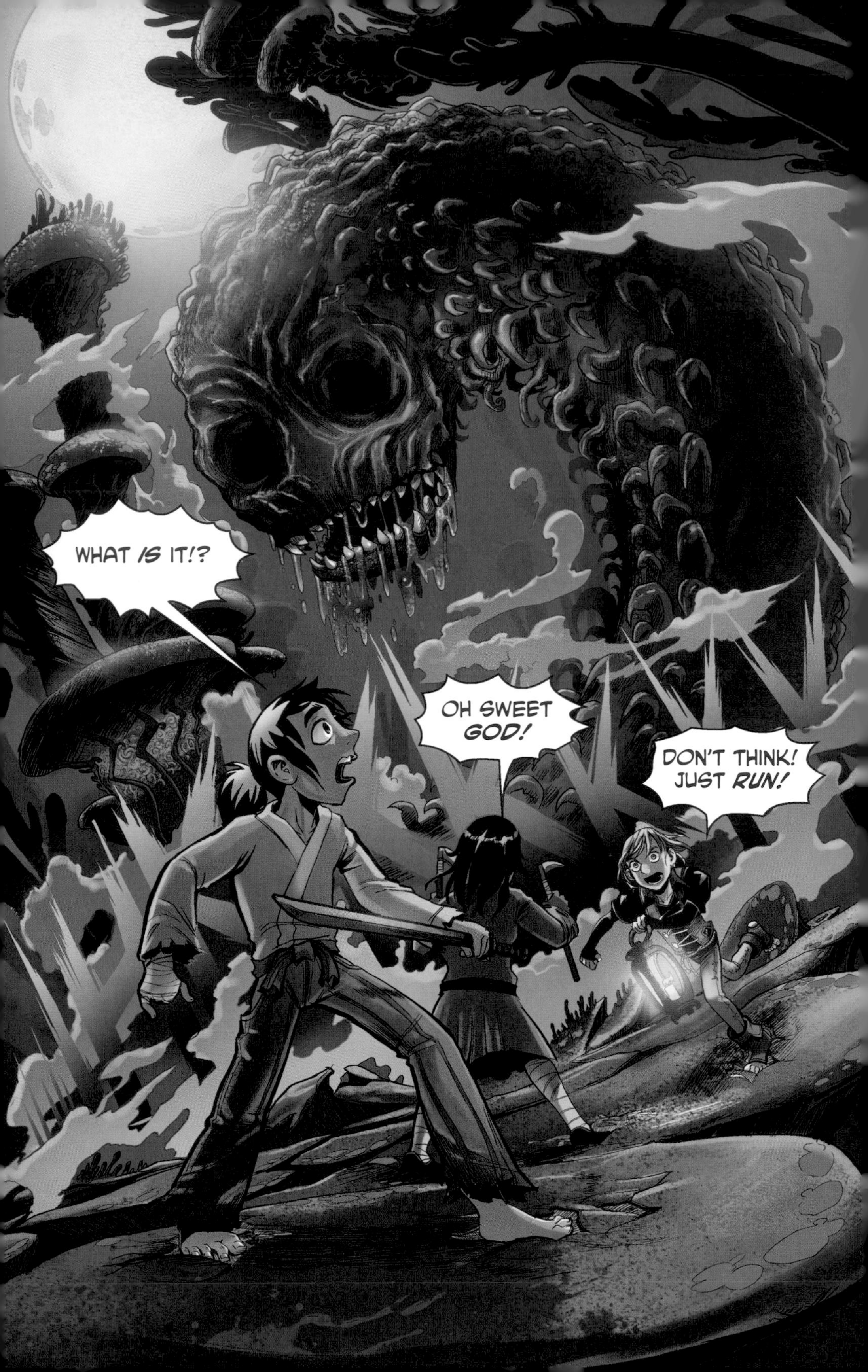
WHAT *IS* IT!?
OH SWEET *GOD!*
DON'T THINK! JUST *RUN!*

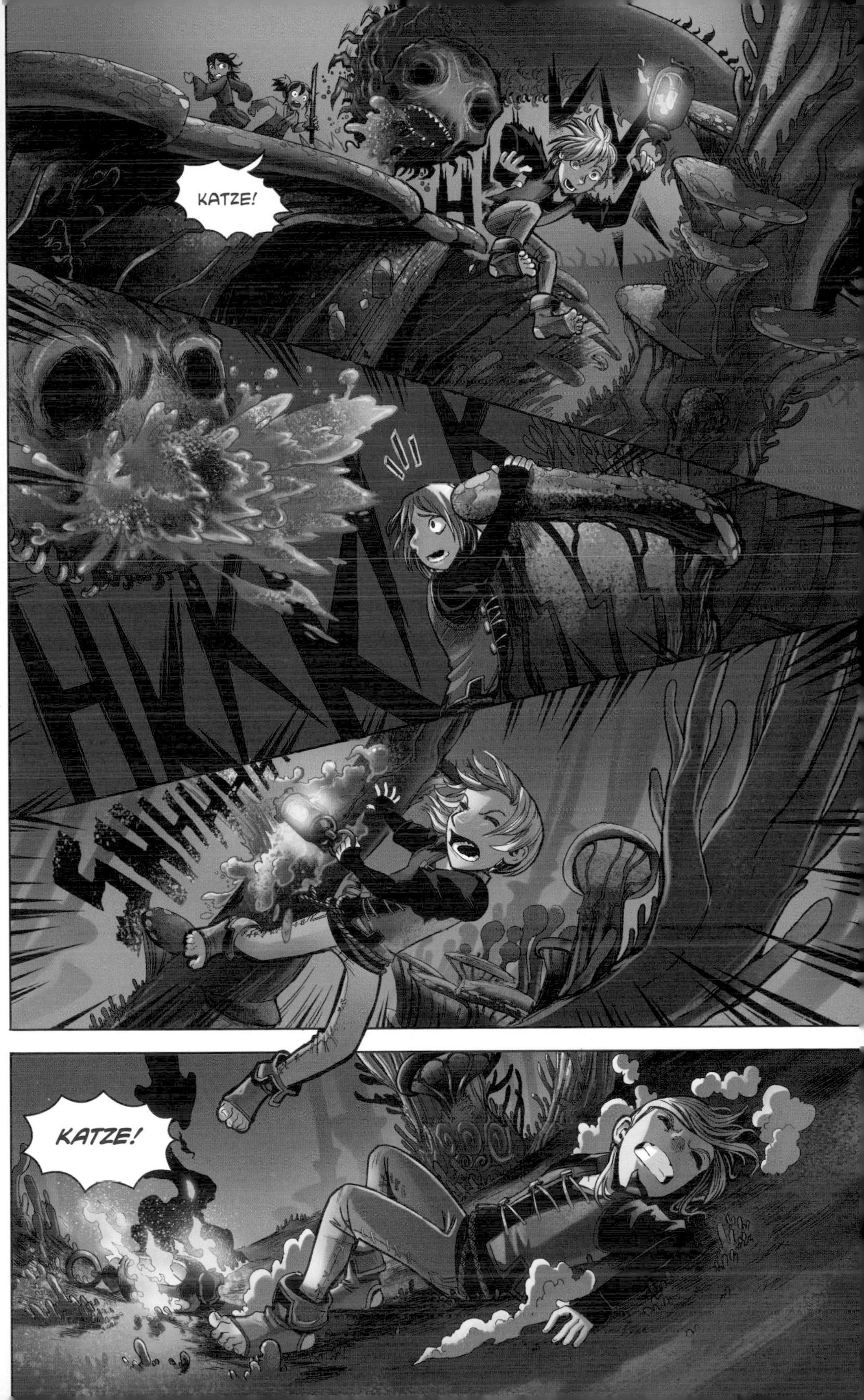
KATZE!
KATZE!

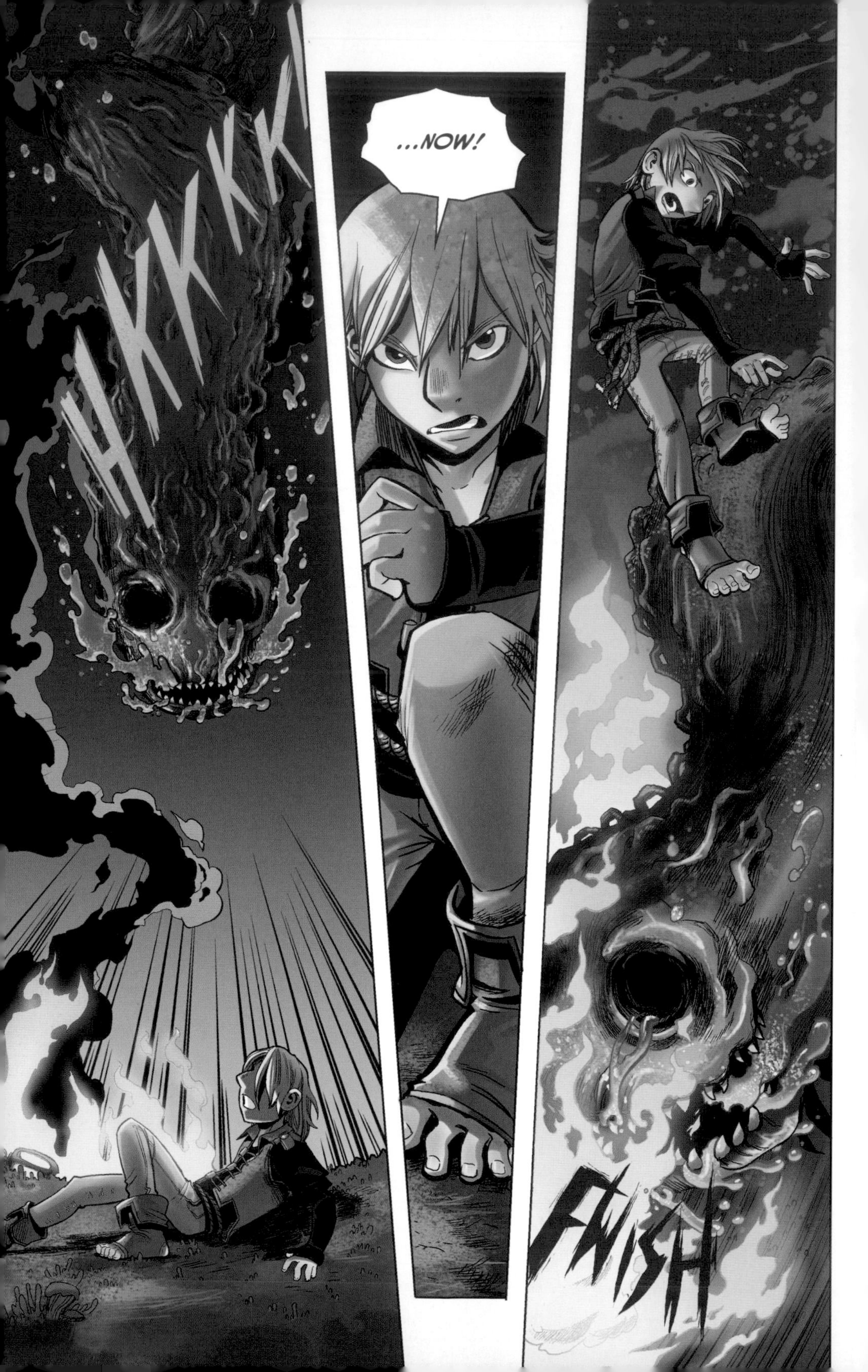
HKKKK!
...NOW!
FWISH

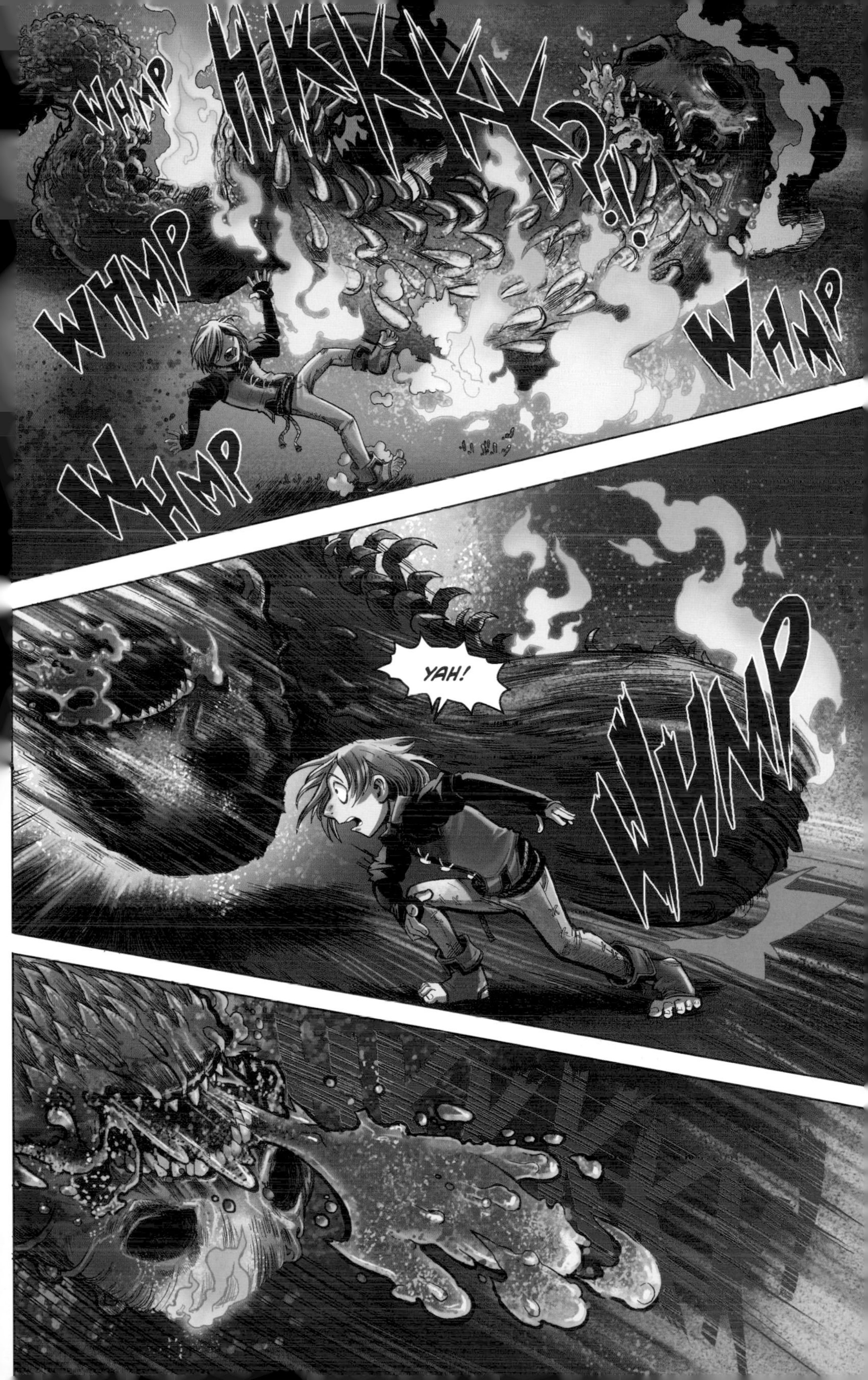
WHMP
HKKKK?!!
WHMP
WHMP
WHMP
WHMP
YAH!
WHUMP

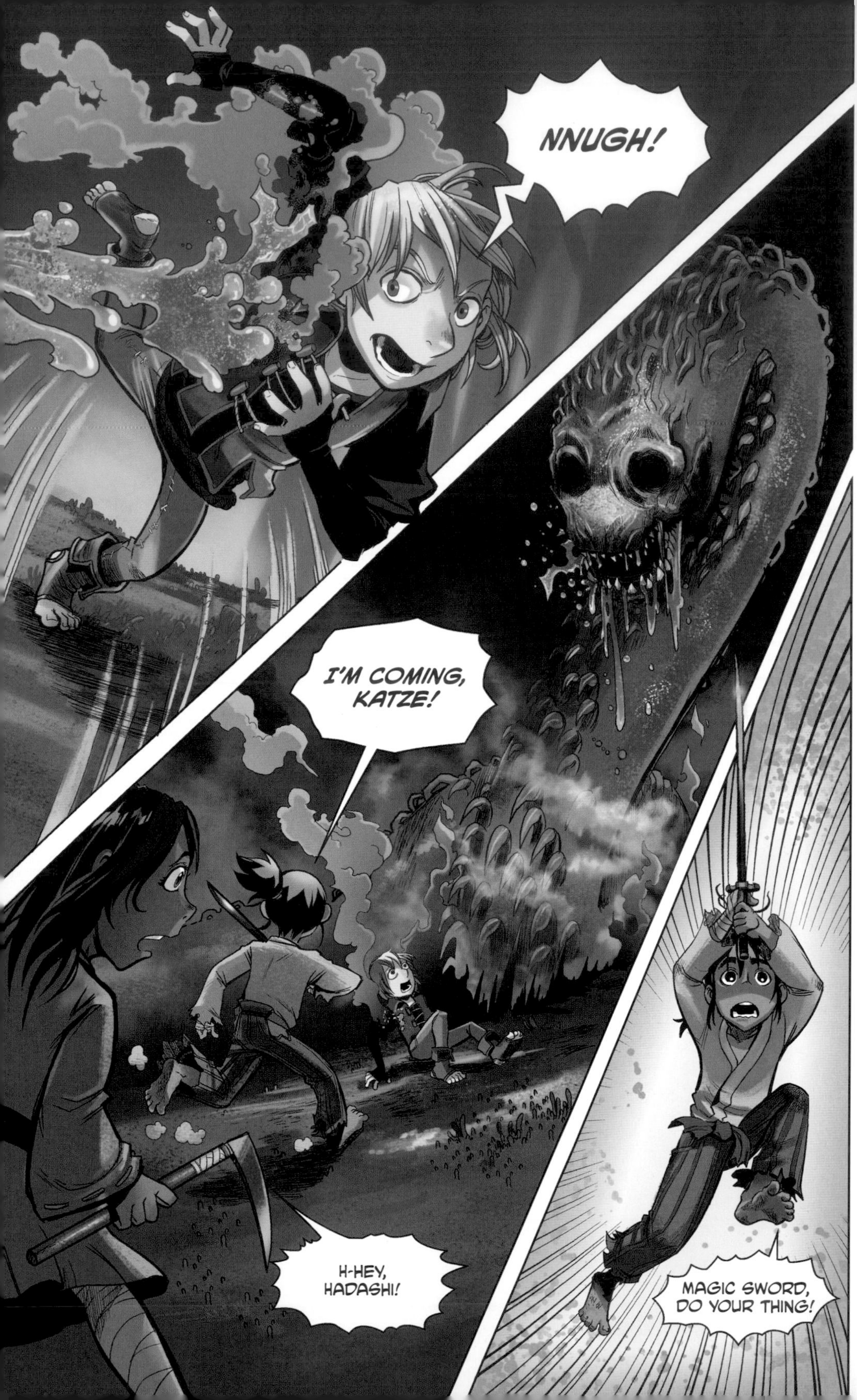
NNUGH!
I'M COMING, KATZE!
H-HEY, HADASHI!
MAGIC SWORD, DO YOUR THING!

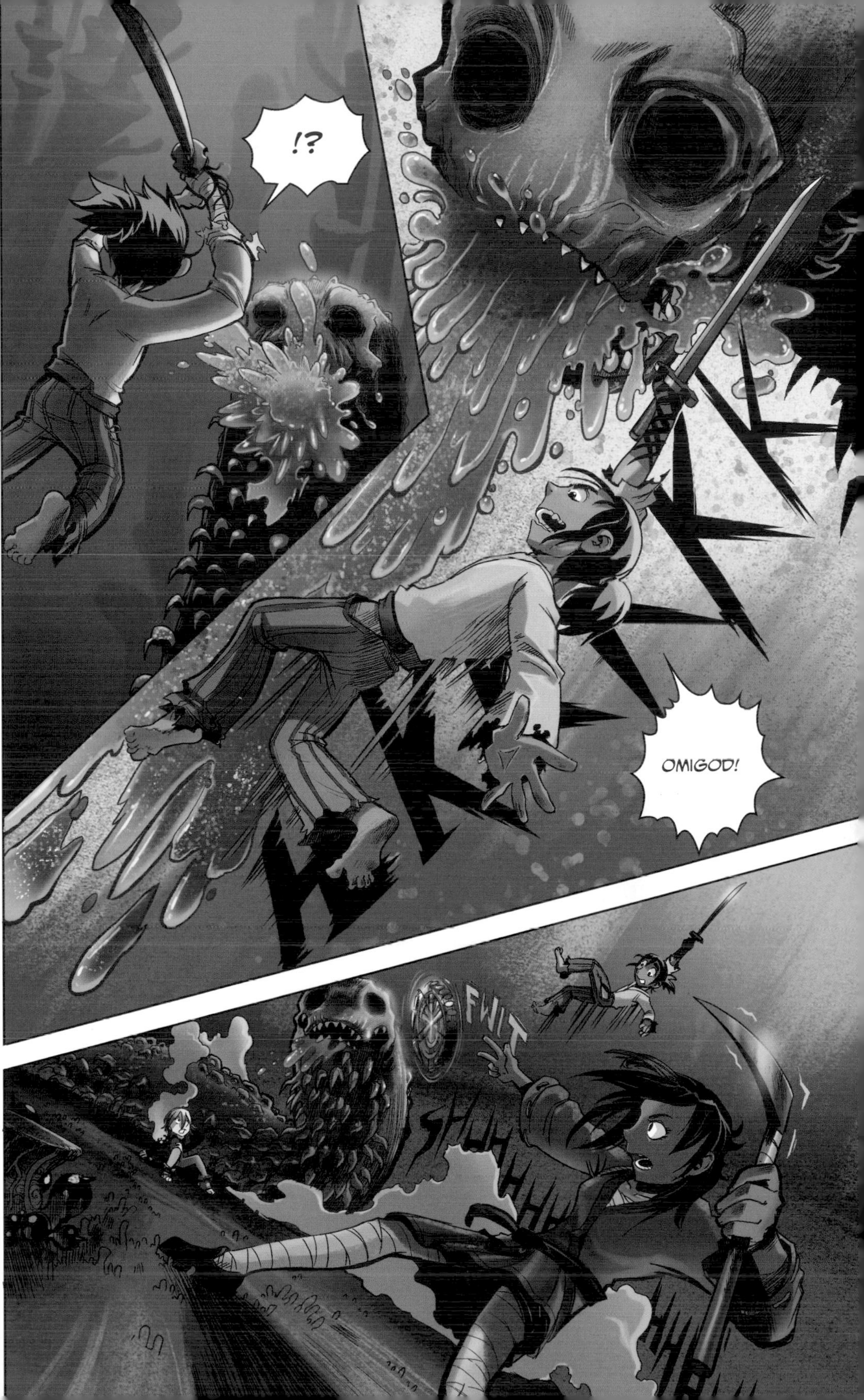
!?
OMIGOD!
FWIT
SHHHHHHHHH

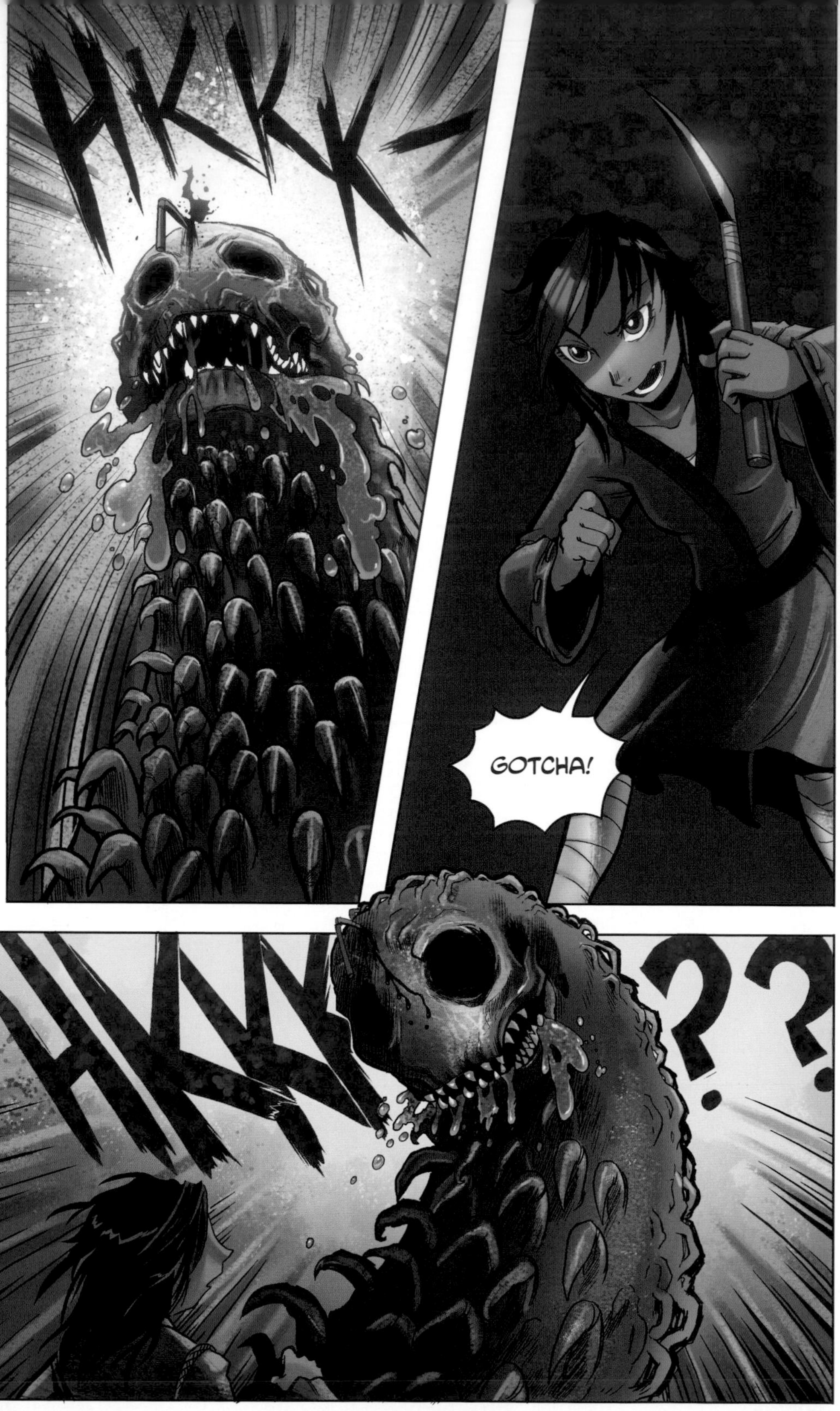
PIKKK-
GOTCHA!
??

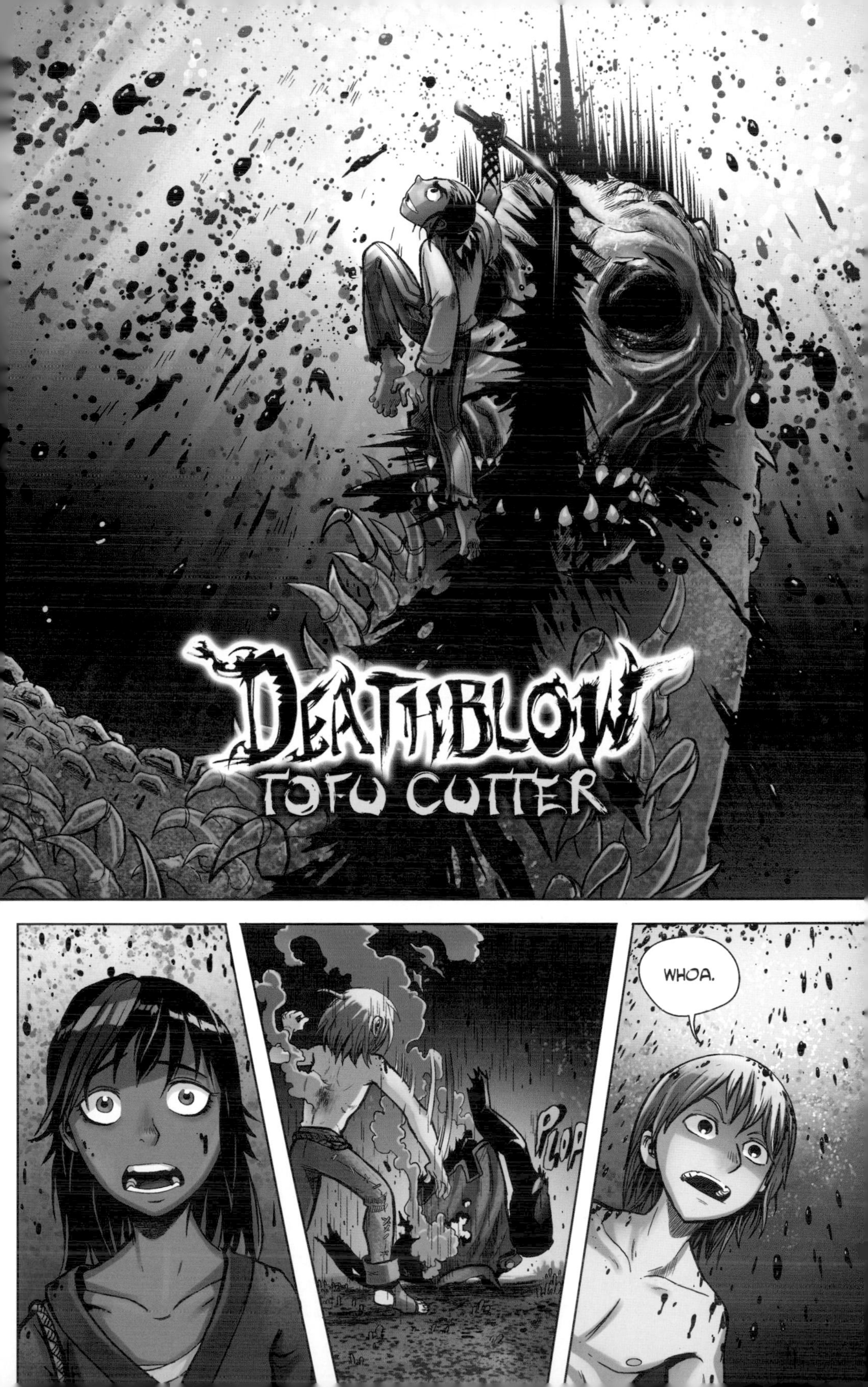
DEATHBLOW
TOFU CUTTER
PLOP
WHOA.

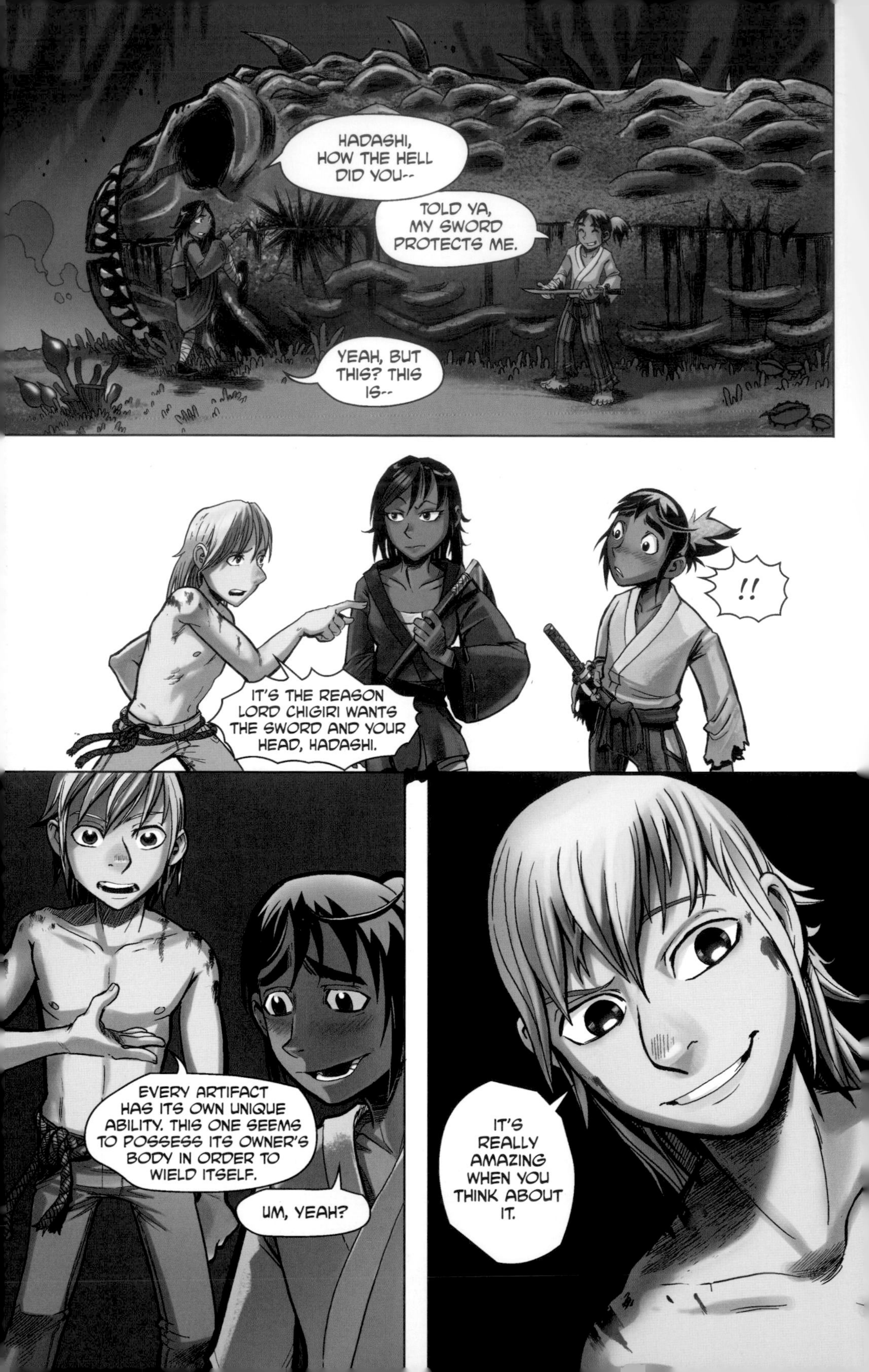
HADASHI, HOW THE HELL DID YOU--
TOLD YA, MY SWORD PROTECTS ME.
YEAH, BUT THIS? THIS IS--
!!
IT'S THE REASON LORD CHIGIRI WANTS THE SWORD AND YOUR HEAD, HADASHI.
EVERY ARTIFACT HAS ITS OWN UNIQUE ABILITY. THIS ONE SEEMS TO POSSESS ITS OWNER'S BODY IN ORDER TO WIELD ITSELF.
UM, YEAH?
IT'S REALLY AMAZING WHEN YOU THINK ABOUT IT.

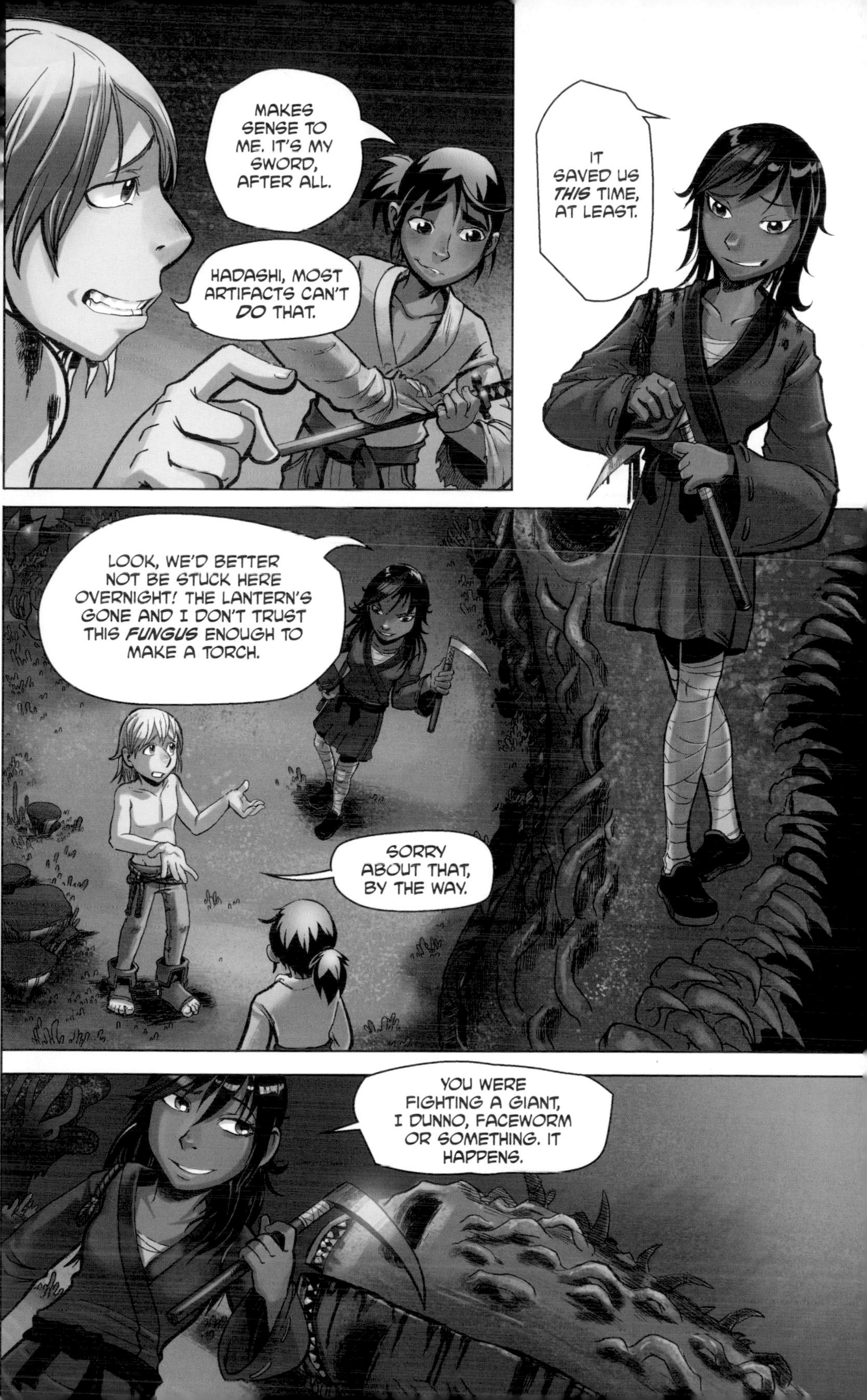

MAKES SENSE TO ME. IT'S MY SWORD, AFTER ALL.
HADASHI, MOST ARTIFACTS CAN'T *DO* THAT.
IT SAVED US *THIS* TIME, AT LEAST.
LOOK, WE'D BETTER NOT BE STUCK HERE OVERNIGHT! THE LANTERN'S GONE AND I DON'T TRUST THIS *FUNGUS* ENOUGH TO MAKE A TORCH.
SORRY ABOUT THAT, BY THE WAY.
YOU WERE FIGHTING A GIANT, I DUNNO, FACEWORM OR SOMETHING. IT HAPPENS.

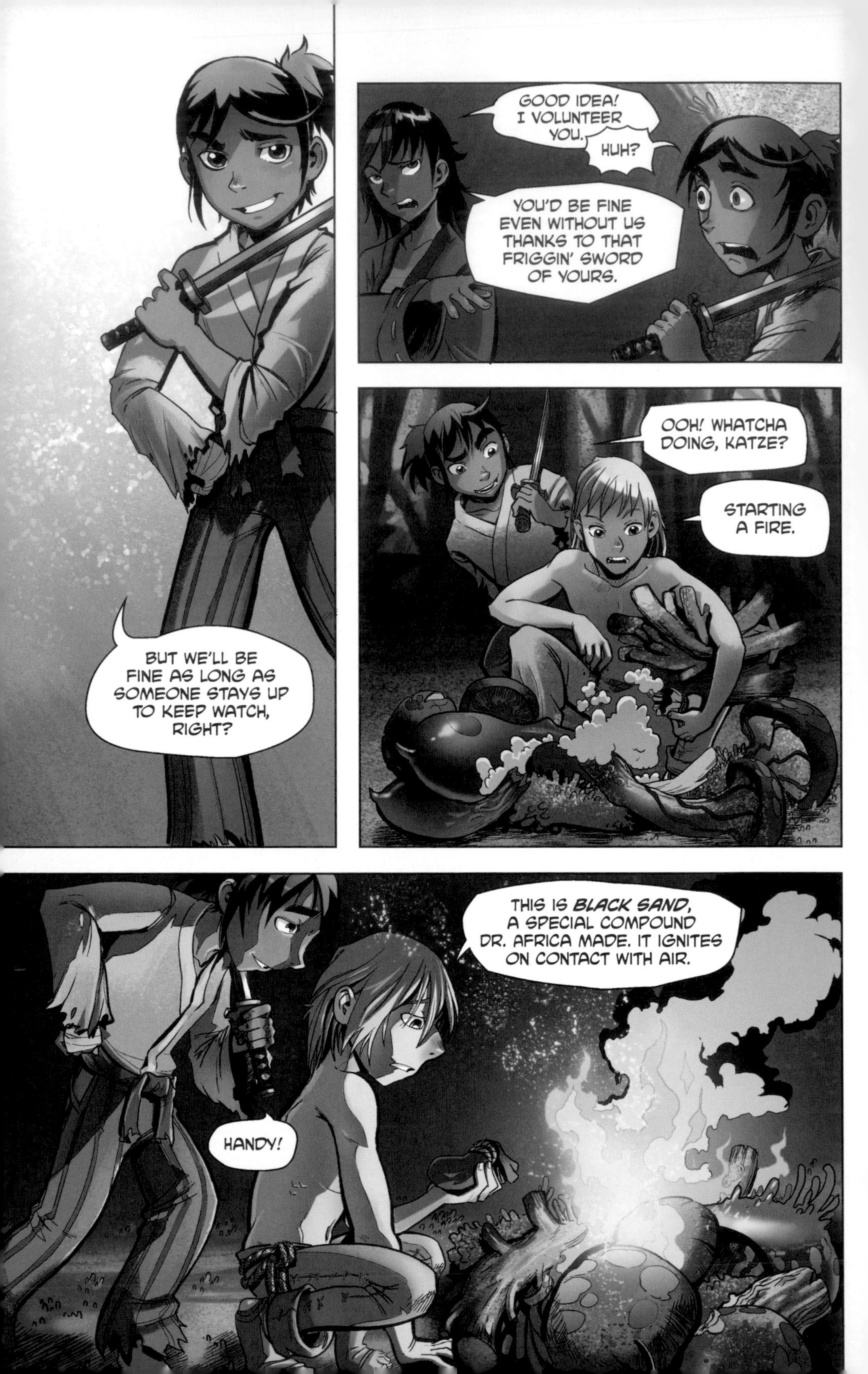
BUT WE'LL BE FINE AS LONG AS SOMEONE STAYS UP TO KEEP WATCH, RIGHT?
GOOD IDEA! I VOLUNTEER YOU.
HUH?
YOU'D BE FINE EVEN WITHOUT US THANKS TO THAT FRIGGIN' SWORD OF YOURS.
OOH! WHATCHA DOING, KATZE?
STARTING A FIRE.
THIS IS *BLACK SAND*, A SPECIAL COMPOUND DR. AFRICA MADE. IT IGNITES ON CONTACT WITH AIR.
HANDY!

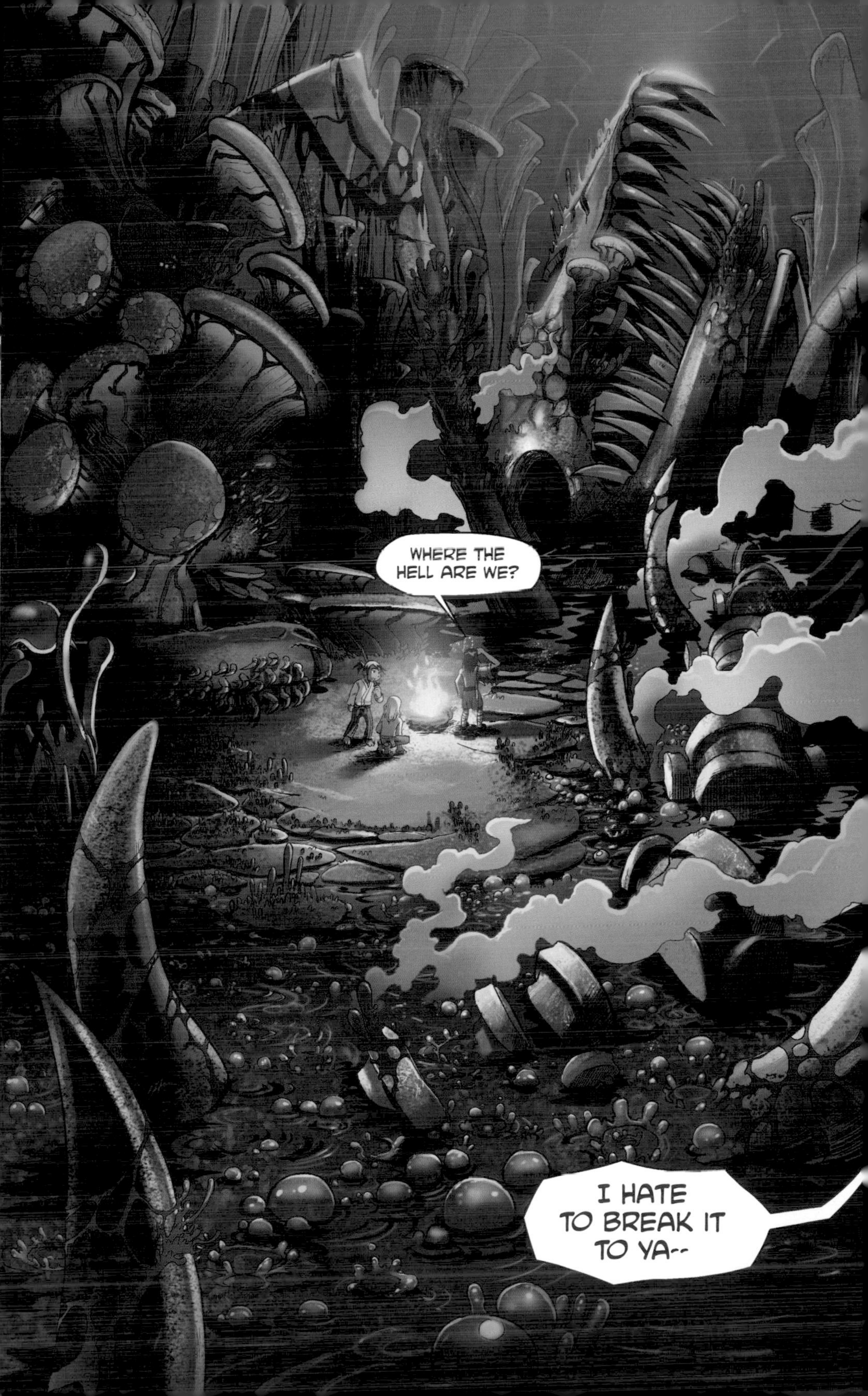
WHERE THE HELL ARE WE?
I HATE TO BREAK IT TO YA--

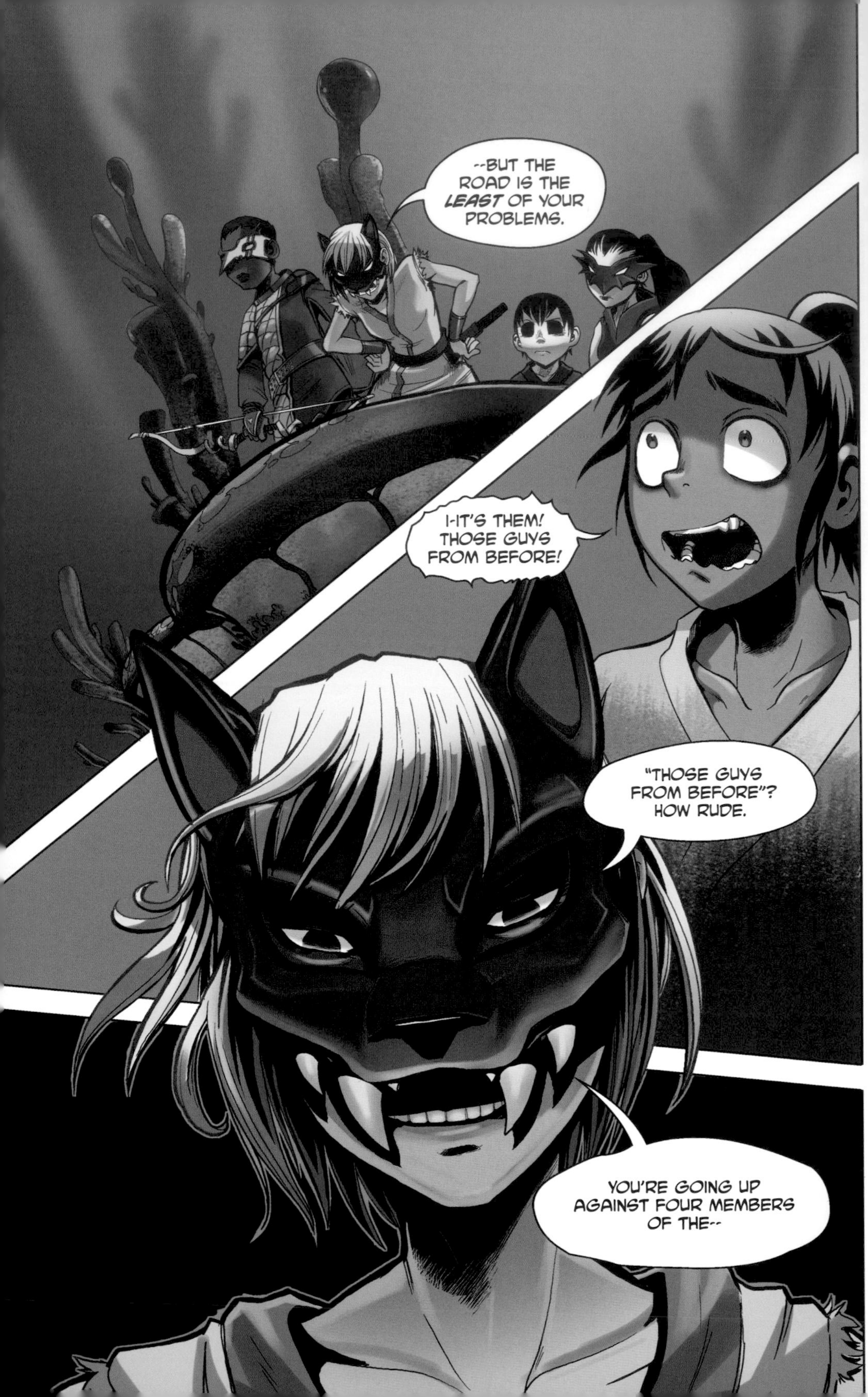
--BUT THE ROAD IS THE *LEAST* OF YOUR PROBLEMS.
I-IT'S THEM! THOSE GUYS FROM BEFORE!
"THOSE GUYS FROM BEFORE"? HOW RUDE.
YOU'RE GOING UP AGAINST FOUR MEMBERS OF THE--

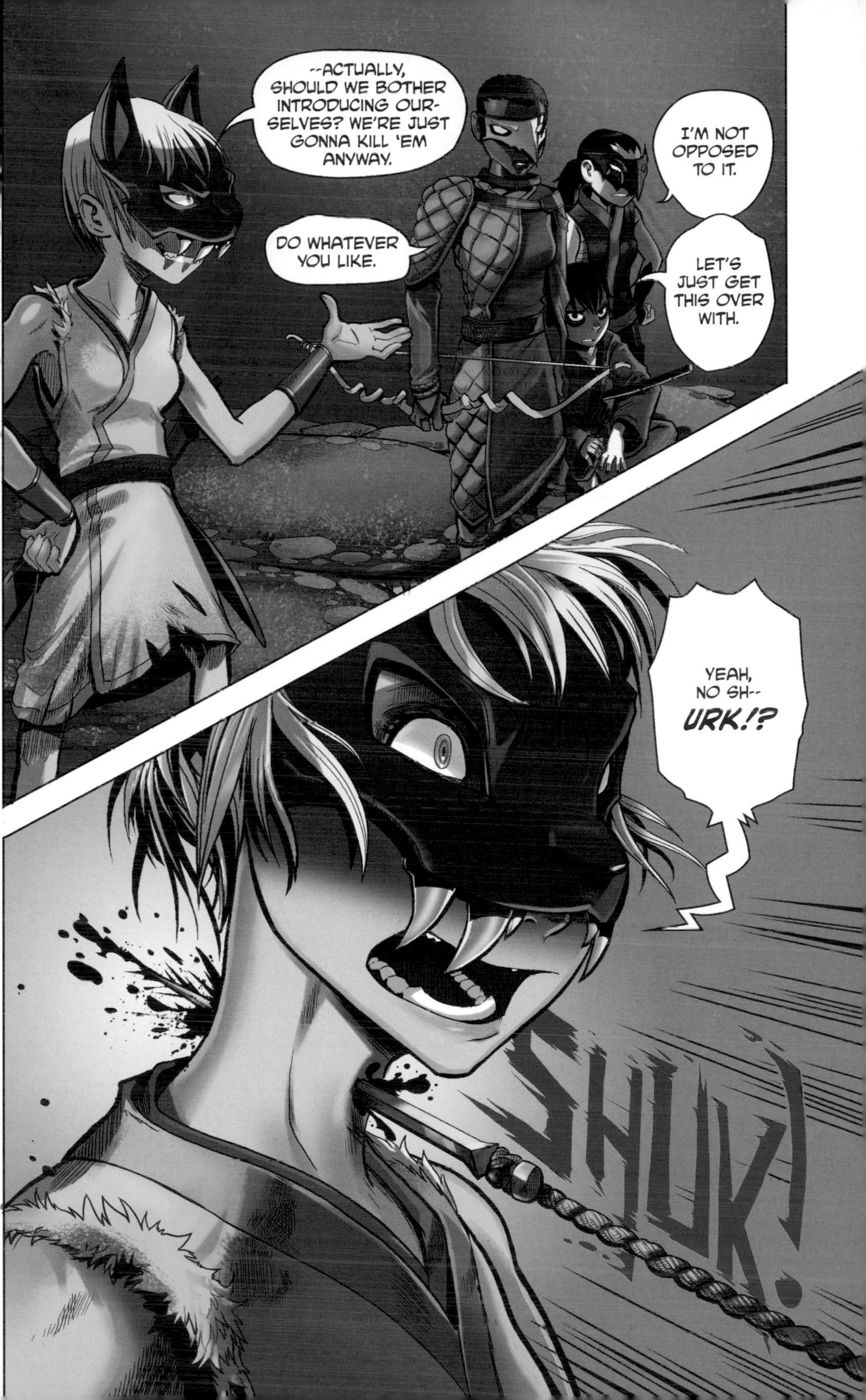
--ACTUALLY, SHOULD WE BOTHER INTRODUCING OUR-SELVES? WE'RE JUST GONNA KILL 'EM ANYWAY.
I'M NOT OPPOSED TO IT.
DO WHATEVER YOU LIKE.
LET'S JUST GET THIS OVER WITH.
YEAH, NO SH-- URK!?
SHUK!

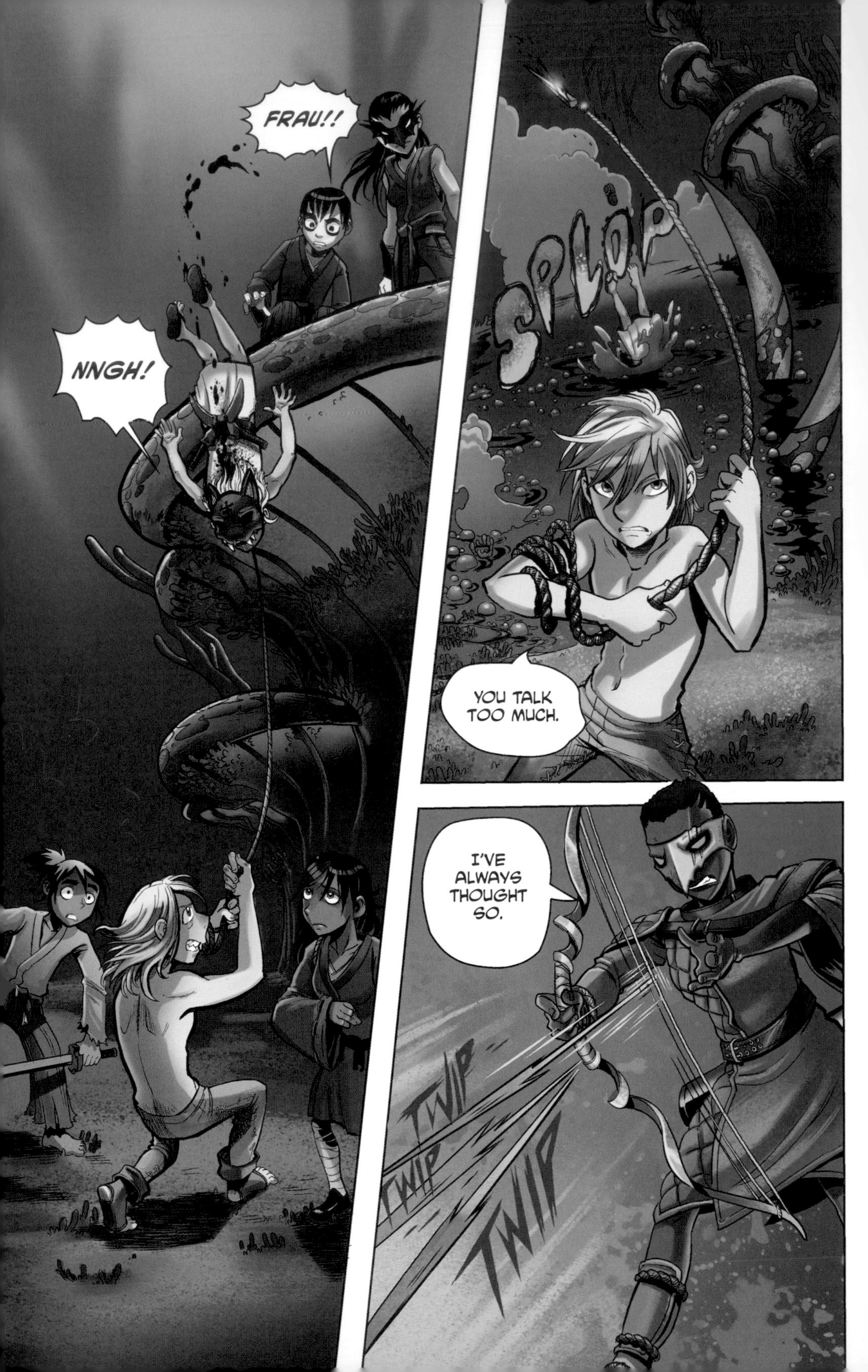
FRAU!!
NNGH!
SPLOP
YOU TALK TOO MUCH.
I'VE ALWAYS THOUGHT SO.
TWIP
TWIP
TWIP

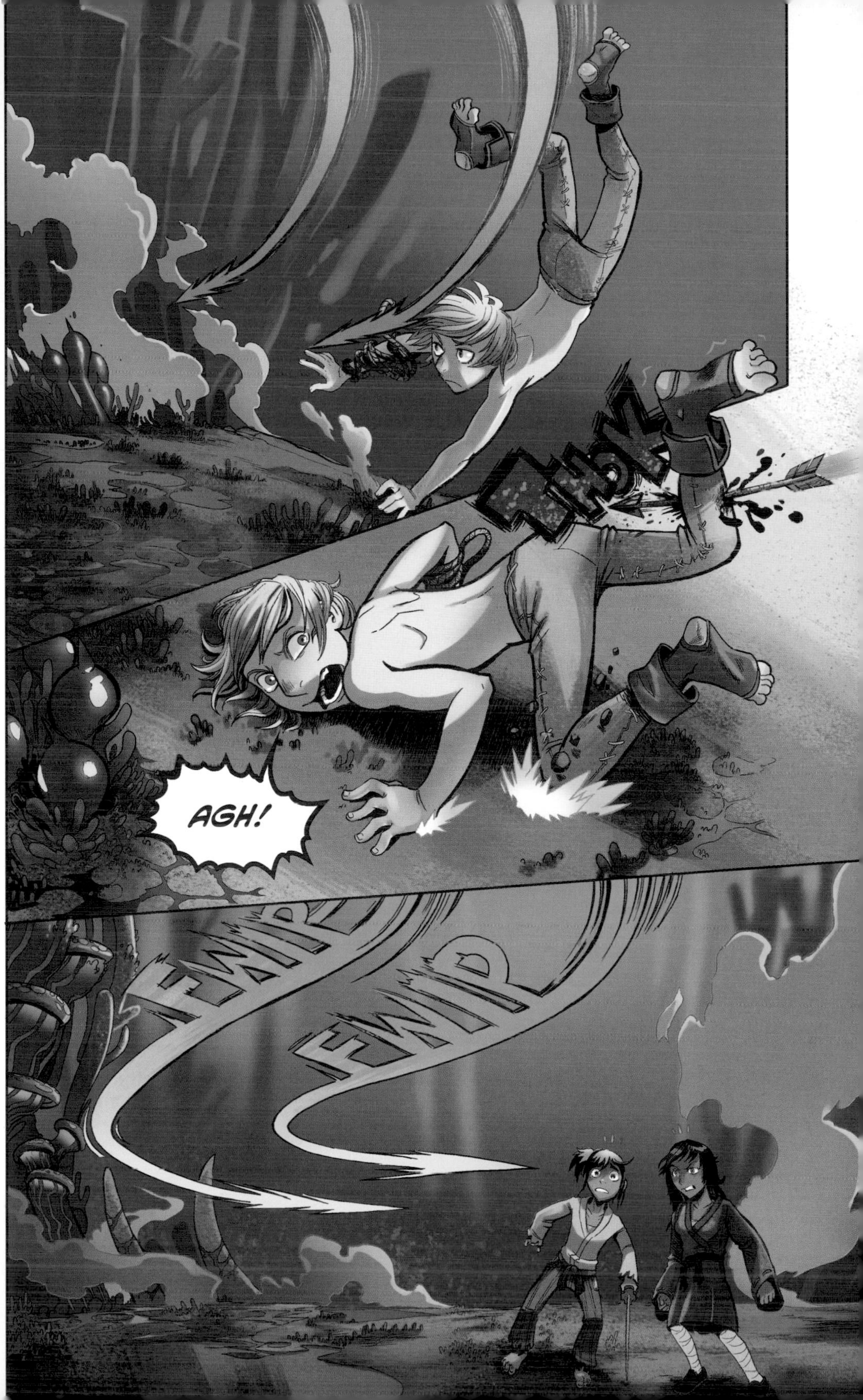
AGH!
FWIP
FWIP

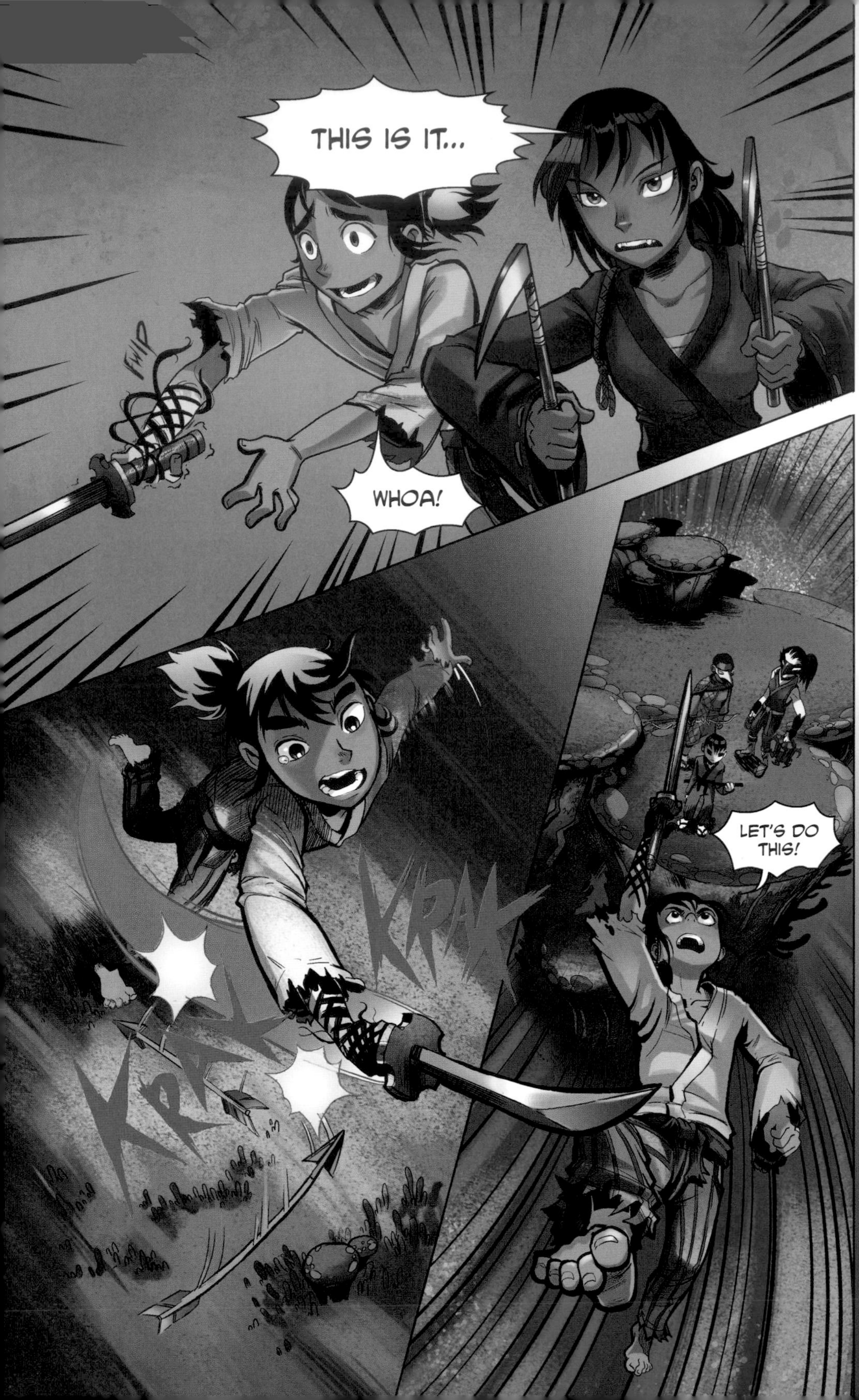
THIS IS IT...
FWIP
WHOA!
KRAK
KRAK
LET'S DO THIS!

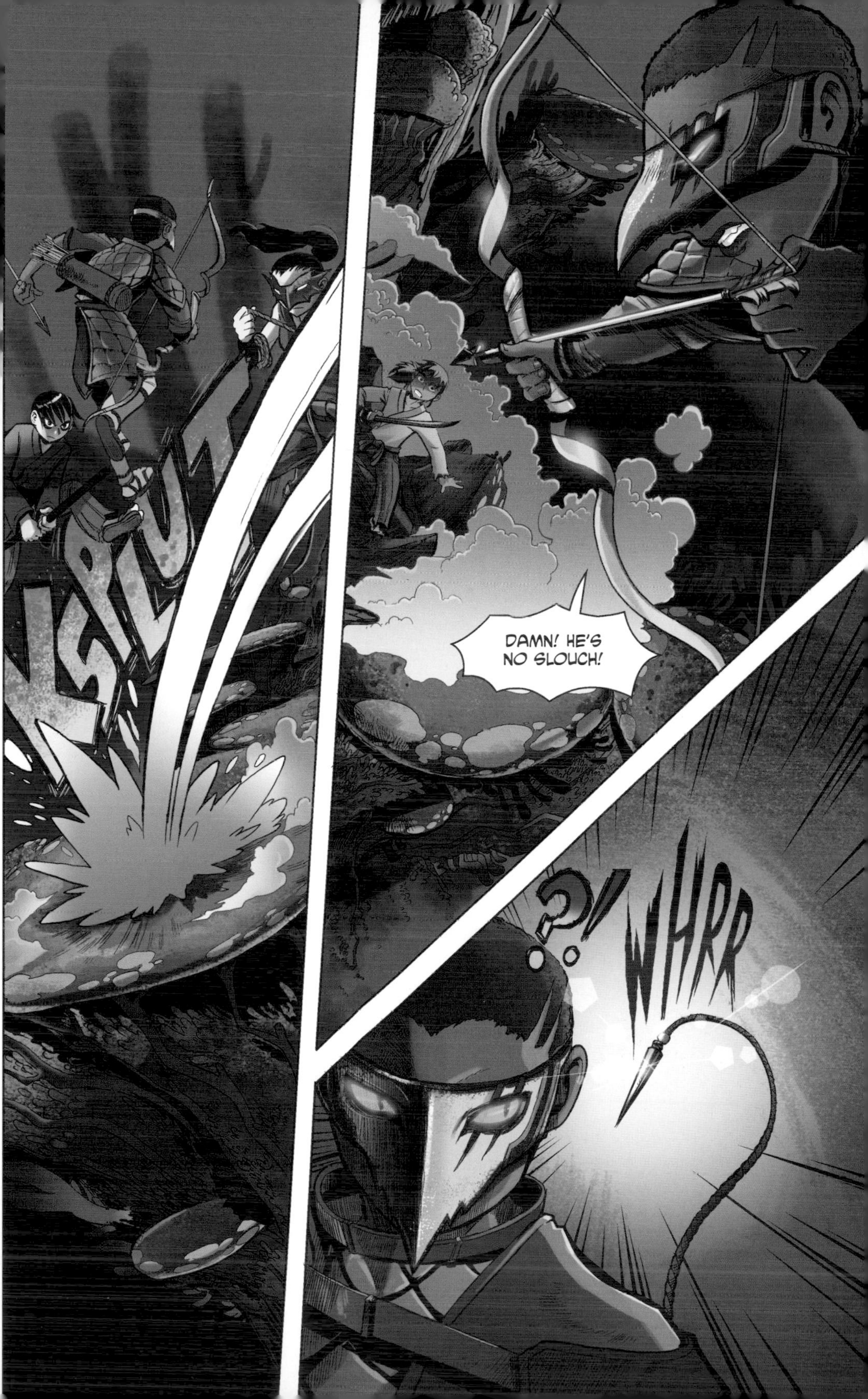
KSPLUT
DAMN! HE'S NO SLOUCH!
?!
WHRR

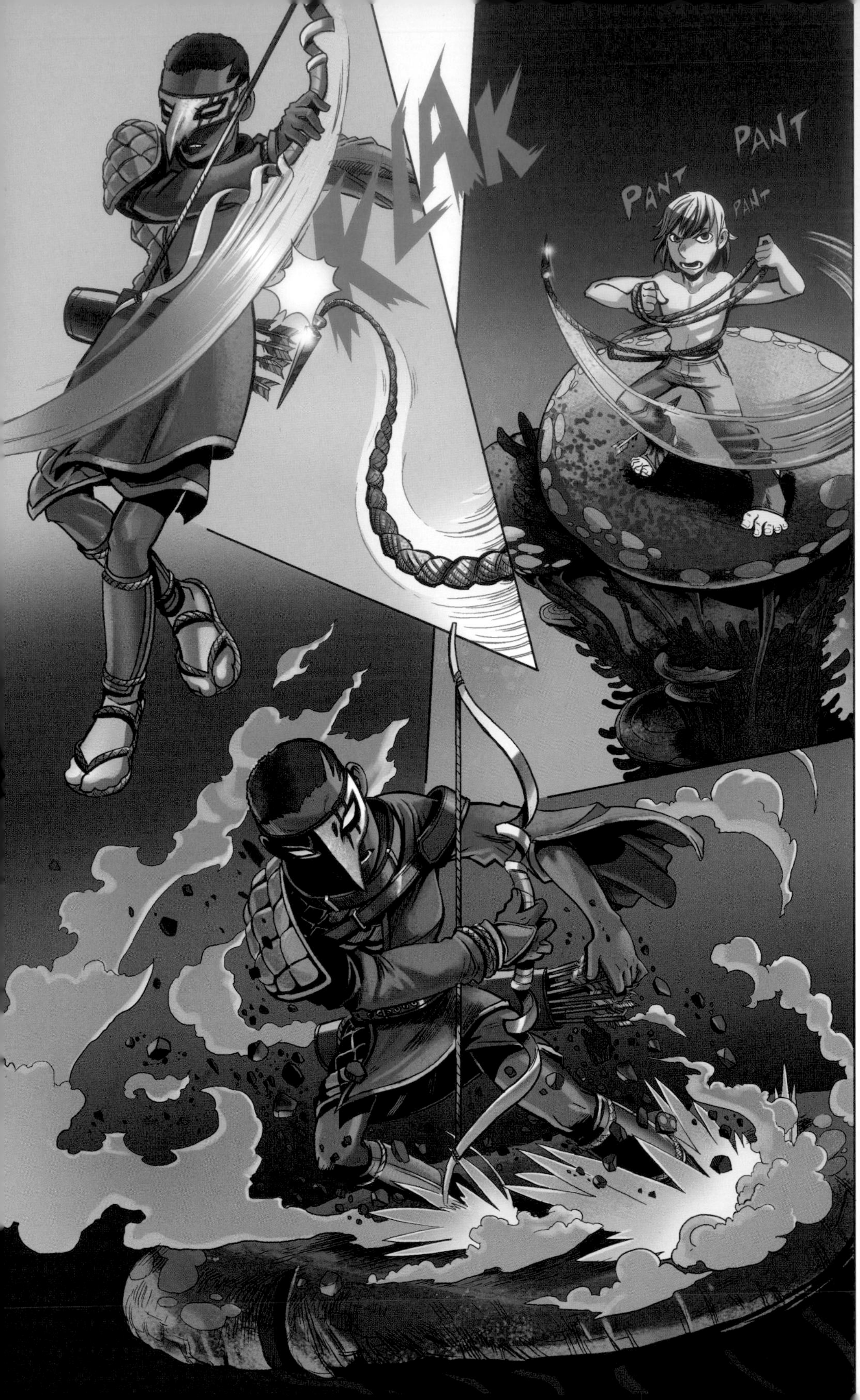
KLAK
PANT
PANT
PANT

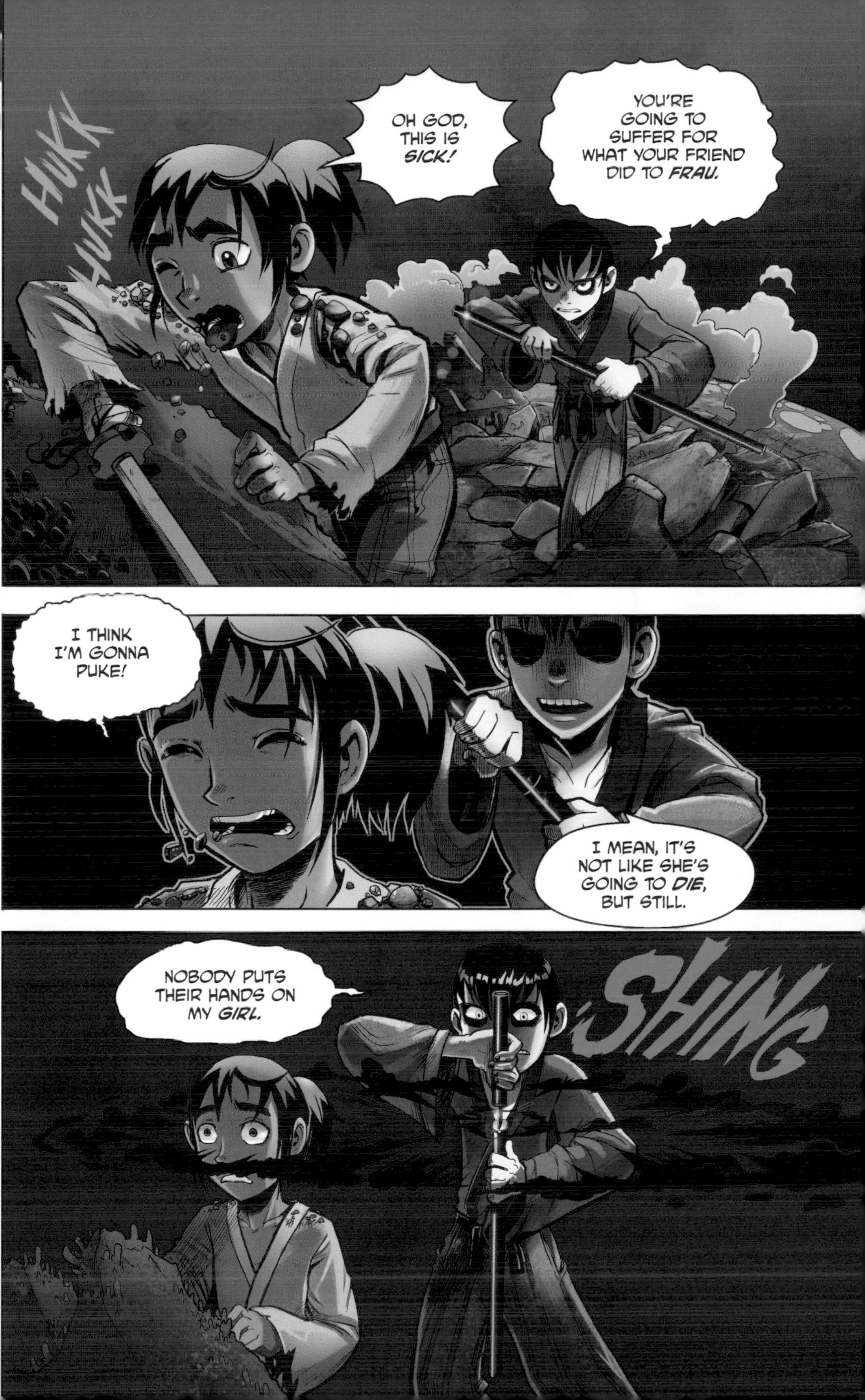
HUKK HUKK
OH GOD, THIS IS SICK!
YOU'RE GOING TO SUFFER FOR WHAT YOUR FRIEND DID TO FRAU.
I THINK I'M GONNA PUKE!
I MEAN, IT'S NOT LIKE SHE'S GOING TO DIE, BUT STILL.
NOBODY PUTS THEIR HANDS ON MY GIRL.
SHING

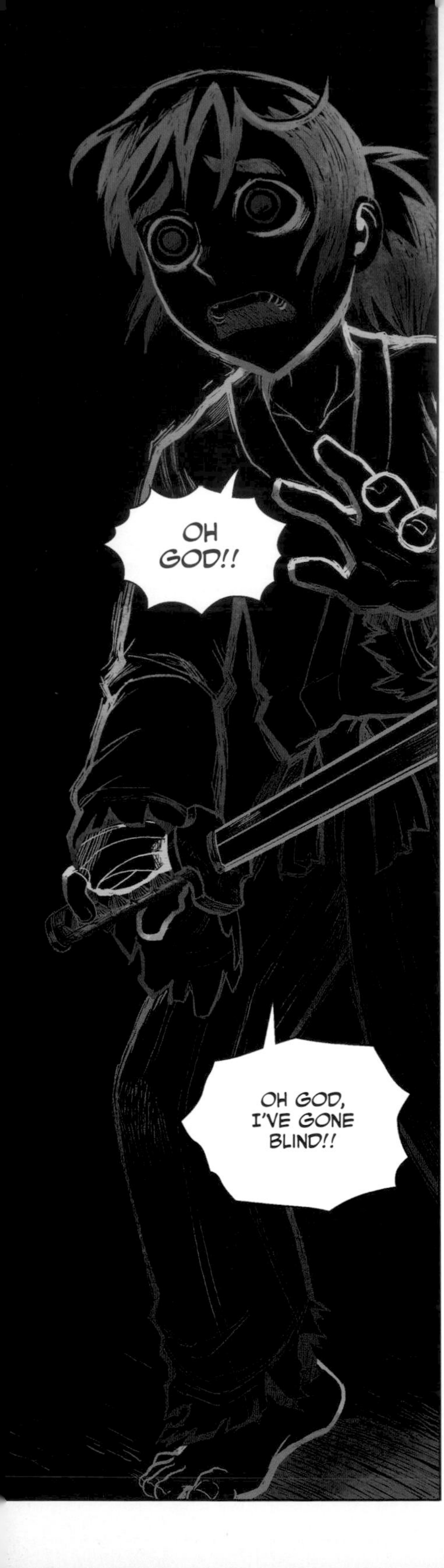
OH GOD!!
OH GOD, I'VE GONE BLIND!!

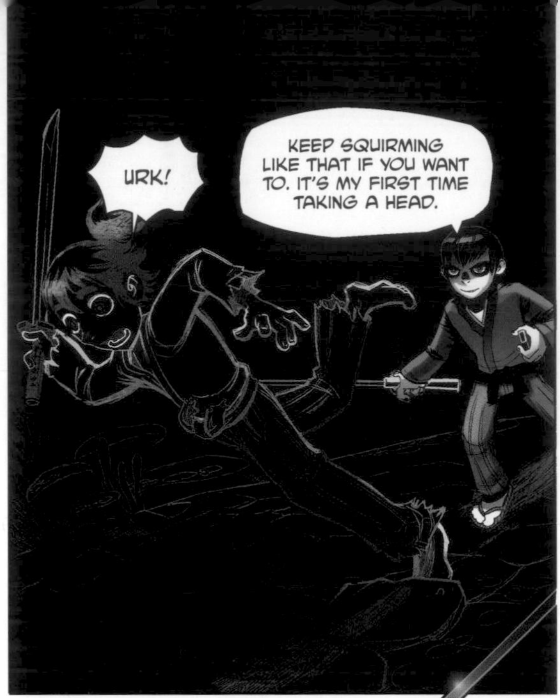
URK!
KEEP SQUIRMING LIKE THAT IF YOU WANT TO. IT'S MY FIRST TIME TAKING A HEAD.

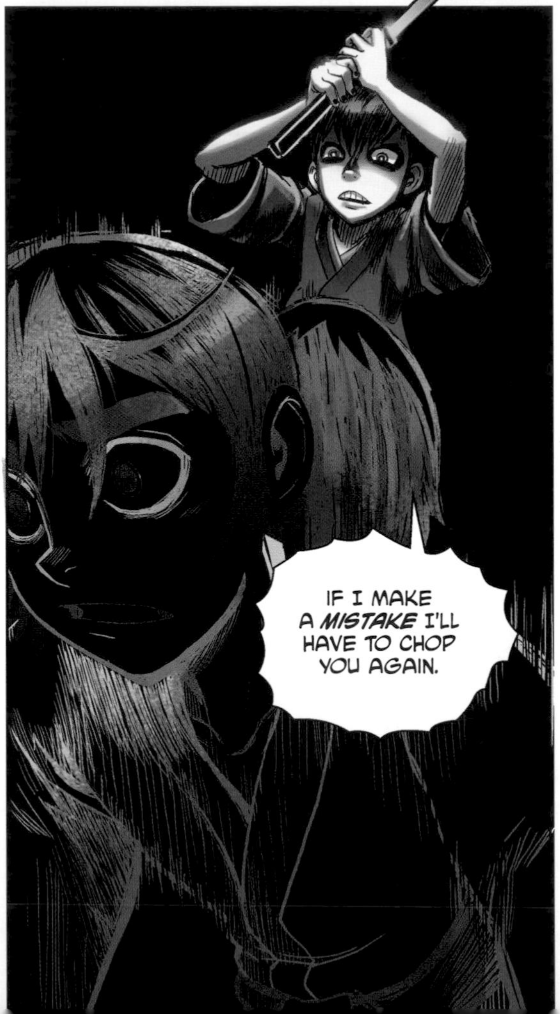
IF I MAKE A *MISTAKE* I'LL HAVE TO CHOP YOU AGAIN.

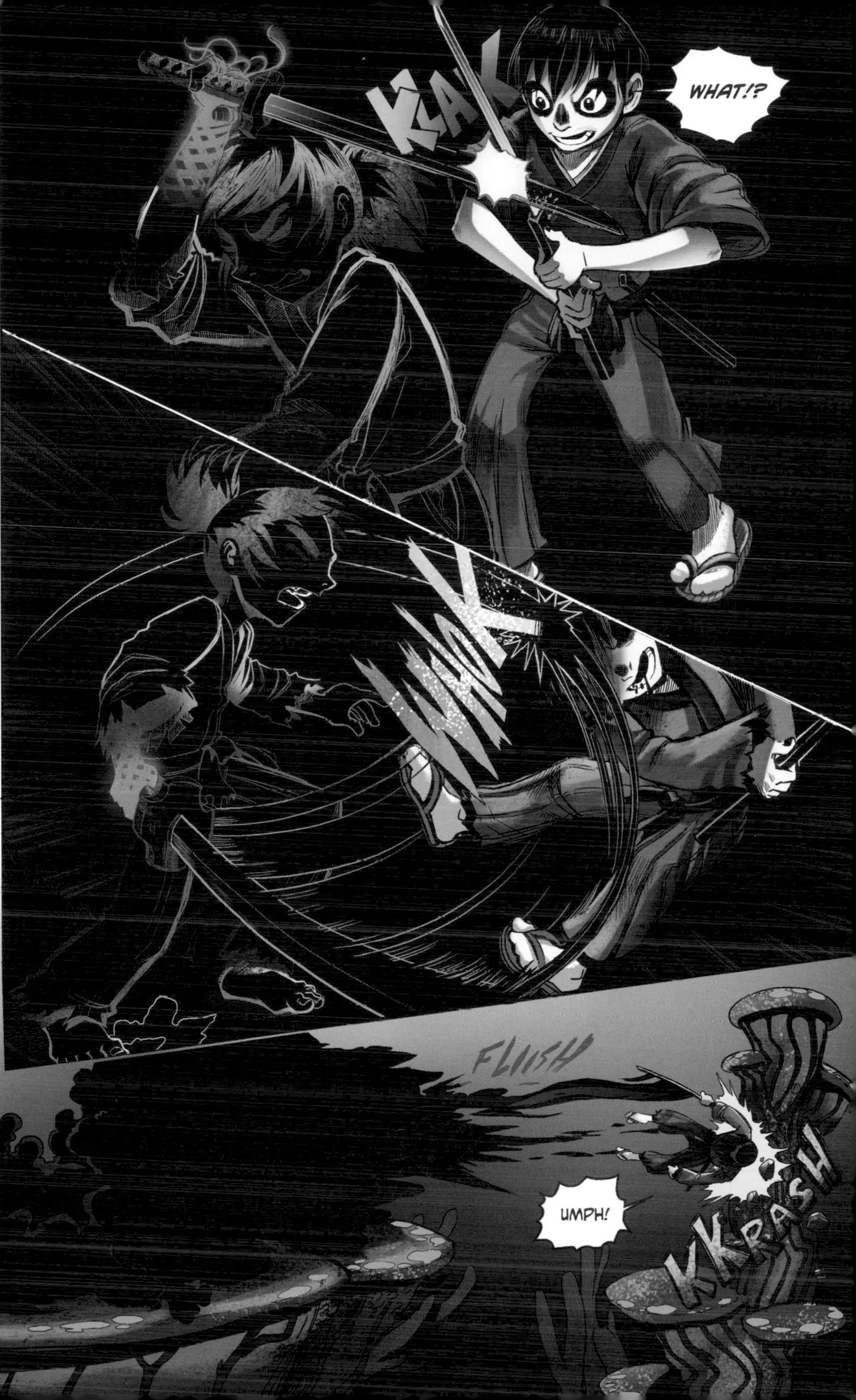
KLAK
WHAT!?
WHOK
FLUSH
UMPH!
KKRASH

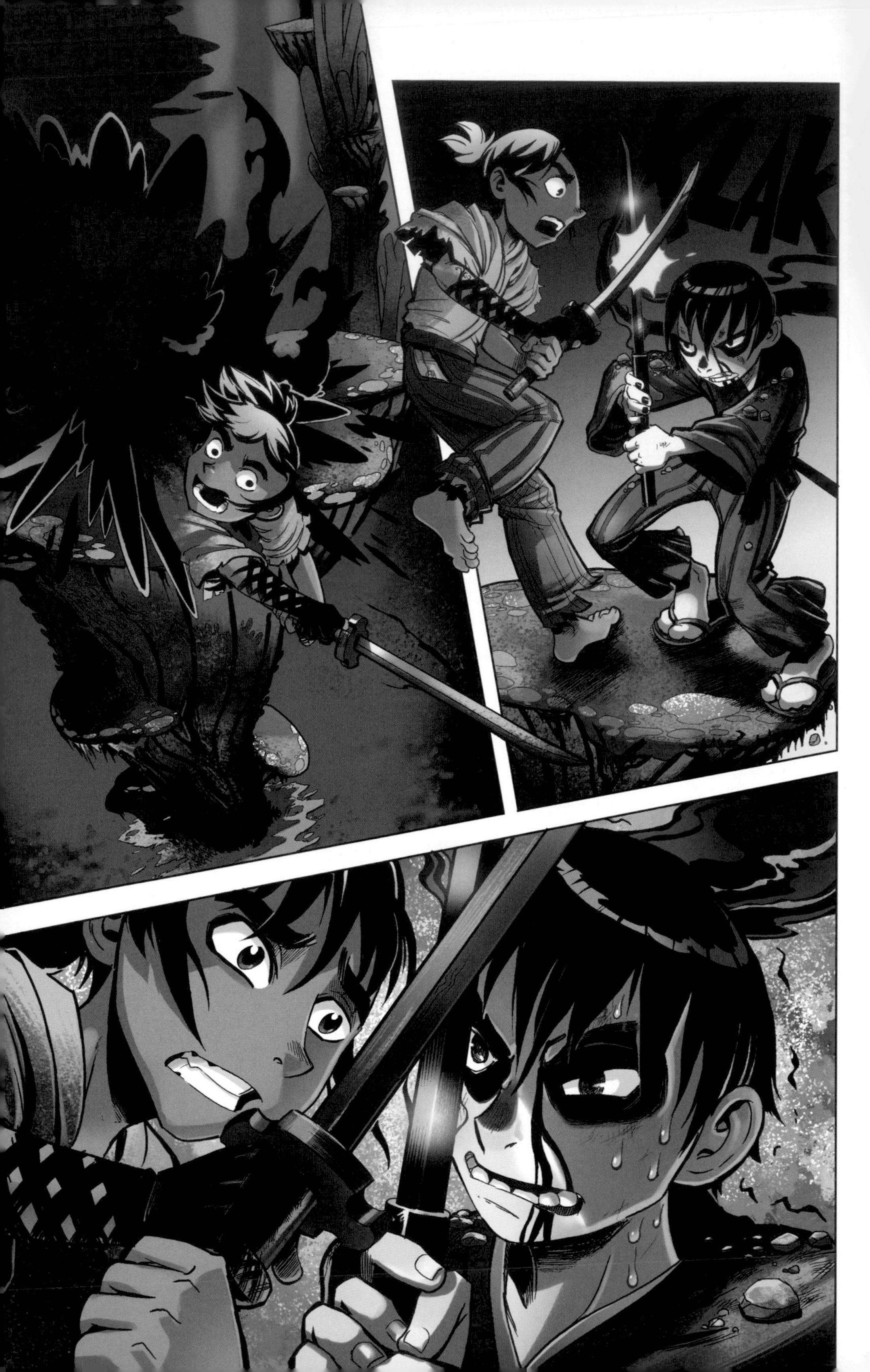
LAK

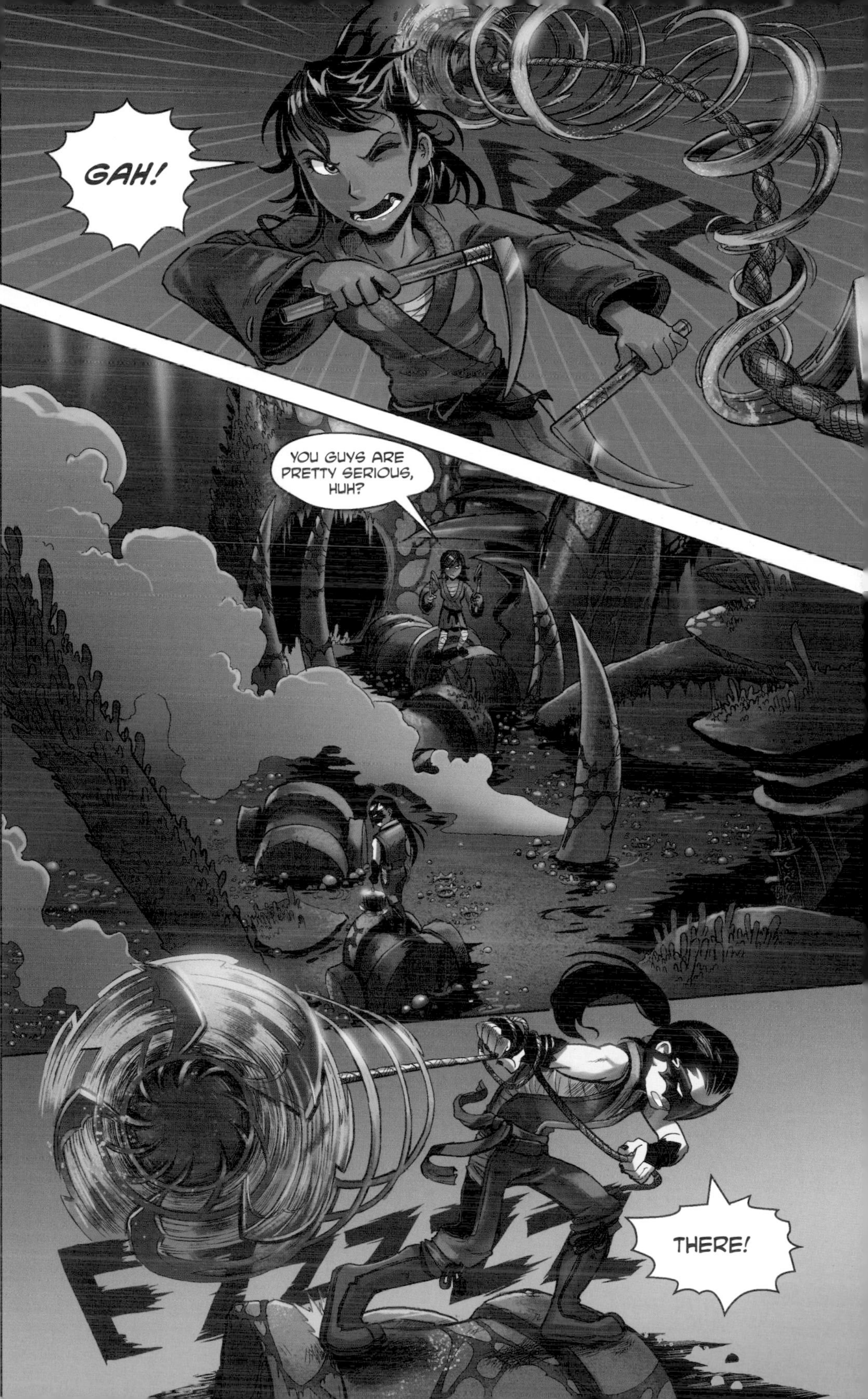
GAH!
YOU GUYS ARE PRETTY SERIOUS, HUH?
THERE!

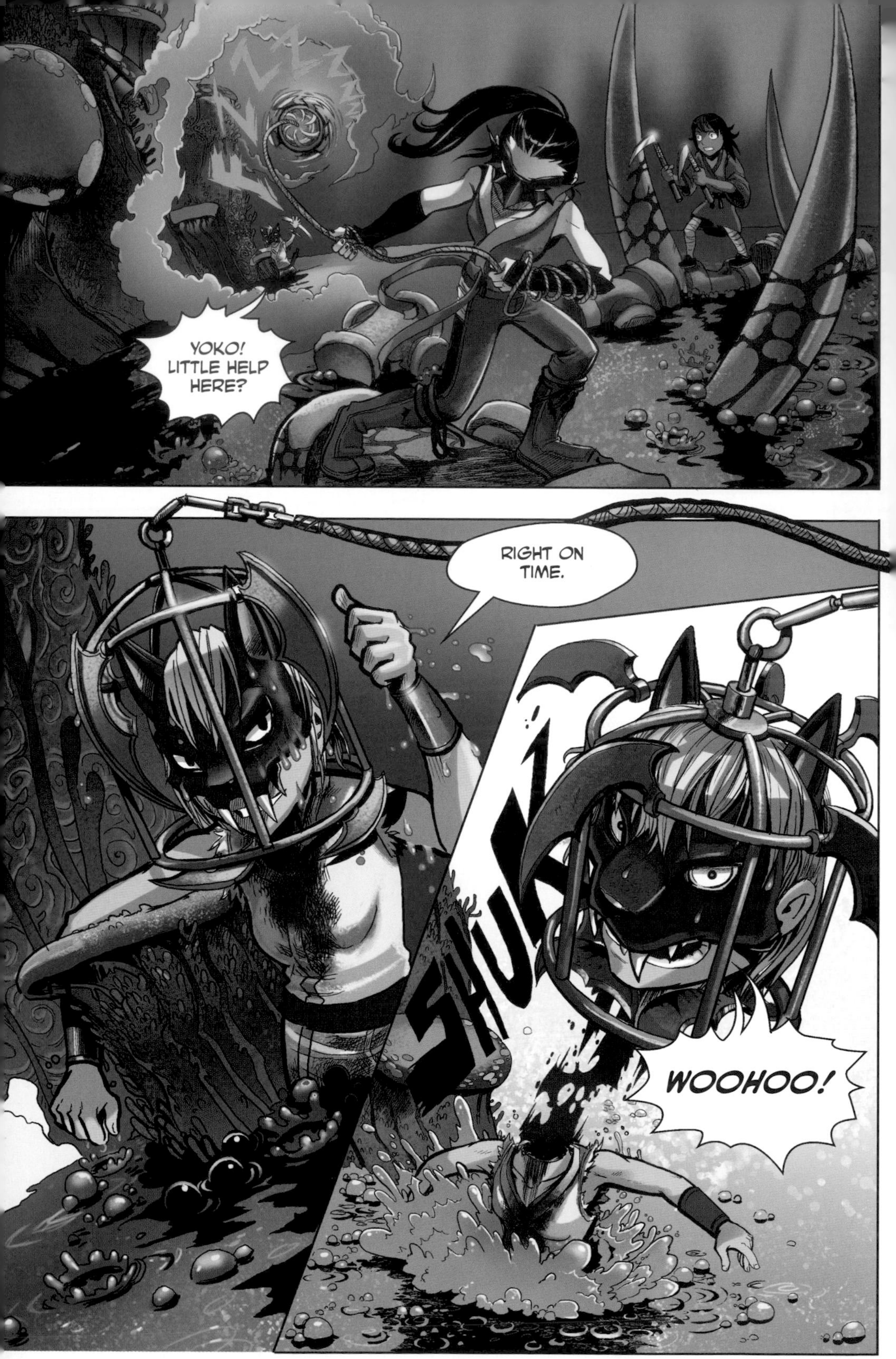
YOKO! LITTLE HELP HERE?
RIGHT ON TIME.
WOOHOO!

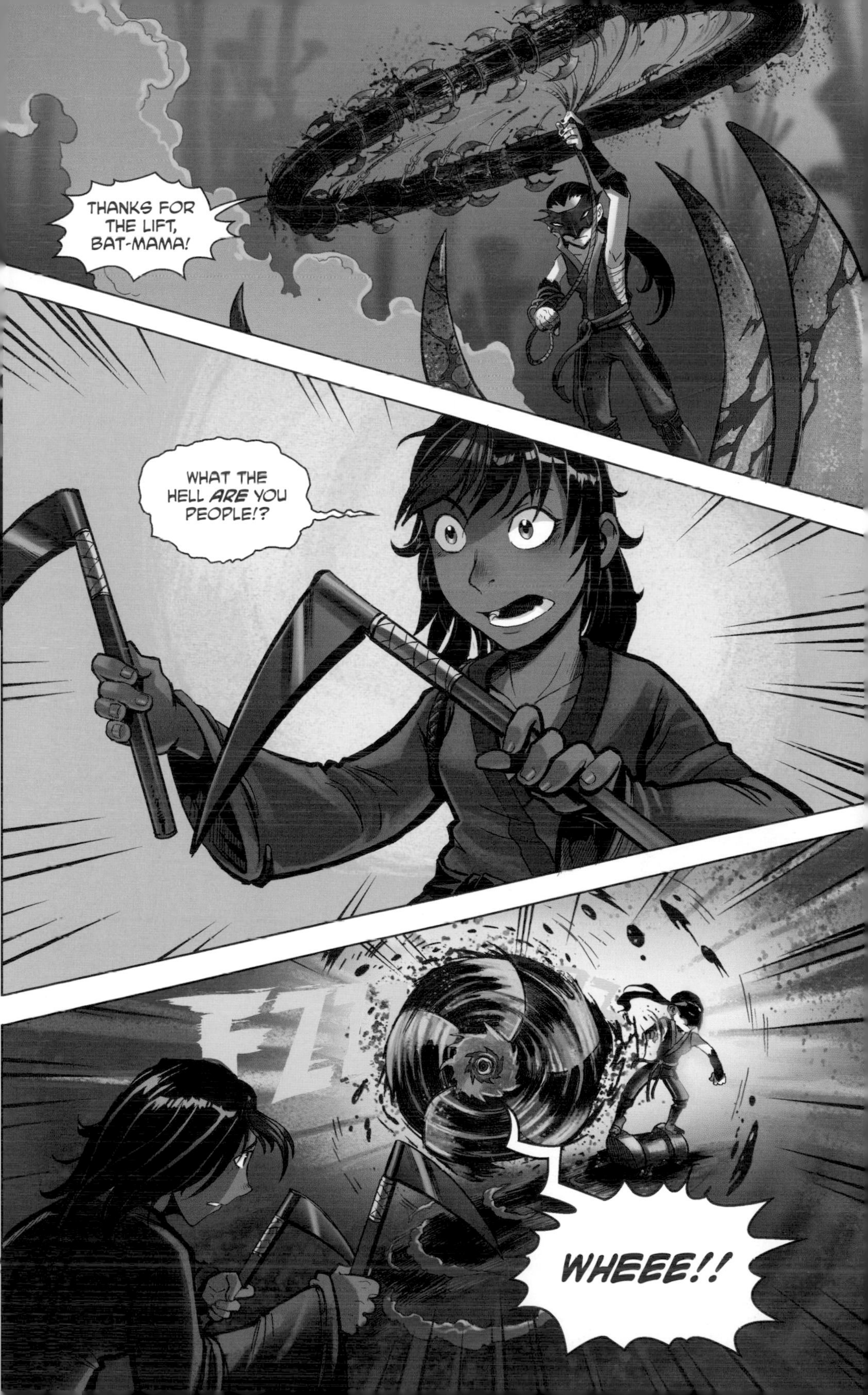
THANKS FOR THE LIFT, BAT-MAMA!
WHAT THE HELL *ARE* YOU PEOPLE!?
WHEEE!!

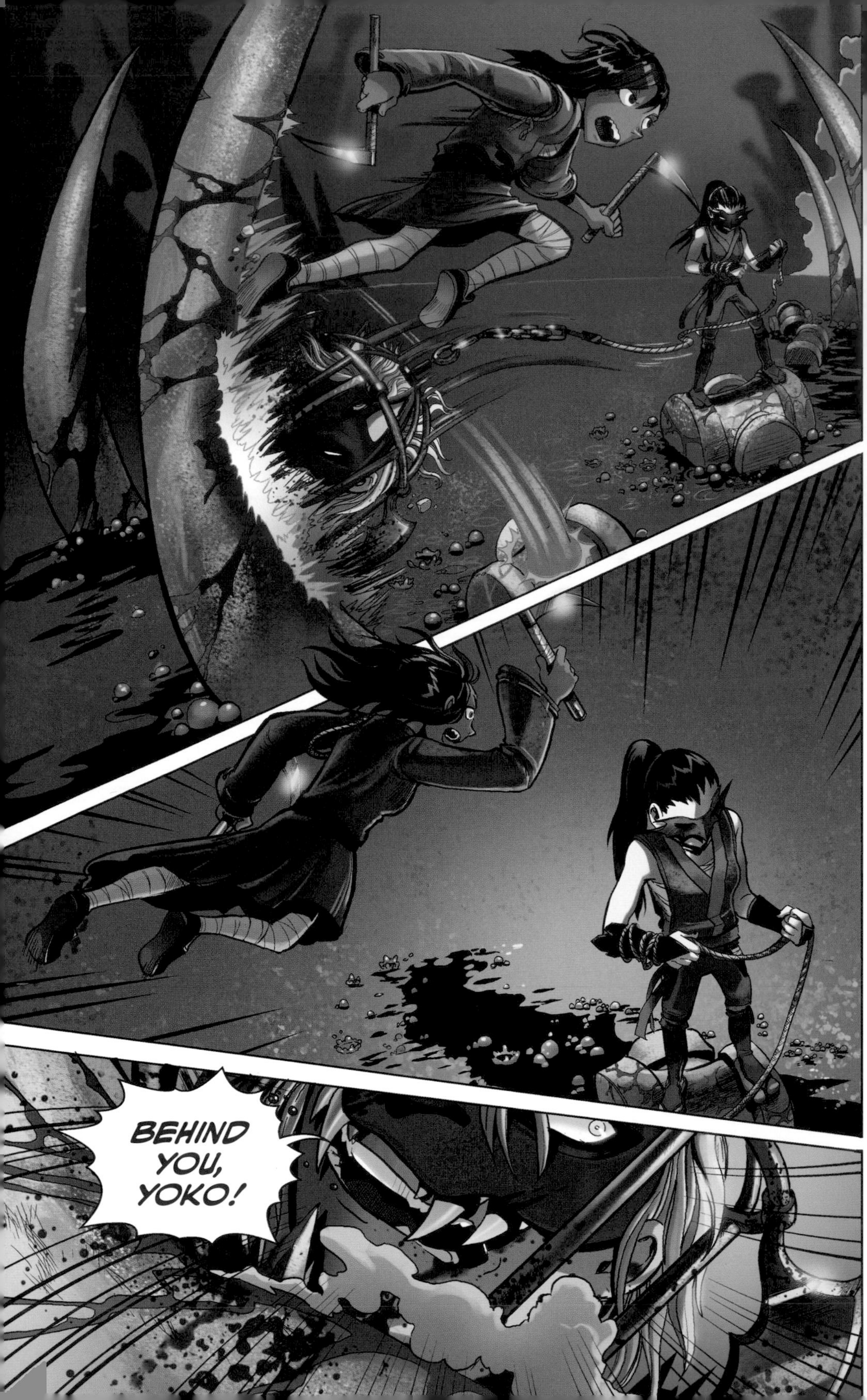
BEHIND YOU, YOKO!

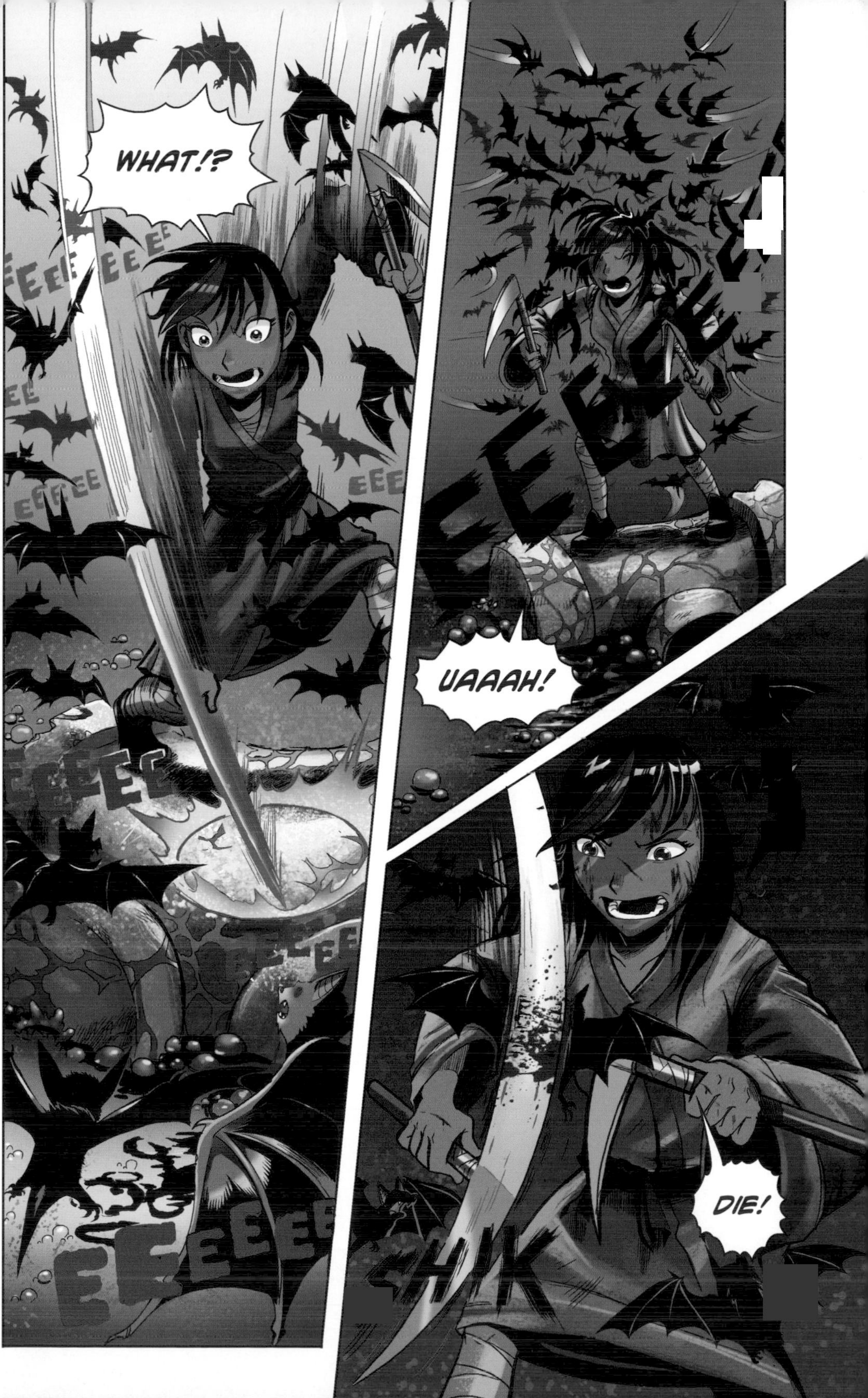
WHAT!?
EEEE
EEEEE
UAAAH!
DIE!

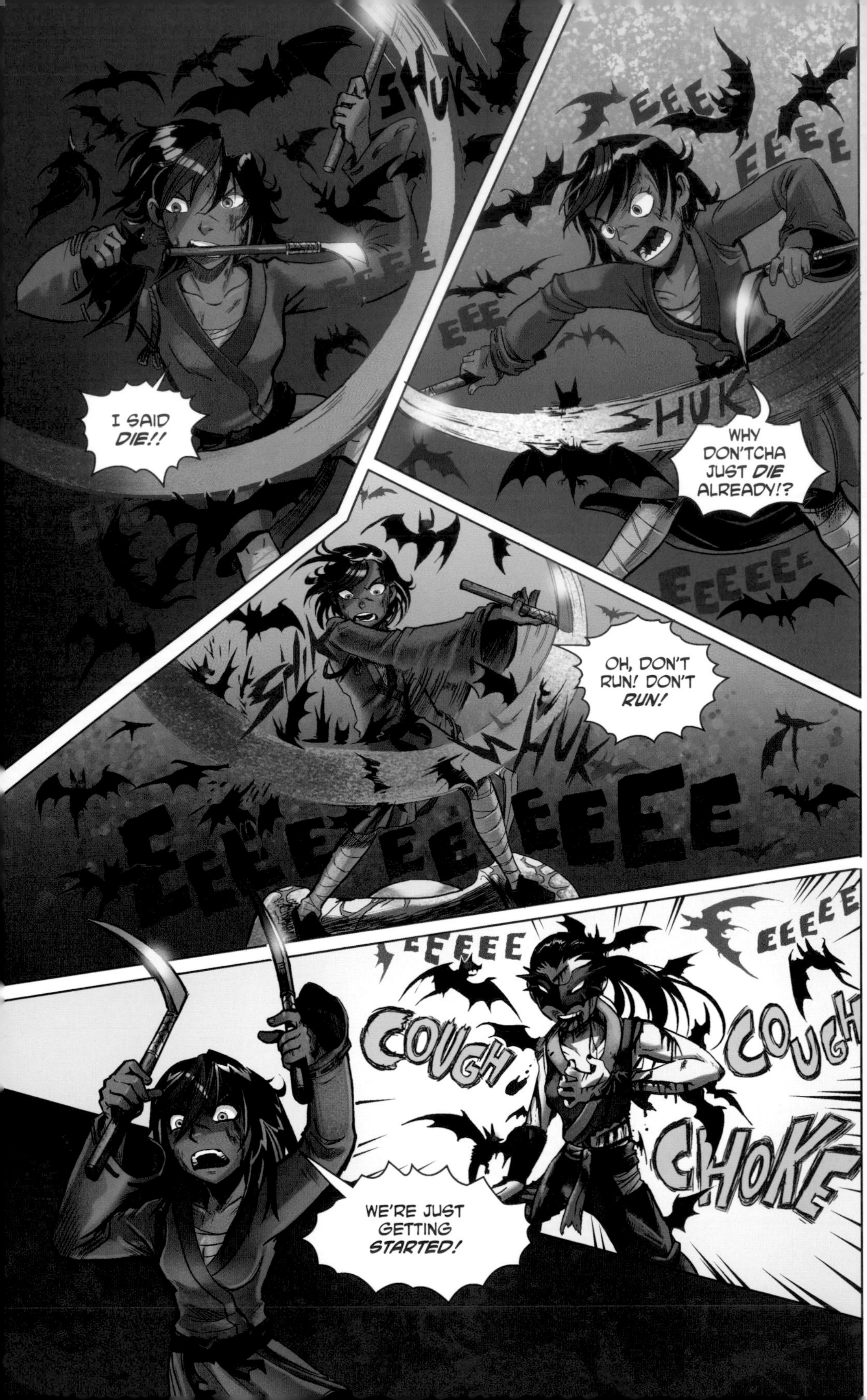
SHUK
EEEEE
I SAID DIE!!
EEEE
EEEE
EEE
SHUK
WHY DON'TCHA JUST DIE ALREADY!?
EEEEEE
OH, DON'T RUN! DON'T RUN!
SHUK
EEEEEEEEE
EEEEE
EEEEE
COUGH
COUGH
CHOKE
WE'RE JUST GETTING STARTED!

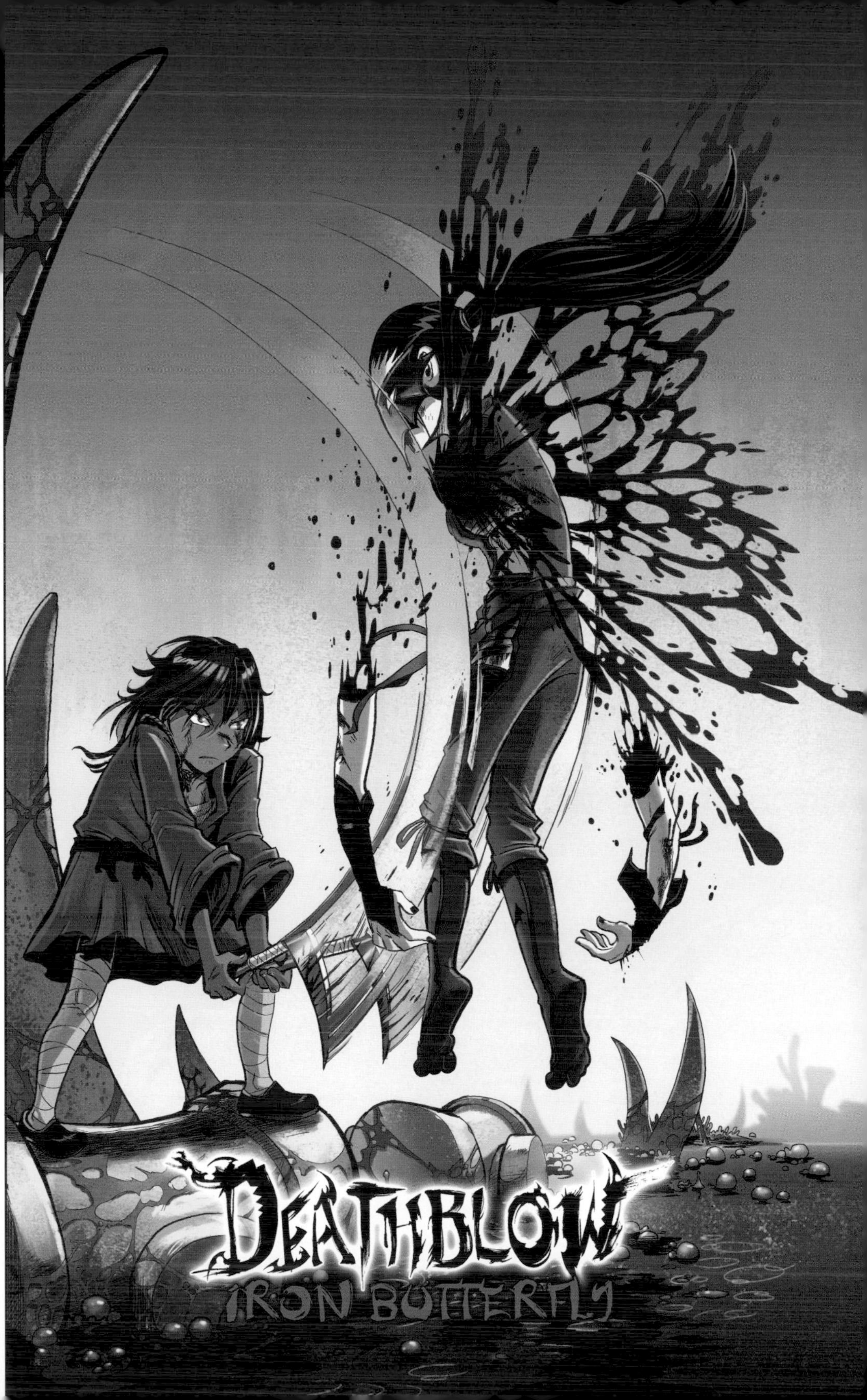
DEATHBLOW
IRON BUTTERFLY

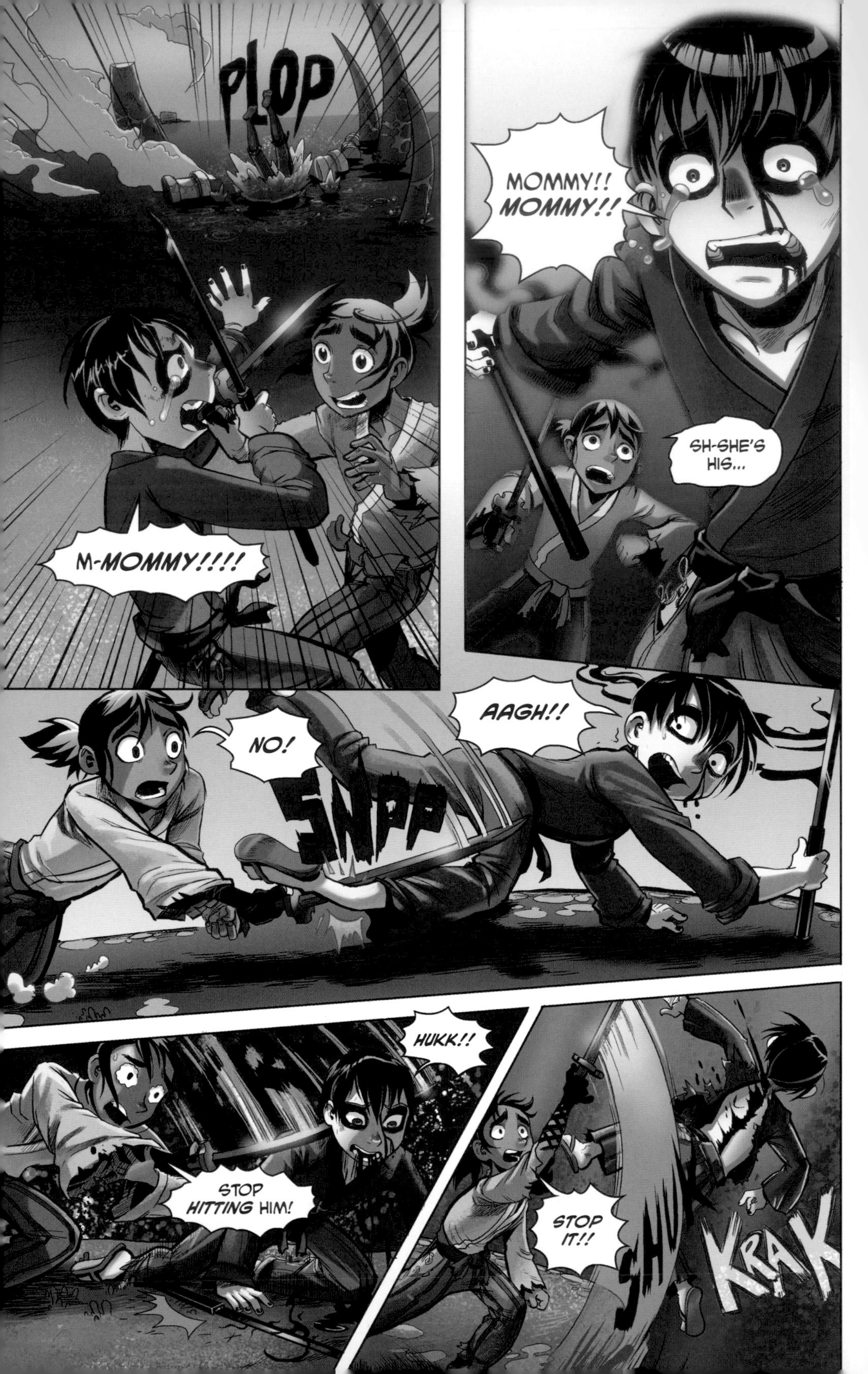
PLOP
M-MOMMY!!!!!
MOMMY!! MOMMY!!
SH-SHE'S HIS...
NO!
SNPP
AAGH!!
HUKK!!
STOP HITTING HIM!
STOP IT!!
SHU
KRAK

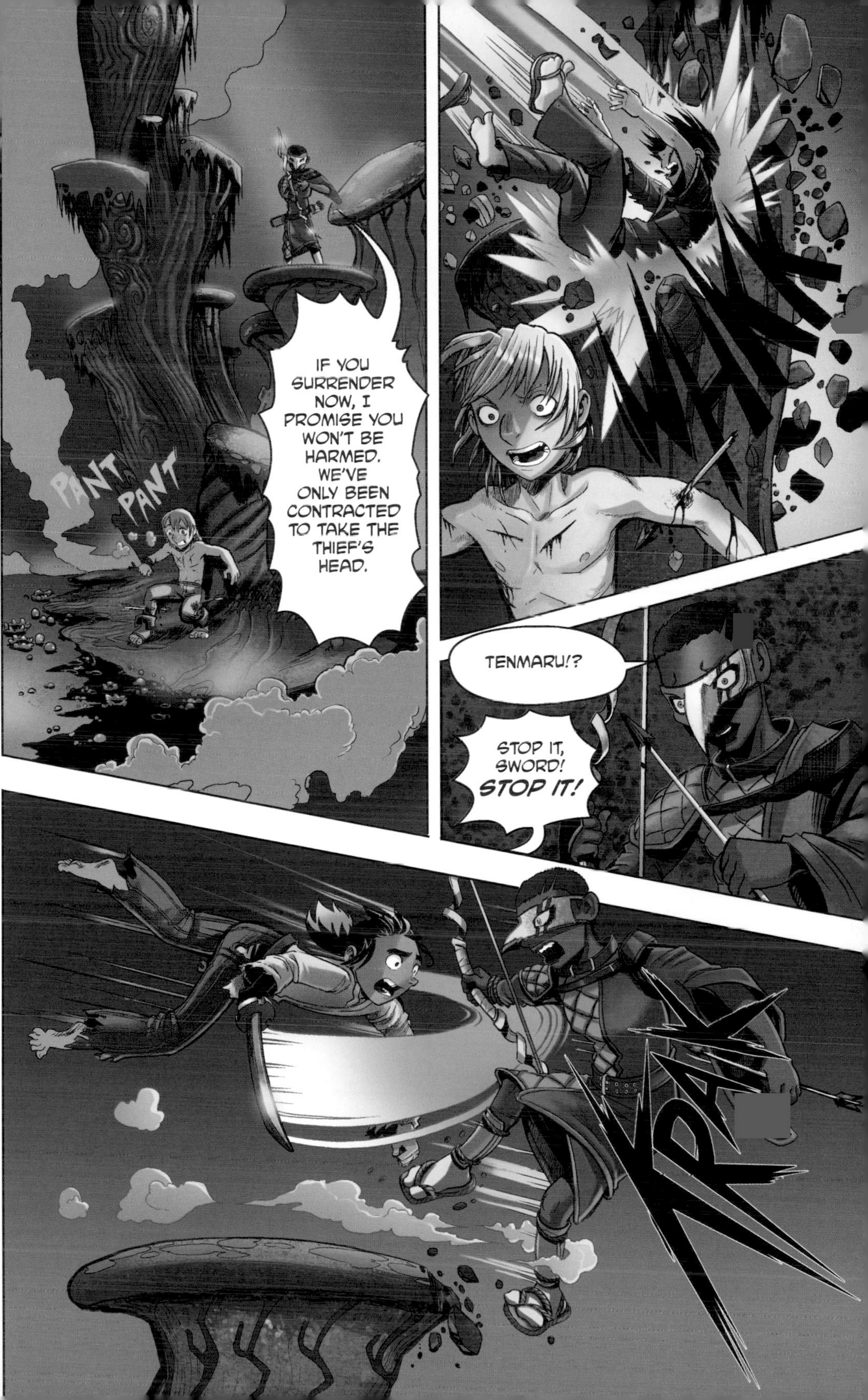

PANT PANT
IF YOU SURRENDER NOW, I PROMISE YOU WON'T BE HARMED. WE'VE ONLY BEEN CONTRACTED TO TAKE THE THIEF'S HEAD.
TENMARU!?
STOP IT, SWORD! STOP IT!
KRAK

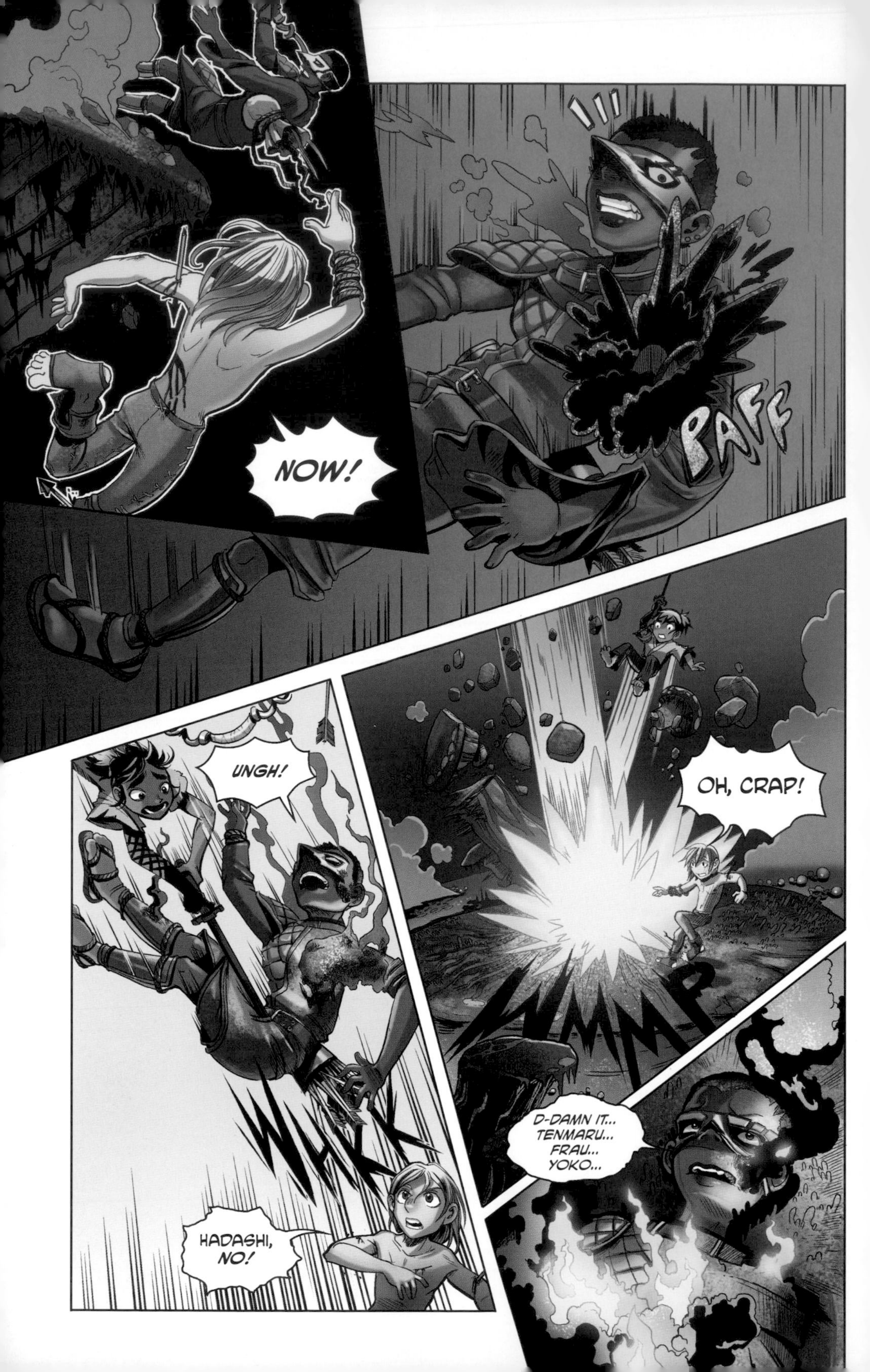
NOW!
PAFF
OH, CRAP!
UNGH!
WHAM
HADASHI,
NO!
D-DAMN IT...
TENMARU...
FRAU...
YOKO...

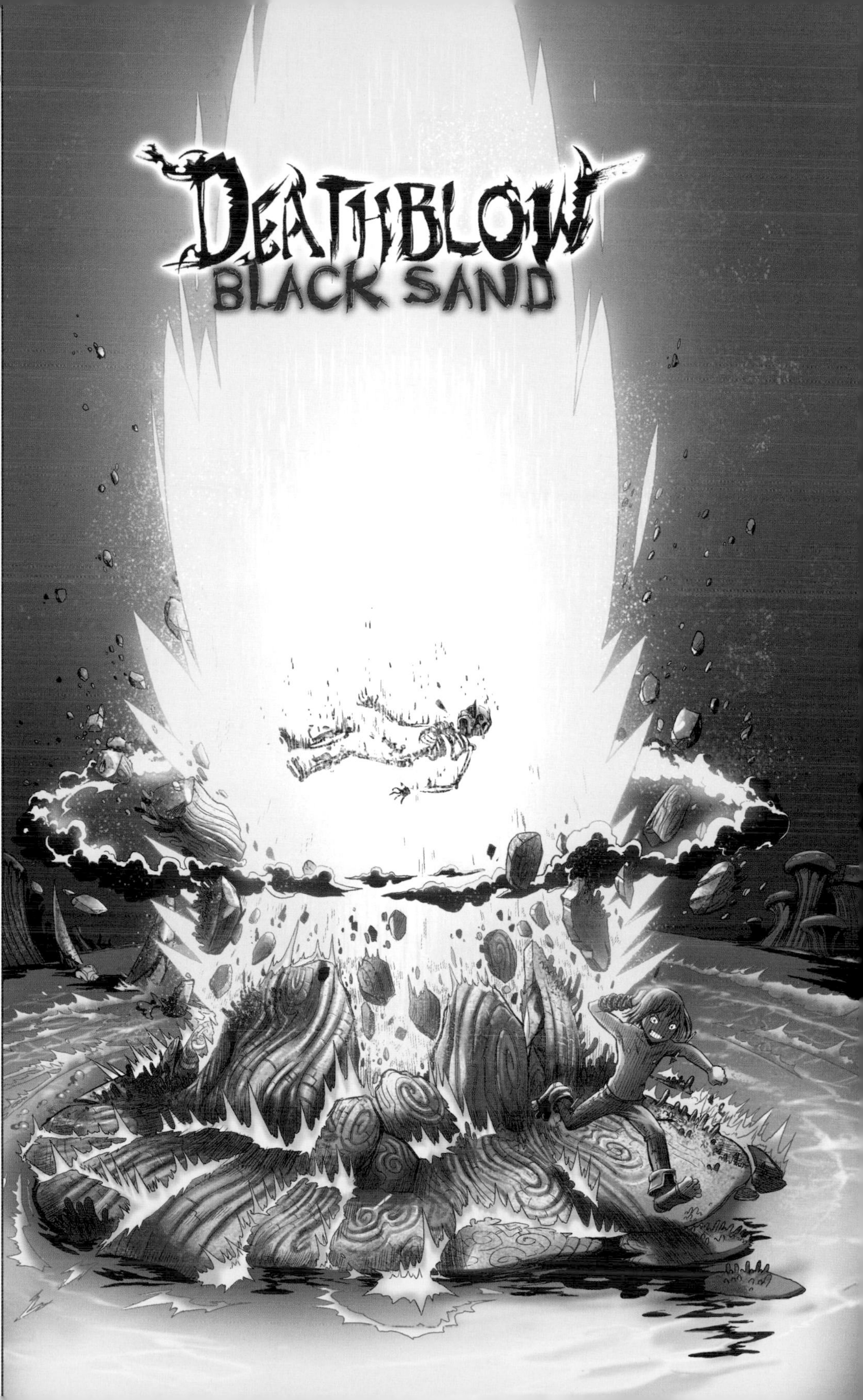
DEATHBLOW
BLACK SAND

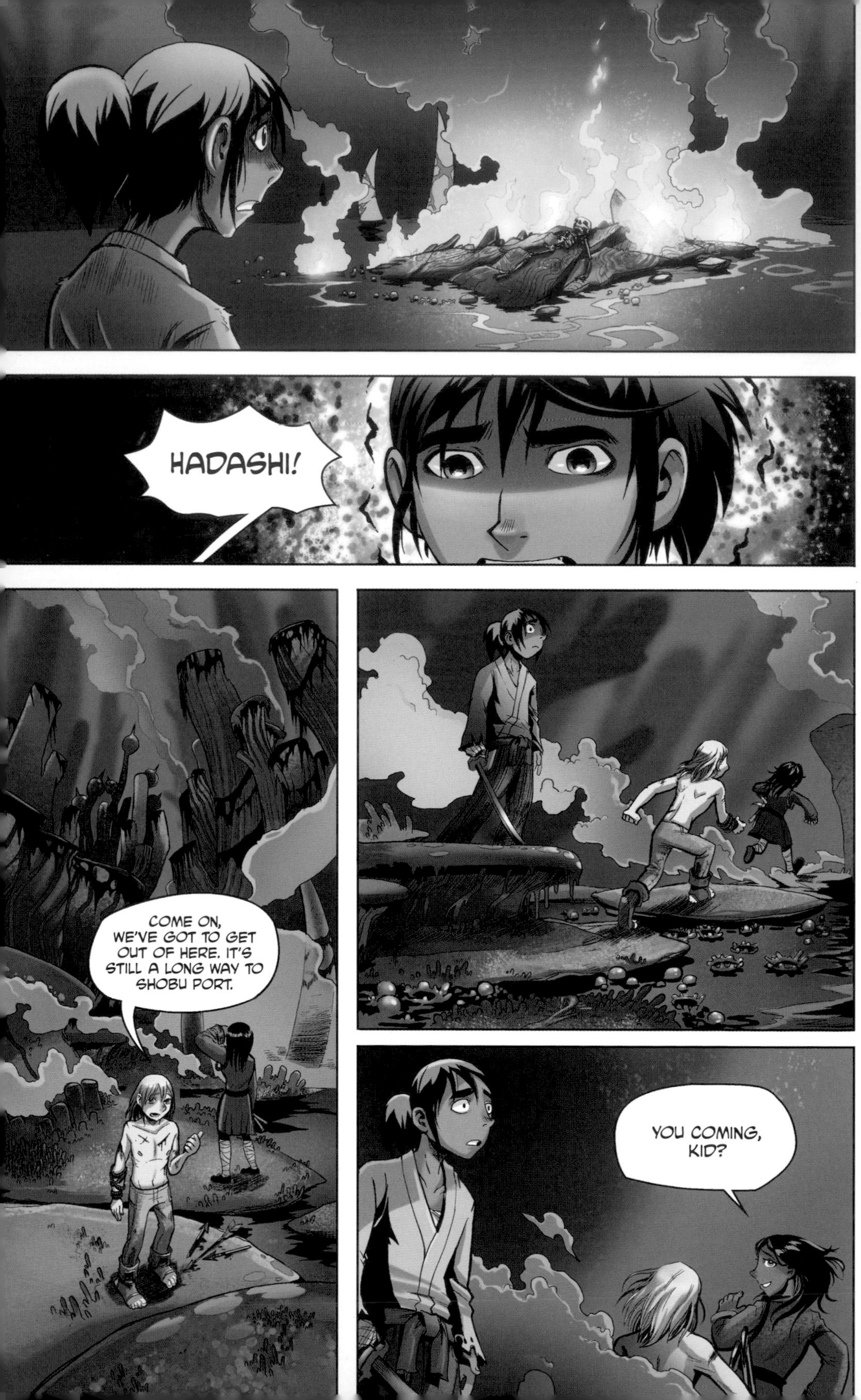
HADASHI!
COME ON, WE'VE GOT TO GET OUT OF HERE. IT'S STILL A LONG WAY TO SHOBU PORT.
YOU COMING, KID?

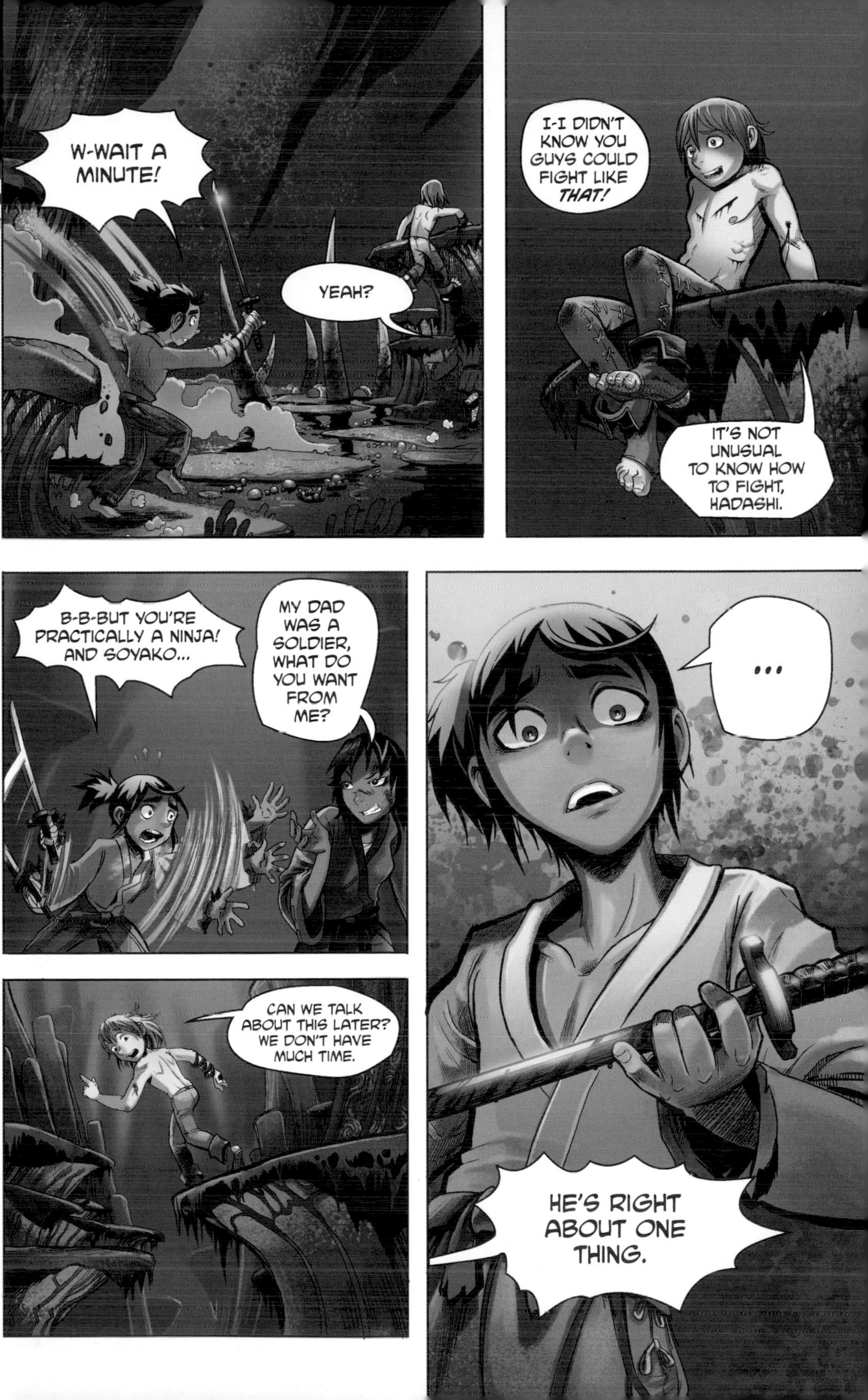
W-WAIT A MINUTE!
YEAH?
I-I DIDN'T KNOW YOU GUYS COULD FIGHT LIKE *THAT!*
IT'S NOT UNUSUAL TO KNOW HOW TO FIGHT, HADASHI.
B-B-BUT YOU'RE PRACTICALLY A NINJA! AND SOYAKO...
MY DAD WAS A SOLDIER, WHAT DO YOU WANT FROM ME?
CAN WE TALK ABOUT THIS LATER? WE DON'T HAVE MUCH TIME.
...
HE'S RIGHT ABOUT ONE THING.

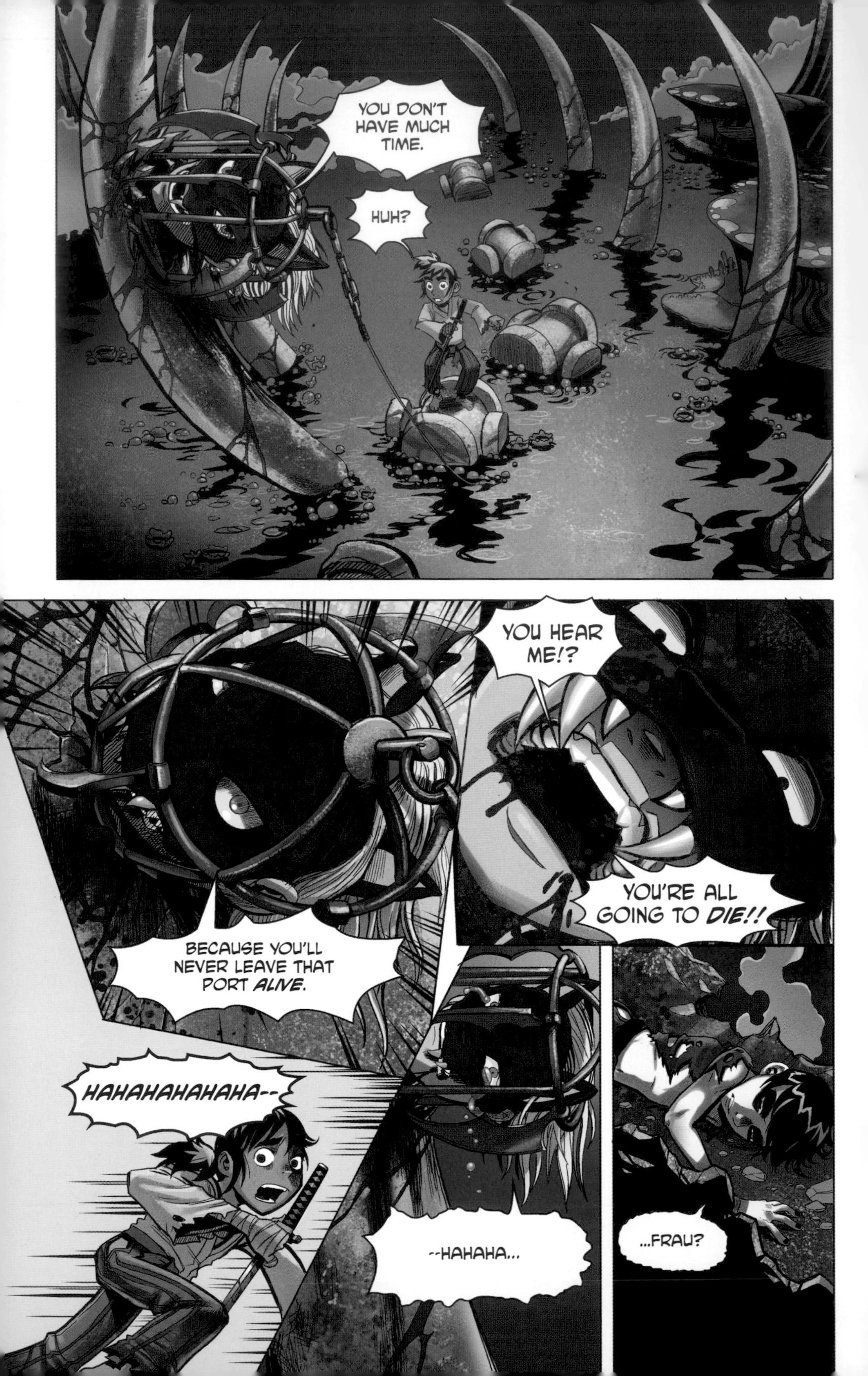
YOU DON'T HAVE MUCH TIME.
HUH?
YOU HEAR ME!?
YOU'RE ALL GOING TO *DIE!!*
BECAUSE YOU'LL NEVER LEAVE THAT PORT *ALIVE*.
HAHAHAHAHAHA--
--HAHAHA...
...FRAU?

CHAPTER 3:
NO ESCAPE, NO REGRETS

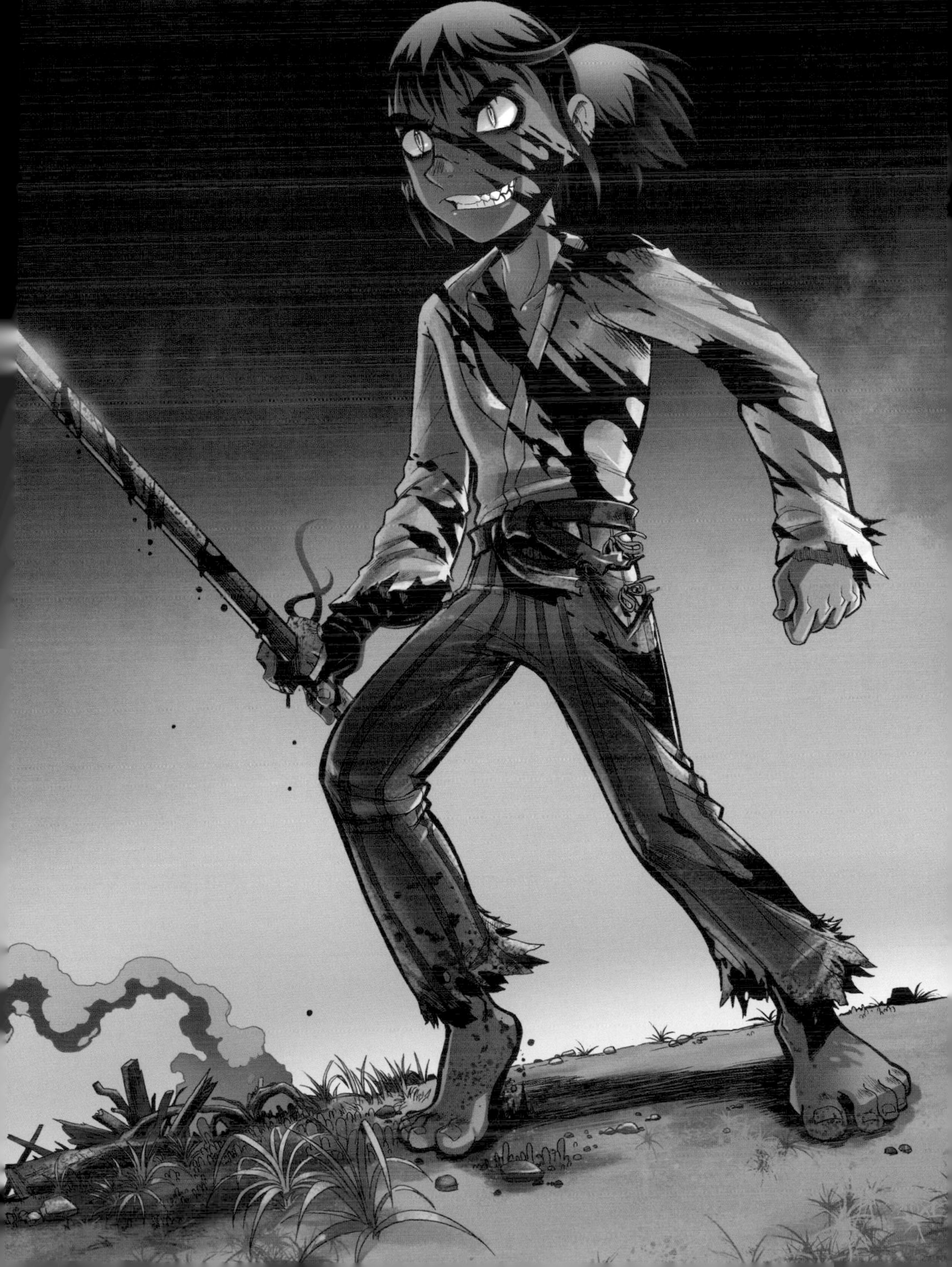

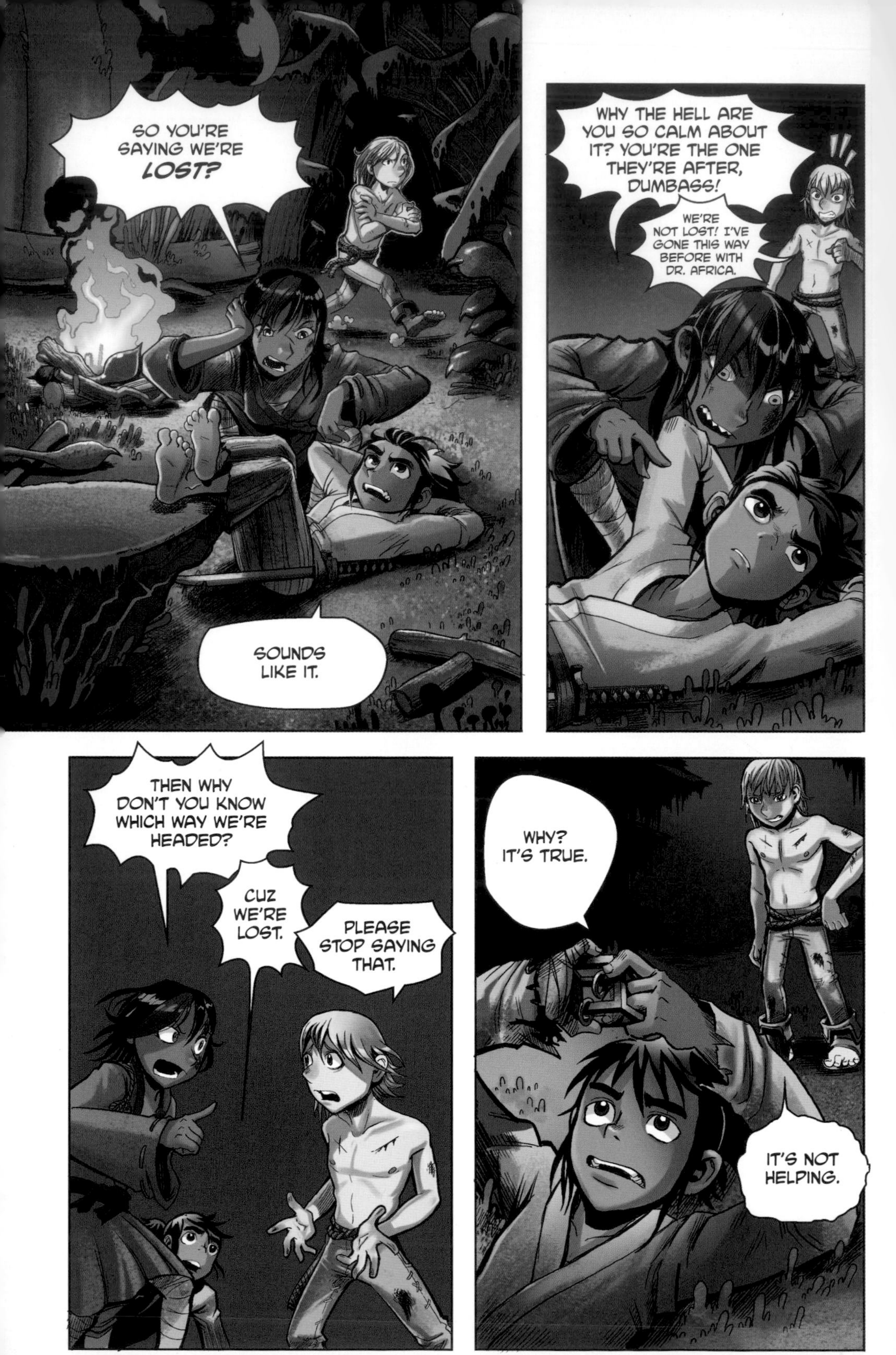
SO YOU'RE SAYING WE'RE LOST?
SOUNDS LIKE IT.
WHY THE HELL ARE YOU SO CALM ABOUT IT? YOU'RE THE ONE THEY'RE AFTER, DUMBASS!
WE'RE NOT LOST! I'VE GONE THIS WAY BEFORE WITH DR. AFRICA.
THEN WHY DON'T YOU KNOW WHICH WAY WE'RE HEADED?
CUZ WE'RE LOST.
PLEASE STOP SAYING THAT.
WHY? IT'S TRUE.
IT'S NOT HELPING.

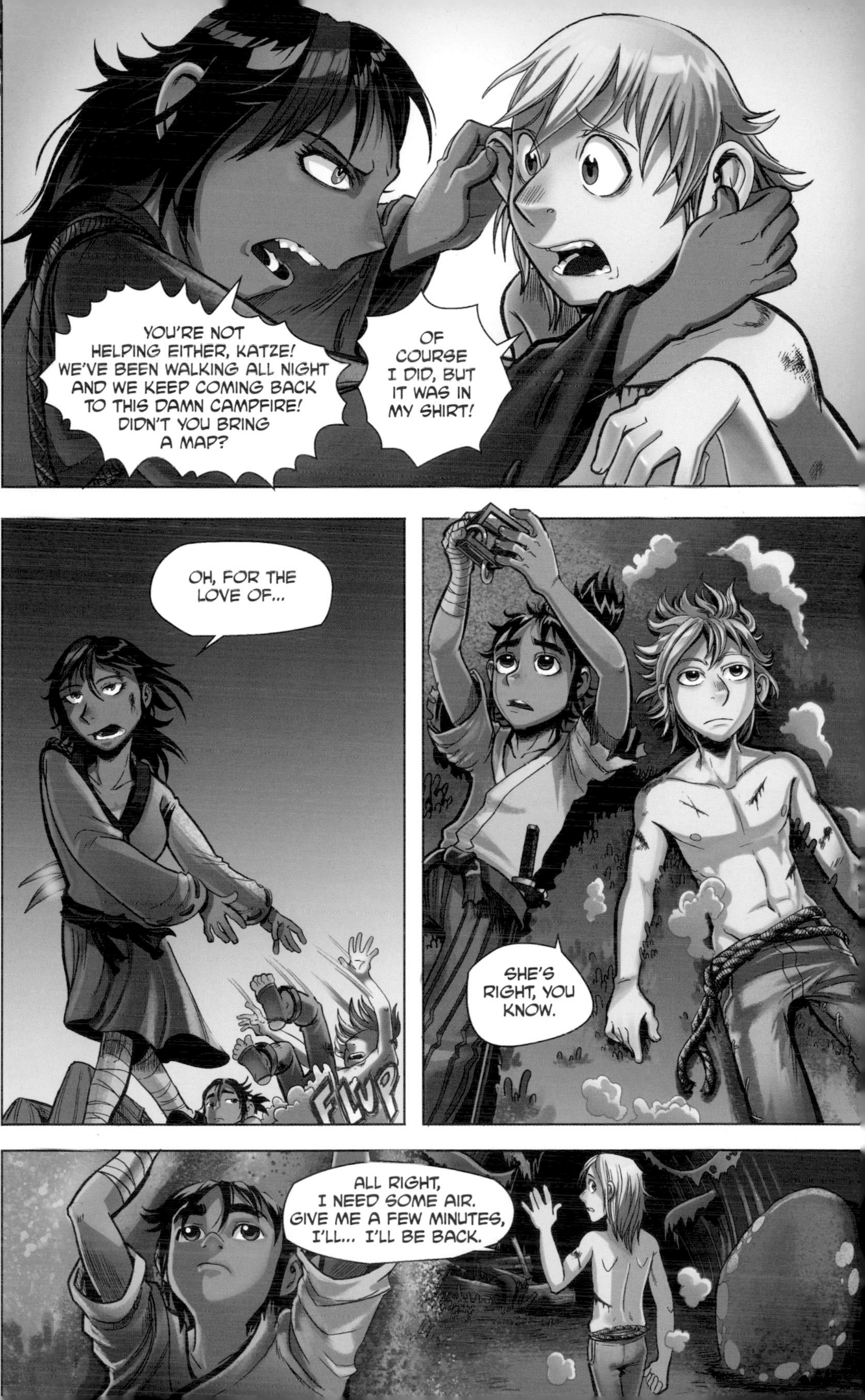
YOU'RE NOT HELPING EITHER, KATZE! WE'VE BEEN WALKING ALL NIGHT AND WE KEEP COMING BACK TO THIS DAMN CAMPFIRE! DIDN'T YOU BRING A MAP?
OF COURSE I DID, BUT IT WAS IN MY SHIRT!
OH, FOR THE LOVE OF...
FLUP
SHE'S RIGHT, YOU KNOW.
ALL RIGHT, I NEED SOME AIR. GIVE ME A FEW MINUTES, I'LL... I'LL BE BACK.

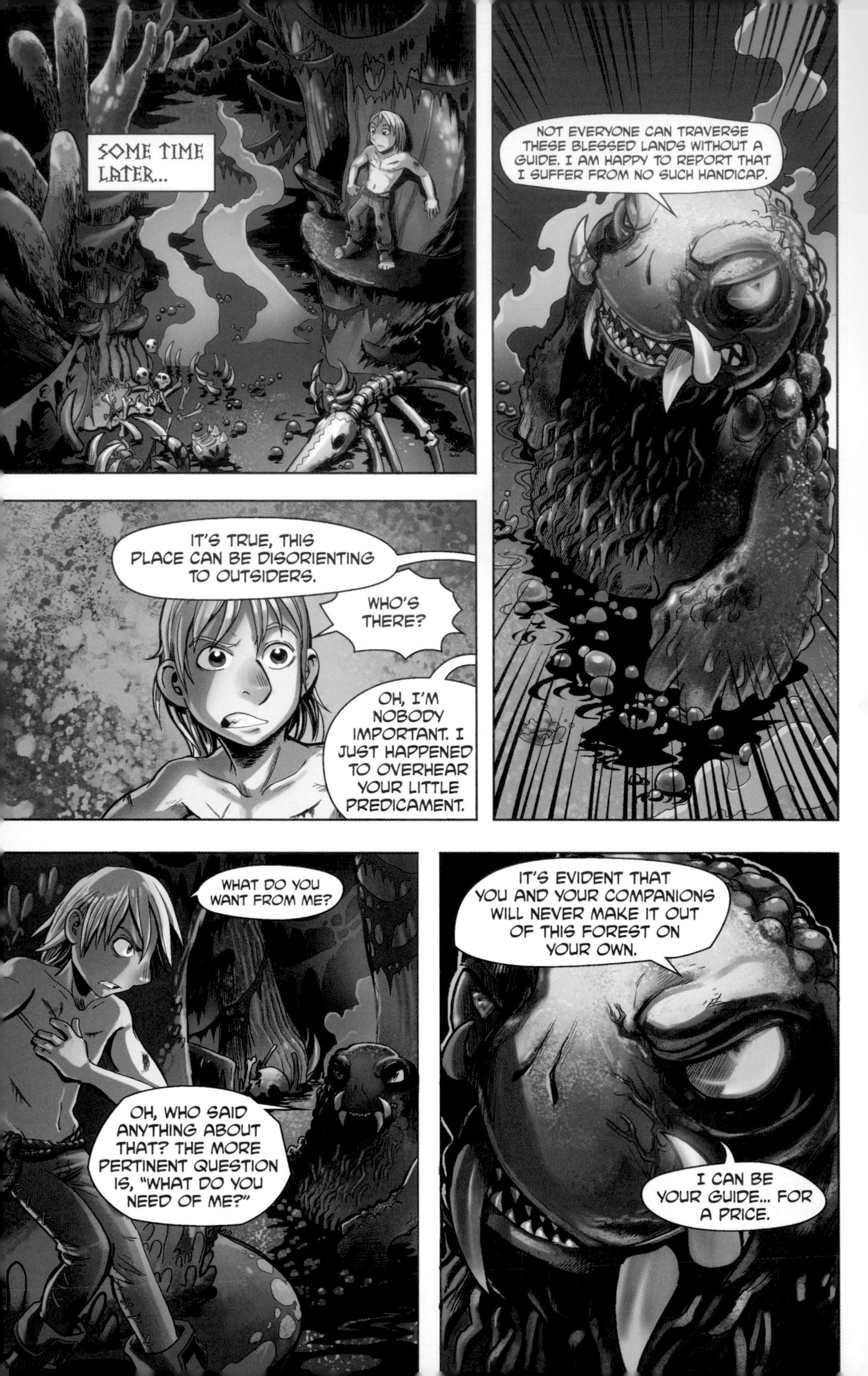
SOME TIME LATER...
NOT EVERYONE CAN TRAVERSE THESE BLESSED LANDS WITHOUT A GUIDE. I AM HAPPY TO REPORT THAT I SUFFER FROM NO SUCH HANDICAP.
IT'S TRUE, THIS PLACE CAN BE DISORIENTING TO OUTSIDERS.
WHO'S THERE?
OH, I'M NOBODY IMPORTANT. I JUST HAPPENED TO OVERHEAR YOUR LITTLE PREDICAMENT.
WHAT DO YOU WANT FROM ME?
OH, WHO SAID ANYTHING ABOUT THAT? THE MORE PERTINENT QUESTION IS, "WHAT DO YOU NEED OF ME?"
IT'S EVIDENT THAT YOU AND YOUR COMPANIONS WILL NEVER MAKE IT OUT OF THIS FOREST ON YOUR OWN.
I CAN BE YOUR GUIDE... FOR A PRICE.

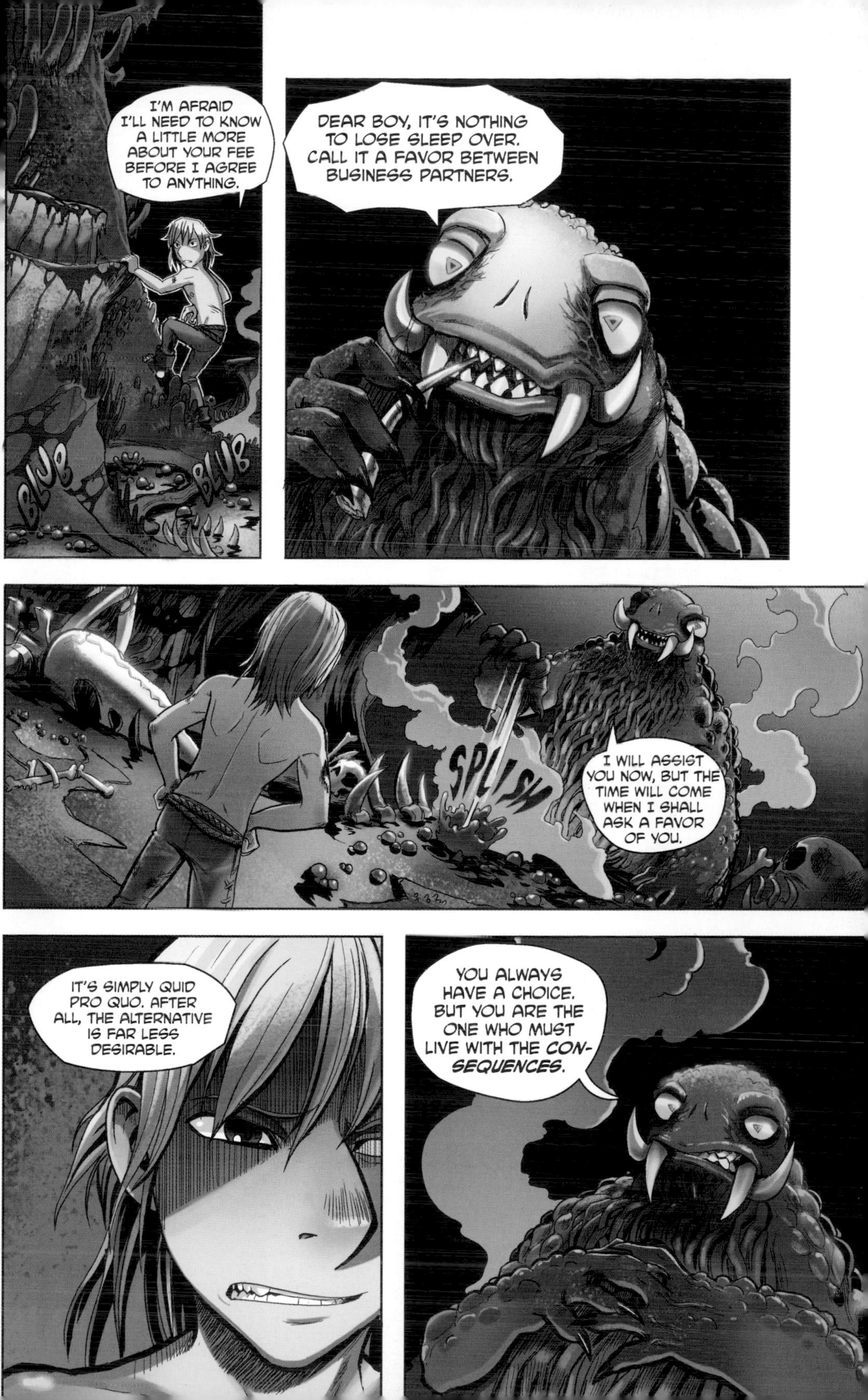
I'M AFRAID I'LL NEED TO KNOW A LITTLE MORE ABOUT YOUR FEE BEFORE I AGREE TO ANYTHING.
DEAR BOY, IT'S NOTHING TO LOSE SLEEP OVER. CALL IT A FAVOR BETWEEN BUSINESS PARTNERS.
BLUB
BLUB
SPLISH
I WILL ASSIST YOU NOW, BUT THE TIME WILL COME WHEN I SHALL ASK A FAVOR OF YOU.
IT'S SIMPLY QUID PRO QUO. AFTER ALL, THE ALTERNATIVE IS FAR LESS DESIRABLE.
YOU ALWAYS HAVE A CHOICE. BUT YOU ARE THE ONE WHO MUST LIVE WITH THE CON-SEQUENCES.

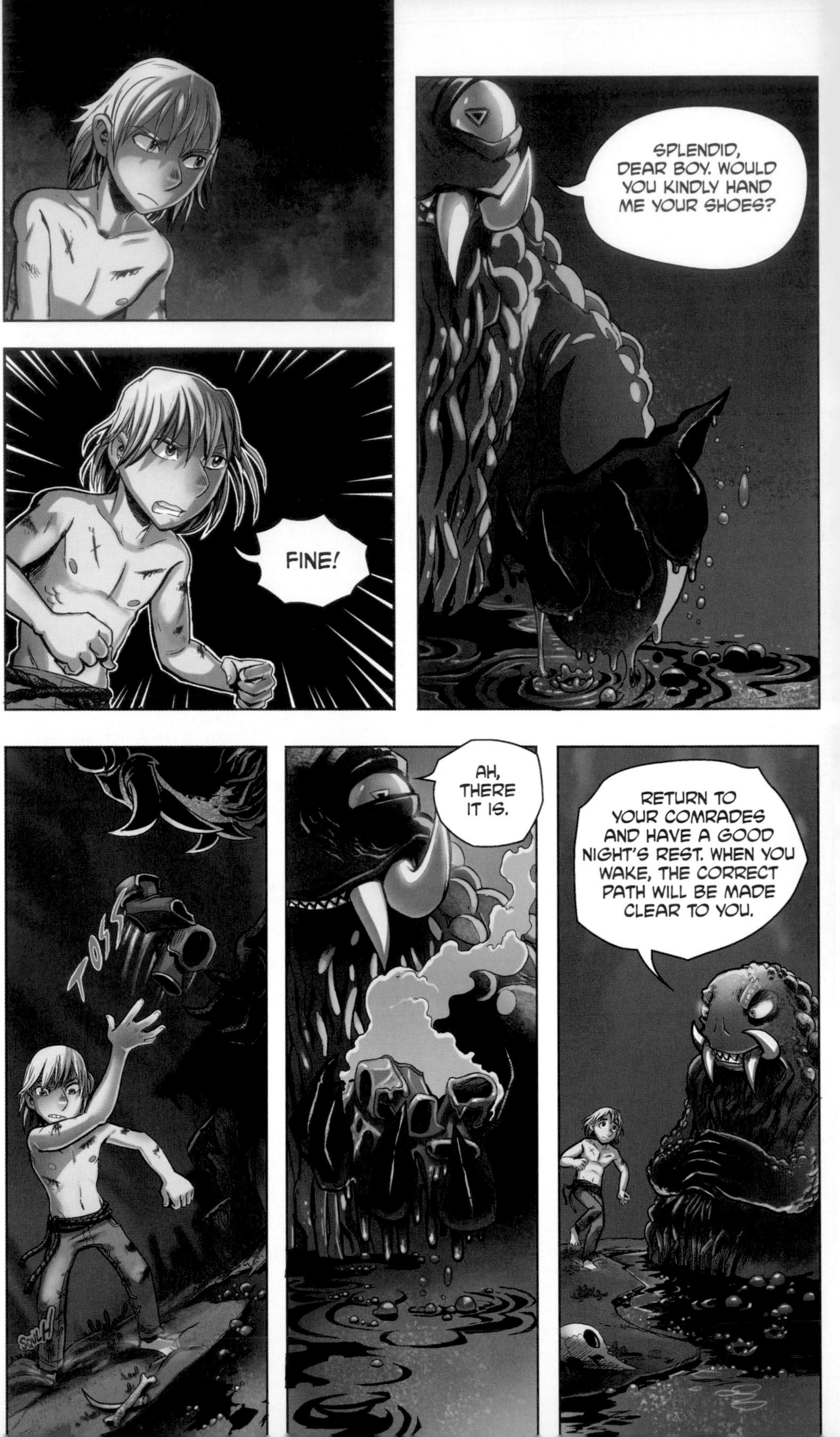
SPLENDID, DEAR BOY. WOULD YOU KINDLY HAND ME YOUR SHOES?
FINE!
TOSS
AH, THERE IT IS.
RETURN TO YOUR COMRADES AND HAVE A GOOD NIGHT'S REST. WHEN YOU WAKE, THE CORRECT PATH WILL BE MADE CLEAR TO YOU.

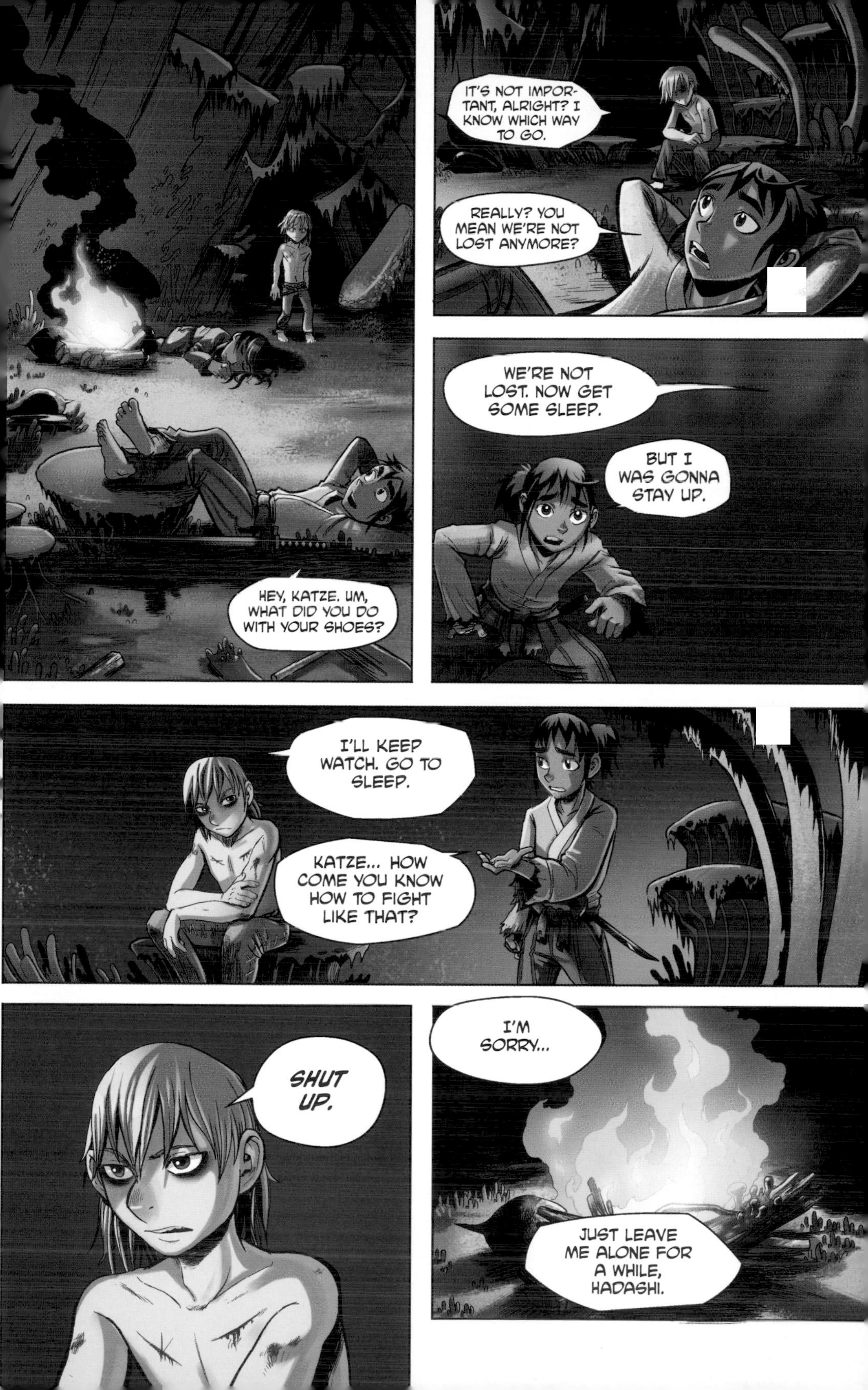
HEY, KATZE. UM, WHAT DID YOU DO WITH YOUR SHOES?
IT'S NOT IMPORTANT, ALRIGHT? I KNOW WHICH WAY TO GO.
REALLY? YOU MEAN WE'RE NOT LOST ANYMORE?
WE'RE NOT LOST. NOW GET SOME SLEEP.
BUT I WAS GONNA STAY UP.
I'LL KEEP WATCH. GO TO SLEEP.
KATZE... HOW COME YOU KNOW HOW TO FIGHT LIKE THAT?
SHUT UP.
I'M SORRY...
JUST LEAVE ME ALONE FOR A WHILE, HADASHI.

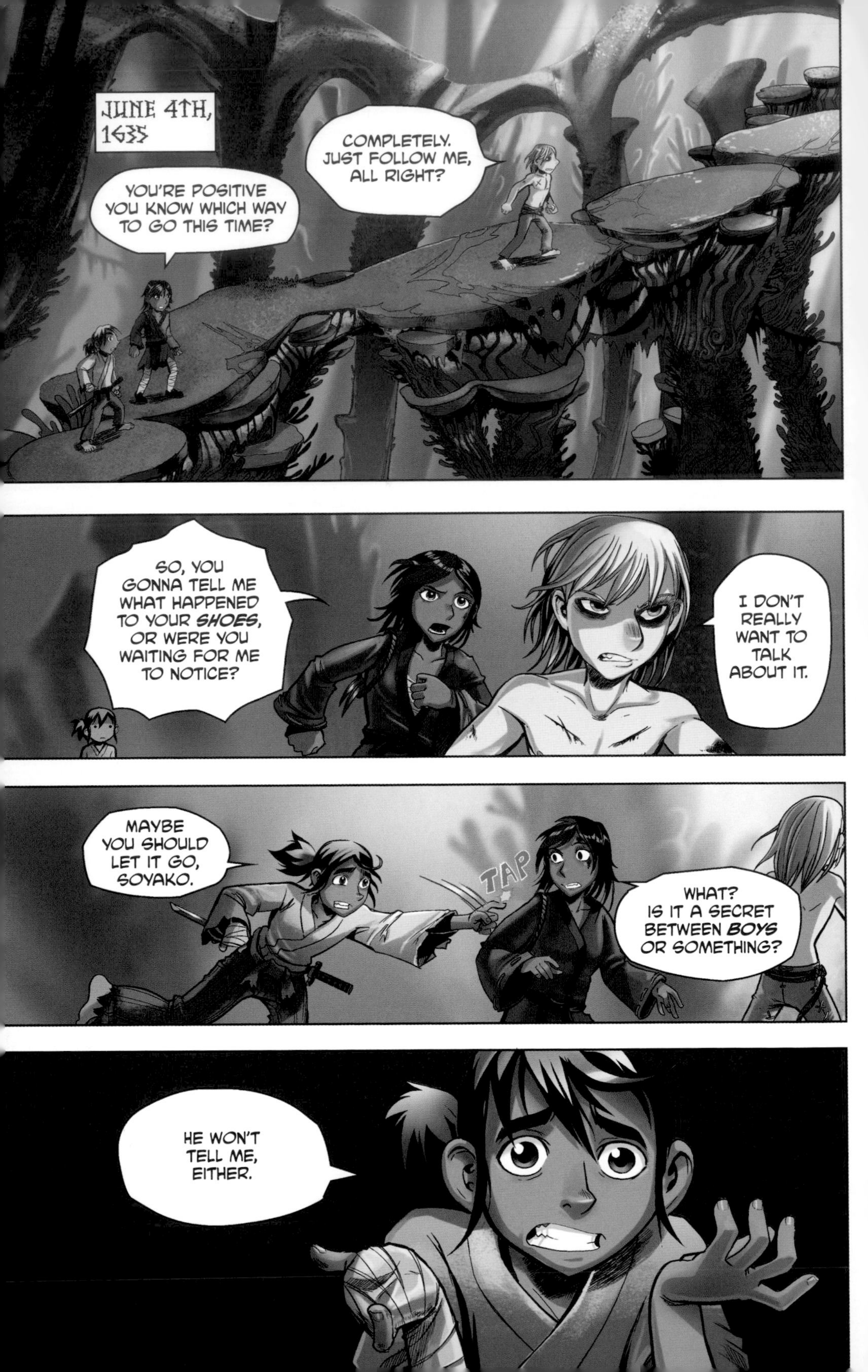
JUNE 4TH, 1635
YOU'RE POSITIVE YOU KNOW WHICH WAY TO GO THIS TIME?
COMPLETELY. JUST FOLLOW ME, ALL RIGHT?
SO, YOU GONNA TELL ME WHAT HAPPENED TO YOUR SHOES, OR WERE YOU WAITING FOR ME TO NOTICE?
I DON'T REALLY WANT TO TALK ABOUT IT.
MAYBE YOU SHOULD LET IT GO, SOYAKO.
TAP
WHAT? IS IT A SECRET BETWEEN BOYS OR SOMETHING?
HE WON'T TELL ME, EITHER.

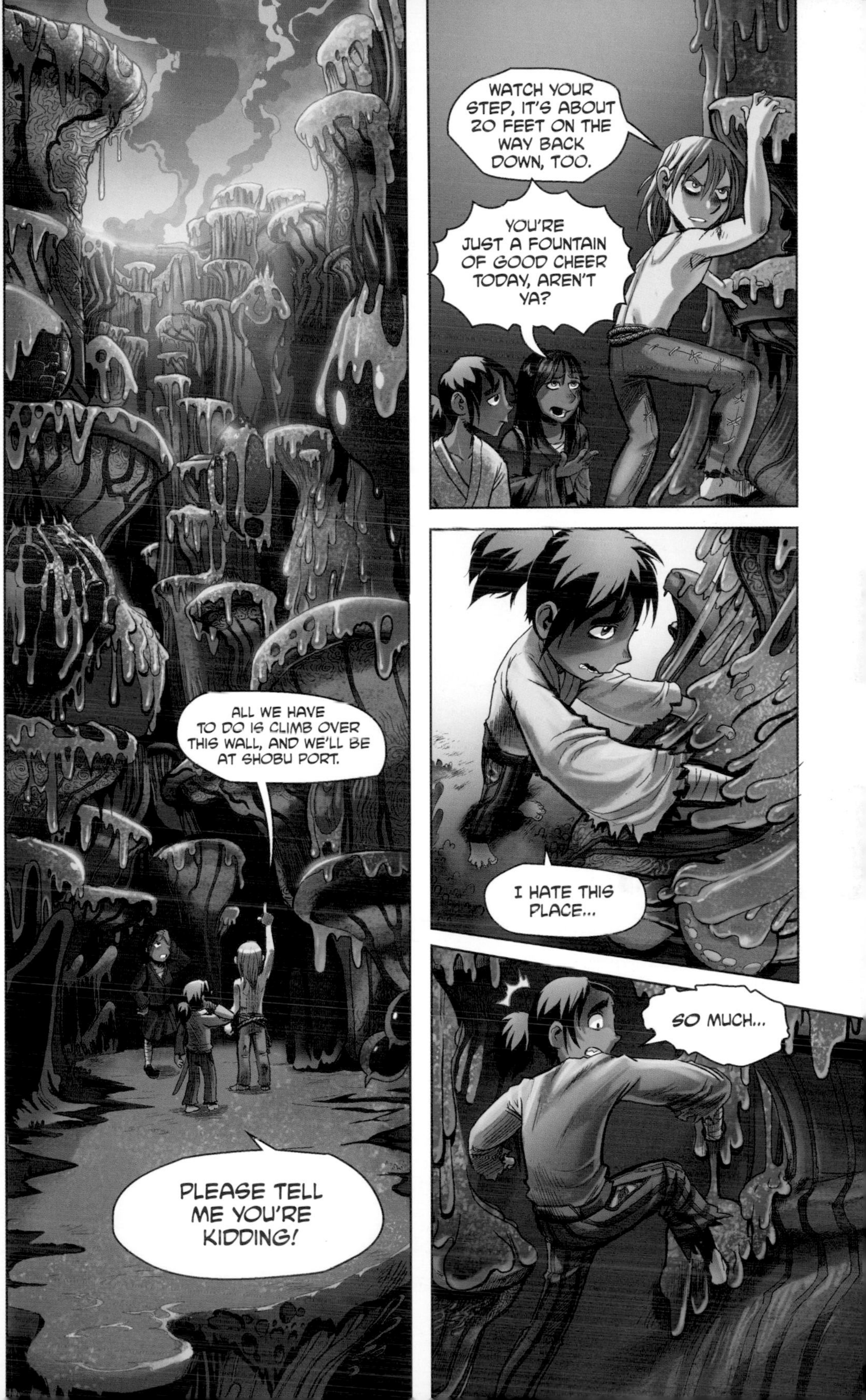
ALL WE HAVE TO DO IS CLIMB OVER THIS WALL, AND WE'LL BE AT SHOBU PORT.
PLEASE TELL ME YOU'RE KIDDING!
WATCH YOUR STEP, IT'S ABOUT 20 FEET ON THE WAY BACK DOWN, TOO.
YOU'RE JUST A FOUNTAIN OF GOOD CHEER TODAY, AREN'T YA?
I HATE THIS PLACE...
SO MUCH...

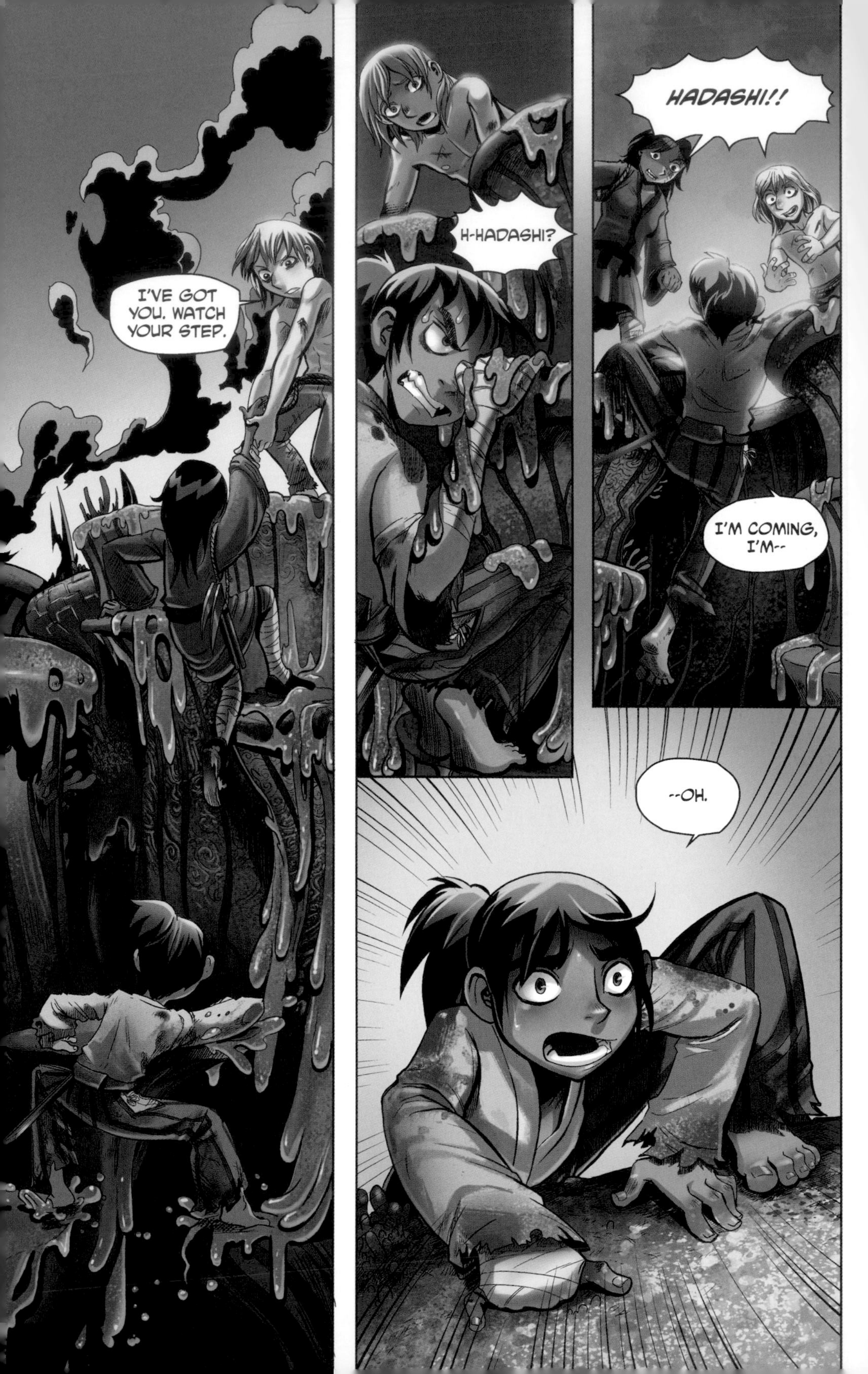
I'VE GOT YOU. WATCH YOUR STEP.
H-HADASHI?
HADASHI!!
I'M COMING, I'M--
--OH.

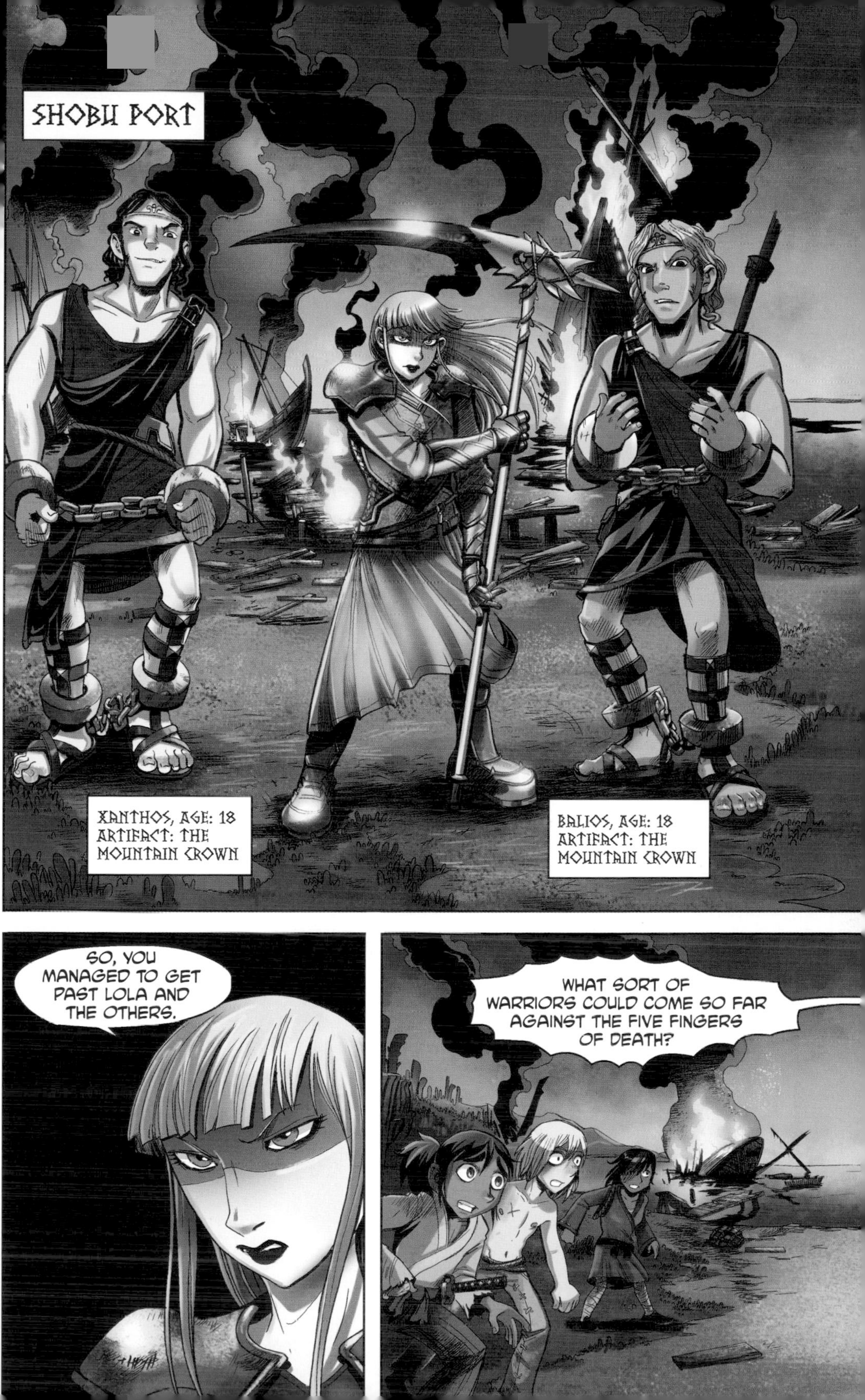
SHOBU PORT
XANTHOS, AGE: 18
ARTIFACT: THE MOUNTAIN CROWN
BALIOS, AGE: 18
ARTIFACT: THE MOUNTAIN CROWN
SO, YOU MANAGED TO GET PAST LOLA AND THE OTHERS.
WHAT SORT OF WARRIORS COULD COME SO FAR AGAINST THE FIVE FINGERS OF DEATH?

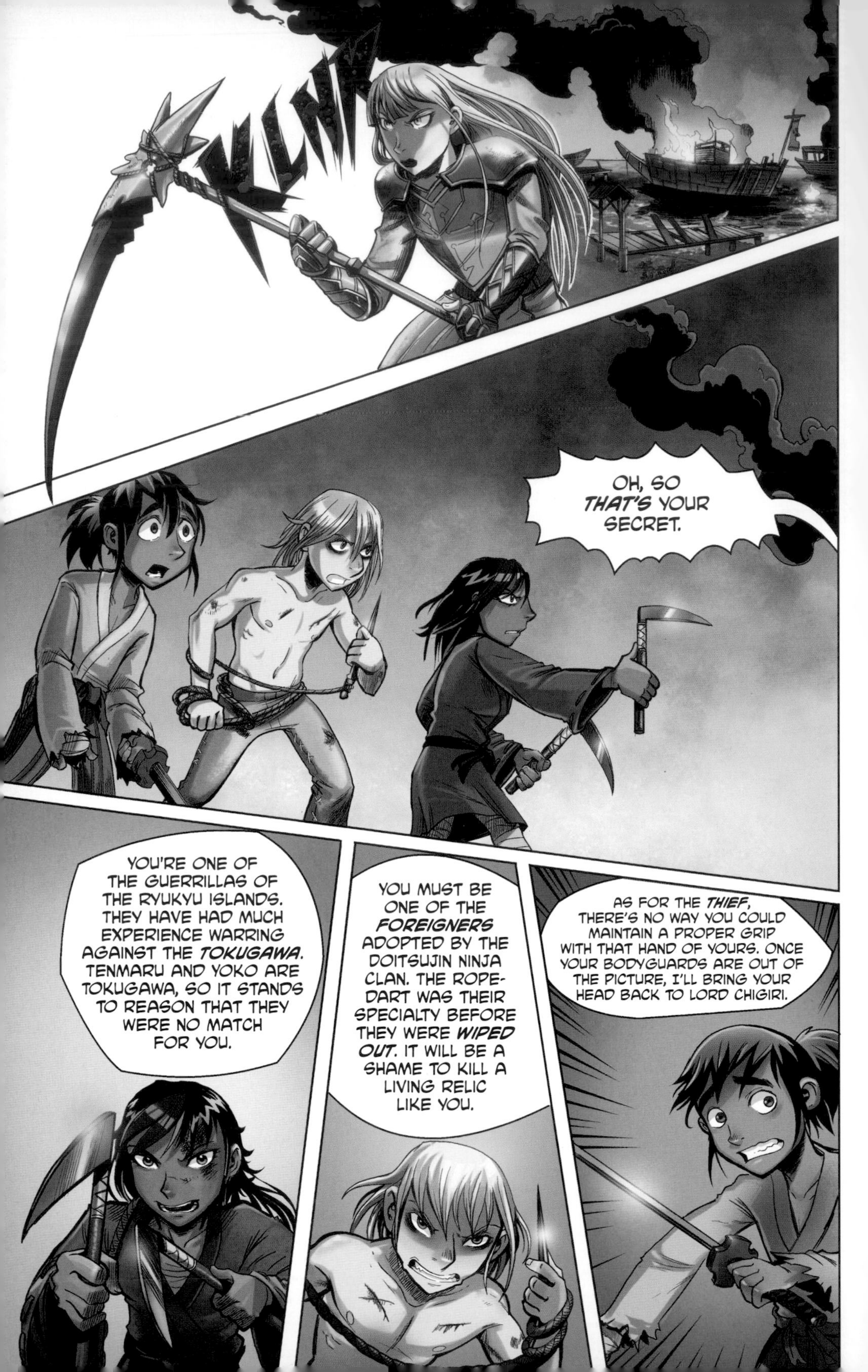
KLNT!
OH, SO THAT'S YOUR SECRET.
YOU'RE ONE OF THE GUERRILLAS OF THE RYUKYU ISLANDS. THEY HAVE HAD MUCH EXPERIENCE WARRING AGAINST THE TOKUGAWA. TENMARU AND YOKO ARE TOKUGAWA, SO IT STANDS TO REASON THAT THEY WERE NO MATCH FOR YOU.
YOU MUST BE ONE OF THE FOREIGNERS ADOPTED BY THE DOITSUJIN NINJA CLAN. THE ROPE-DART WAS THEIR SPECIALTY BEFORE THEY WERE WIPED OUT. IT WILL BE A SHAME TO KILL A LIVING RELIC LIKE YOU.
AS FOR THE THIEF, THERE'S NO WAY YOU COULD MAINTAIN A PROPER GRIP WITH THAT HAND OF YOURS. ONCE YOUR BODYGUARDS ARE OUT OF THE PICTURE, I'LL BRING YOUR HEAD BACK TO LORD CHIGIRI.

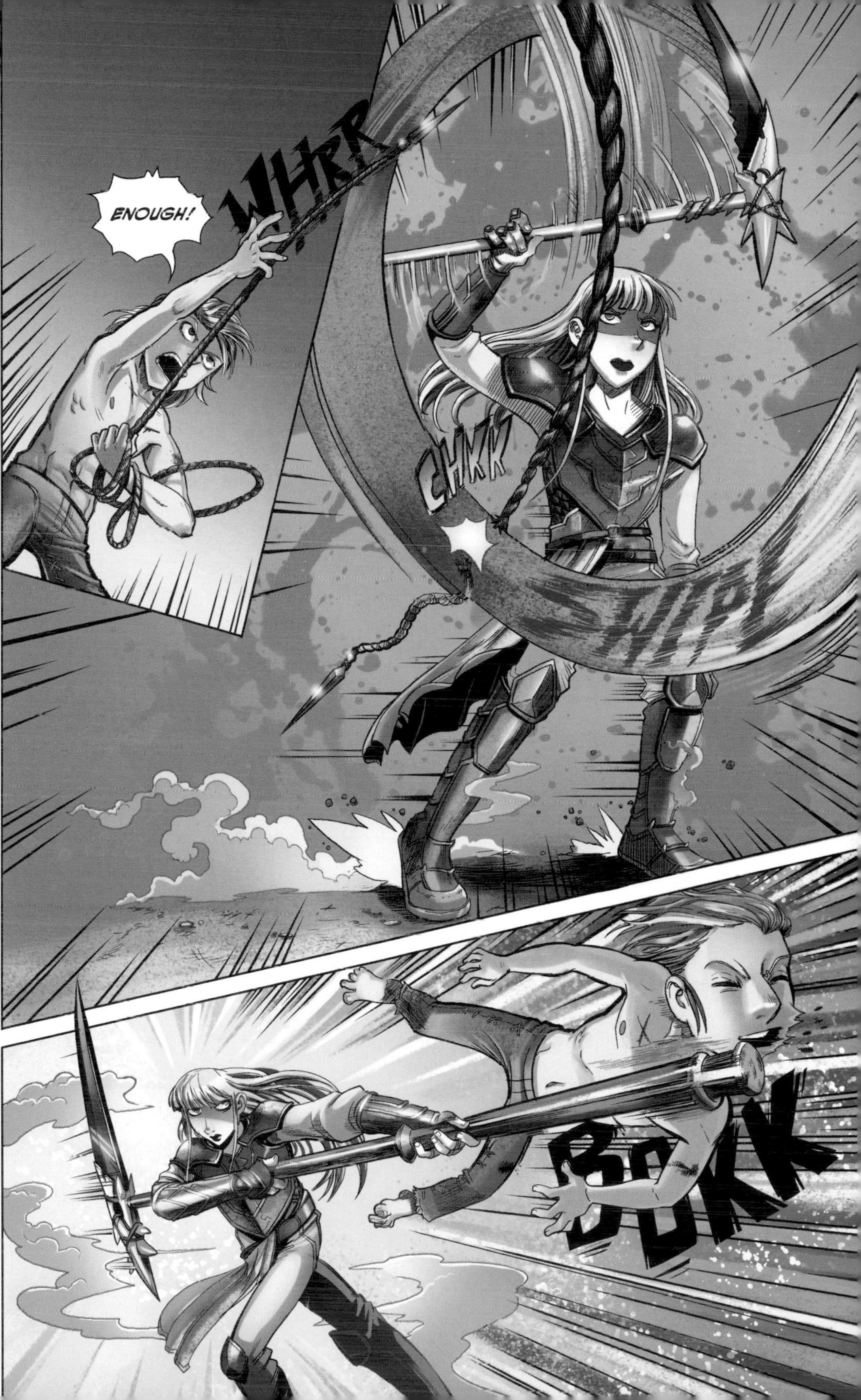
ENOUGH!
WHRR
CHKK
SHIPP
BOKK

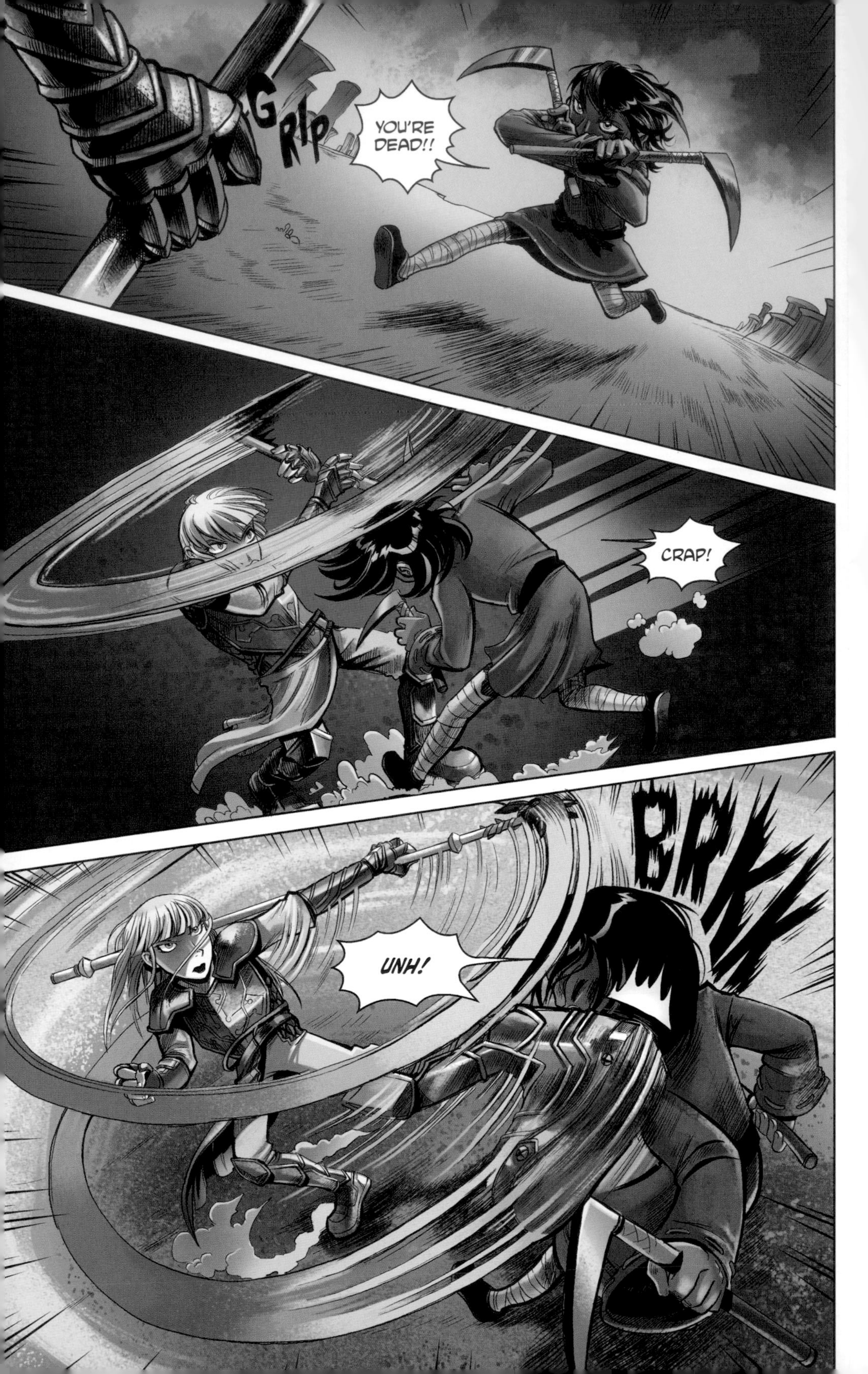
GRIP
YOU'RE DEAD!!
CRAP!
BRK
UNH!

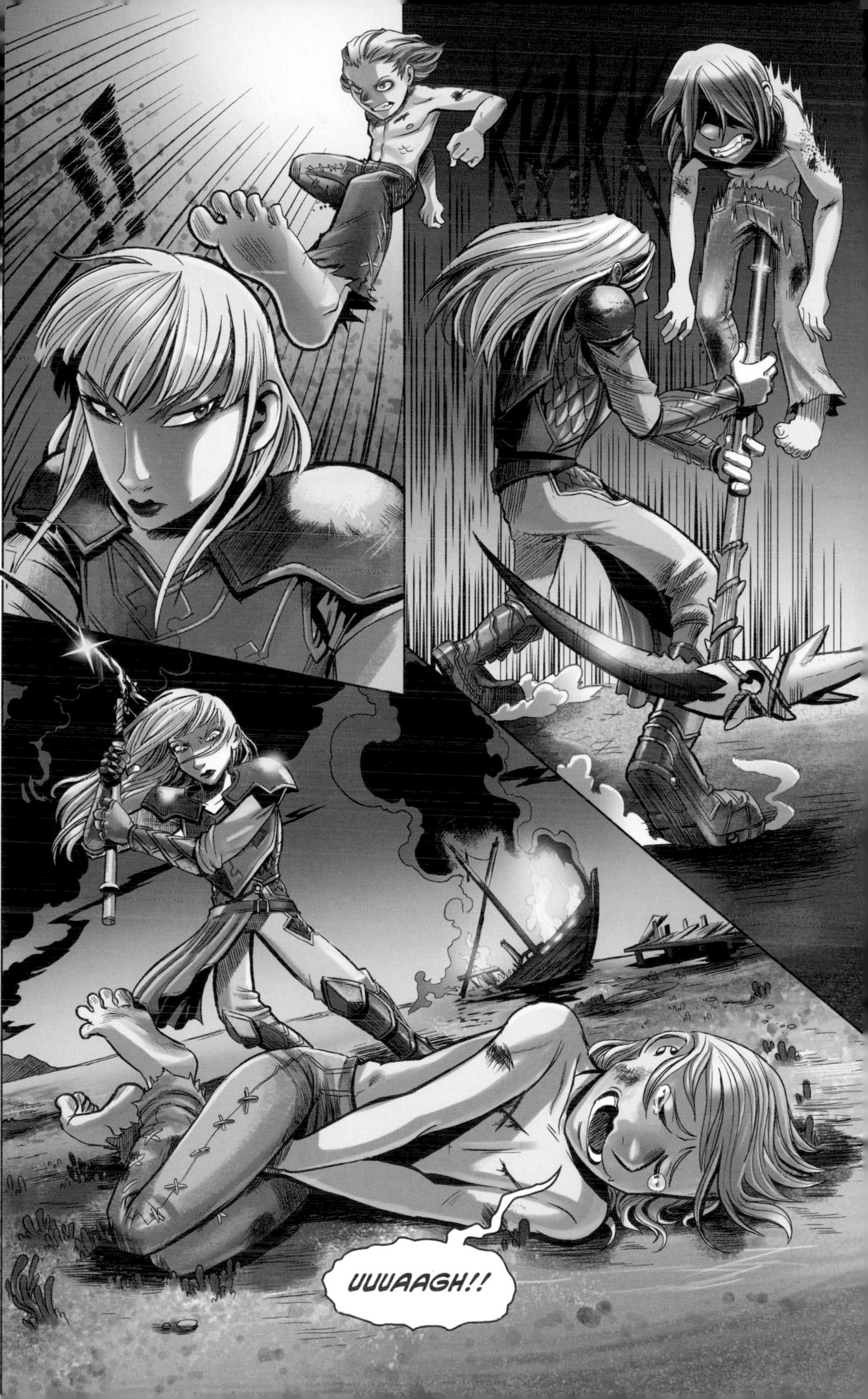
!!
UUUAAGH!!

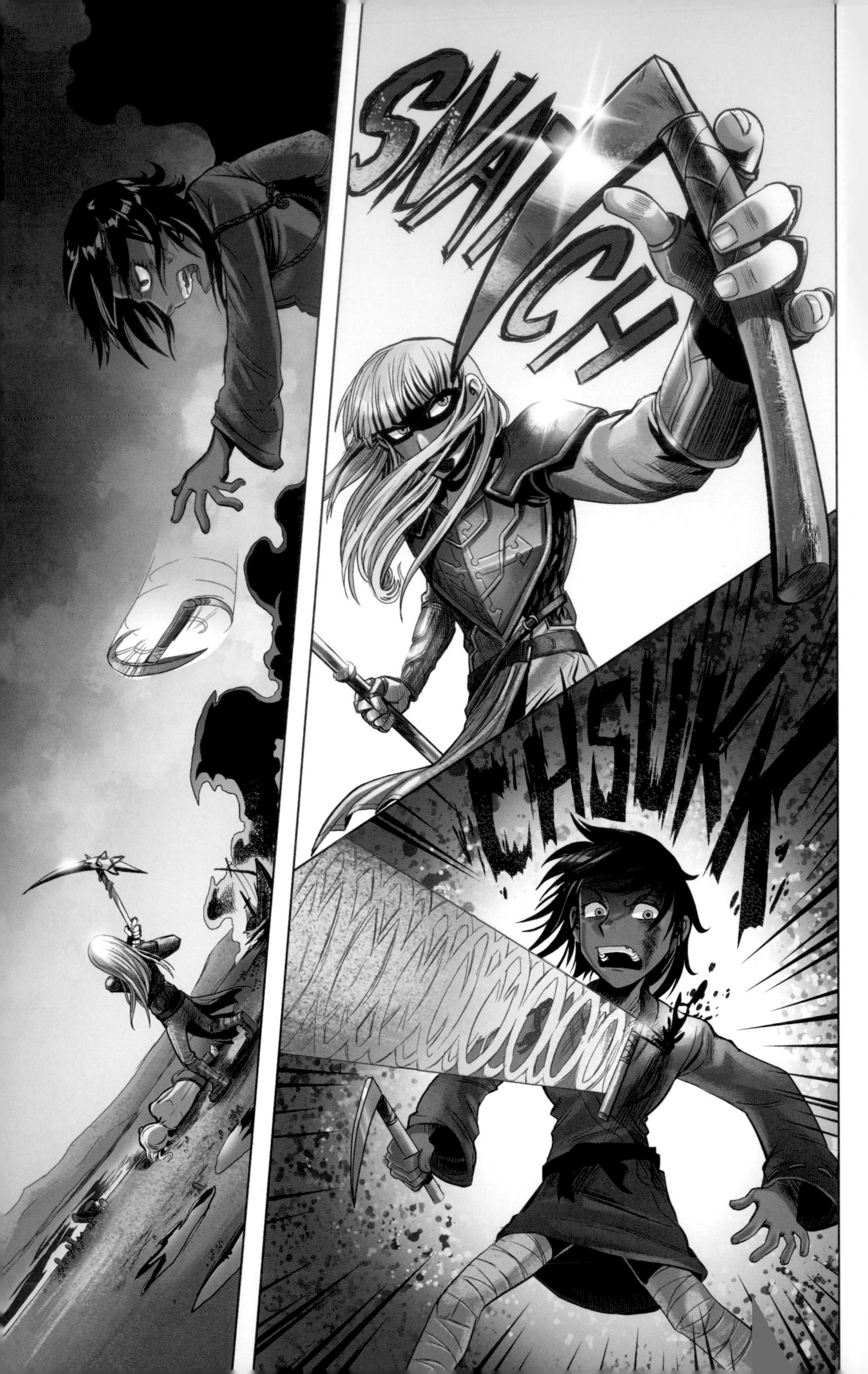
SNATCH
CHSUK

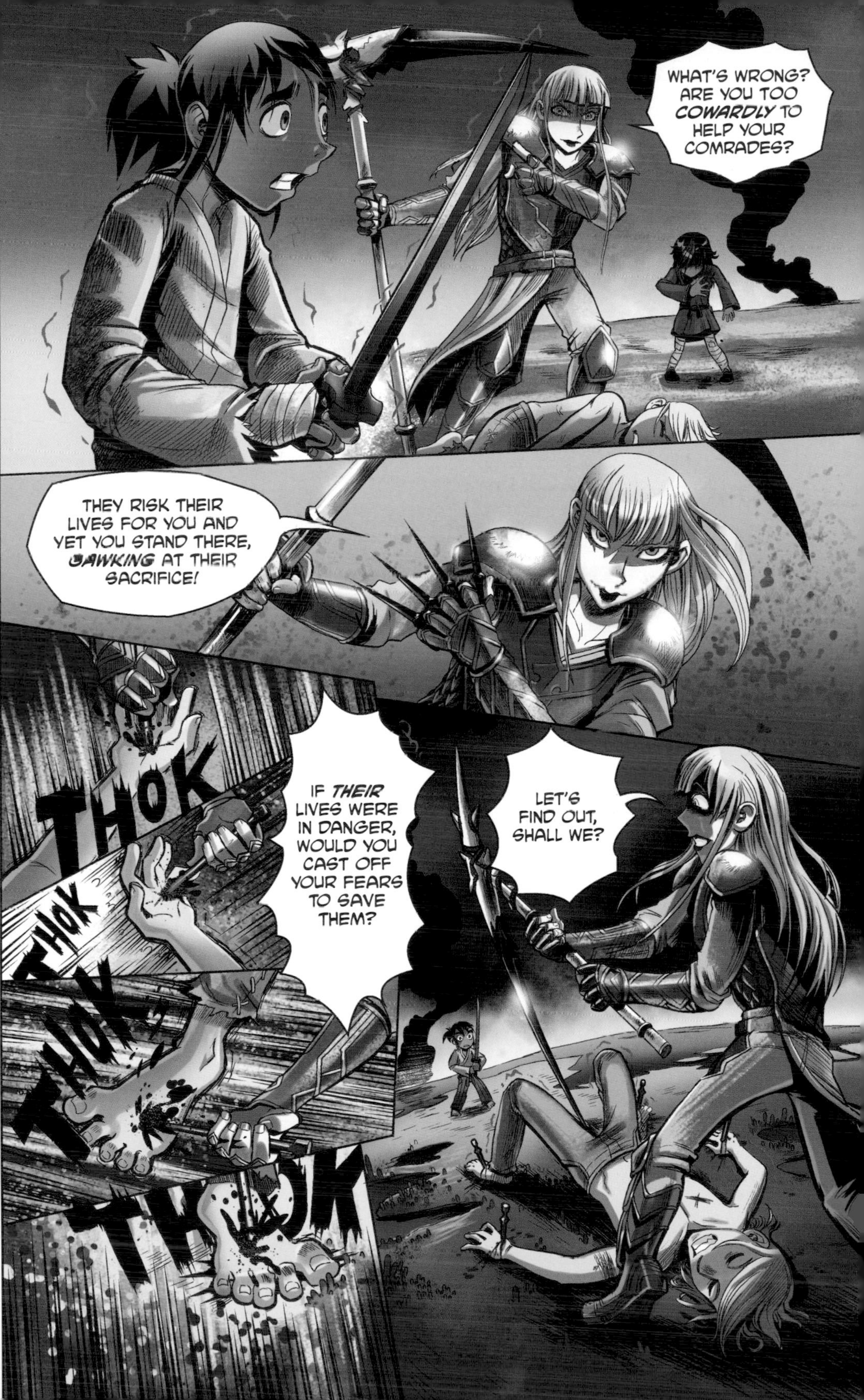
WHAT'S WRONG? ARE YOU TOO *COWARDLY* TO HELP YOUR COMRADES?
THEY RISK THEIR LIVES FOR YOU AND YET YOU STAND THERE, *GAWKING* AT THEIR SACRIFICE!
THOK
THOK
THOK
THOK
IF *THEIR* LIVES WERE IN DANGER, WOULD YOU CAST OFF YOUR FEARS TO SAVE THEM?
LET'S FIND OUT, SHALL WE?

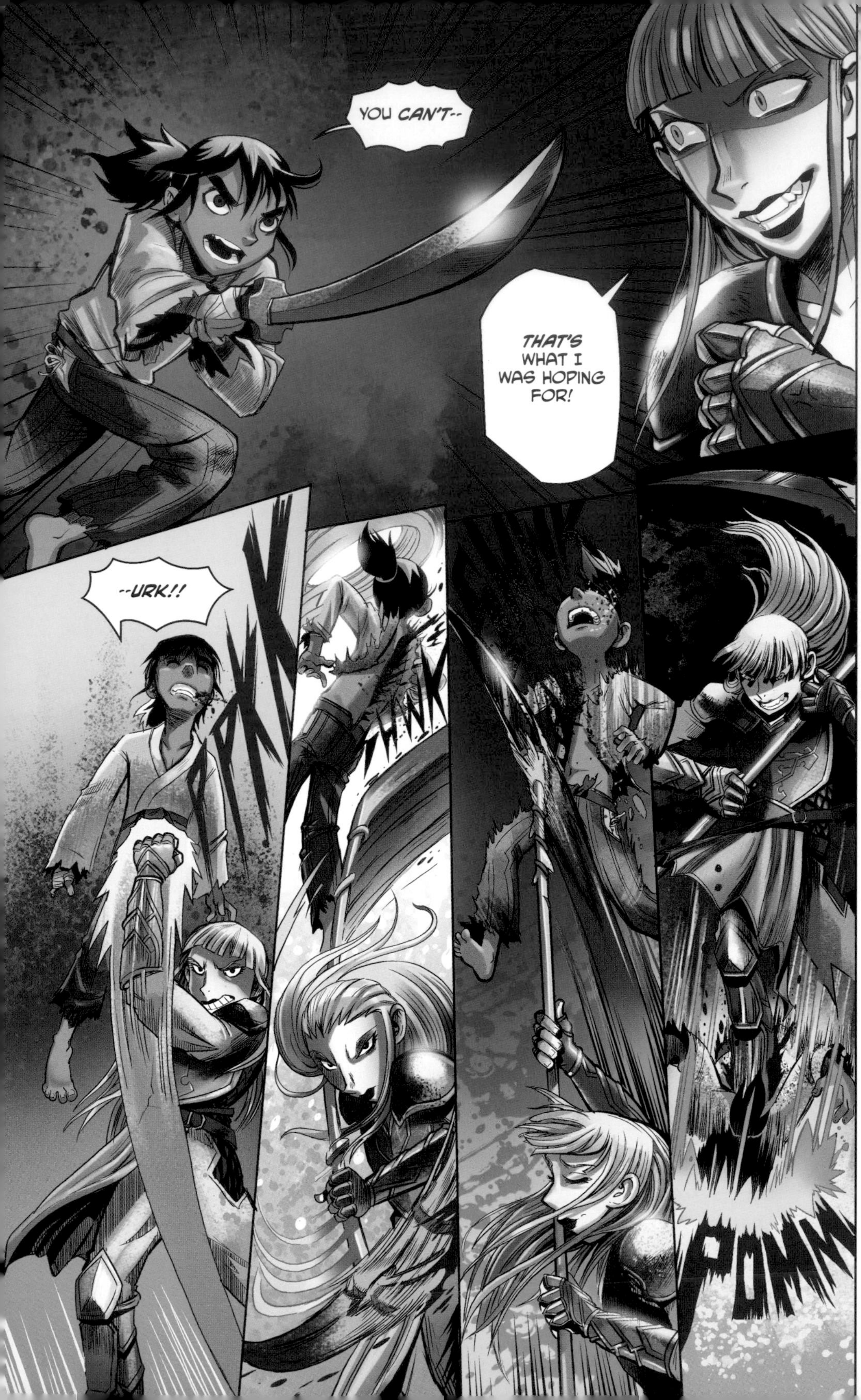
YOU CAN'T--
THAT'S WHAT I WAS HOPING FOR!
--URK!!
THWK
POMM

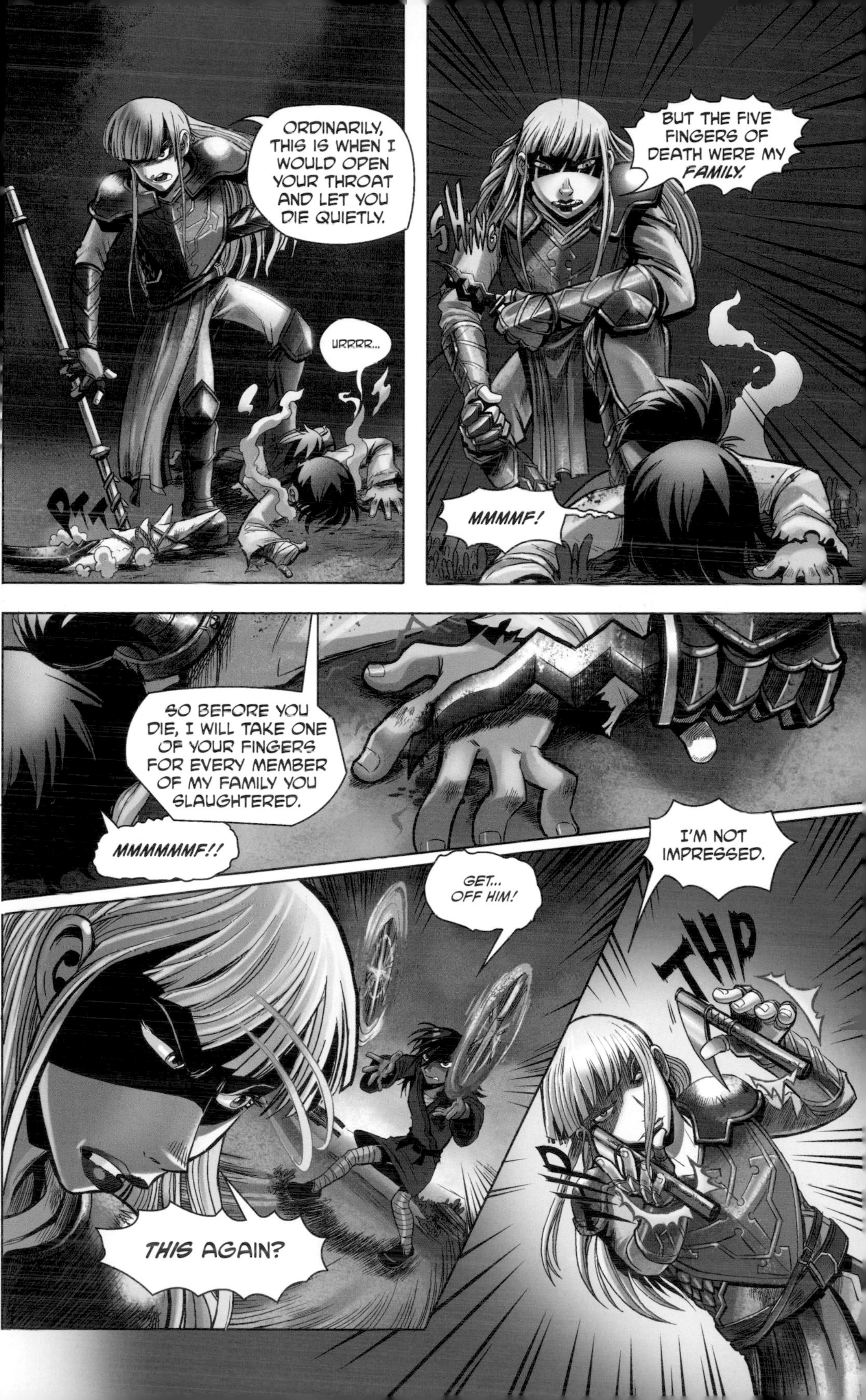
ORDINARILY, THIS IS WHEN I WOULD OPEN YOUR THROAT AND LET YOU DIE QUIETLY.
URRRR...
SHING
BUT THE FIVE FINGERS OF DEATH WERE MY *FAMILY.*
MMMMF!
SO BEFORE YOU DIE, I WILL TAKE ONE OF YOUR FINGERS FOR EVERY MEMBER OF MY FAMILY YOU SLAUGHTERED.
MMMMMMF!!
GET... OFF HIM!
I'M NOT IMPRESSED.
THP
THIS AGAIN?

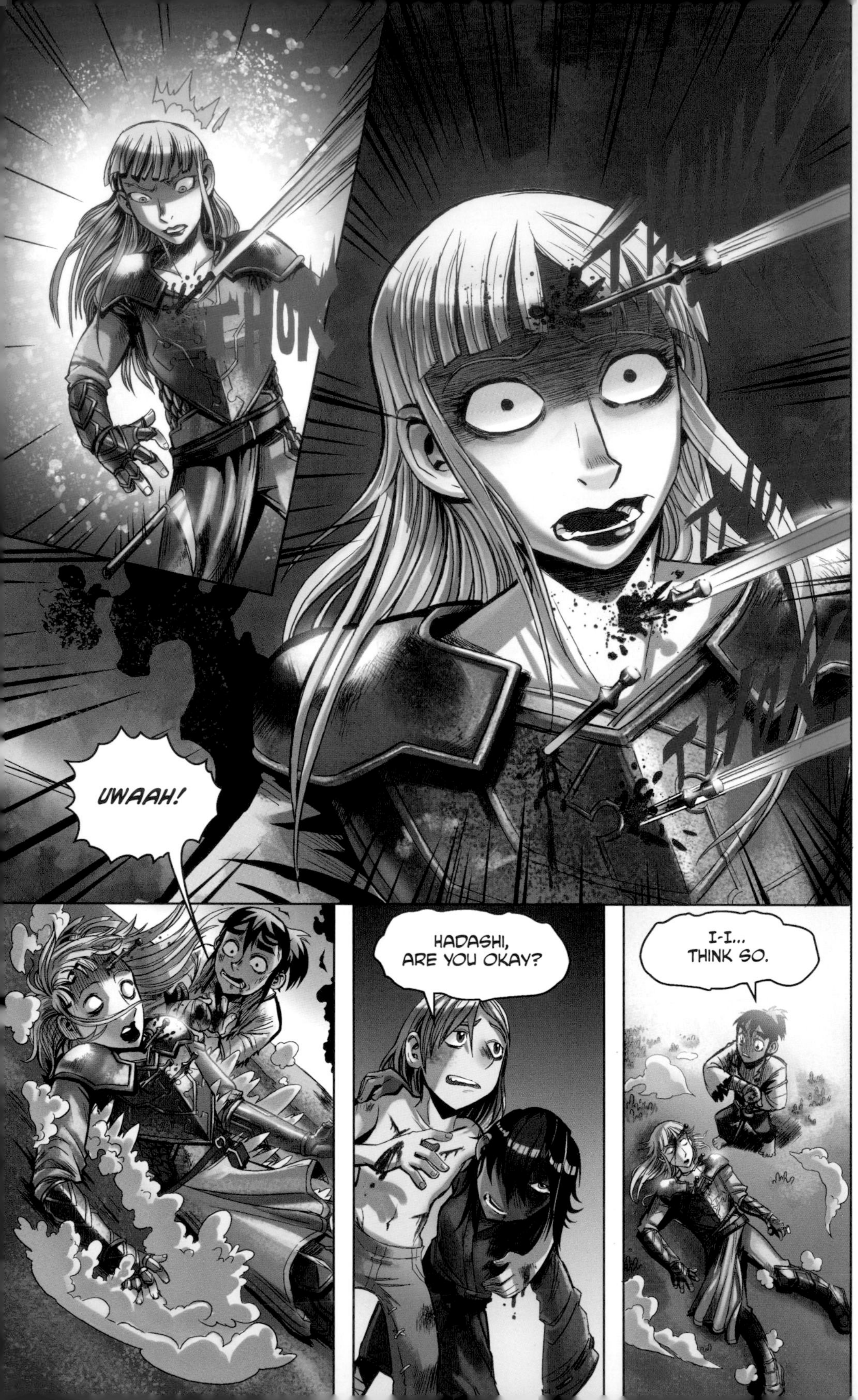
THUK
THK
THUK
THUK
UWAAH!
HADASHI, ARE YOU OKAY?
I-I... THINK SO.

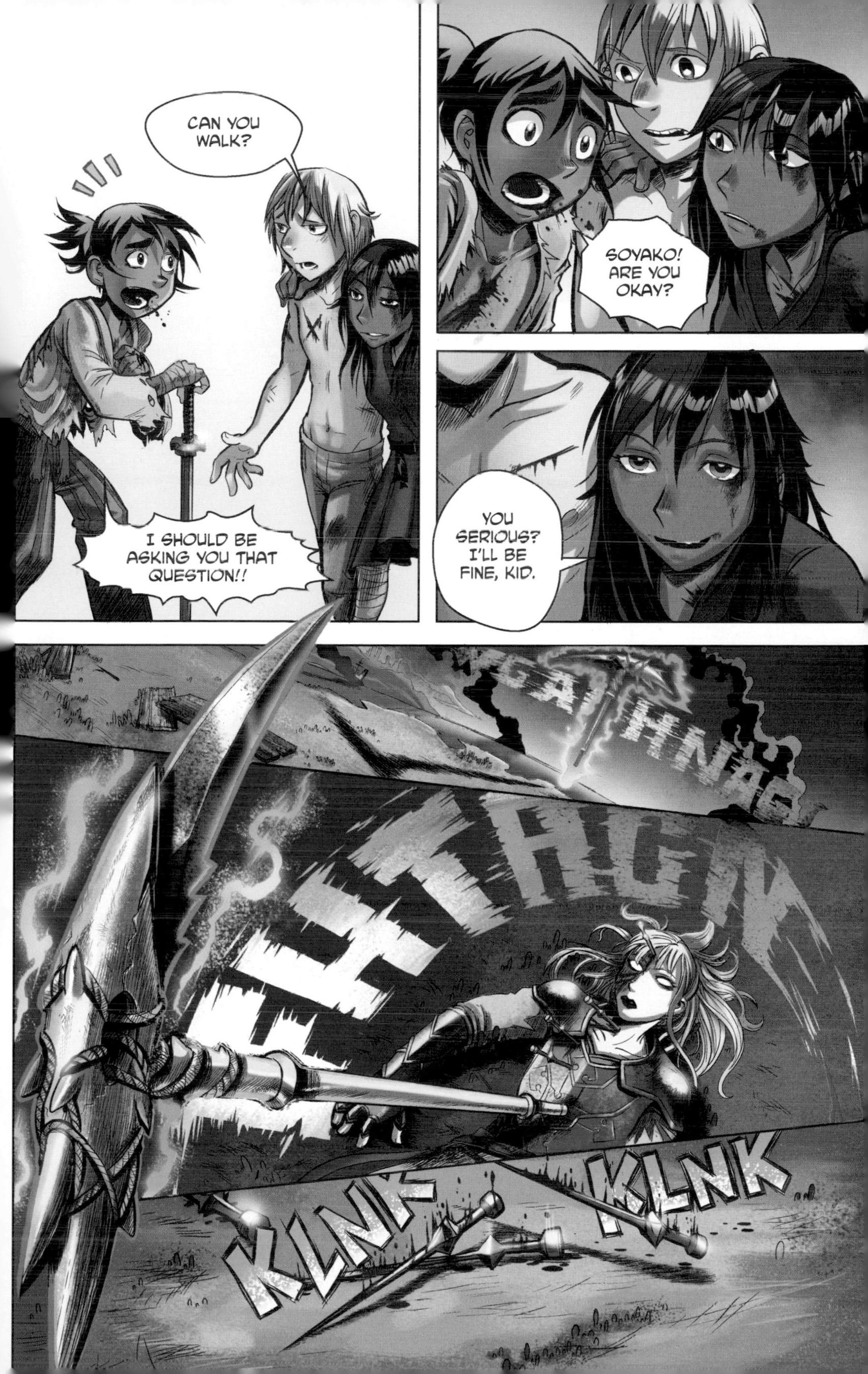
CAN YOU WALK?
I SHOULD BE ASKING YOU THAT QUESTION!!
SOYAKO! ARE YOU OKAY?
YOU SERIOUS? I'LL BE FINE, KID.
KLNK
KLNK

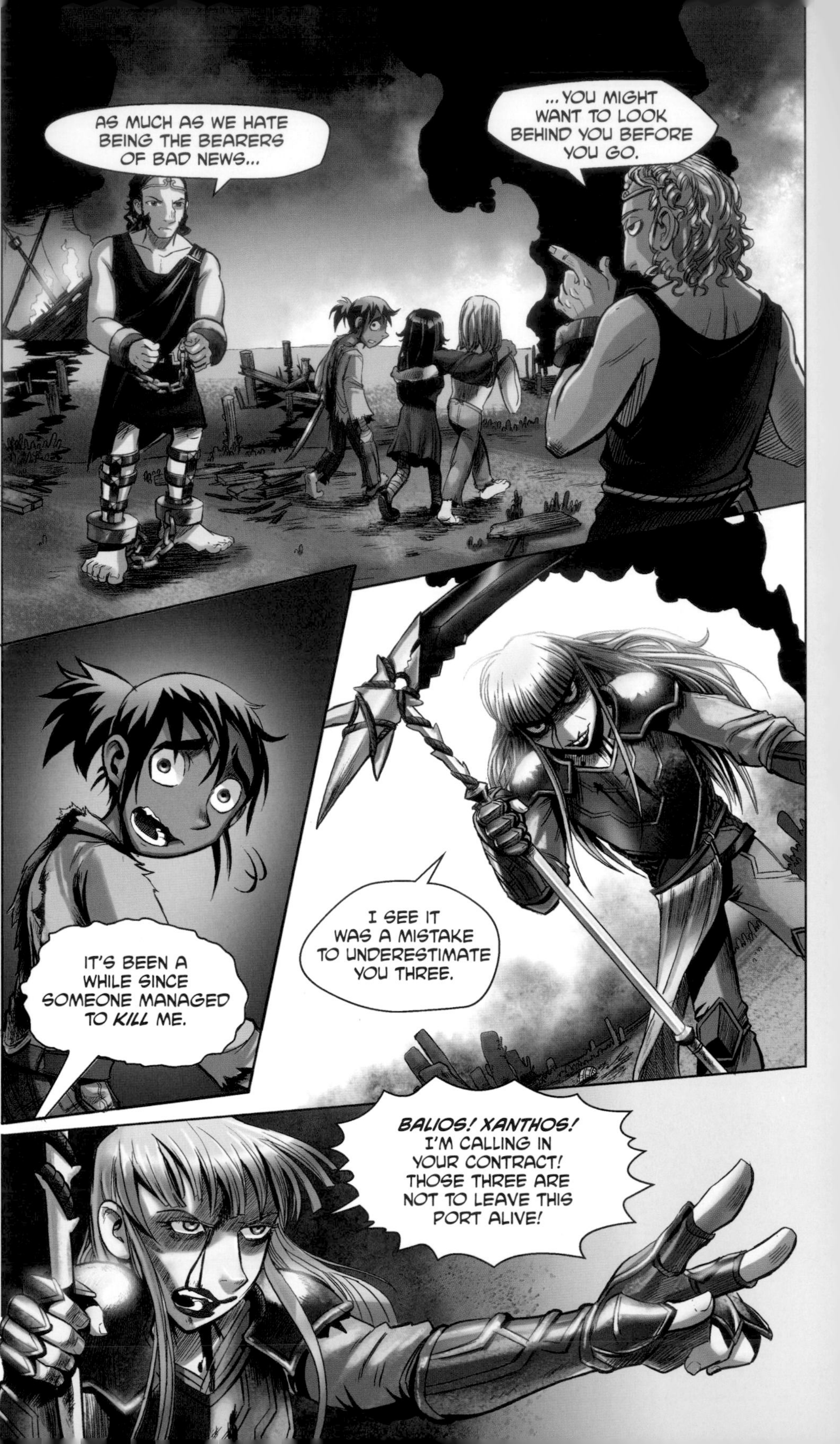
AS MUCH AS WE HATE BEING THE BEARERS OF BAD NEWS...
...YOU MIGHT WANT TO LOOK BEHIND YOU BEFORE YOU GO.
IT'S BEEN A WHILE SINCE SOMEONE MANAGED TO *KILL* ME.
I SEE IT WAS A MISTAKE TO UNDERESTIMATE YOU THREE.
BALIOS! XANTHOS! I'M CALLING IN YOUR CONTRACT! THOSE THREE ARE NOT TO LEAVE THIS PORT ALIVE!

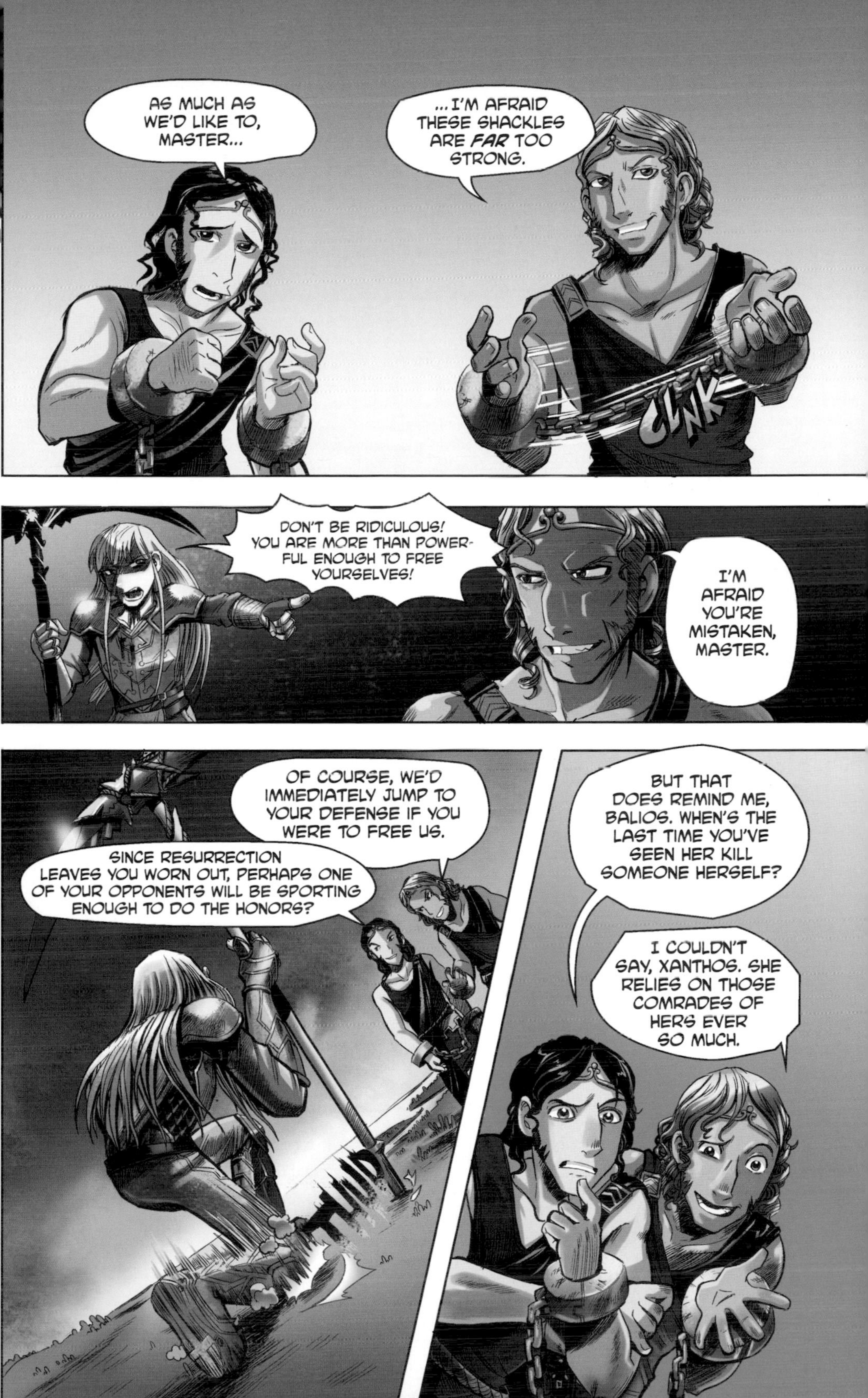
AS MUCH AS WE'D LIKE TO, MASTER...
...I'M AFRAID THESE SHACKLES ARE *FAR* TOO STRONG.
CLINK
DON'T BE RIDICULOUS! YOU ARE MORE THAN POWERFUL ENOUGH TO FREE YOURSELVES!
I'M AFRAID YOU'RE MISTAKEN, MASTER.
OF COURSE, WE'D IMMEDIATELY JUMP TO YOUR DEFENSE IF YOU WERE TO FREE US.
SINCE RESURRECTION LEAVES YOU WORN OUT, PERHAPS ONE OF YOUR OPPONENTS WILL BE SPORTING ENOUGH TO DO THE HONORS?
BUT THAT DOES REMIND ME, BALIOS. WHEN'S THE LAST TIME YOU'VE SEEN HER KILL SOMEONE HERSELF?
I COULDN'T SAY, XANTHOS. SHE RELIES ON THOSE COMRADES OF HERS EVER SO MUCH.

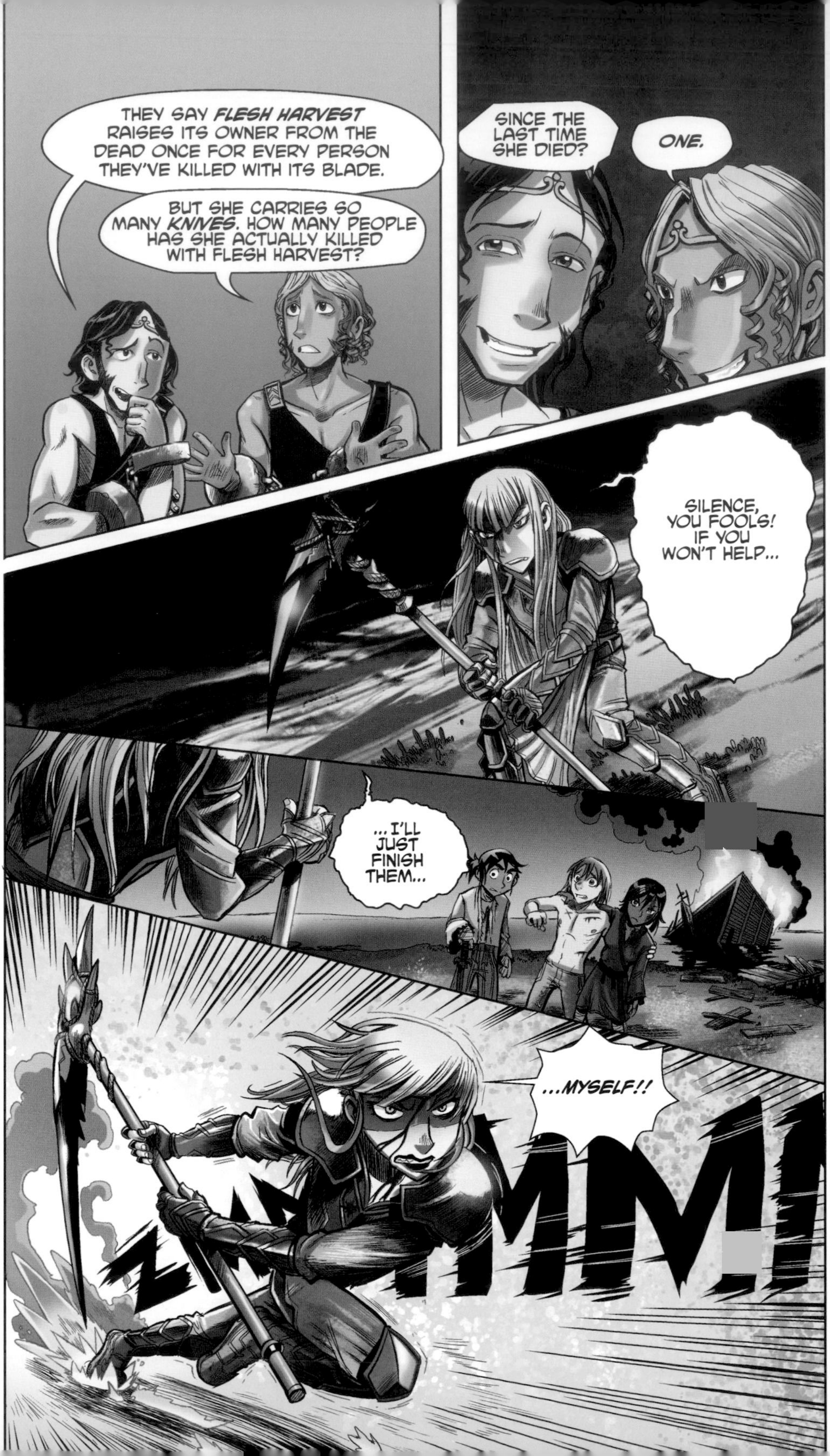
THEY SAY FLESH HARVEST RAISES ITS OWNER FROM THE DEAD ONCE FOR EVERY PERSON THEY'VE KILLED WITH ITS BLADE.
BUT SHE CARRIES SO MANY KNIVES. HOW MANY PEOPLE HAS SHE ACTUALLY KILLED WITH FLESH HARVEST?
SINCE THE LAST TIME SHE DIED?
ONE.
SILENCE, YOU FOOLS! IF YOU WON'T HELP...
...I'LL JUST FINISH THEM...
...MYSELF!!

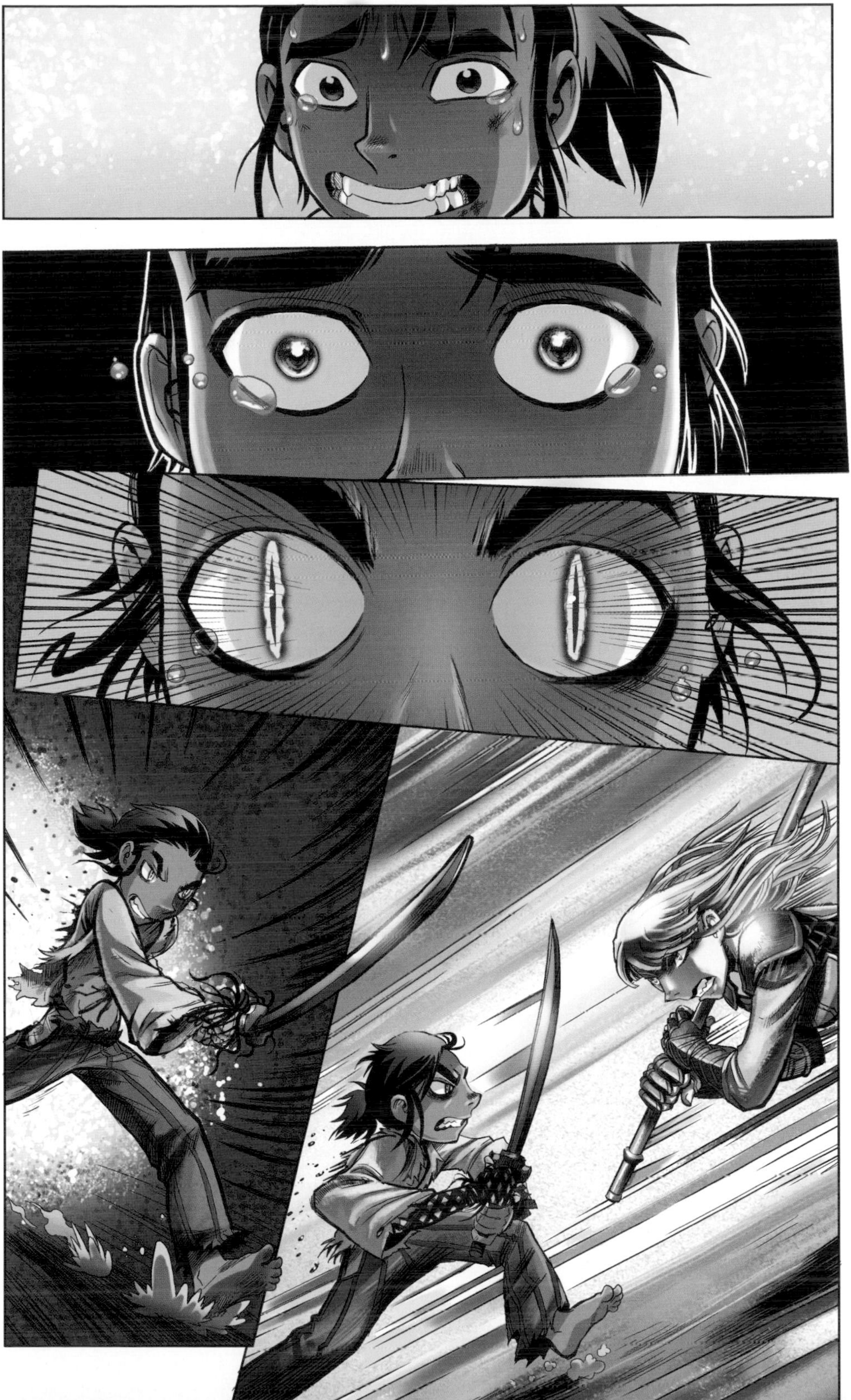

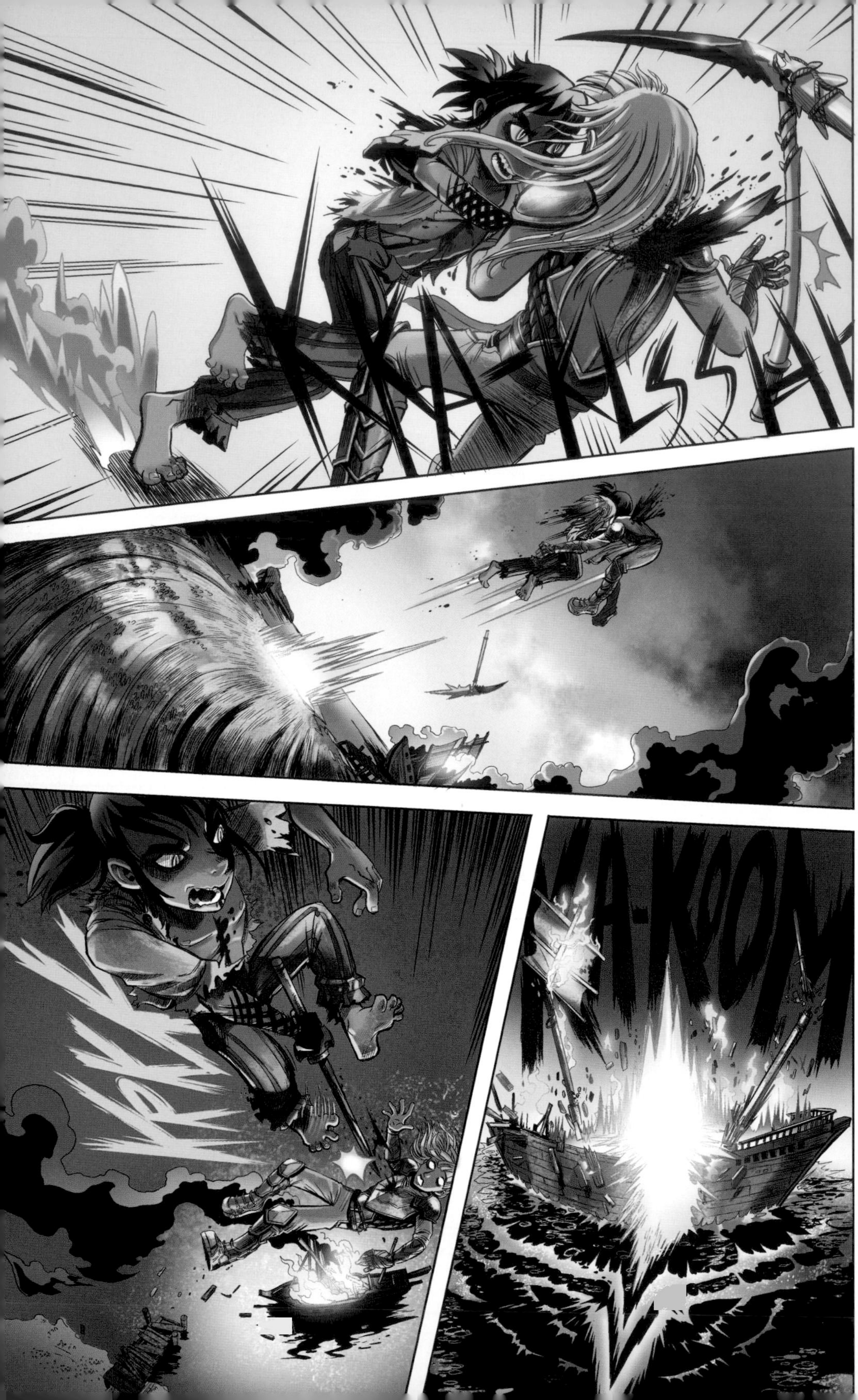
KA-KOOM

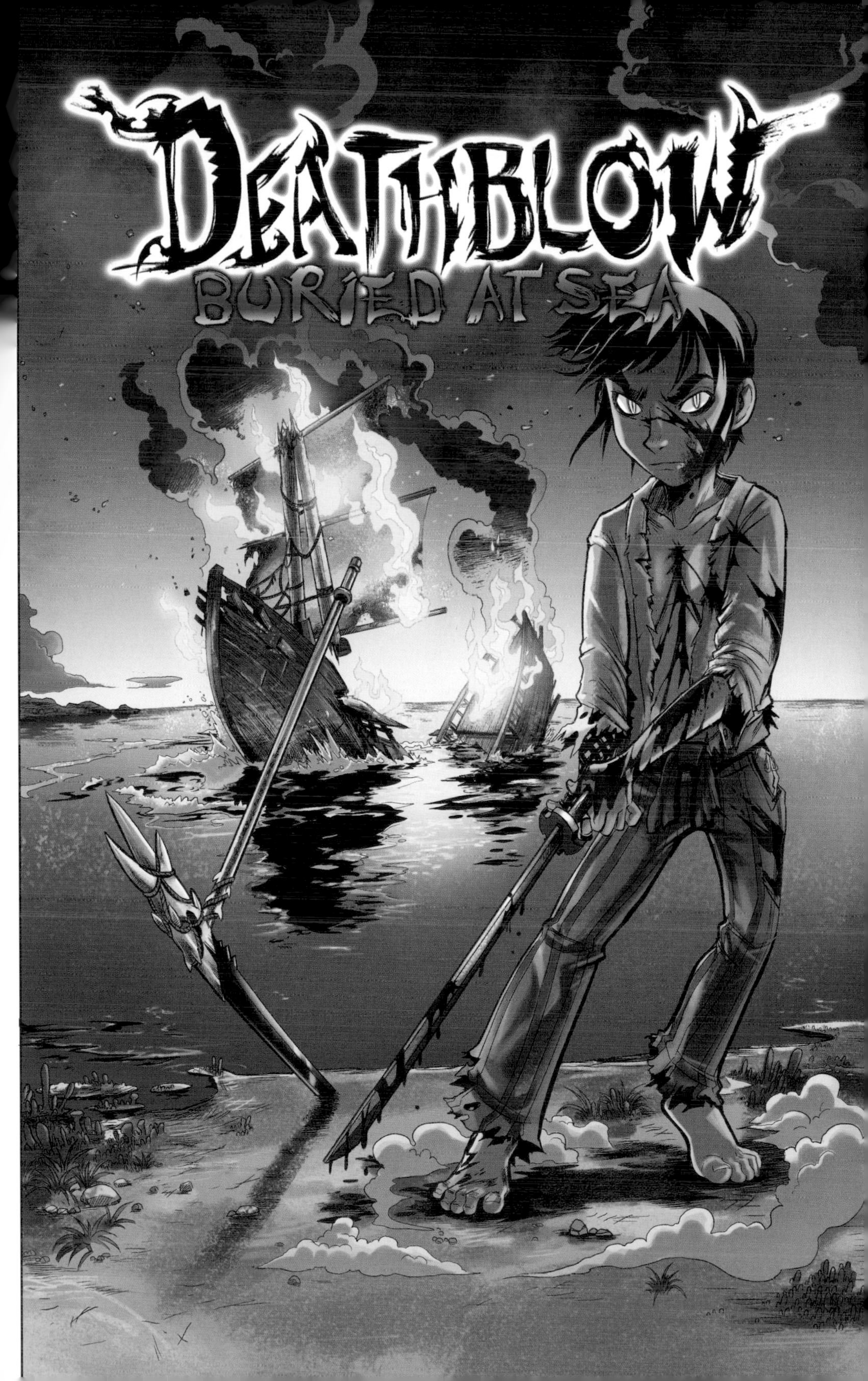
DEATHBLOW
BURIED AT SEA

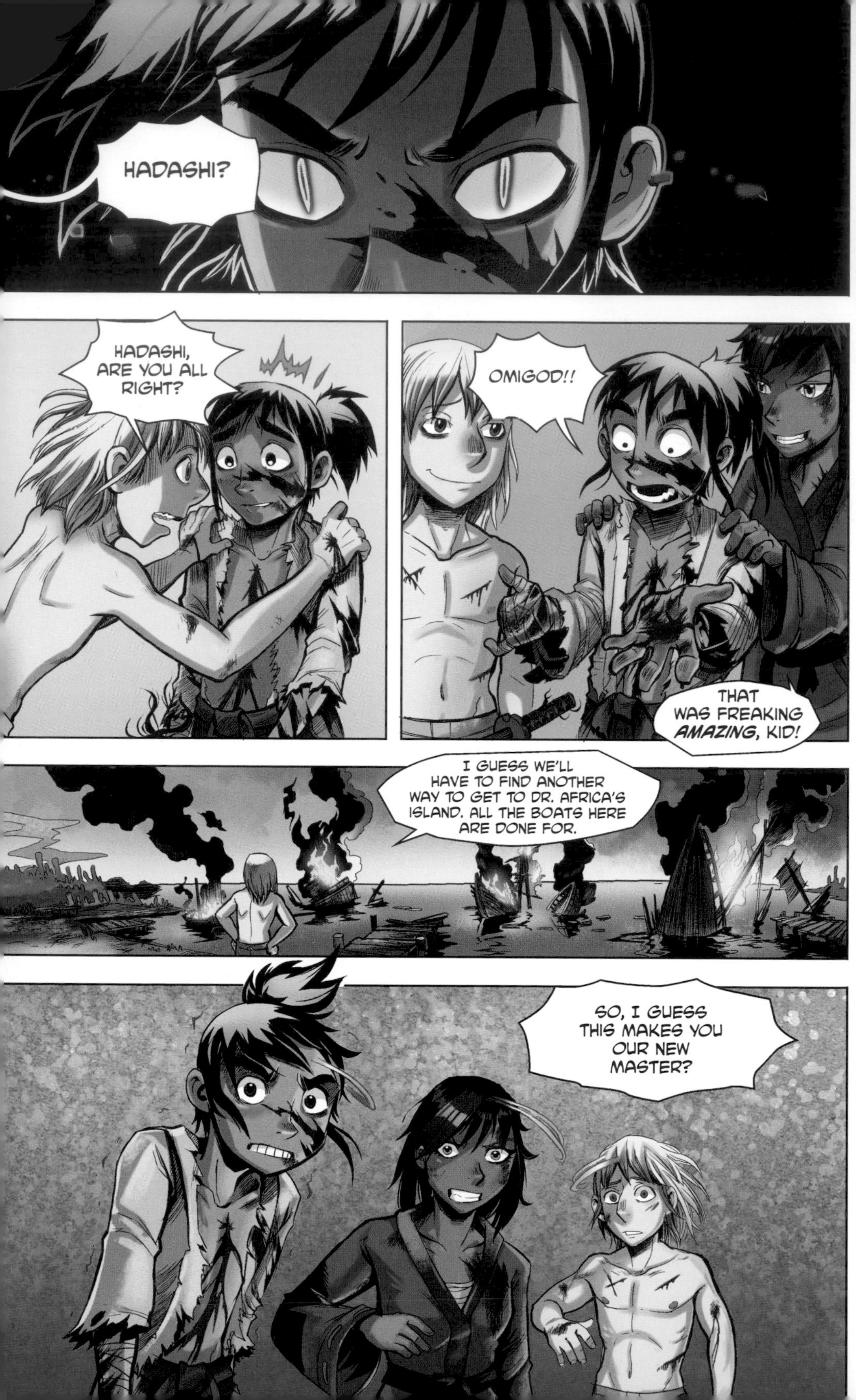
HADASHI?
HADASHI, ARE YOU ALL RIGHT?
OMIGOD!!
THAT WAS FREAKING *AMAZING*, KID!
I GUESS WE'LL HAVE TO FIND ANOTHER WAY TO GET TO DR. AFRICA'S ISLAND. ALL THE BOATS HERE ARE DONE FOR.
SO, I GUESS THIS MAKES YOU OUR NEW MASTER?

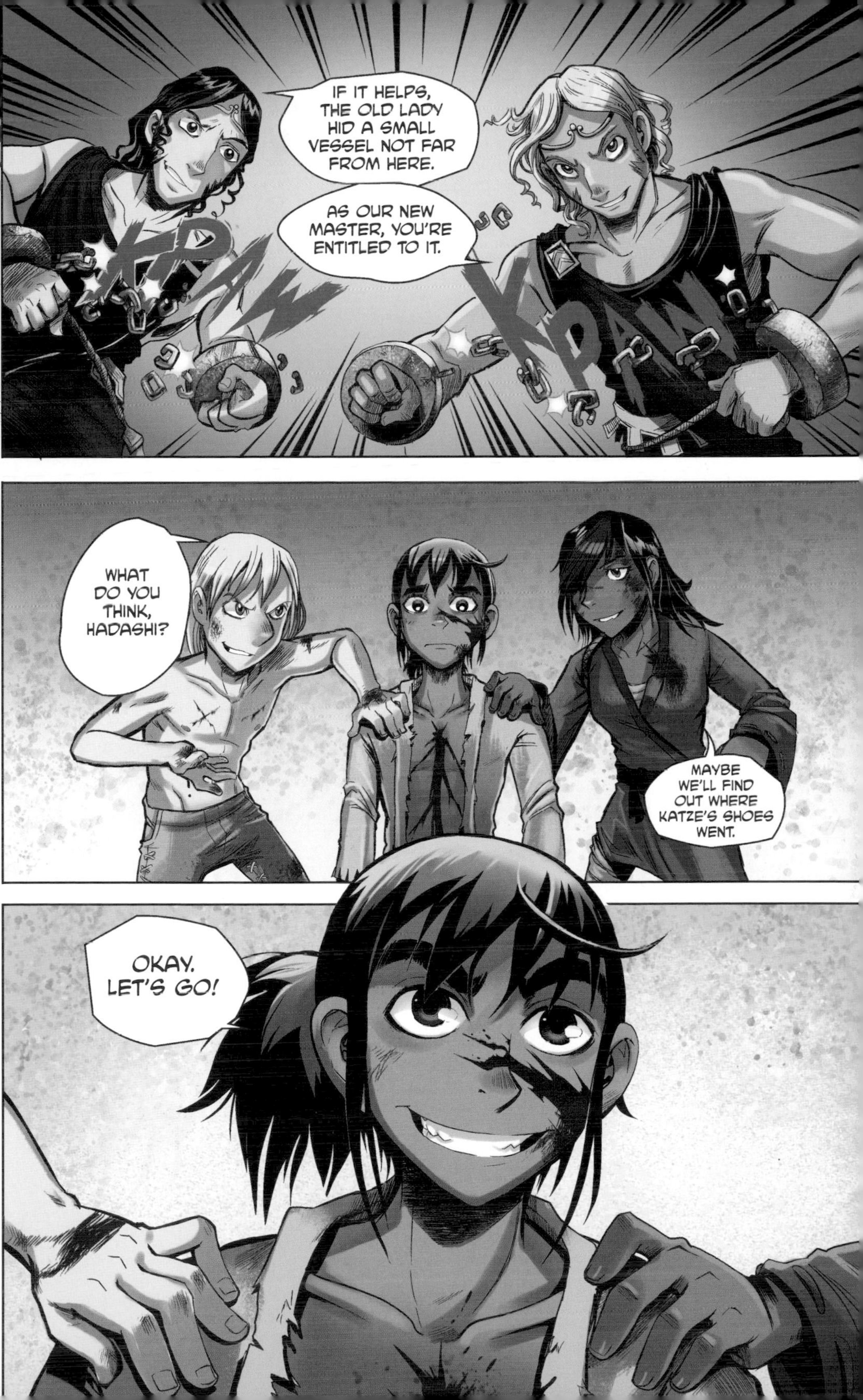
IF IT HELPS, THE OLD LADY HID A SMALL VESSEL NOT FAR FROM HERE.
AS OUR NEW MASTER, YOU'RE ENTITLED TO IT.
KPAW
KPAW
WHAT DO YOU THINK, HADASHI?
MAYBE WE'LL FIND OUT WHERE KATZE'S SHOES WENT.
OKAY. LET'S GO!

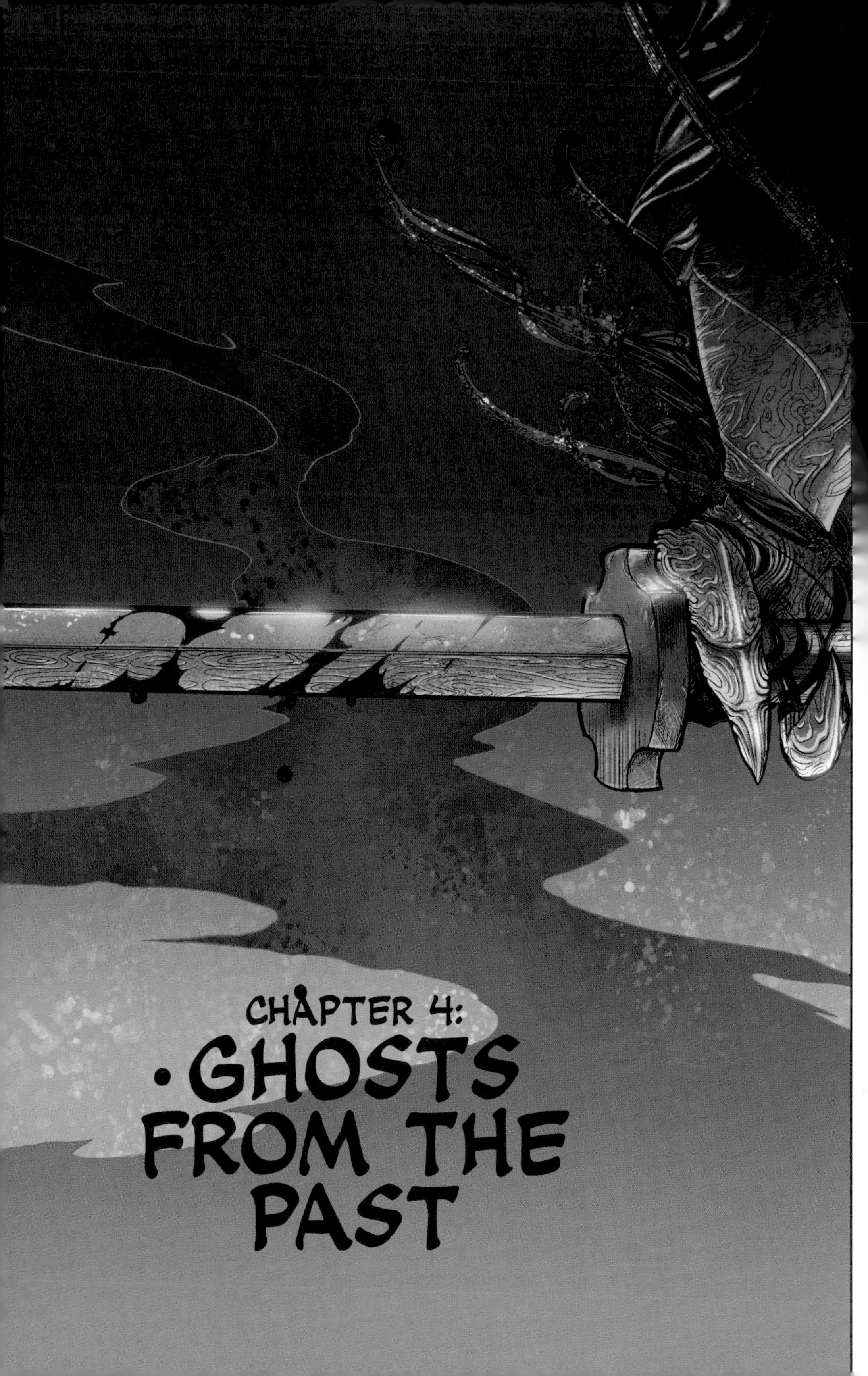
CHAPTER 4:
GHOSTS FROM THE PAST

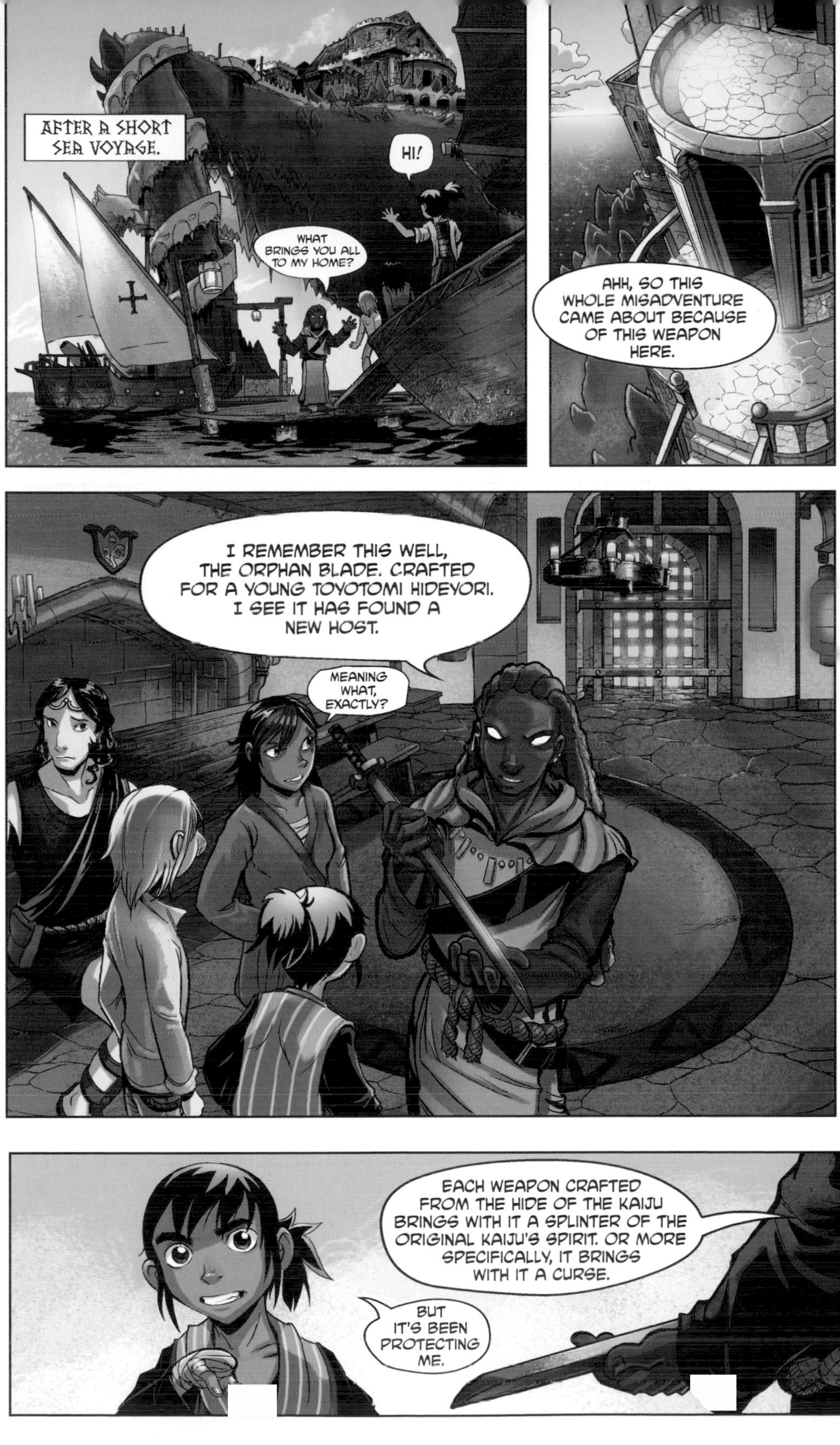
AFTER A SHORT SEA VOYAGE.
HI!
WHAT BRINGS YOU ALL TO MY HOME?
AHH, SO THIS WHOLE MISADVENTURE CAME ABOUT BECAUSE OF THIS WEAPON HERE.
I REMEMBER THIS WELL, THE ORPHAN BLADE. CRAFTED FOR A YOUNG TOYOTOMI HIDEYORI. I SEE IT HAS FOUND A NEW HOST.
MEANING WHAT, EXACTLY?
EACH WEAPON CRAFTED FROM THE HIDE OF THE KAIJU BRINGS WITH IT A SPLINTER OF THE ORIGINAL KAIJU'S SPIRIT. OR MORE SPECIFICALLY, IT BRINGS WITH IT A CURSE.
BUT IT'S BEEN PROTECTING ME.

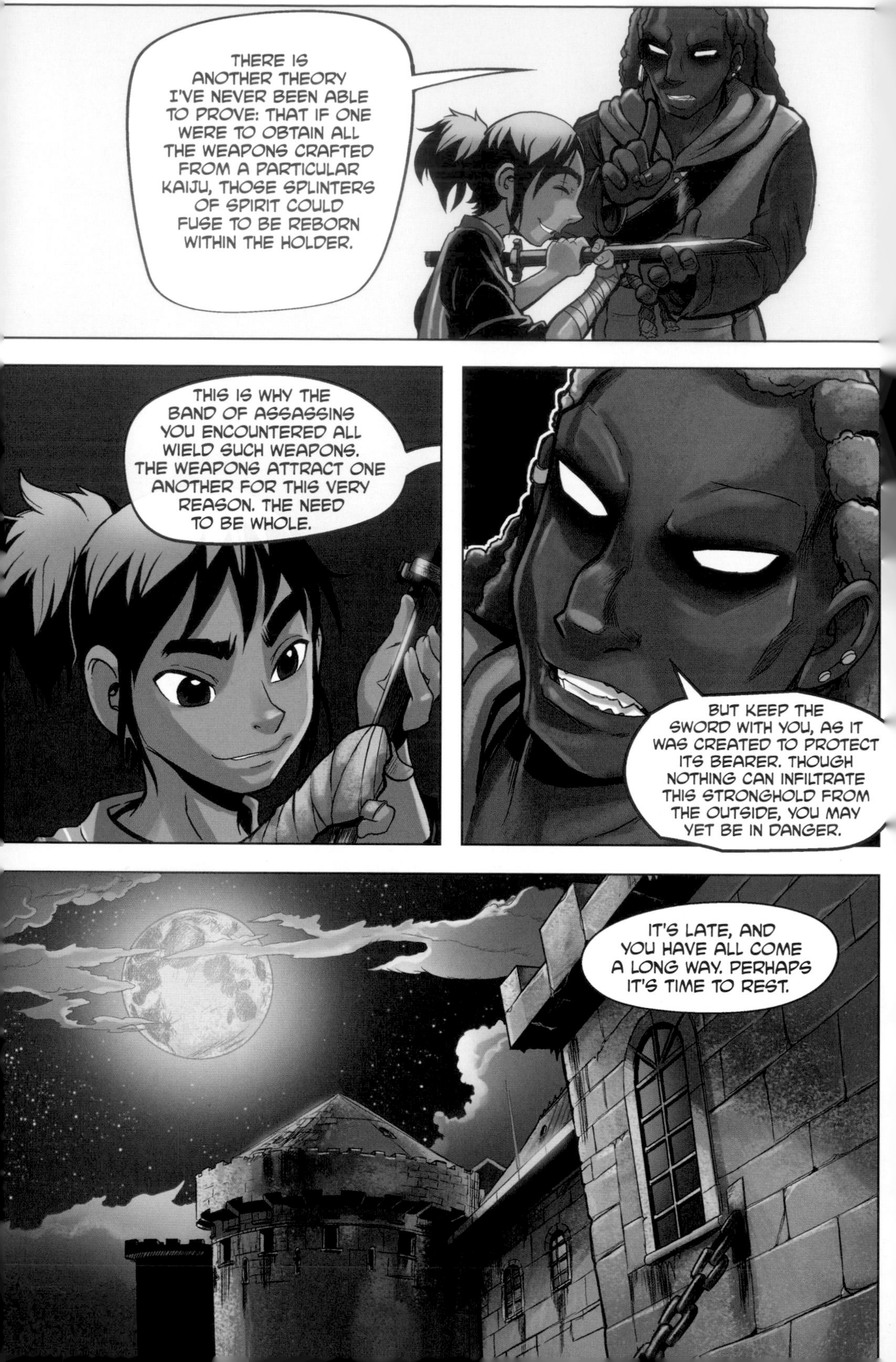
THERE IS ANOTHER THEORY I'VE NEVER BEEN ABLE TO PROVE: THAT IF ONE WERE TO OBTAIN ALL THE WEAPONS CRAFTED FROM A PARTICULAR KAIJU, THOSE SPLINTERS OF SPIRIT COULD FUSE TO BE REBORN WITHIN THE HOLDER.
THIS IS WHY THE BAND OF ASSASSINS YOU ENCOUNTERED ALL WIELD SUCH WEAPONS. THE WEAPONS ATTRACT ONE ANOTHER FOR THIS VERY REASON. THE NEED TO BE WHOLE.
BUT KEEP THE SWORD WITH YOU, AS IT WAS CREATED TO PROTECT ITS BEARER. THOUGH NOTHING CAN INFILTRATE THIS STRONGHOLD FROM THE OUTSIDE, YOU MAY YET BE IN DANGER.
IT'S LATE, AND YOU HAVE ALL COME A LONG WAY. PERHAPS IT'S TIME TO REST.

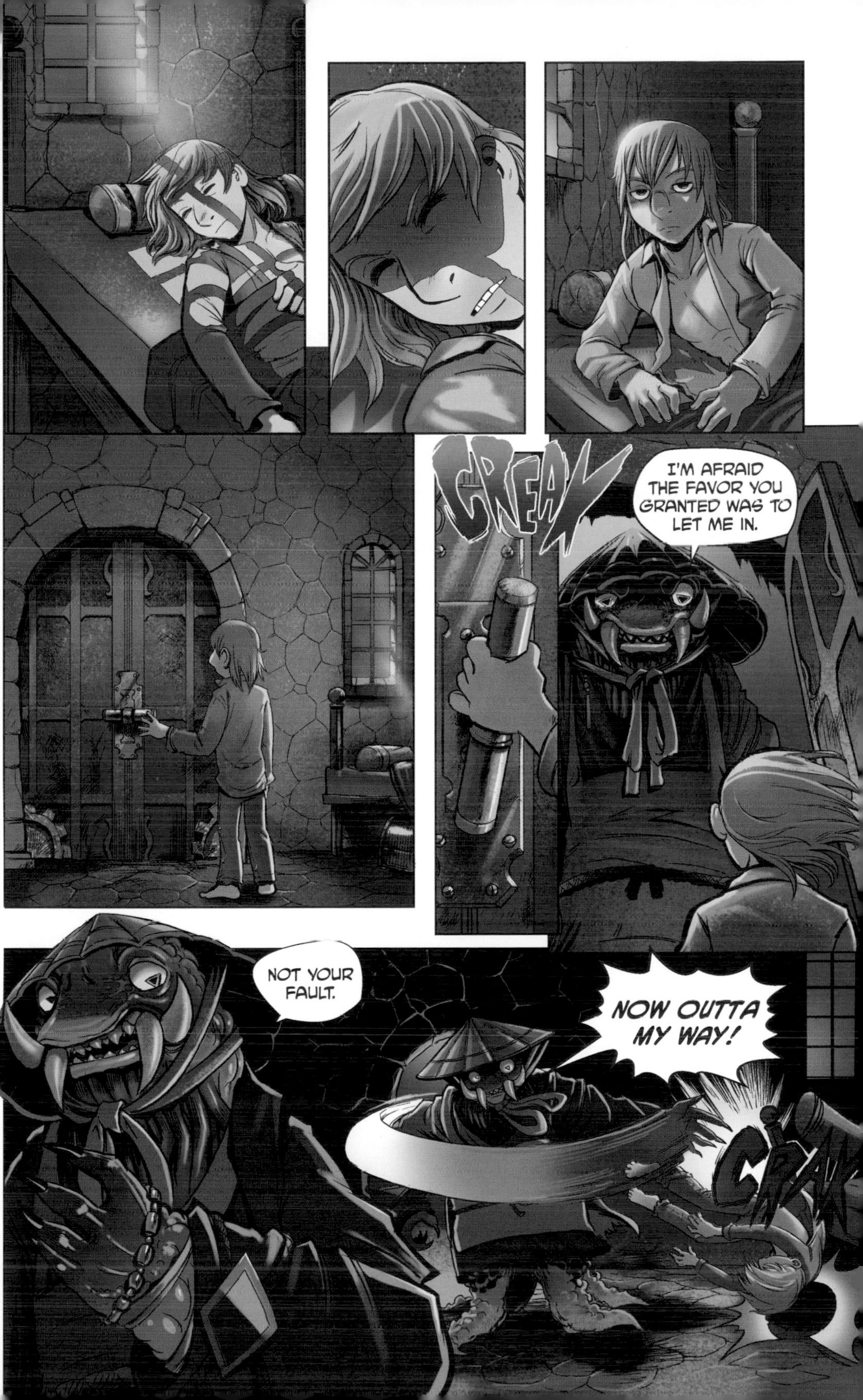
CREAK
I'M AFRAID THE FAVOR YOU GRANTED WAS TO LET ME IN.
NOT YOUR FAULT.
NOW OUTTA MY WAY!
CRAK

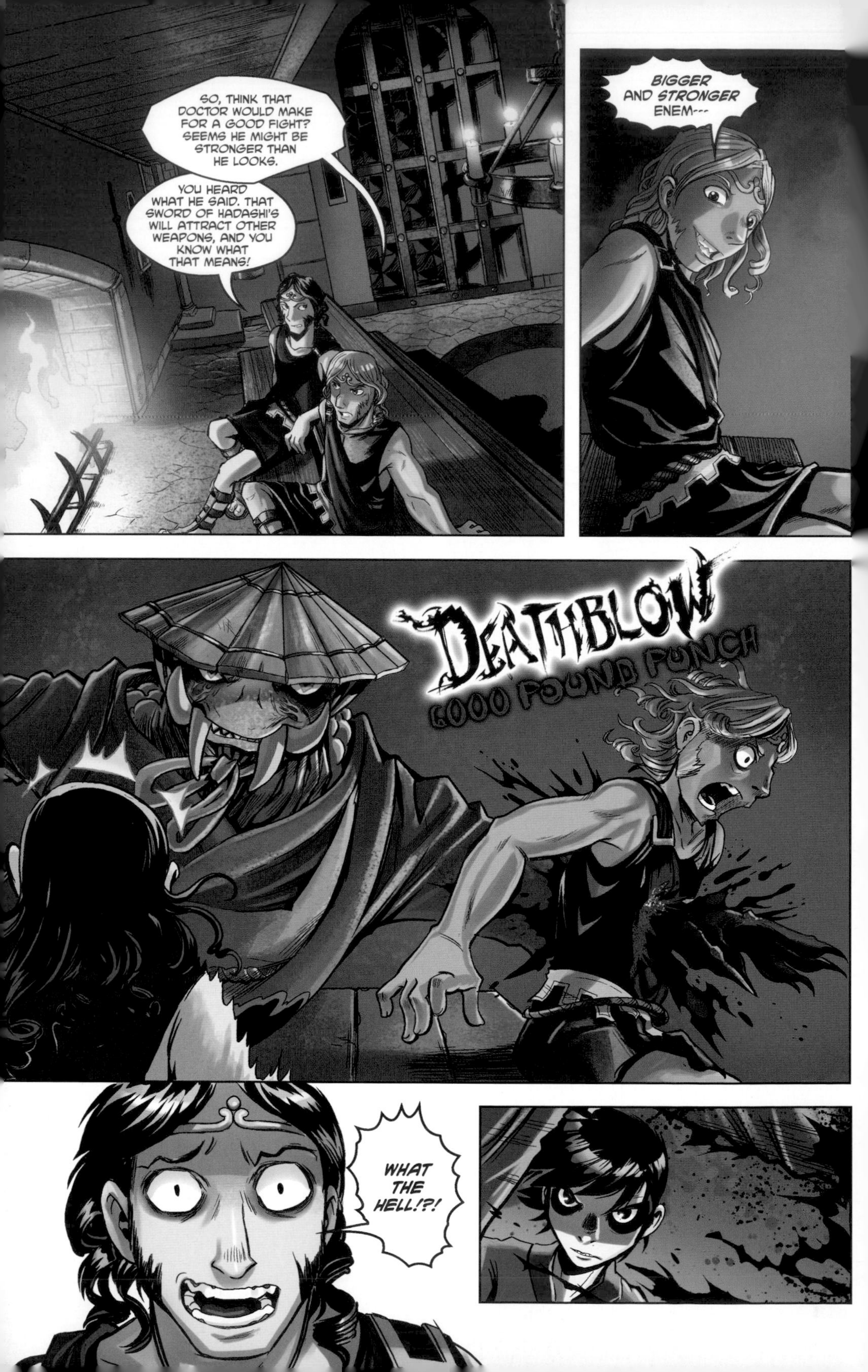
SO, THINK THAT DOCTOR WOULD MAKE FOR A GOOD FIGHT? SEEMS HE MIGHT BE STRONGER THAN HE LOOKS.
YOU HEARD WHAT HE SAID. THAT SWORD OF HADASHI'S WILL ATTRACT OTHER WEAPONS, AND YOU KNOW WHAT THAT MEANS!
BIGGER AND STRONGER ENEM---
DEATHBLOW
6000 POUND PUNCH
WHAT THE HELL!?!

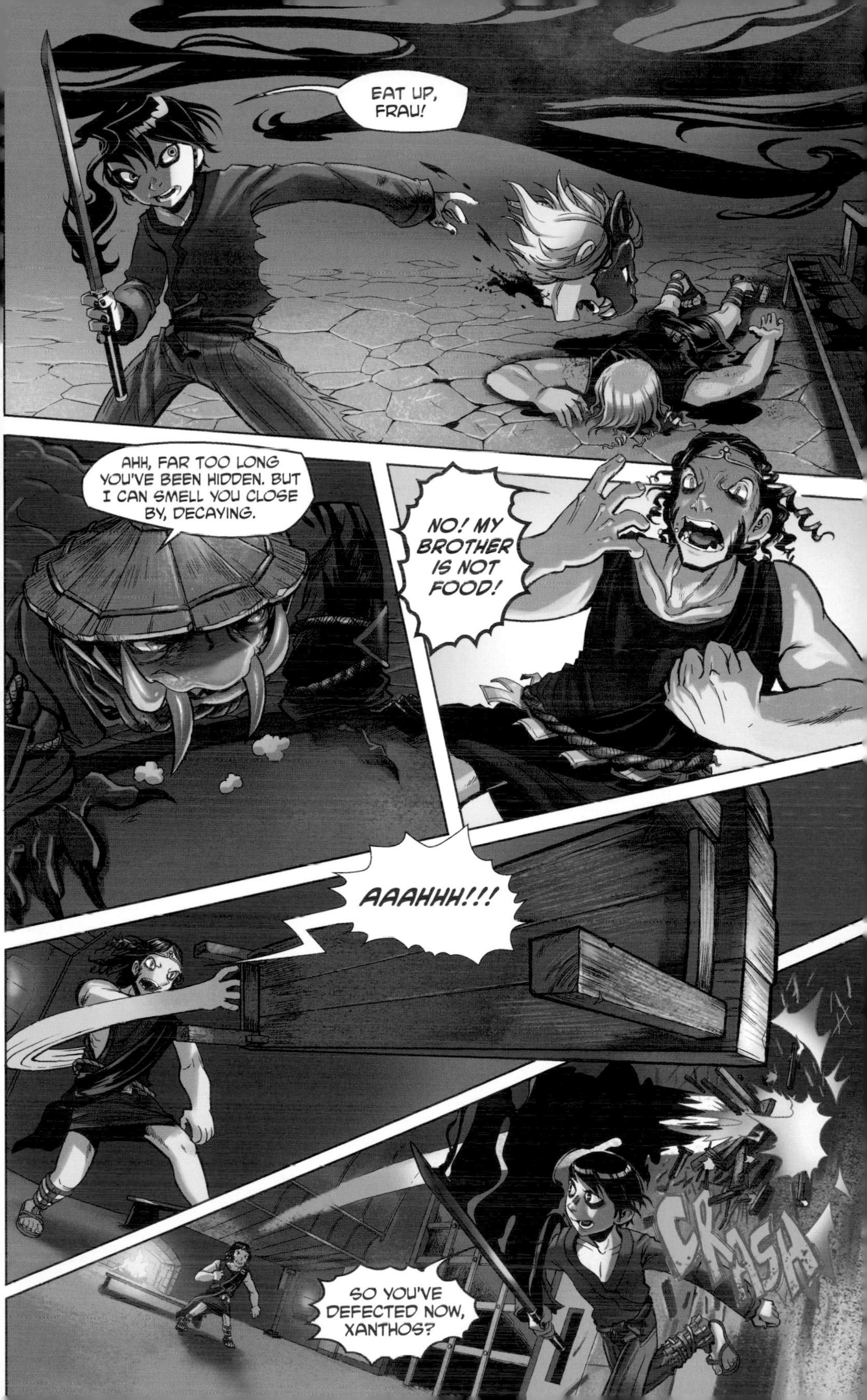
EAT UP, FRAU!
AHH, FAR TOO LONG YOU'VE BEEN HIDDEN. BUT I CAN SMELL YOU CLOSE BY, DECAYING.
NO! MY BROTHER IS NOT FOOD!
AAAHHH!!!
CRASH
SO YOU'VE DEFECTED NOW, XANTHOS?

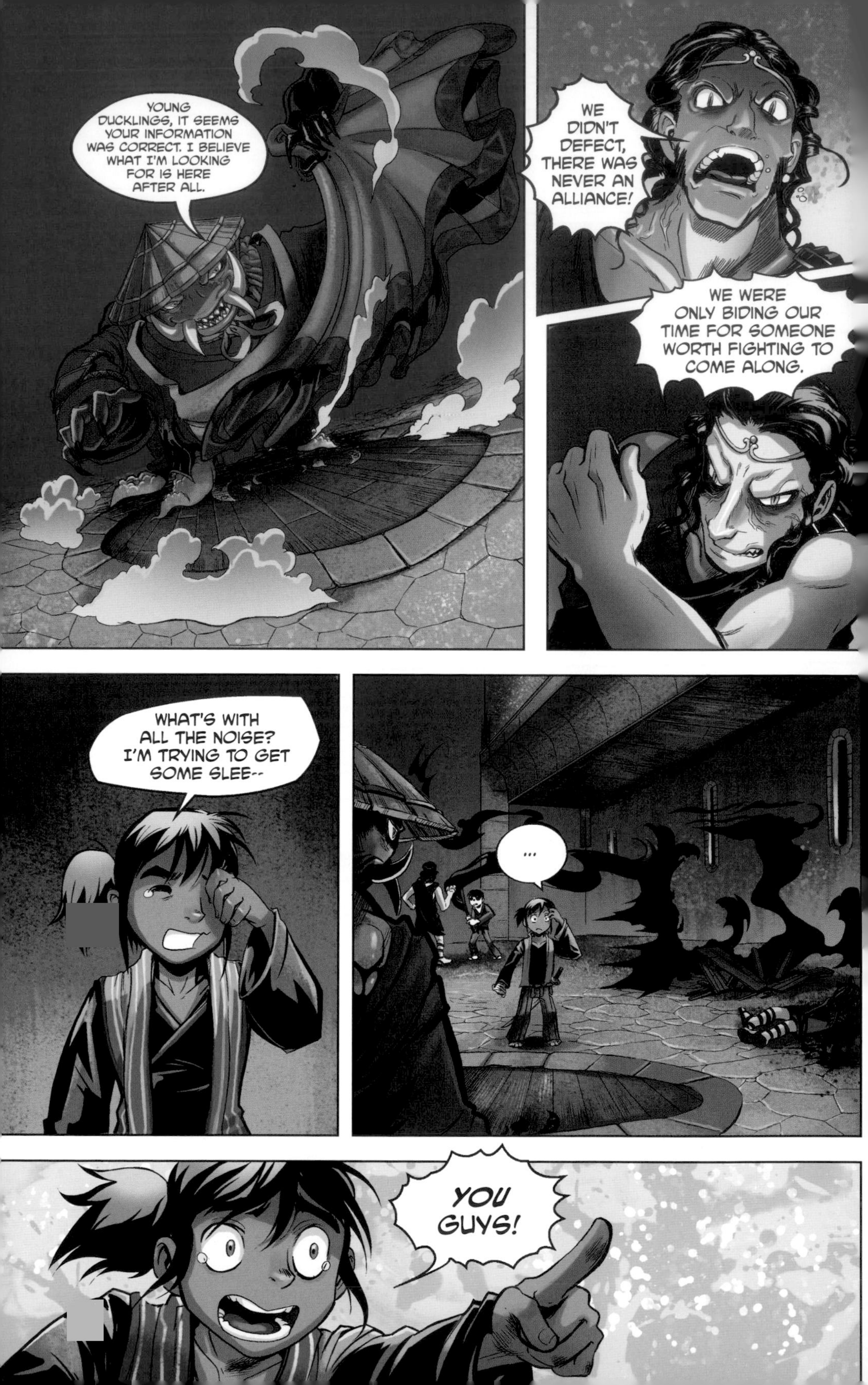
YOUNG DUCKLINGS, IT SEEMS YOUR INFORMATION WAS CORRECT. I BELIEVE WHAT I'M LOOKING FOR IS HERE AFTER ALL.
WE DIDN'T DEFECT, THERE WAS NEVER AN ALLIANCE!
WE WERE ONLY BIDING OUR TIME FOR SOMEONE WORTH FIGHTING TO COME ALONG.
WHAT'S WITH ALL THE NOISE? I'M TRYING TO GET SOME SLEE--
...
YOU GUYS!

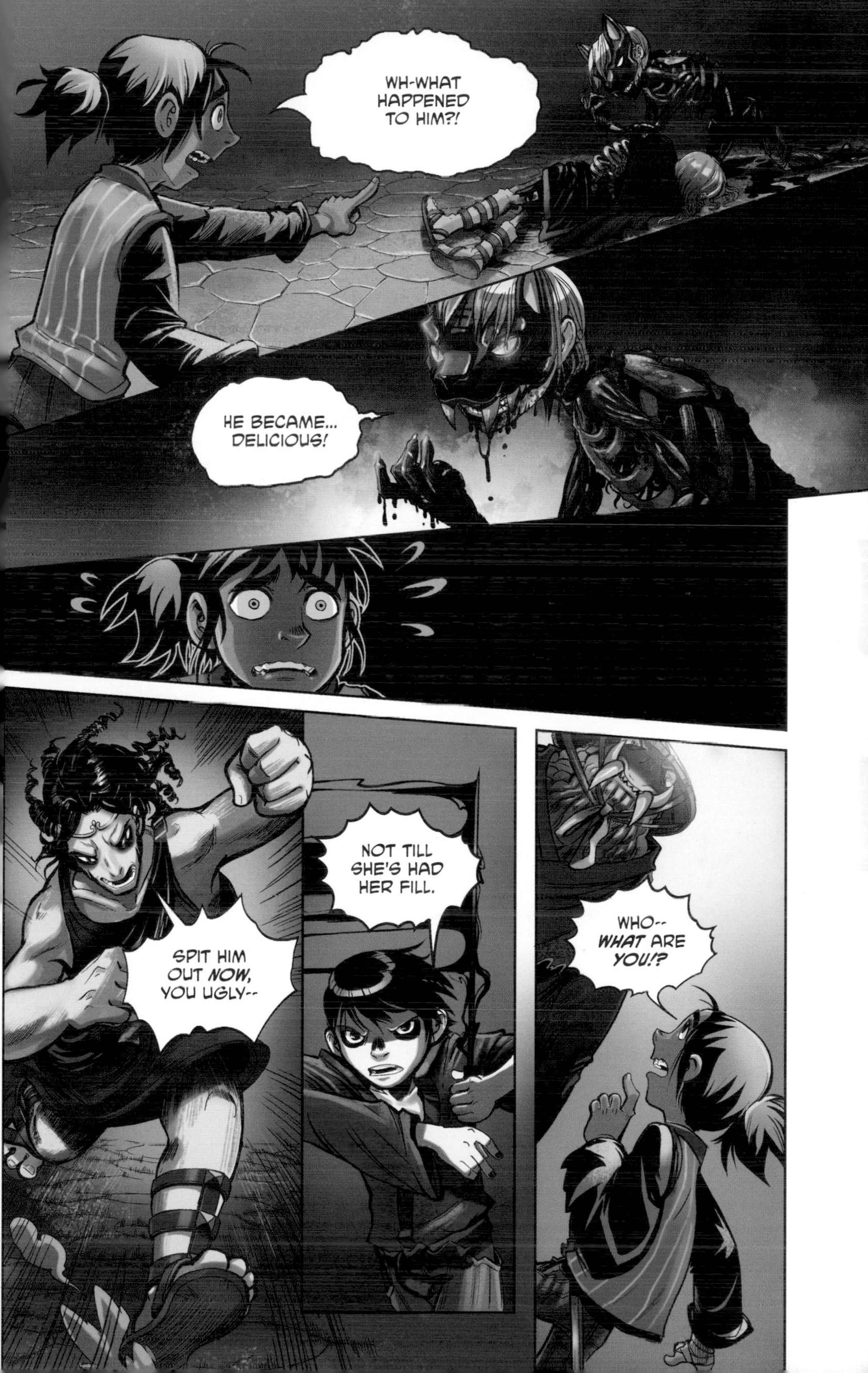
WH-WHAT HAPPENED TO HIM?!
HE BECAME... DELICIOUS!
SPIT HIM OUT *NOW*, YOU UGLY--
NOT TILL SHE'S HAD HER FILL.
WHO-- *WHAT* ARE *YOU!?*

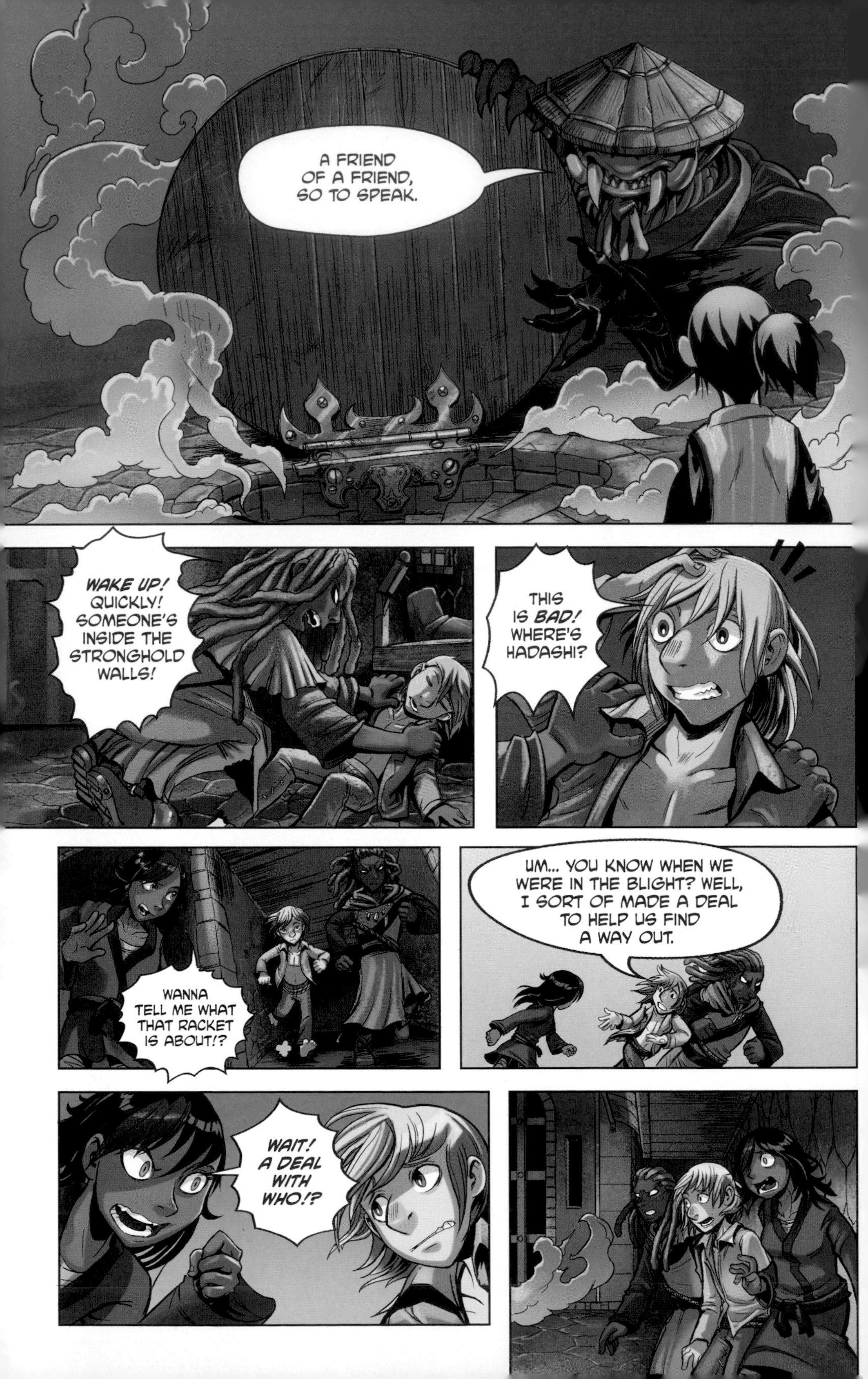
A FRIEND OF A FRIEND, SO TO SPEAK.
WAKE UP! QUICKLY! SOMEONE'S INSIDE THE STRONGHOLD WALLS!
THIS IS *BAD!* WHERE'S HADASHI?
WANNA TELL ME WHAT THAT RACKET IS ABOUT!?
UM... YOU KNOW WHEN WE WERE IN THE BLIGHT? WELL, I SORT OF MADE A DEAL TO HELP US FIND A WAY OUT.
WAIT! A DEAL WITH WHO!?

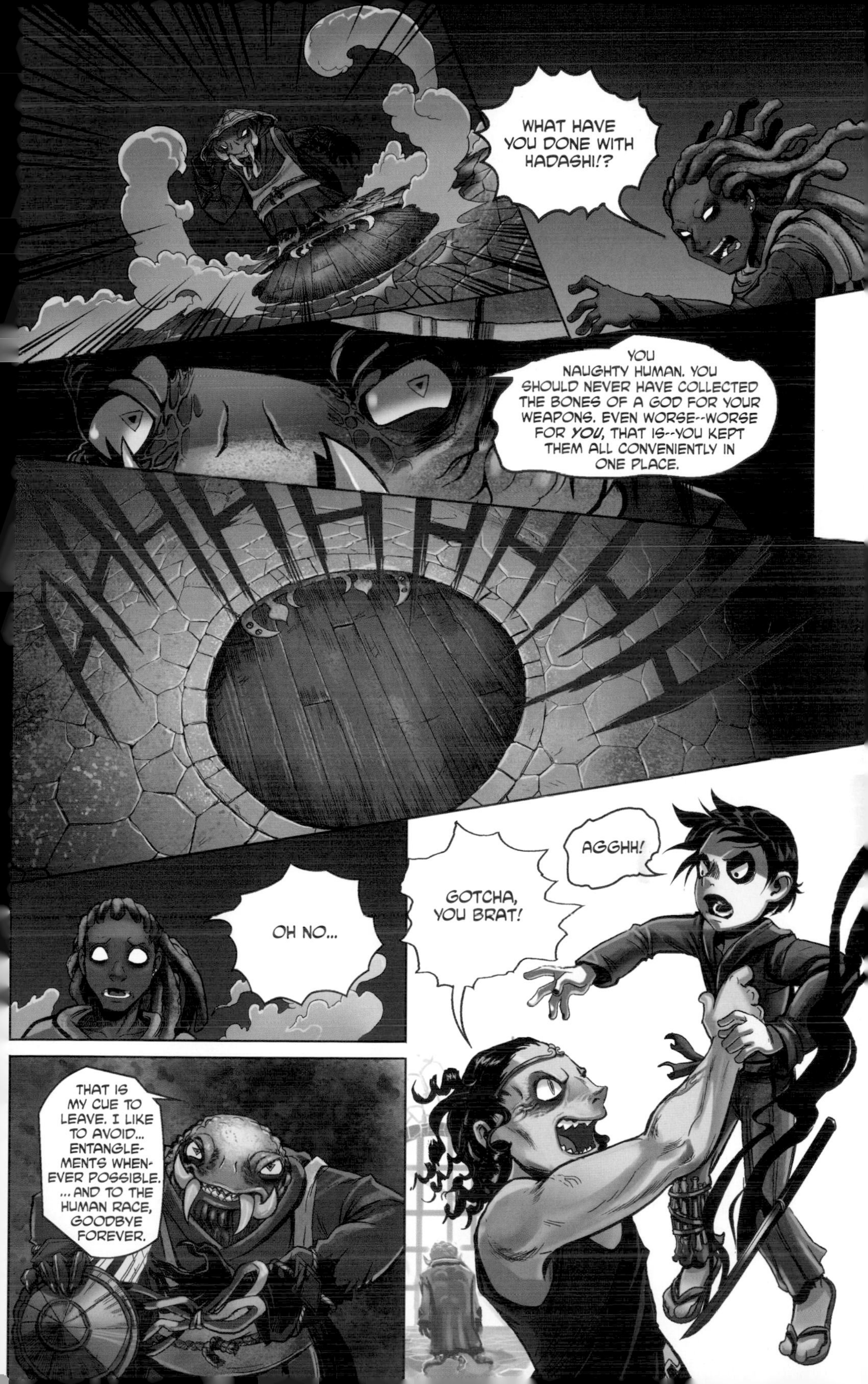
WHAT HAVE YOU DONE WITH HADASHI!?
YOU NAUGHTY HUMAN. YOU SHOULD NEVER HAVE COLLECTED THE BONES OF A GOD FOR YOUR WEAPONS. EVEN WORSE--WORSE FOR *YOU*, THAT IS--YOU KEPT THEM ALL CONVENIENTLY IN ONE PLACE.
AHHHHHHH
OH NO...
AGGHH!
GOTCHA, YOU BRAT!
THAT IS MY CUE TO LEAVE. I LIKE TO AVOID... ENTANGLE-MENTS WHEN-EVER POSSIBLE. ...AND TO THE HUMAN RACE, GOODBYE FOREVER.

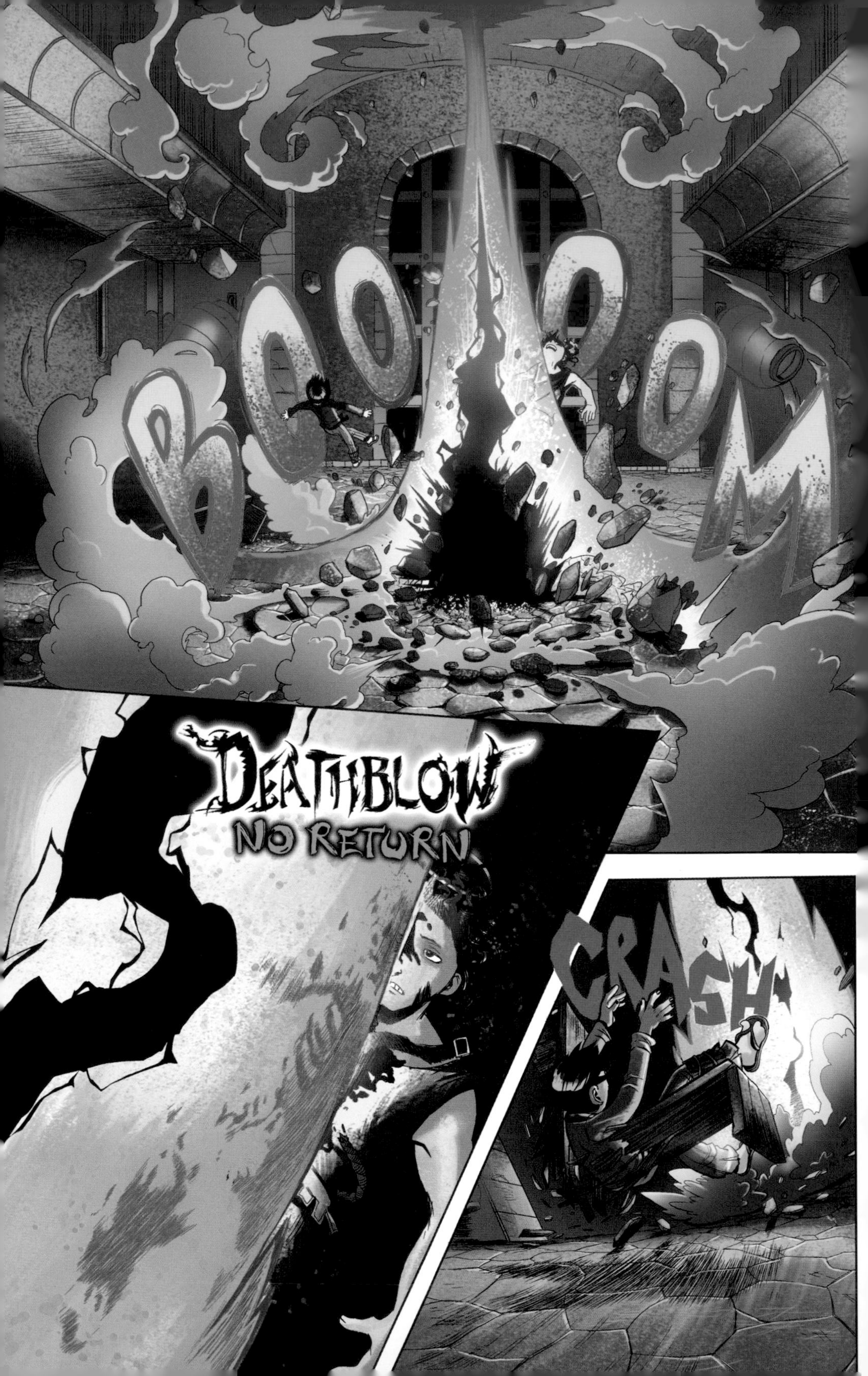
BOOOOOOM
DEATHBLOW
NO RETURN
CRASH

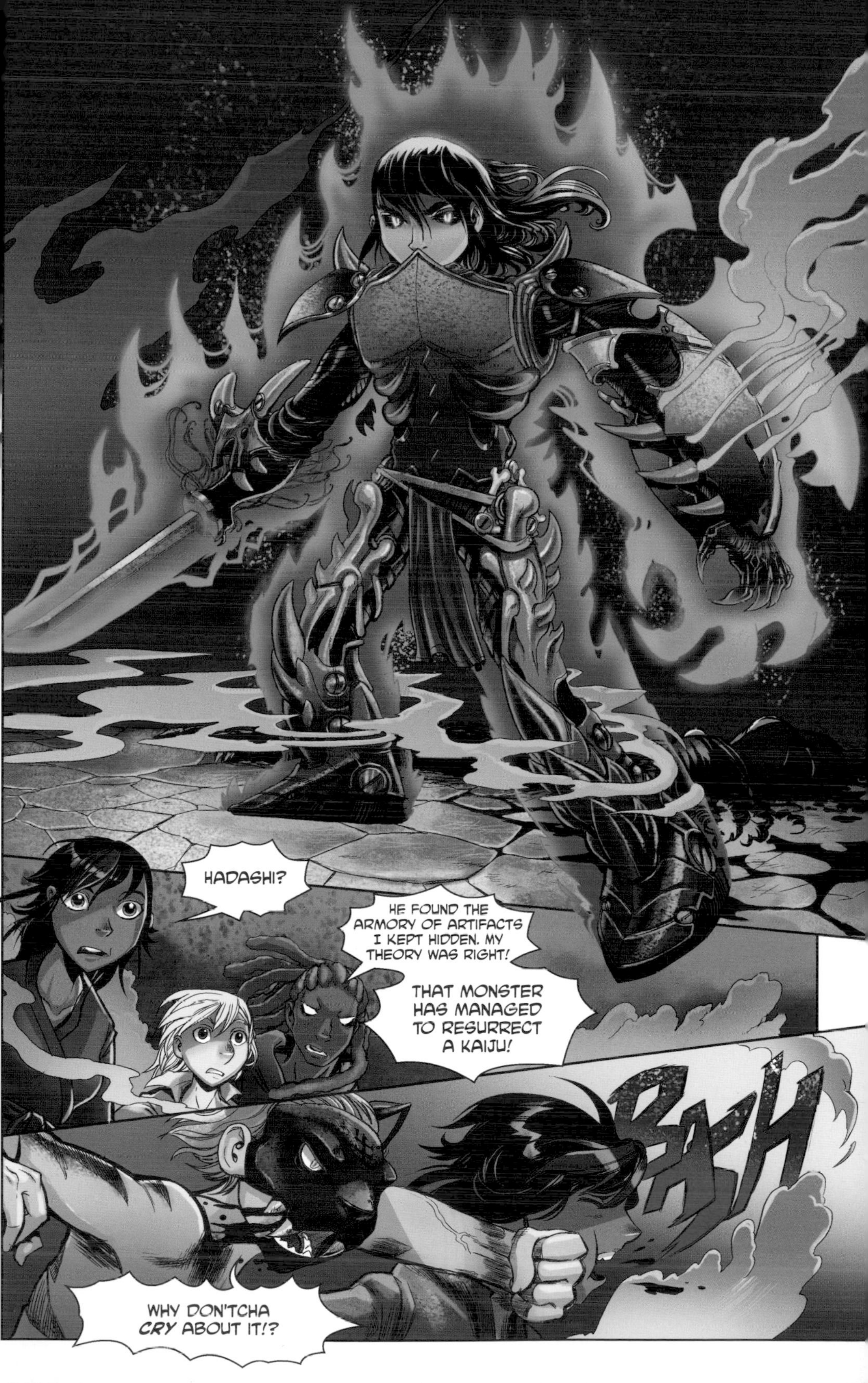
HADASHI?
HE FOUND THE ARMORY OF ARTIFACTS I KEPT HIDDEN. MY THEORY WAS RIGHT!
THAT MONSTER HAS MANAGED TO RESURRECT A KAIJU!
BAKH
WHY DON'TCHA *CRY* ABOUT IT!?

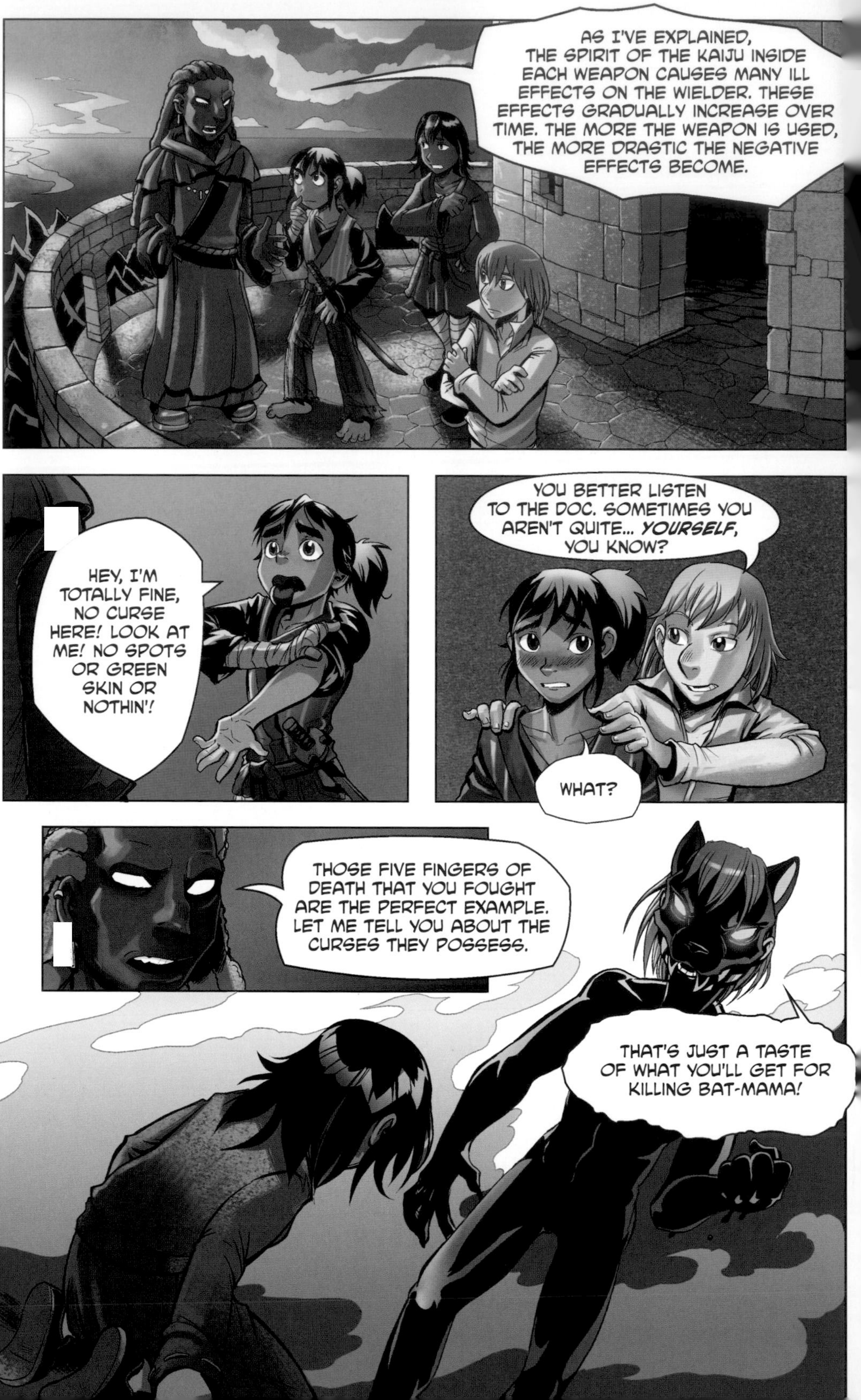
AS I'VE EXPLAINED, THE SPIRIT OF THE KAIJU INSIDE EACH WEAPON CAUSES MANY ILL EFFECTS ON THE WIELDER. THESE EFFECTS GRADUALLY INCREASE OVER TIME. THE MORE THE WEAPON IS USED, THE MORE DRASTIC THE NEGATIVE EFFECTS BECOME.
HEY, I'M TOTALLY FINE, NO CURSE HERE! LOOK AT ME! NO SPOTS OR GREEN SKIN OR NOTHIN'!
YOU BETTER LISTEN TO THE DOC. SOMETIMES YOU AREN'T QUITE... *YOURSELF*, YOU KNOW?
WHAT?
THOSE FIVE FINGERS OF DEATH THAT YOU FOUGHT ARE THE PERFECT EXAMPLE. LET ME TELL YOU ABOUT THE CURSES THEY POSSESS.
THAT'S JUST A TASTE OF WHAT YOU'LL GET FOR KILLING BAT-MAMA!

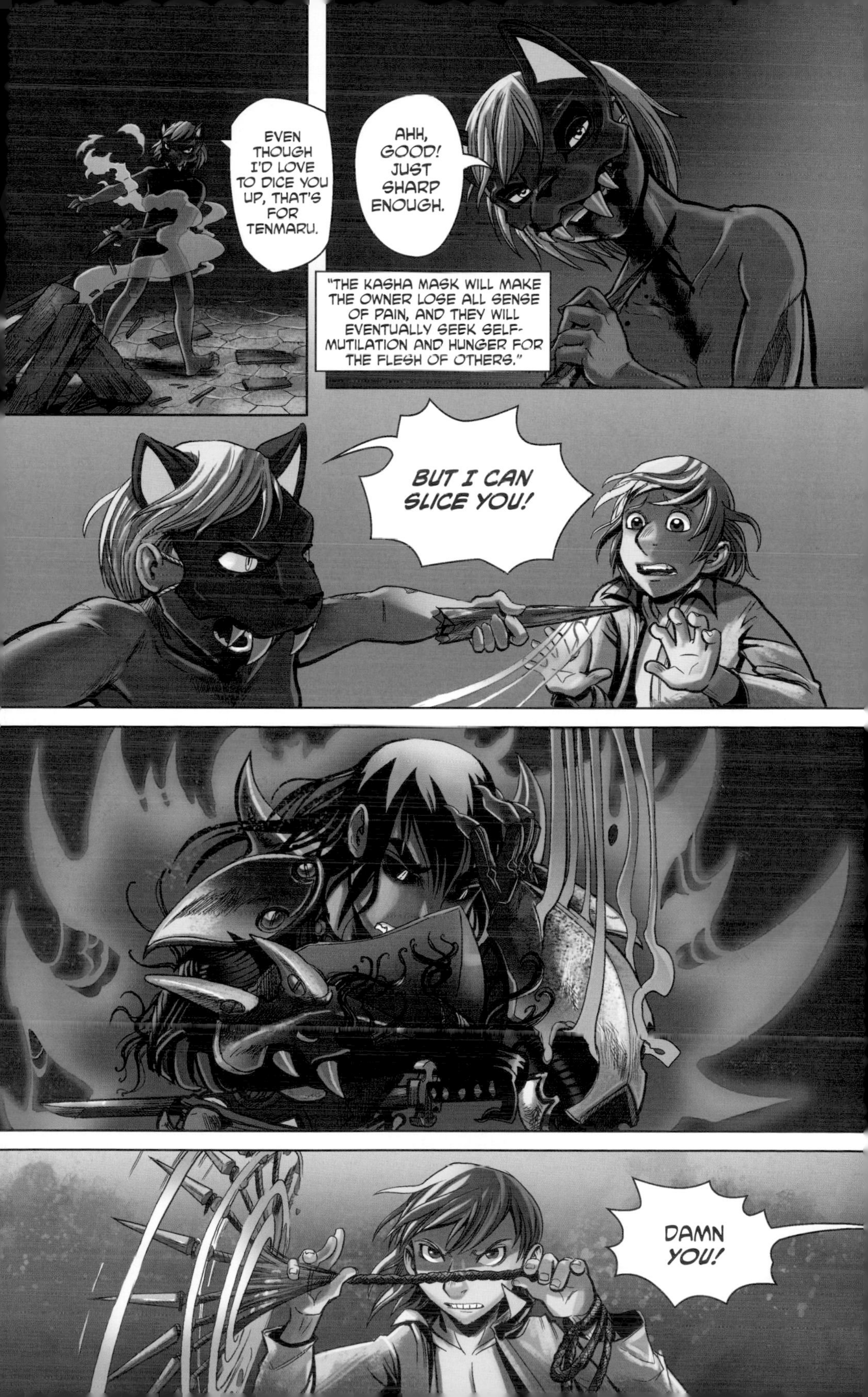
EVEN THOUGH I'D LOVE TO DICE YOU UP, THAT'S FOR TENMARU.
AHH, GOOD! JUST SHARP ENOUGH.
"THE KASHA MASK WILL MAKE THE OWNER LOSE ALL SENSE OF PAIN, AND THEY WILL EVENTUALLY SEEK SELF-MUTILATION AND HUNGER FOR THE FLESH OF OTHERS."
BUT I CAN SLICE YOU!
DAMN YOU!

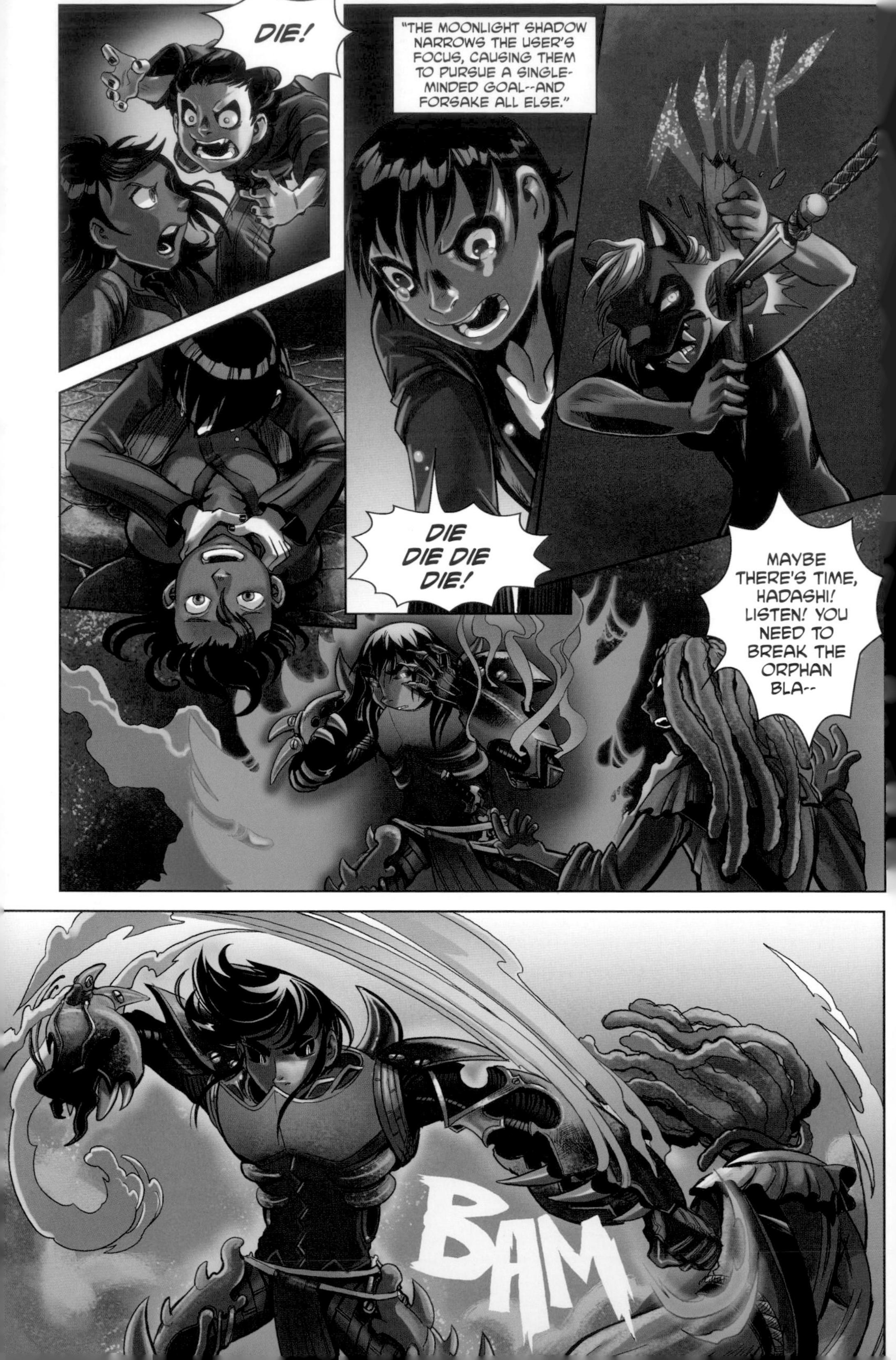
DIE!
"THE MOONLIGHT SHADOW NARROWS THE USER'S FOCUS, CAUSING THEM TO PURSUE A SINGLE-MINDED GOAL--AND FORSAKE ALL ELSE."
THOK
DIE DIE DIE DIE!
MAYBE THERE'S TIME, HADASHI! LISTEN! YOU NEED TO BREAK THE ORPHAN BLA--
BAM

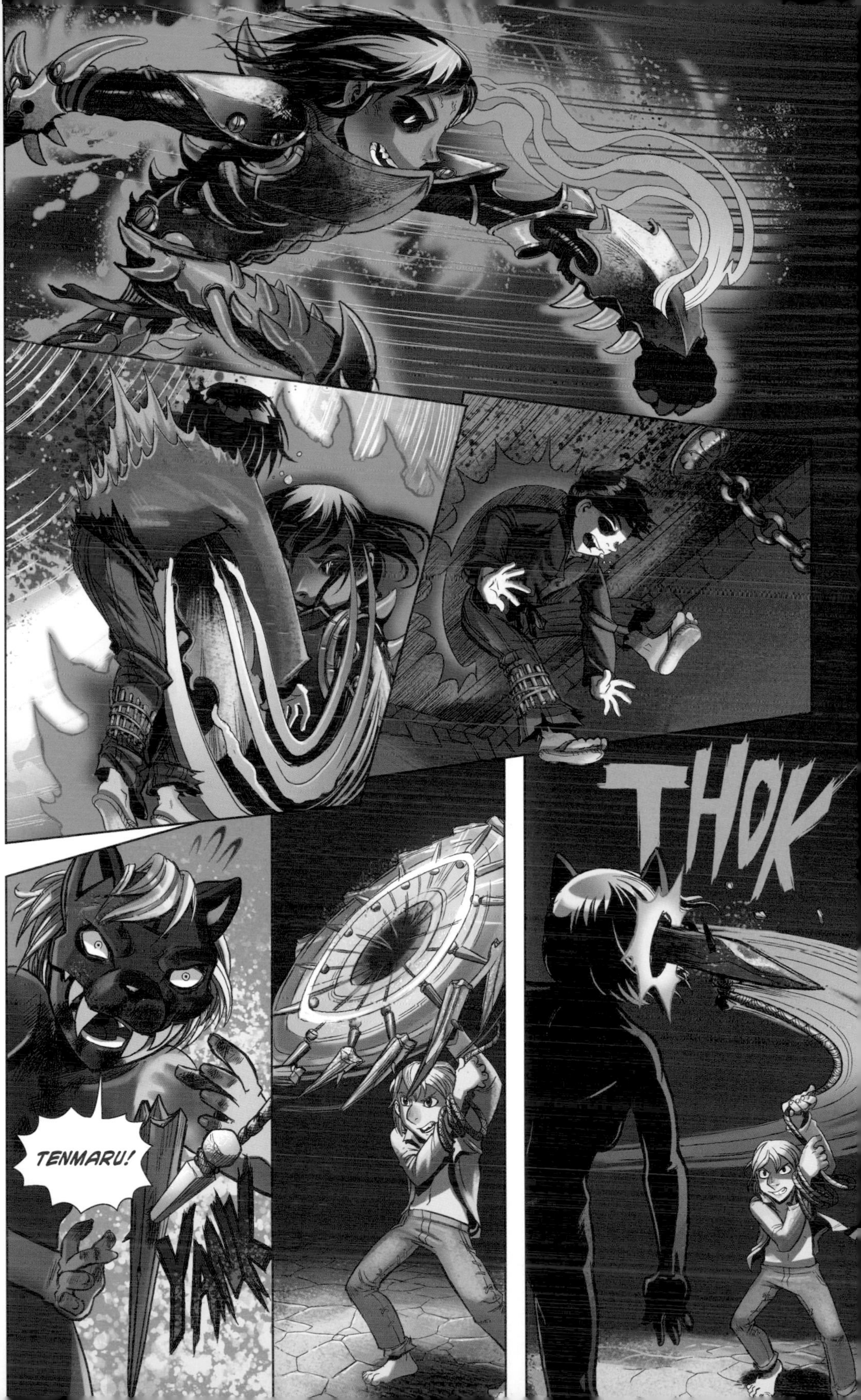

THOK
TENMARU!
YAH!

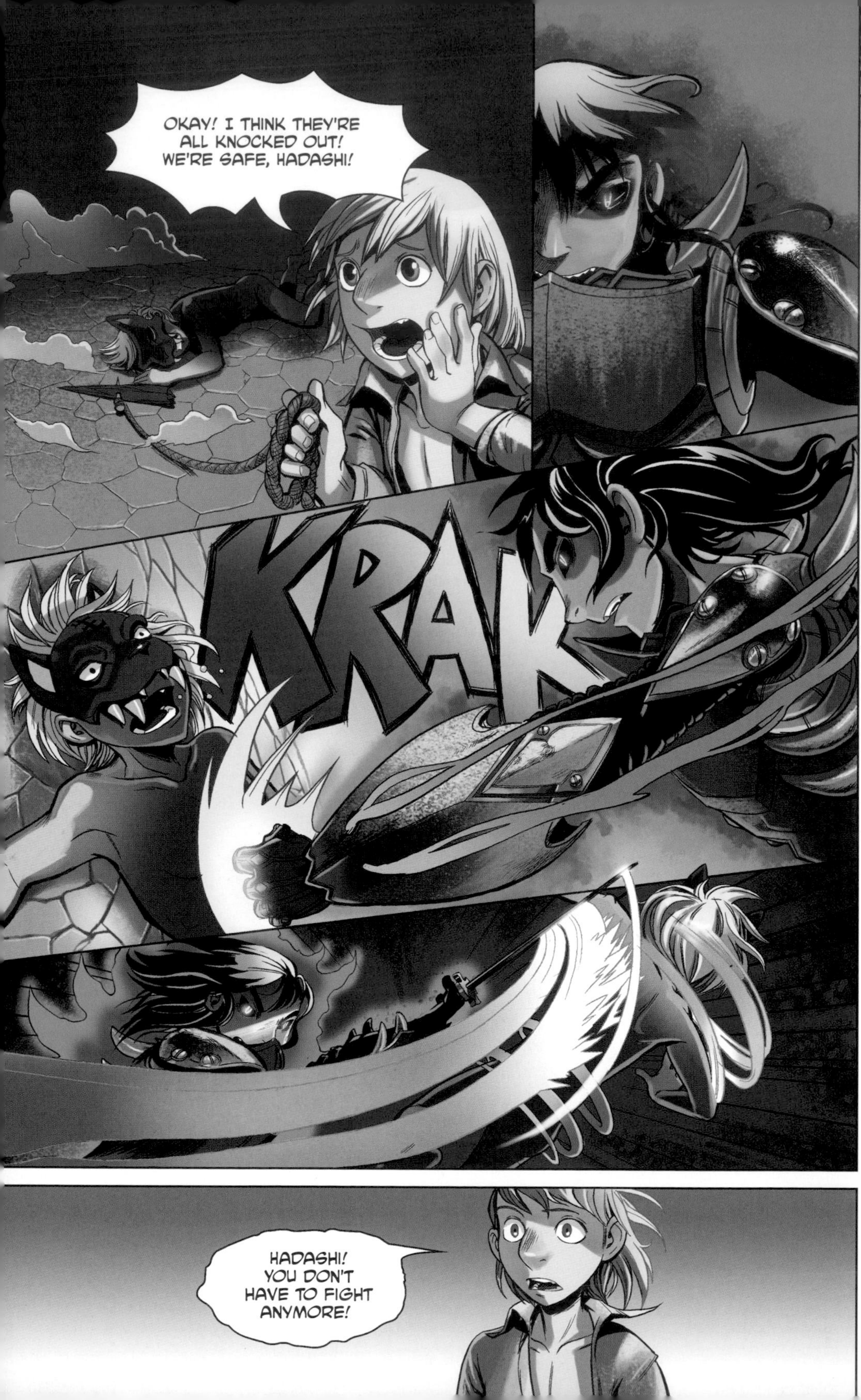
OKAY! I THINK THEY'RE ALL KNOCKED OUT! WE'RE SAFE, HADASHI!
KRAK
HADASHI! YOU DON'T HAVE TO FIGHT ANYMORE!

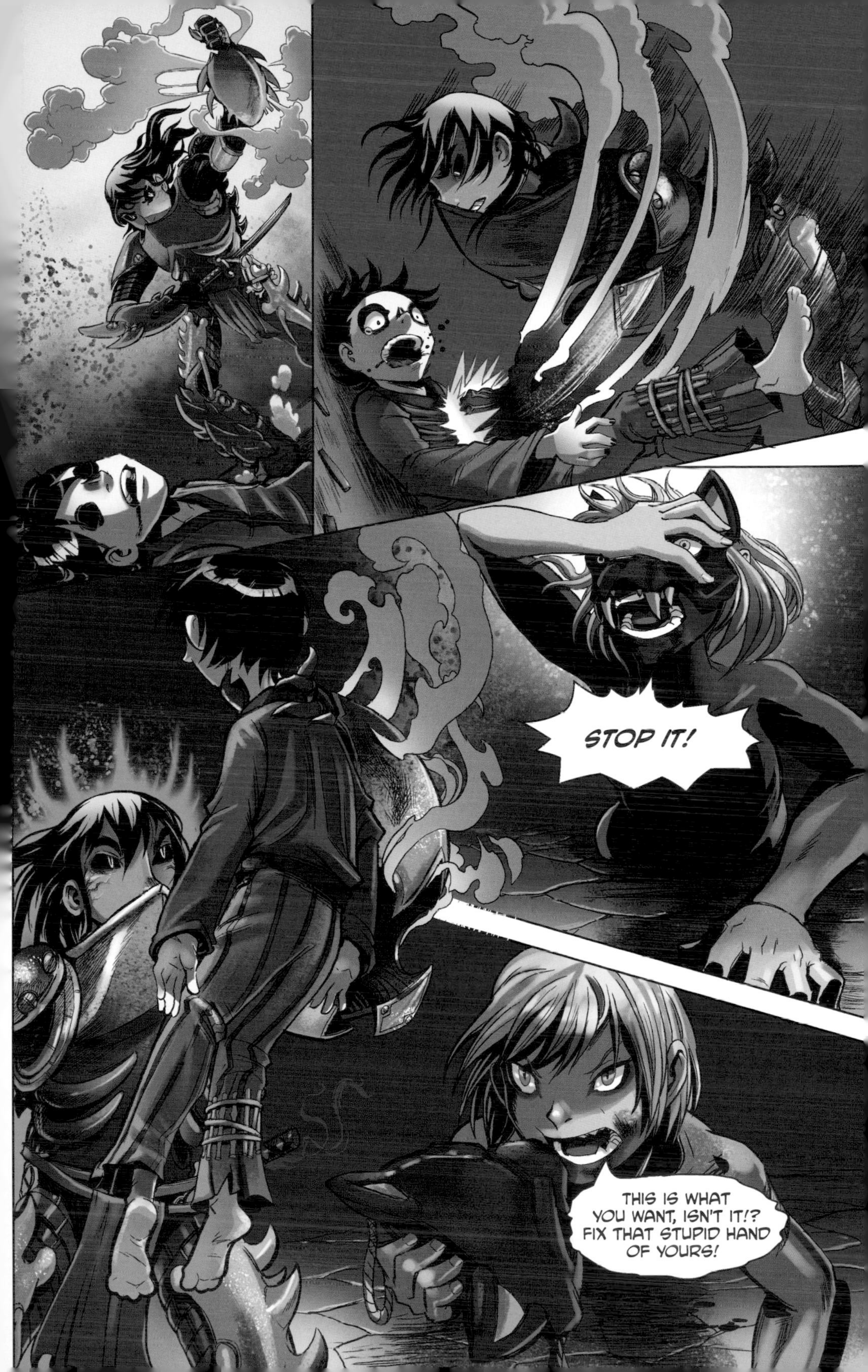
STOP IT!
THIS IS WHAT YOU WANT, ISN'T IT!? FIX THAT STUPID HAND OF YOURS!

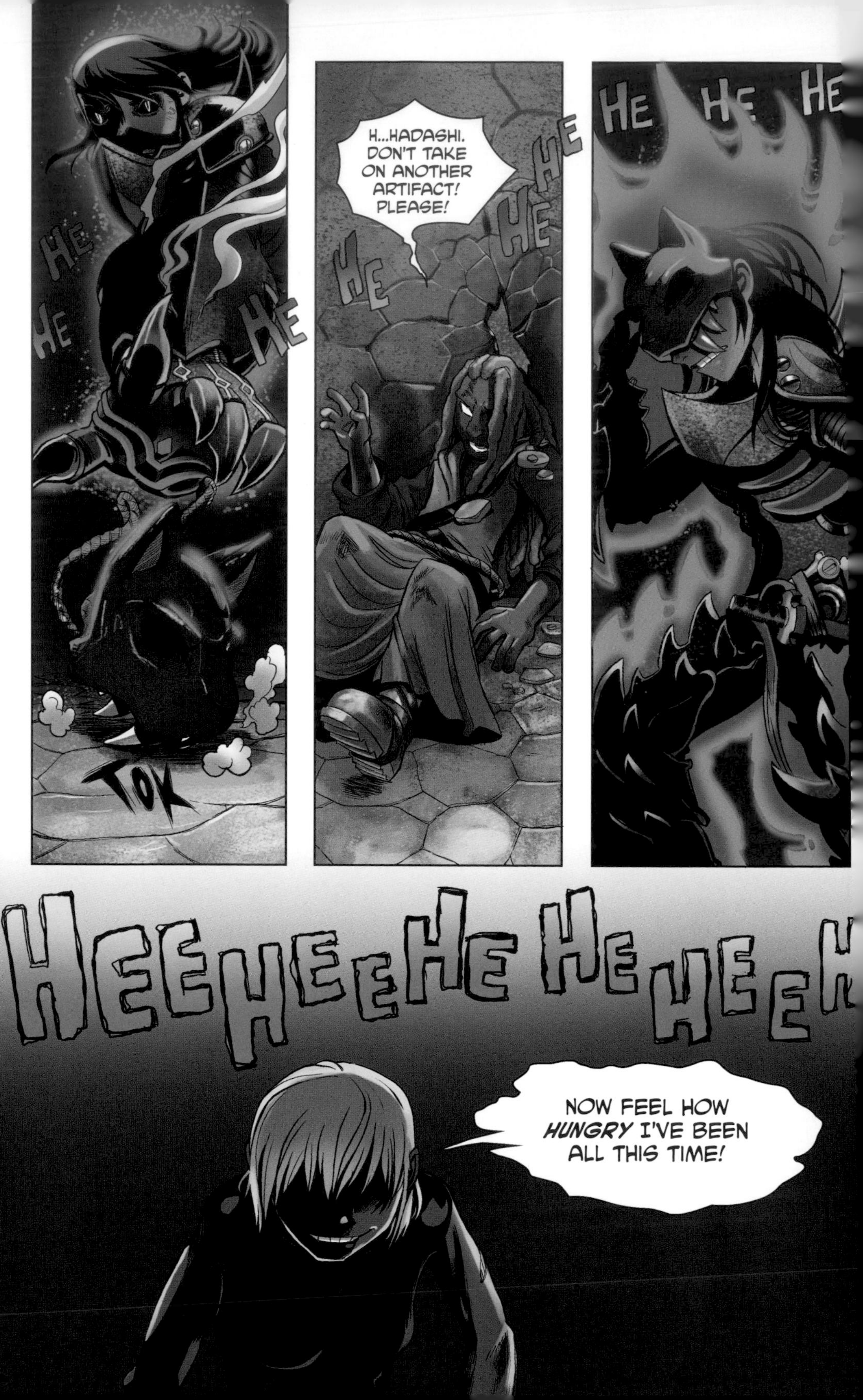
HE
HE
HE
TOK
H...HADASHI. DON'T TAKE ON ANOTHER ARTIFACT! PLEASE!
HE
HE
HE
HE
HE
HE
HE
HEEHEEHEHEHEEH
NOW FEEL HOW *HUNGRY* I'VE BEEN ALL THIS TIME!

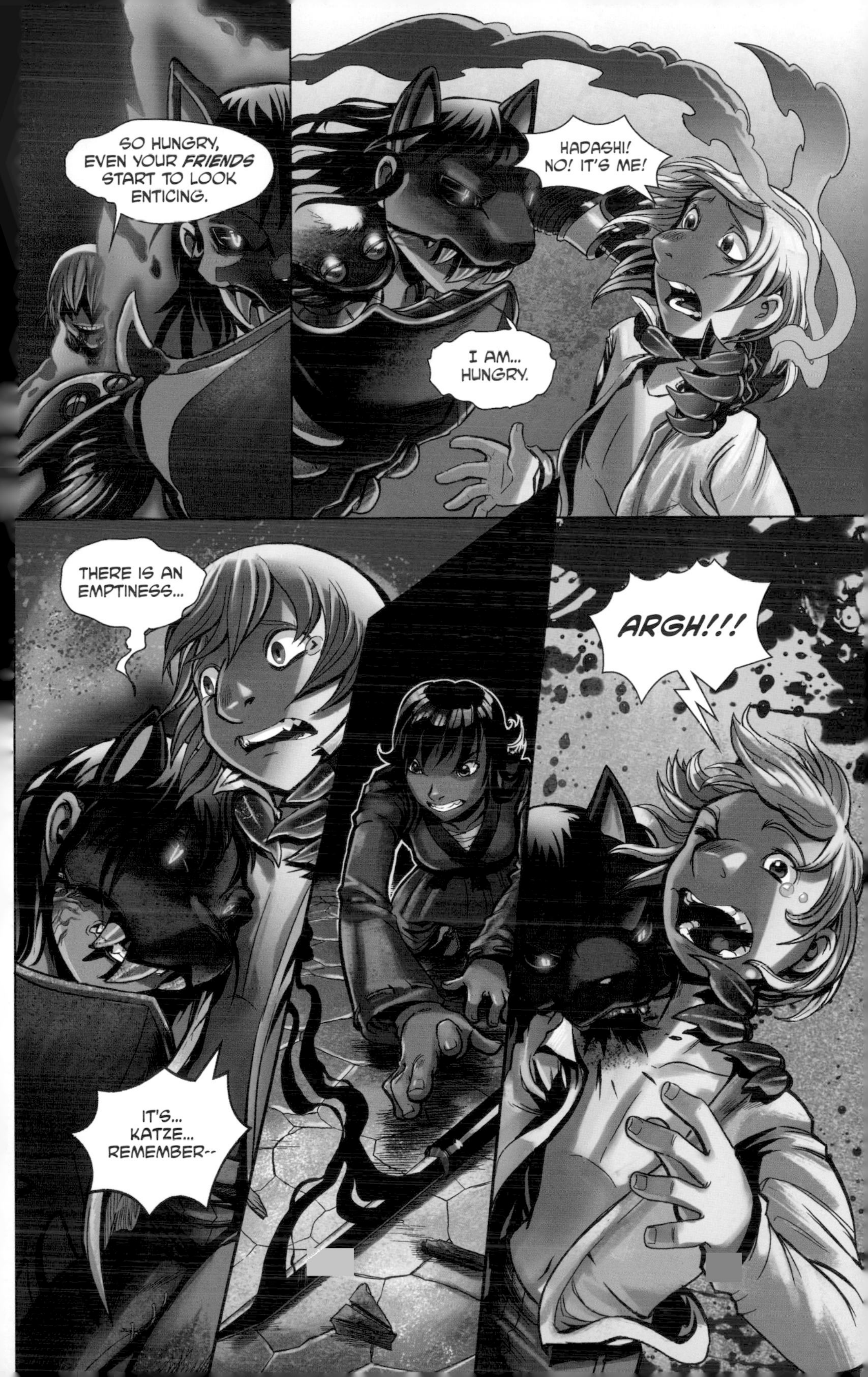
SO HUNGRY, EVEN YOUR *FRIENDS* START TO LOOK ENTICING.
HADASHI! NO! IT'S ME!
I AM... HUNGRY.
THERE IS AN EMPTINESS...
ARGH!!!
IT'S... KATZE... REMEMBER--

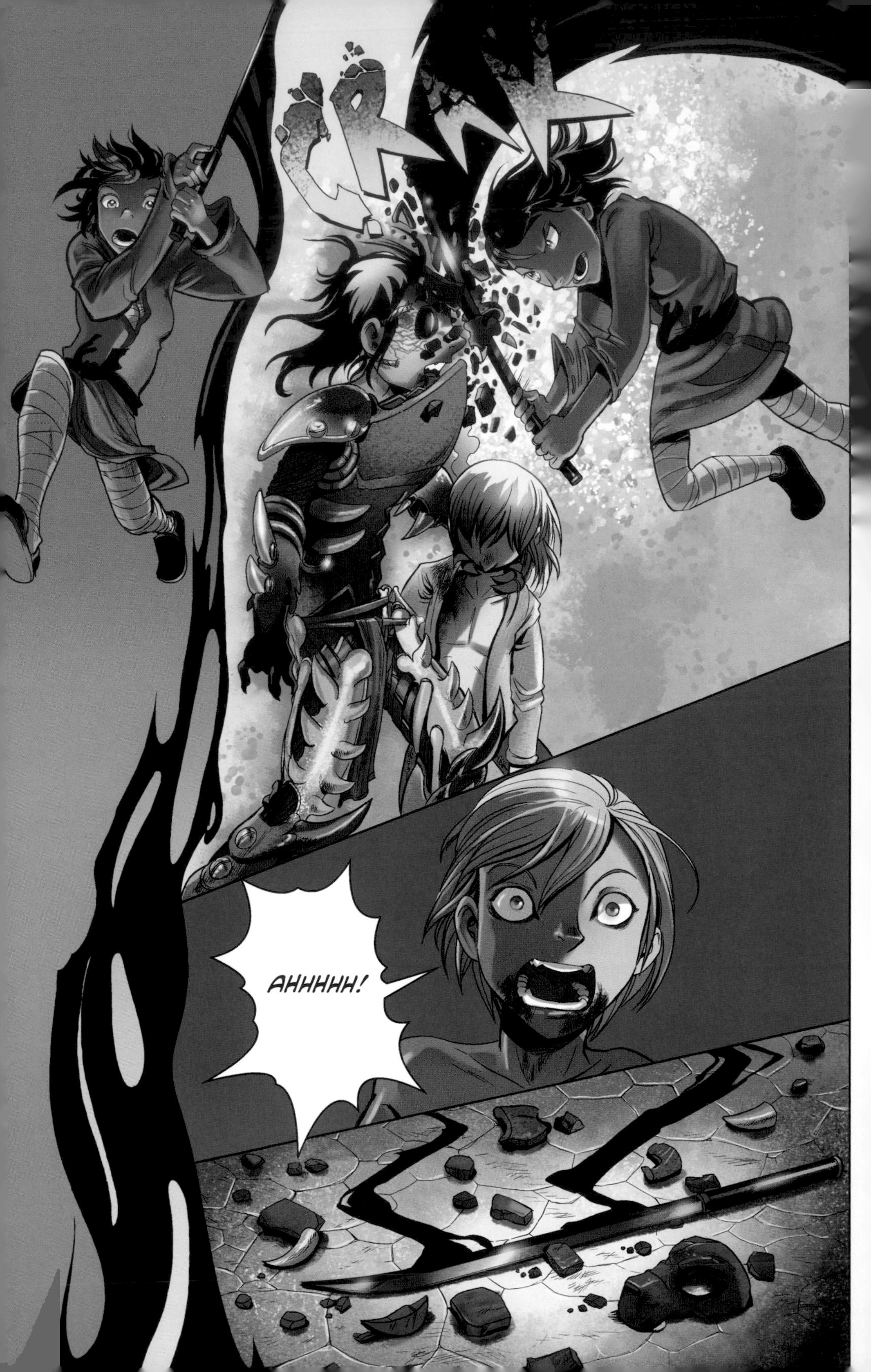
AHHHHH!

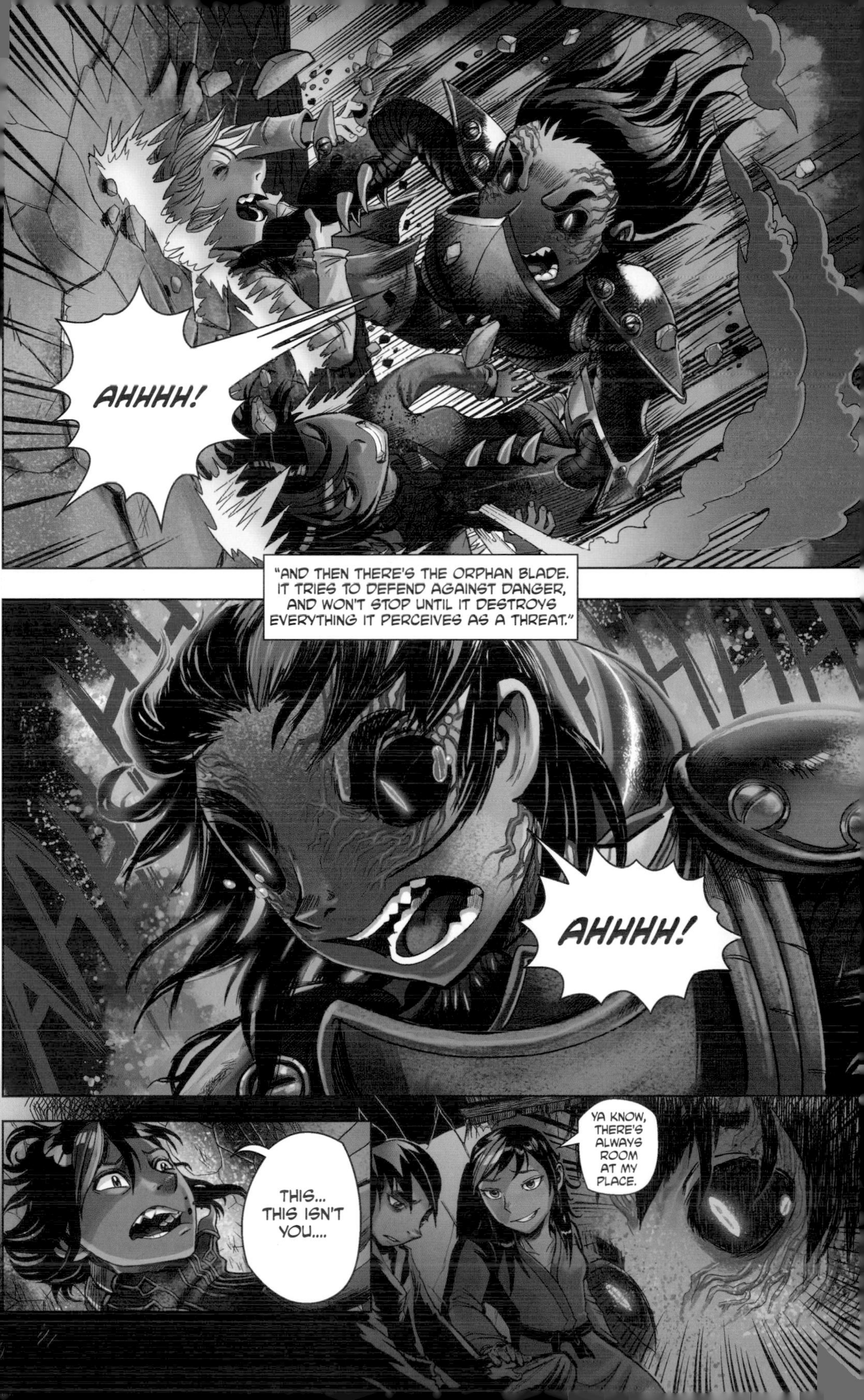
AHHHH!
"AND THEN THERE'S THE ORPHAN BLADE. IT TRIES TO DEFEND AGAINST DANGER, AND WON'T STOP UNTIL IT DESTROYS EVERYTHING IT PERCEIVES AS A THREAT."
AHHHH!
THIS... THIS ISN'T YOU....
YA KNOW, THERE'S ALWAYS ROOM AT MY PLACE.

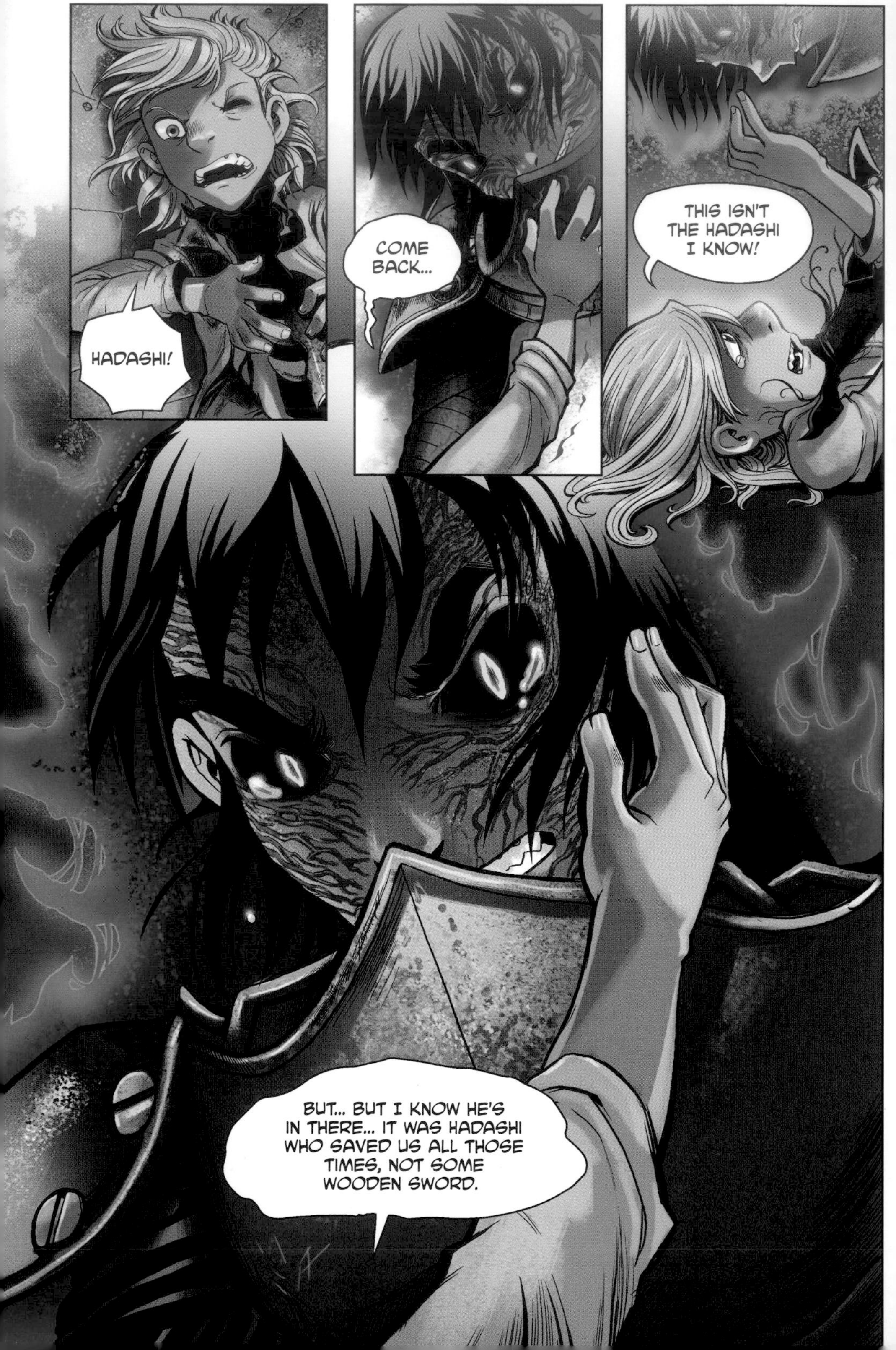
HADASHI!
COME BACK...
THIS ISN'T THE HADASHI I KNOW!
BUT... BUT I KNOW HE'S IN THERE... IT WAS HADASHI WHO SAVED US ALL THOSE TIMES, NOT SOME WOODEN SWORD.

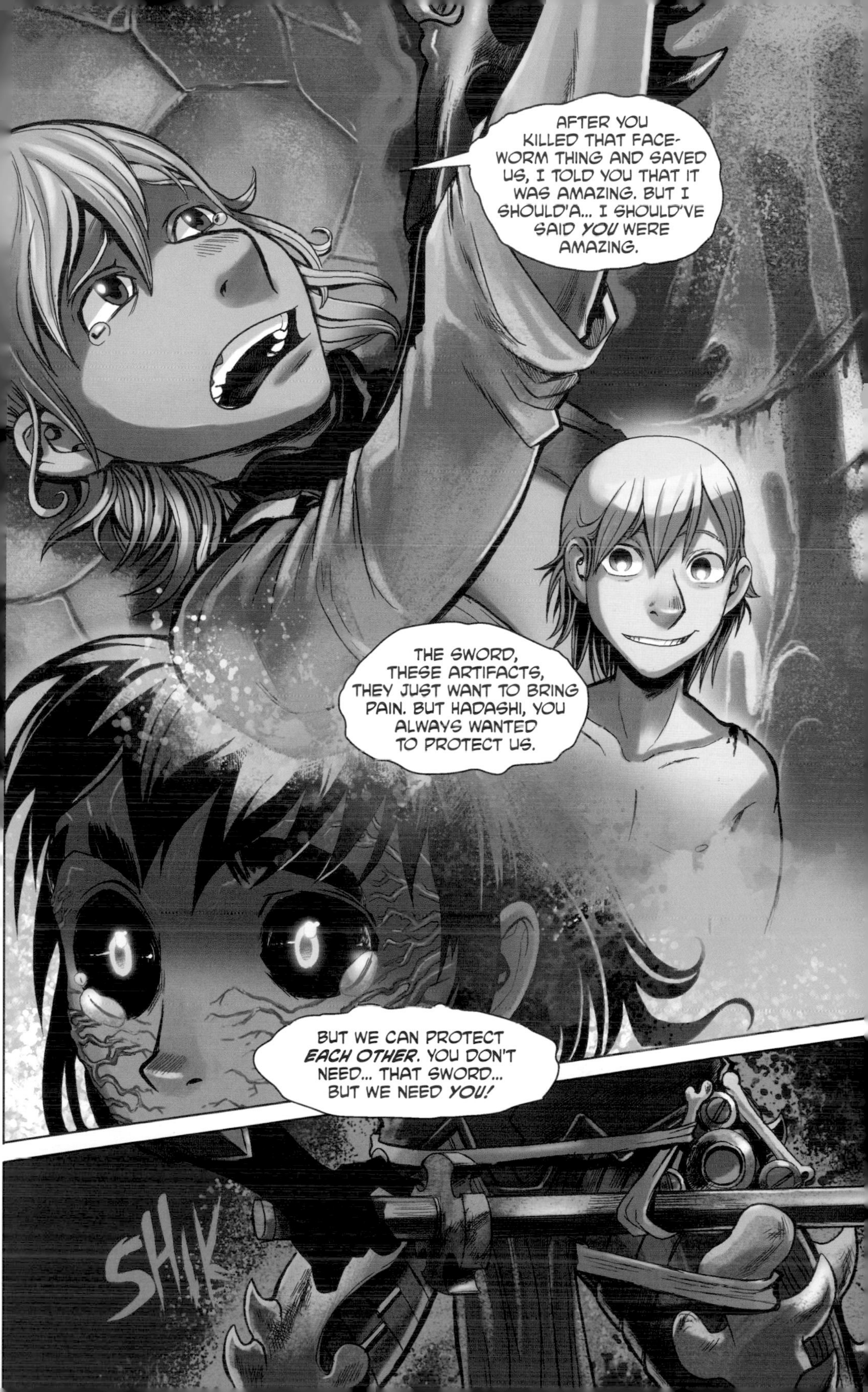
AFTER YOU KILLED THAT FACE-WORM THING AND SAVED US, I TOLD YOU THAT IT WAS AMAZING. BUT I SHOULD'A... I SHOULD'VE SAID *YOU* WERE AMAZING.
THE SWORD, THESE ARTIFACTS, THEY JUST WANT TO BRING PAIN. BUT HADASHI, YOU ALWAYS WANTED TO PROTECT US.
BUT WE CAN PROTECT *EACH OTHER*. YOU DON'T NEED... THAT SWORD... BUT WE NEED *YOU!*
SHIK

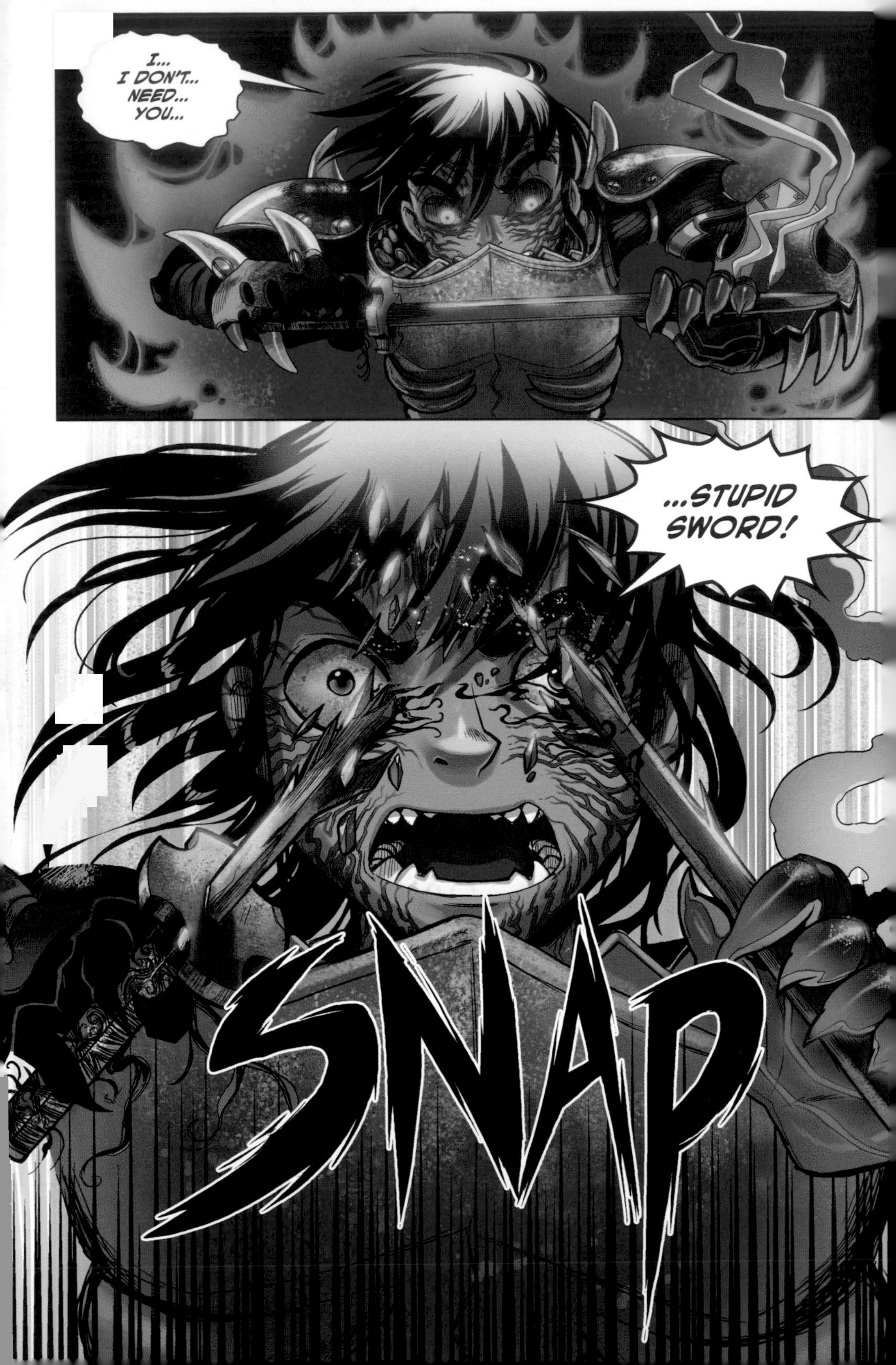
I... I DON'T... NEED... YOU...
...STUPID SWORD!
SNAP

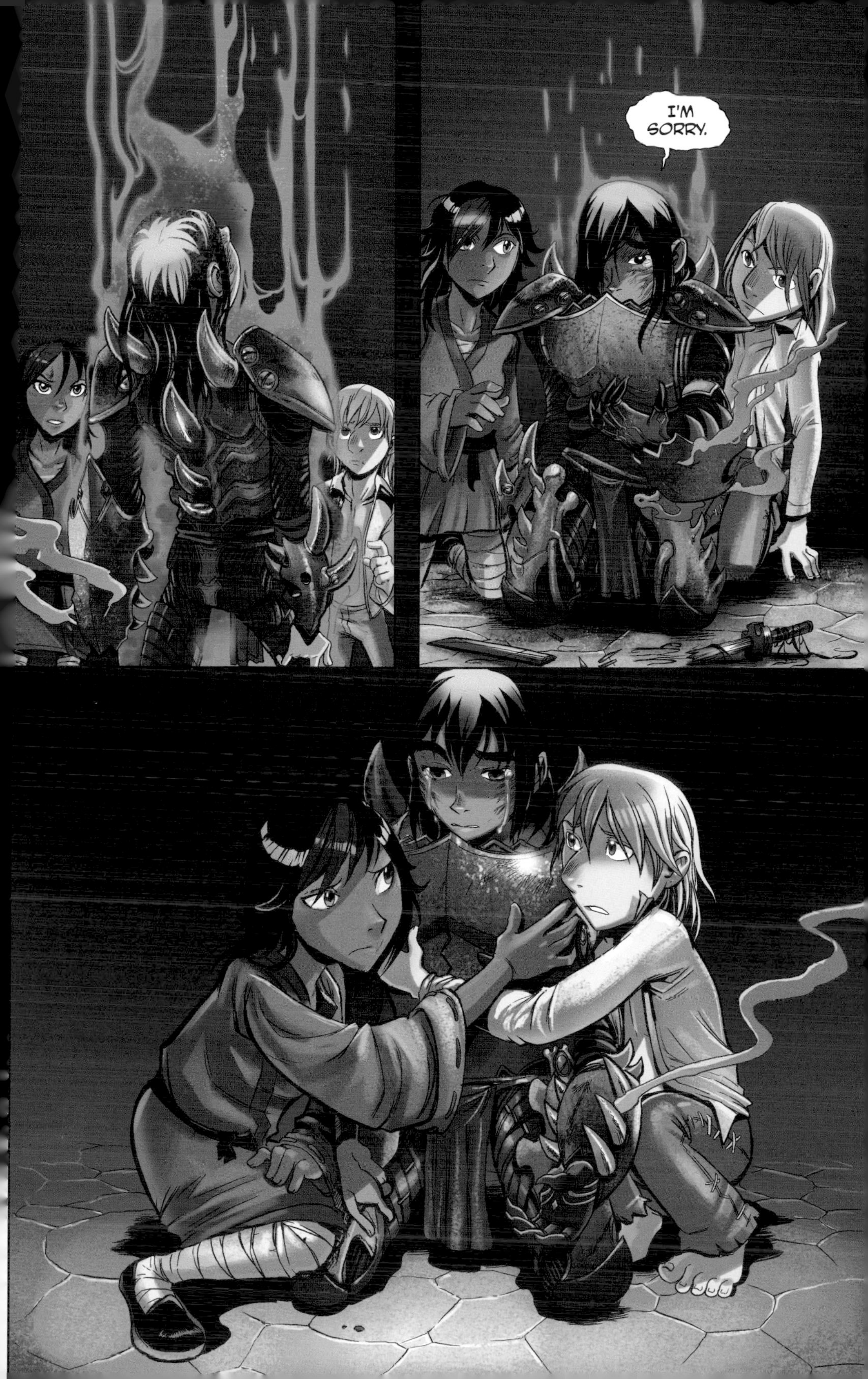
I'M SORRY.

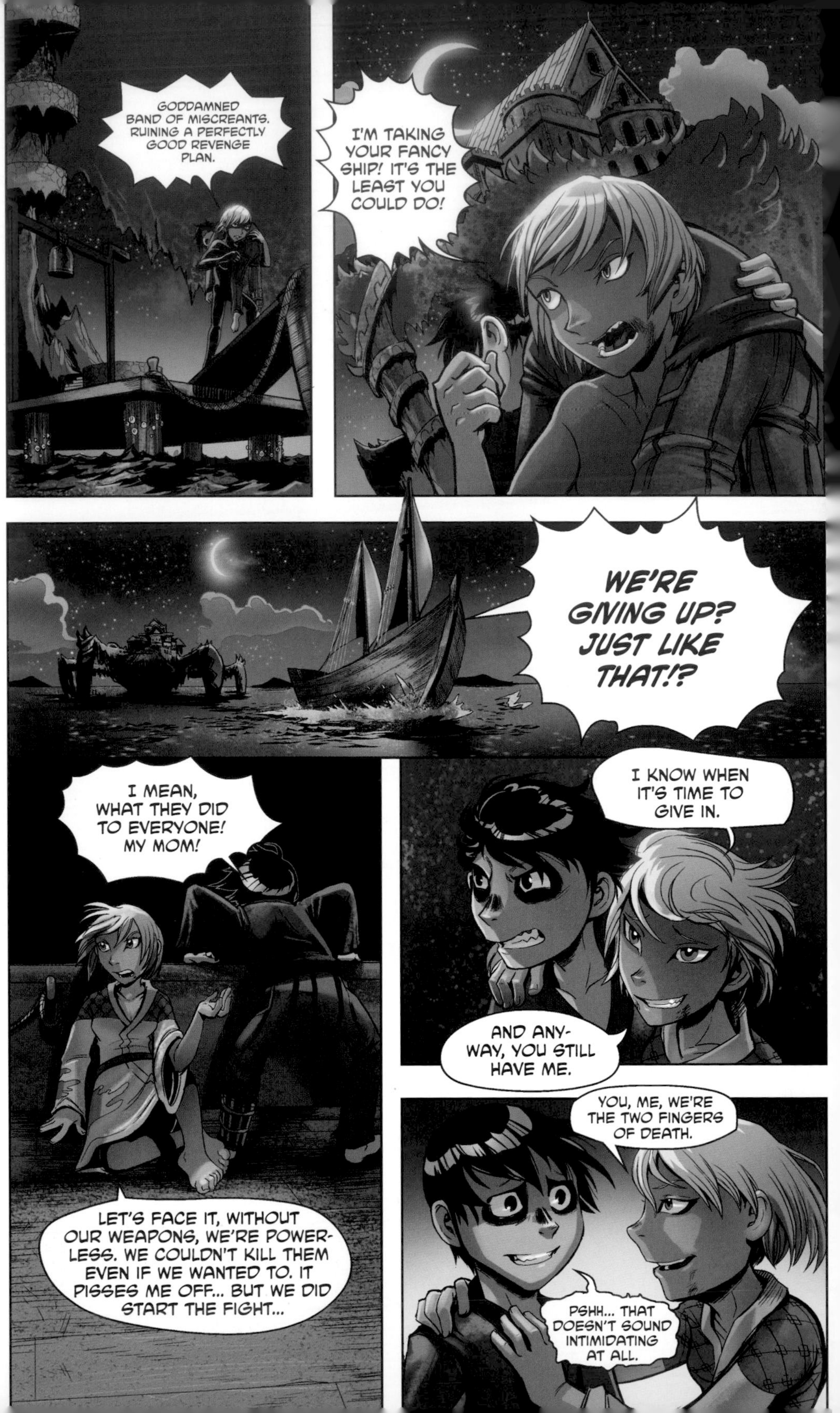
GODDAMNED BAND OF MISCREANTS. RUINING A PERFECTLY GOOD REVENGE PLAN.
I'M TAKING YOUR FANCY SHIP! IT'S THE LEAST YOU COULD DO!
WE'RE GIVING UP? JUST LIKE THAT!?
I MEAN, WHAT THEY DID TO EVERYONE! MY MOM!
LET'S FACE IT, WITHOUT OUR WEAPONS, WE'RE POWER-LESS. WE COULDN'T KILL THEM EVEN IF WE WANTED TO. IT PISSES ME OFF... BUT WE DID START THE FIGHT...
I KNOW WHEN IT'S TIME TO GIVE IN.
AND ANY-WAY, YOU STILL HAVE ME.
YOU, ME, WE'RE THE TWO FINGERS OF DEATH.
PSHH... THAT DOESN'T SOUND INTIMIDATING AT ALL.

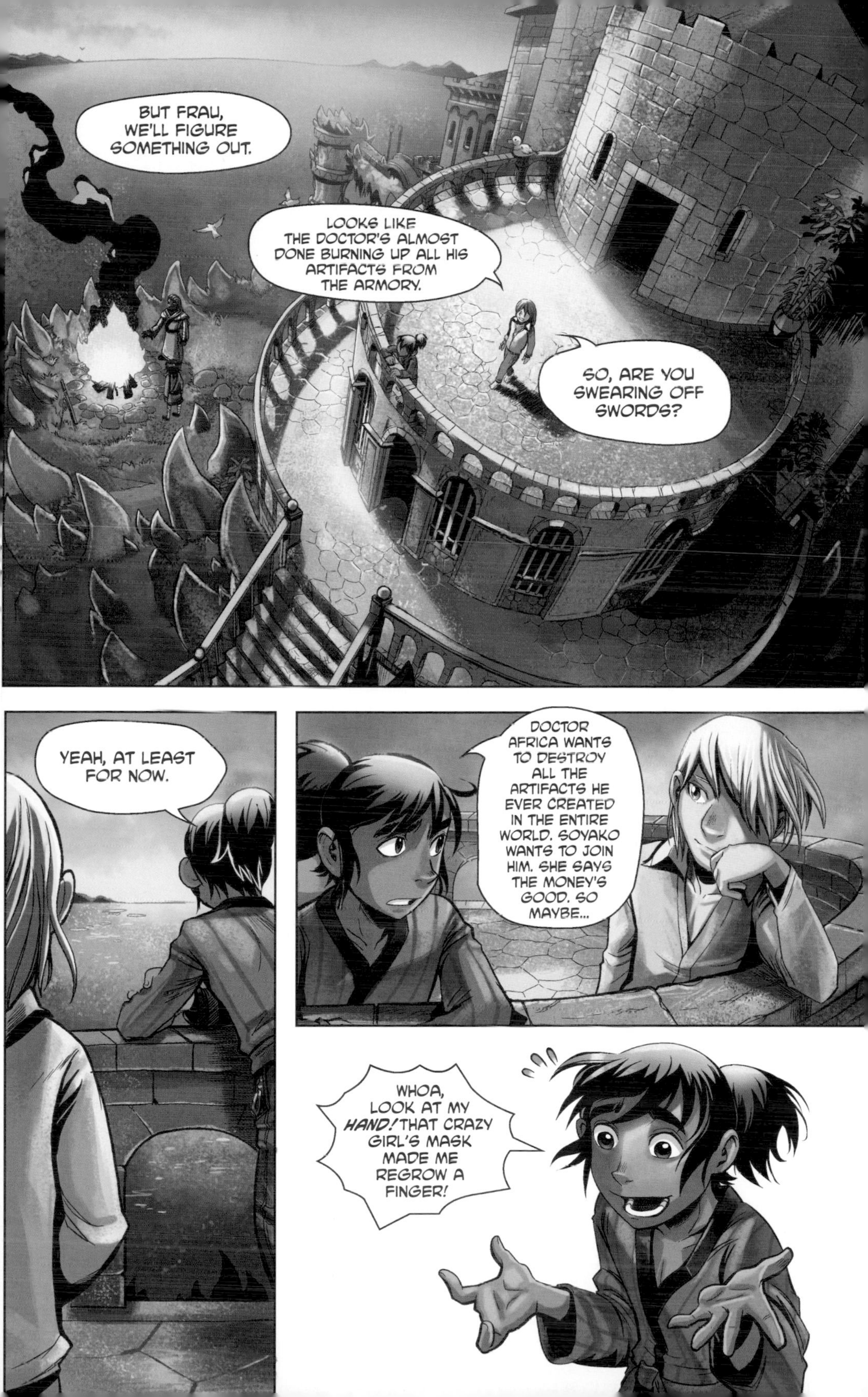
BUT FRAU, WE'LL FIGURE SOMETHING OUT.
LOOKS LIKE THE DOCTOR'S ALMOST DONE BURNING UP ALL HIS ARTIFACTS FROM THE ARMORY.
SO, ARE YOU SWEARING OFF SWORDS?
YEAH, AT LEAST FOR NOW.
DOCTOR AFRICA WANTS TO DESTROY ALL THE ARTIFACTS HE EVER CREATED IN THE ENTIRE WORLD. SOYAKO WANTS TO JOIN HIM. SHE SAYS THE MONEY'S GOOD. SO MAYBE...
WHOA, LOOK AT MY *HAND!* THAT CRAZY GIRL'S MASK MADE ME REGROW A FINGER!

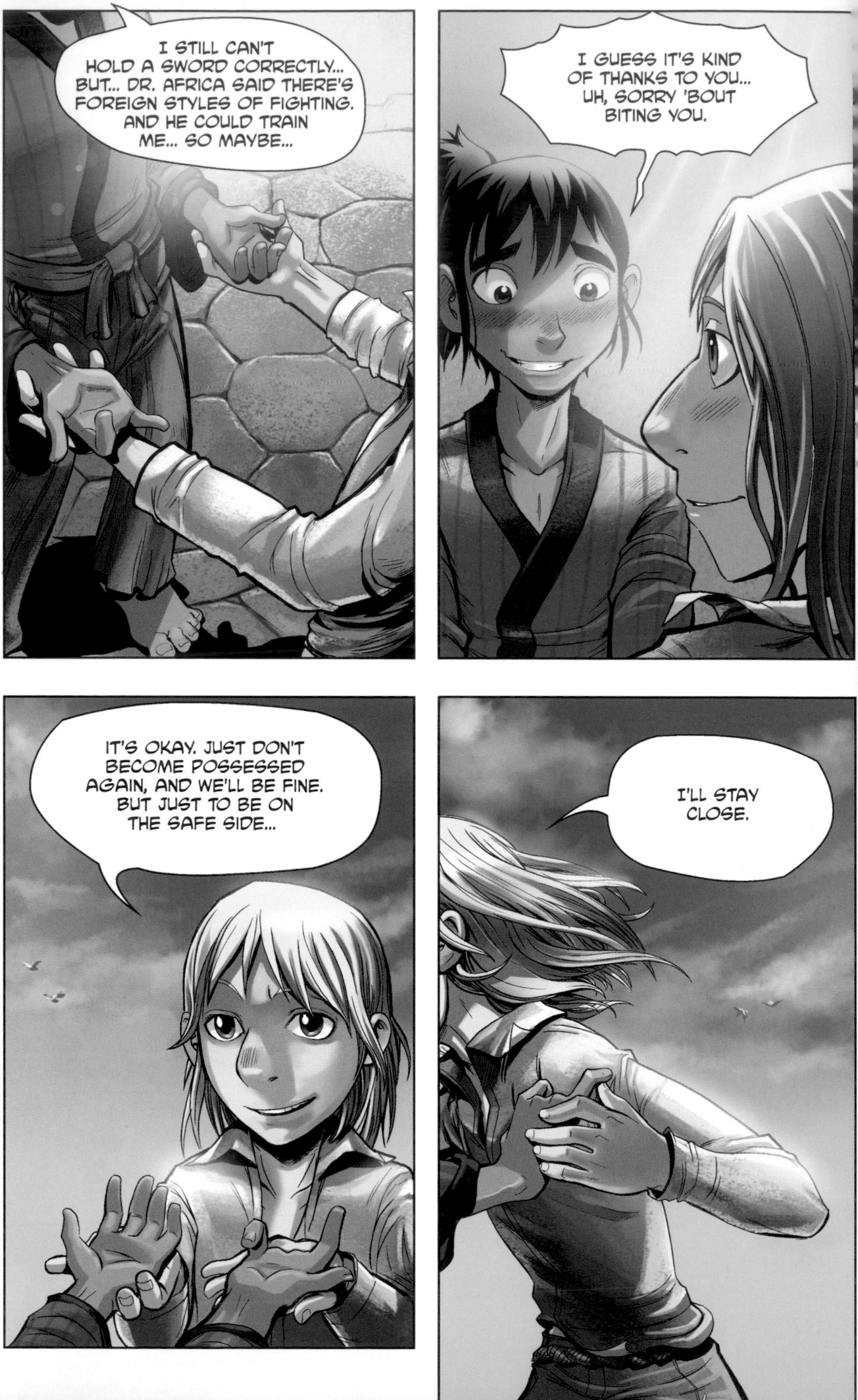
I STILL CAN'T HOLD A SWORD CORRECTLY... BUT... DR. AFRICA SAID THERE'S FOREIGN STYLES OF FIGHTING. AND HE COULD TRAIN ME... SO MAYBE...
I GUESS IT'S KIND OF THANKS TO YOU... UH, SORRY 'BOUT BITING YOU.
IT'S OKAY. JUST DON'T BECOME POSSESSED AGAIN, AND WE'LL BE FINE. BUT JUST TO BE ON THE SAFE SIDE...
I'LL STAY CLOSE.

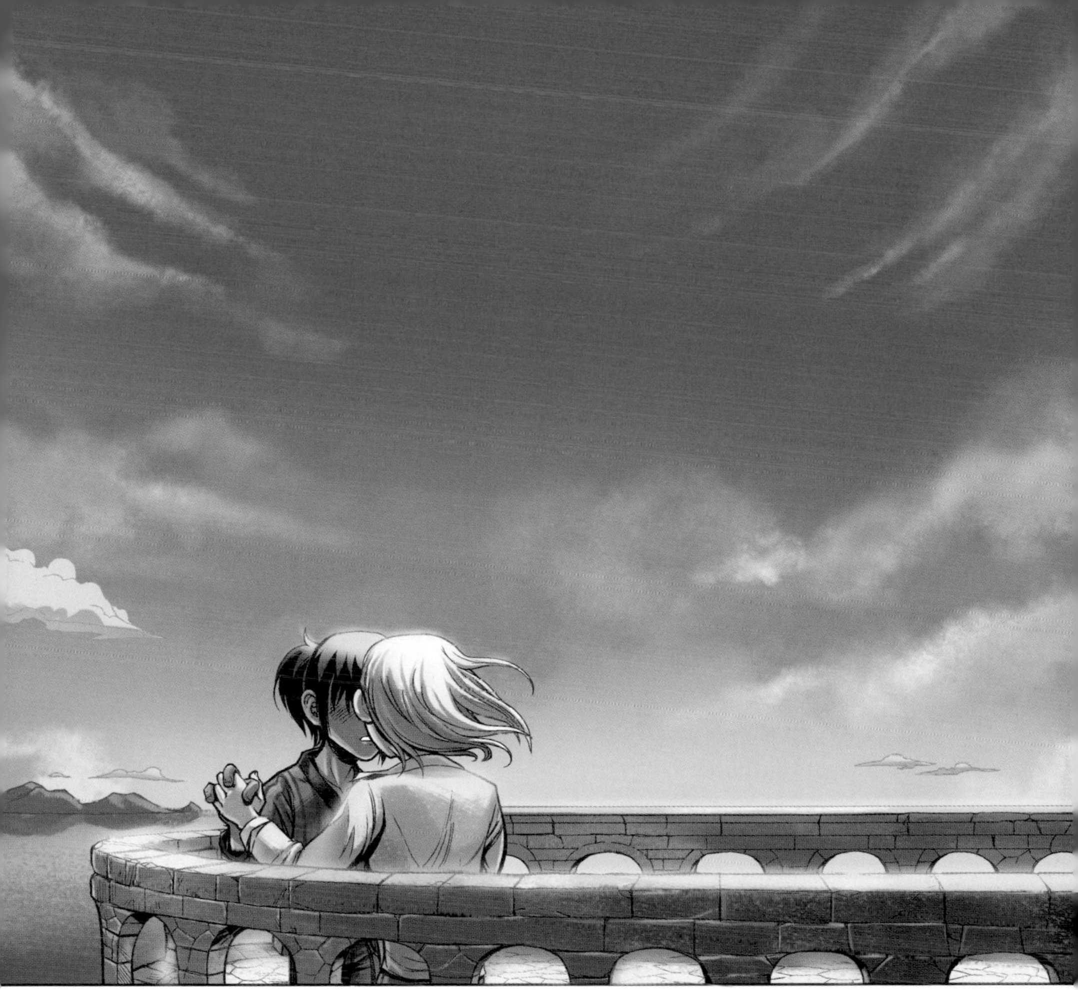

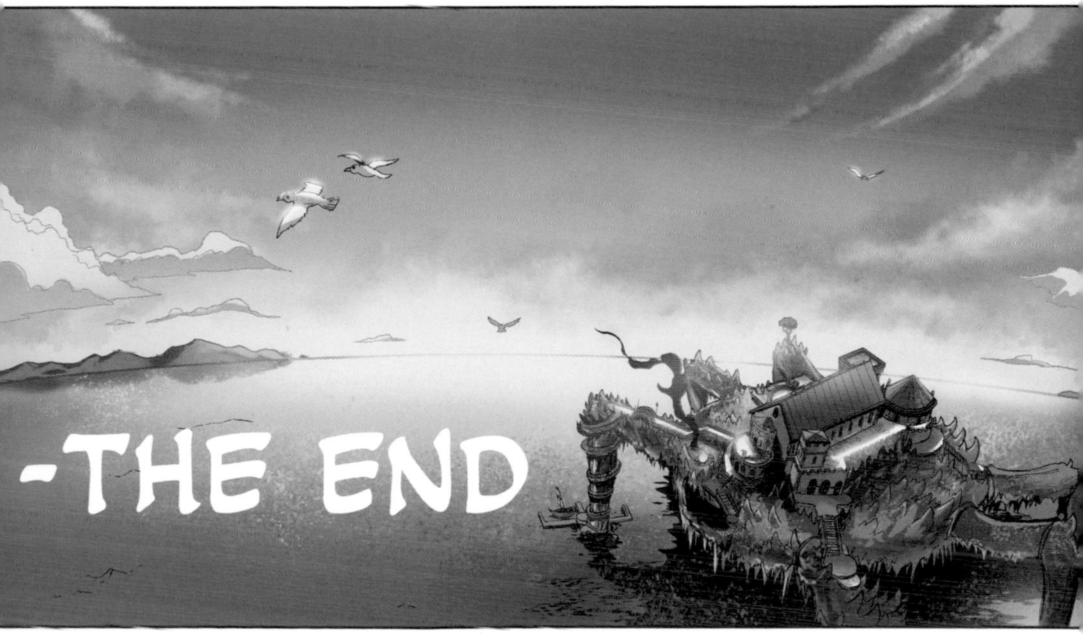
-THE END

Marcus "Nick" Almand was a talented writer with a big heart and an even bigger imagination.

In 2006, he turned his writing attention to comics, eventually creating the independent comic book *Razor Kid*, as well as contributing to the Harvey Award-nominated anthology *Unique Tales*. Nick was also the creator and author of the YA science fiction novel and short story series *Sons of Nowhere*.

Some of Nick's favorite movies included *Pacific Rim*, *Let the Right One In* (also *Let Me In*), and *X-Men 2*. Inspiring books/comics were Stephen King's *Carrie*, Michael Crichton's *Jurassic Park*, *Neon Genesis Evangelion*, and *Knights of the Dinner Table*. Oddly enough, Nick's first inspiration to write as a child came from the *Mortal Kombat II* video game. Make of that what you will.

Nick passed away in 2013 and is dearly missed by his friends, family, and everyone at Oni Press. *Orphan Blade* was his first book with Oni.

"To the young man whose laughter is now a memorial among us--"

– from *Memorial* by Clifton Gachagua

I wanted this book to come out more than anything because it was the event that brought us together as good friends. I'll miss you, Nick.

– Jake Myler

Nick was one of the kindest, funniest, and most caring people I've ever met. The world is a better place for having had him in it. I miss you, my friend.

– Jill Beaton

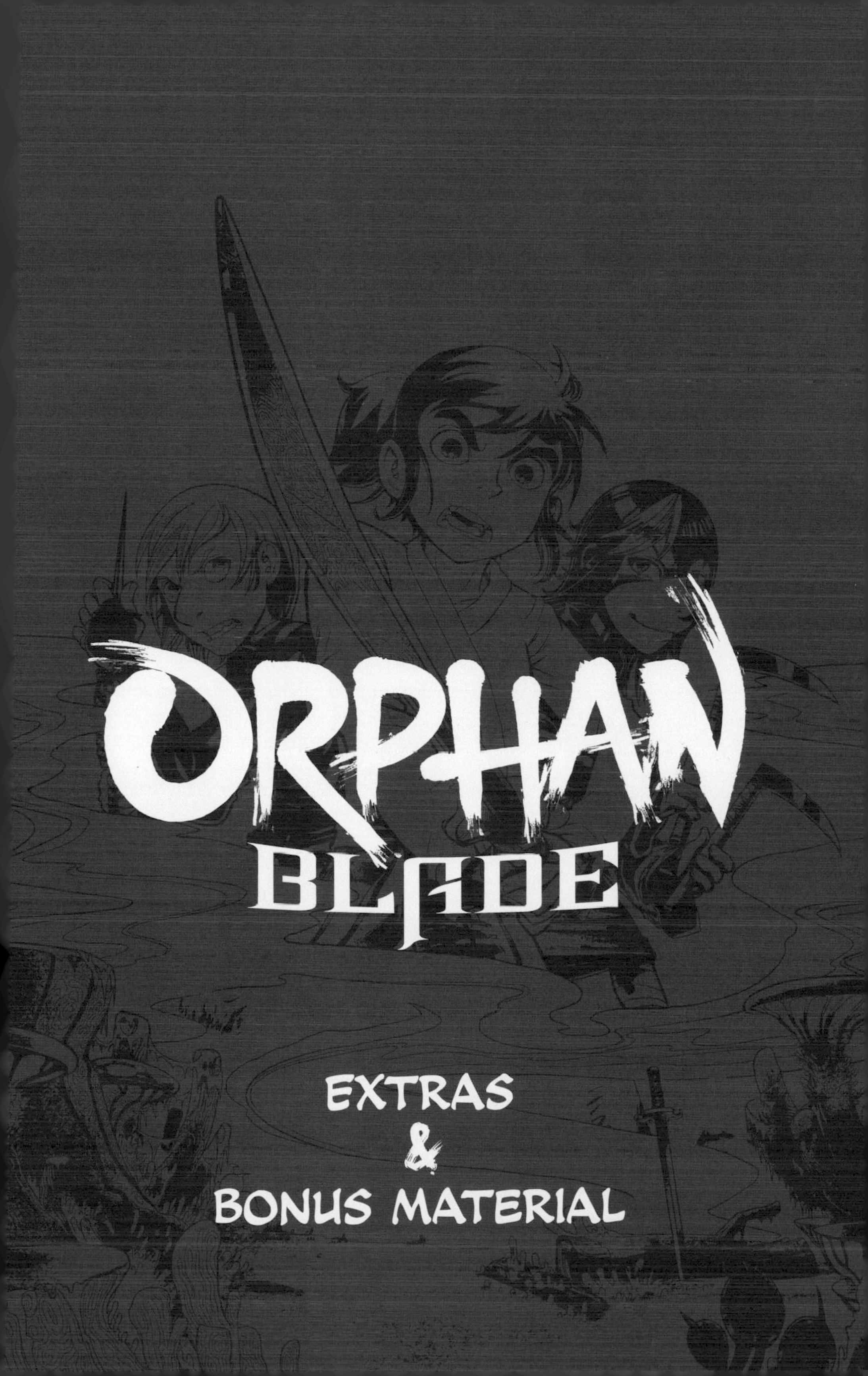
ORPHAN
BLADE
EXTRAS
&
BONUS MATERIAL

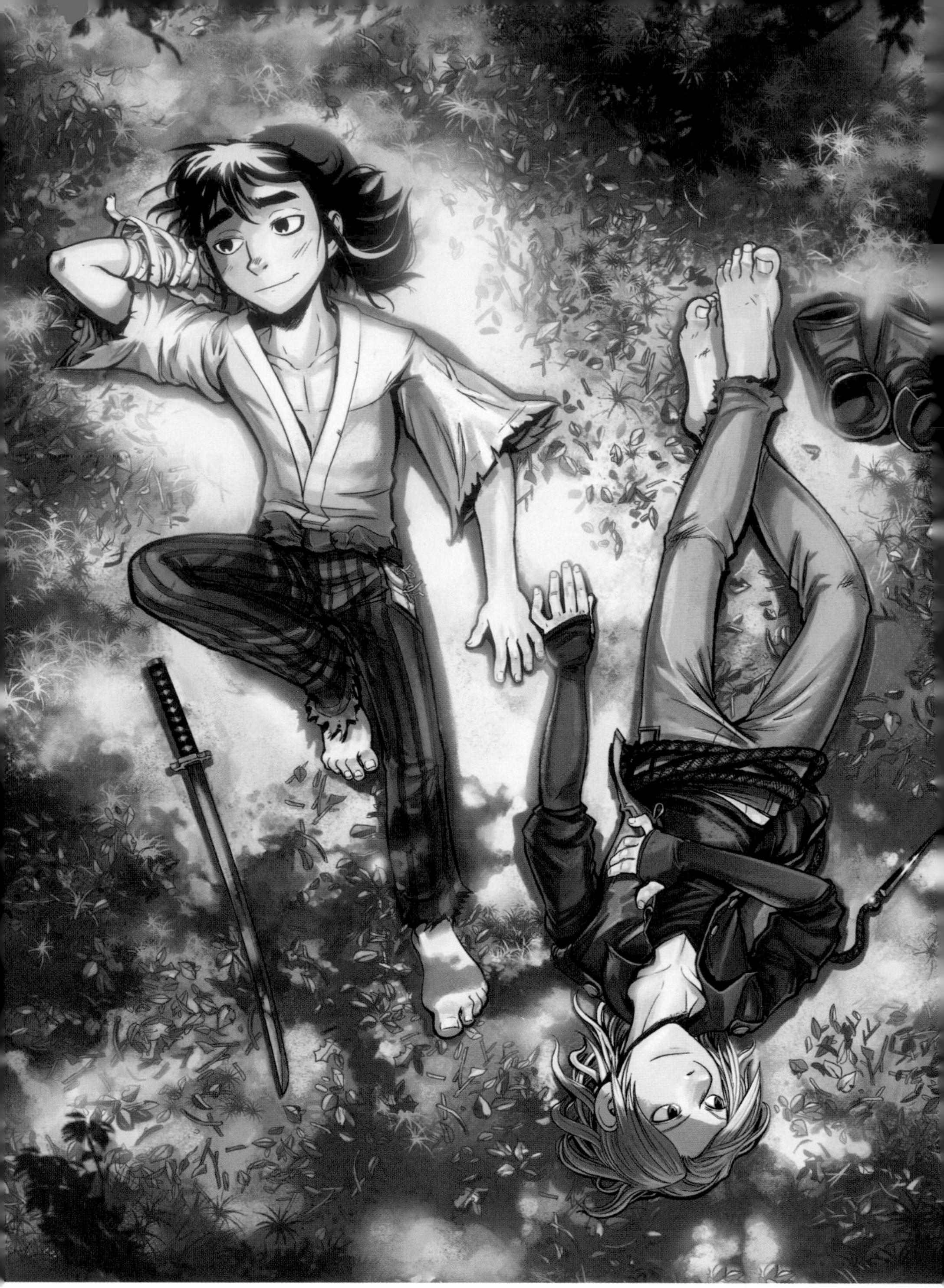

Jake: This is a illustration I made while working on Orphan Blade.

Nick: OMG this is ADORABLE!!!!! >w<

ORPHAN BLADE

CHARACTERS

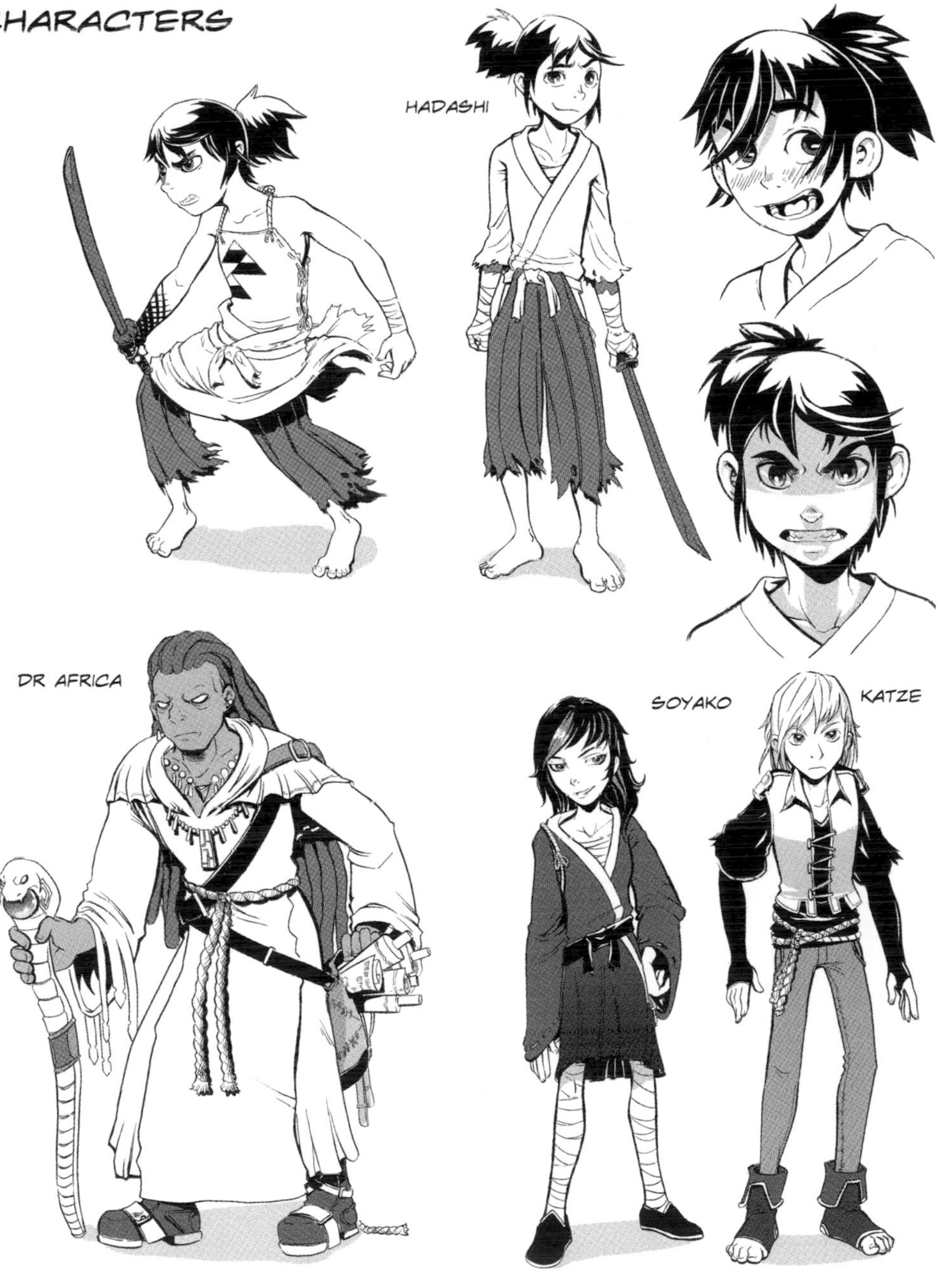
HADASHI
DR AFRICA
SOYAKO
KATZE

Jake: The first character design sheet that I made for Orphan Blade in 2012. I sent a quick email to Jill Beaton [Editor] and Nick: Hello Jill! I think this should be pretty cool to work with you and Marcus on something!

Jill responded: Nick's notes echo anything I have to say on these. And he knows exactly what he wants to see in these designs, so I trust your collaborations to be spot on. :)

4 days later, **Jill** responded again: Hey there, Jake! Congratulations, we've got approval to move forward on Orphan Blade with you attached as artist.

PROCESS FOR CREATING A PAGE!

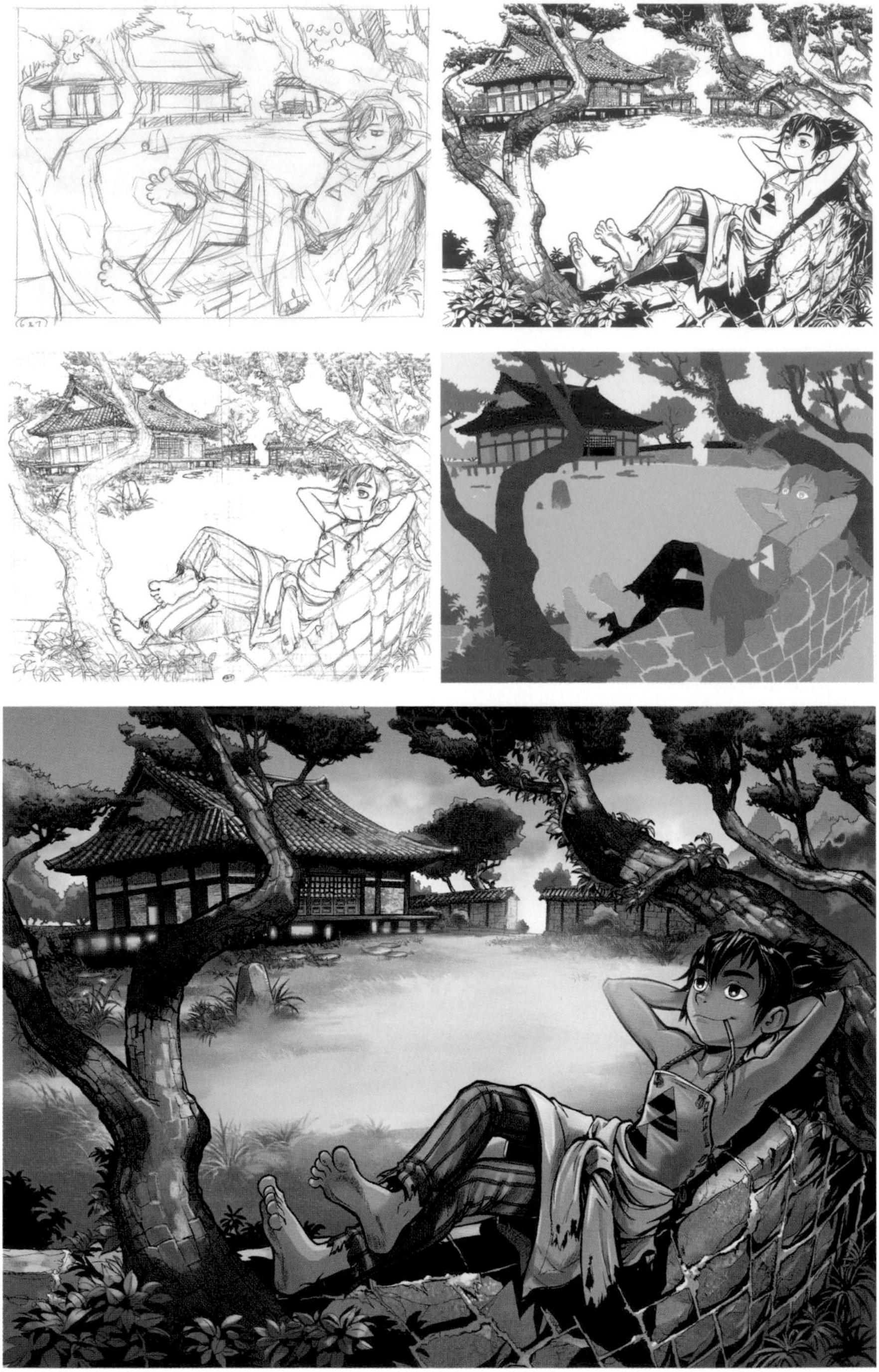

Everything starts with a rough **thumbnail**. Then after the whole book was drawn out quickly this way and approved, I'll go on to drawing it more carefully on a big sheet of bristol paper with a **pencil**. After this, the page is scanned and the black **lines** are added in the computer using a tablet pen. A **flatter** comes in at this point and just fills in everything with various colors that can be used to add the final **colors**.

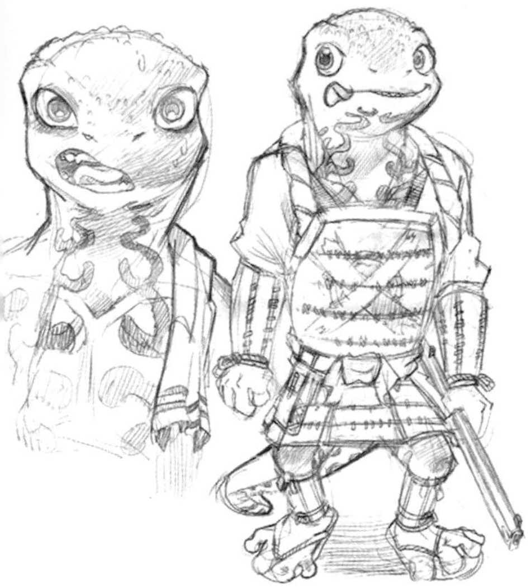

Jake: A character that didn't get put into the book! This guy is called **The Ebon Hunter**. He was basically the Keeper of Vows' bodyguard.

Jake: This is the Keeper of Vows' traveling outfit! He's disguised as a monk! Although his tentacle feet and teeth might be a giveaway to any passerby.

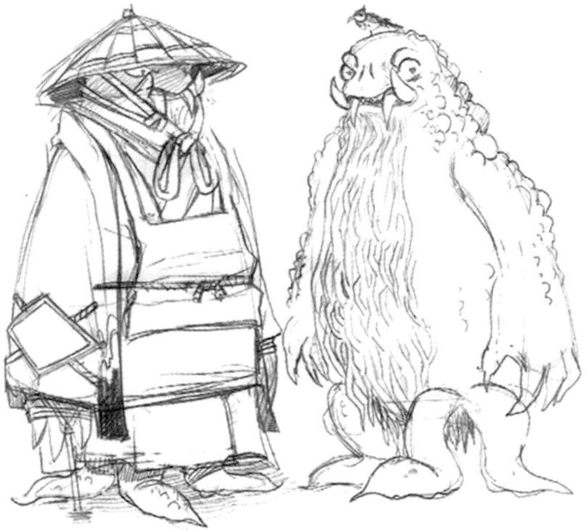

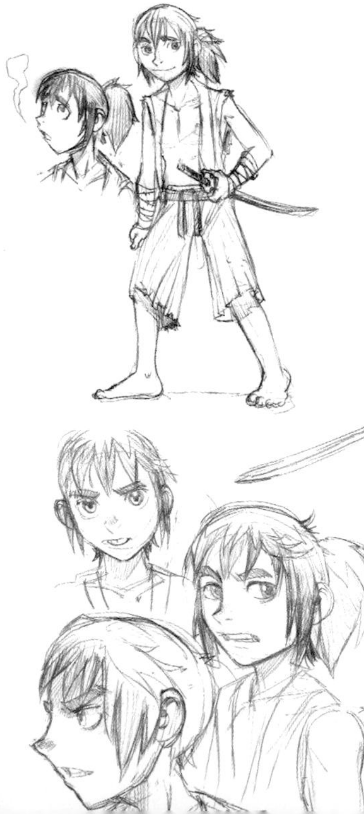

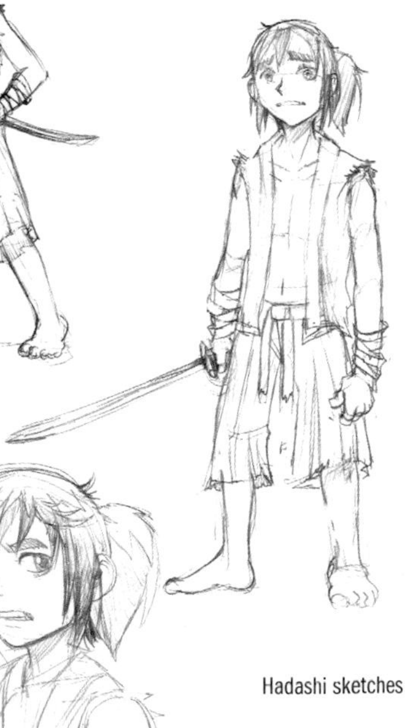

Hadashi sketches

Lola sketches

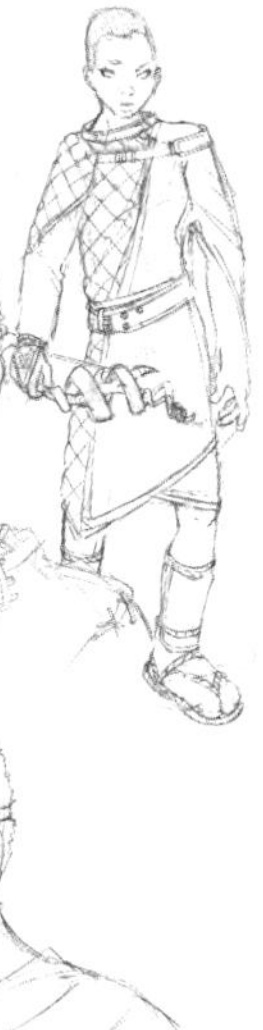

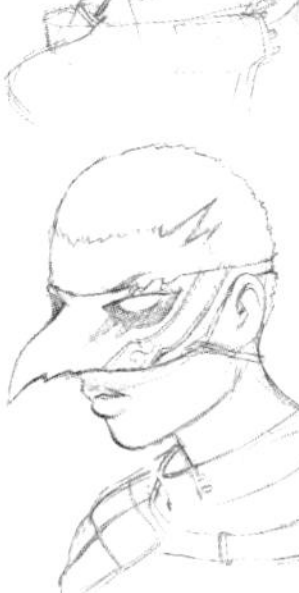

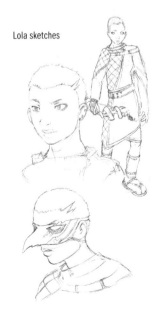

Megane sketches

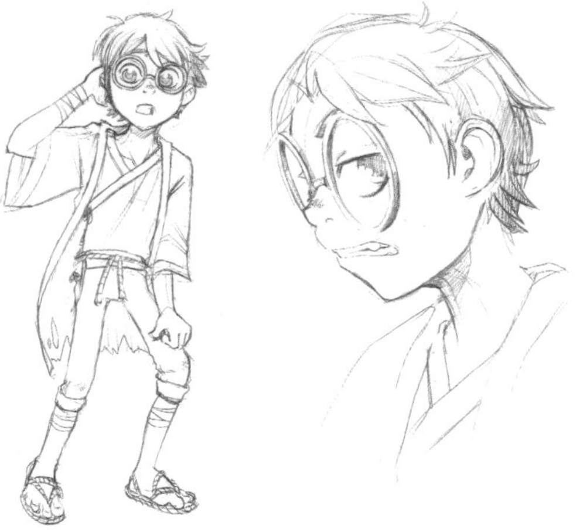

Jake: Tenmaru is my favorite character to draw in the book

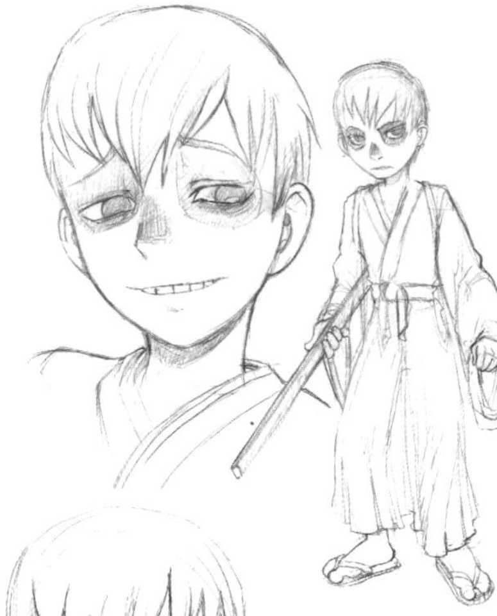

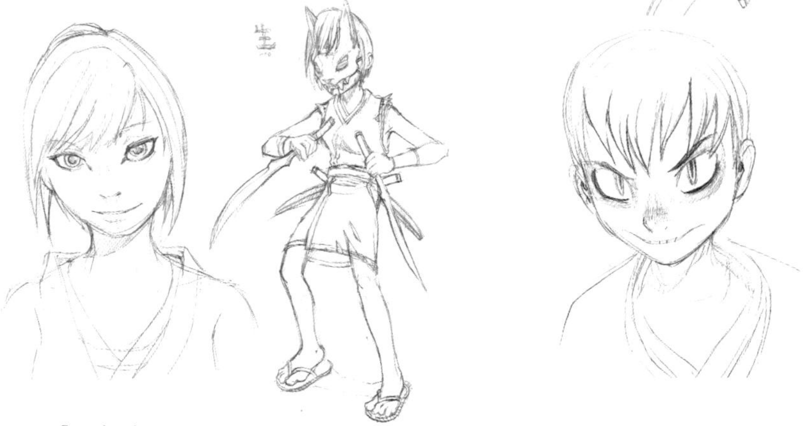

Frau sketches

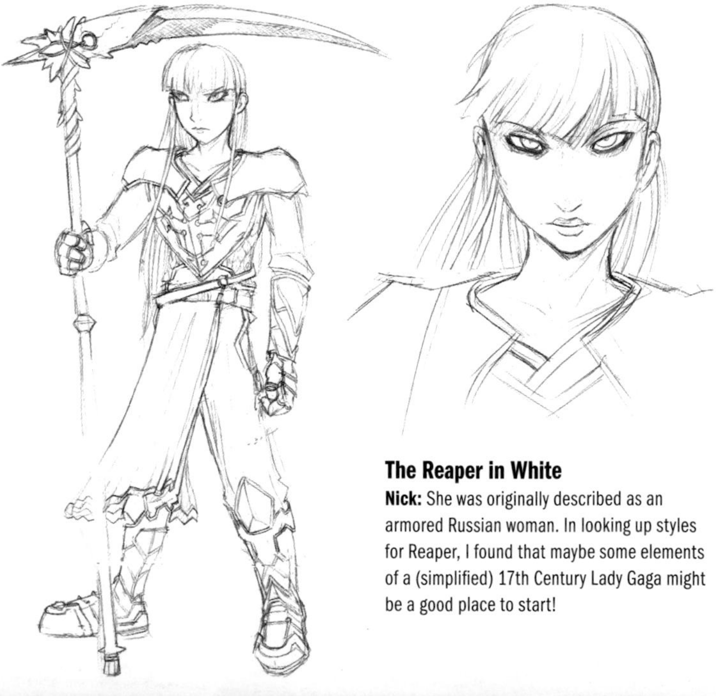

The Reaper in White

Nick: She was originally described as an armored Russian woman. In looking up styles for Reaper, I found that maybe some elements of a (simplified) 17th Century Lady Gaga might be a good place to start!

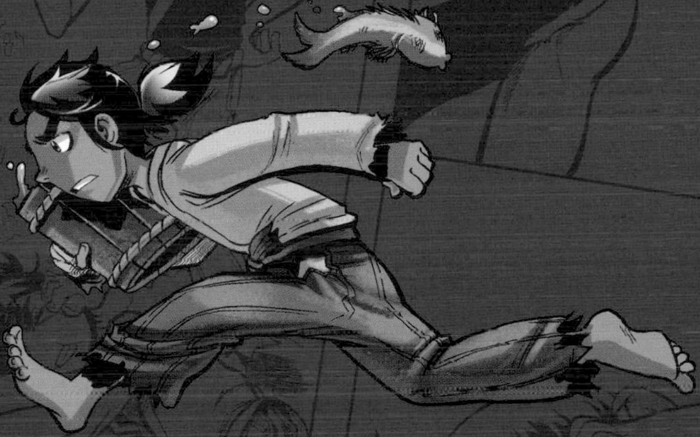

Jake Myler

HOPELESSLY ADDICTED TO COFFEE AND DESPISING SUNLIGHT, IT MAKES PERFECT SENSE THAT JAKE MYLER SETTLED DOWN IN SEATTLE, WASHINGTON. JAKE HAS ILLUSTRATED THE GRAPHIC NOVEL *UNDERTOWN*, WHICH WAS LATER SYNDICATED IN NEWSPAPERS WORLDWIDE. HE HAS ALSO WORKED AS A COVER ARTIST, PENCILLER AND COLORIST FOR MANY DISNEY, PIXAR AND HENSON PROPERTIES AS WELL AS DRAWING INTERIORS FOR A SERIES OF *FINDING NEMO* COMICS.

MORE BOOKS FROM

ONI PRESS

MEGAGOGO, VOLUME 1

By Wook-Jin Clark
176 pages, softcover, black and white interiors
ISBN 978-1-62010-117-9

1
MEGAGOGO
WOOK JIN CLARK

BLACK METAL OMNIBVS

By Rick Spears & Chuck BB
472 pages, softcover, black and white interiors
ISBN 978-1-62010-143-8

RICK SPEARS CHUCK BB
BLACK METAL

SCOTT PILGRIM COLOR HARDCOVER, VOL. 1: PRECIOUS LITTLE LIFE

By Bryan Lee O'Malley
192 pages, hardcover, color interiors
ISBN 978-1-62010-000-4

SCOTT PILGRIM 1
SCOTT PILGRIM'S PRECIOUS LITTLE LIFE
BY BRYAN LEE O'MALLEY
COLOR EDITION

WET MOON, VOL. 1: FEEBLE WANDERINGS

By Ross Campbell
176 pages, softcover, black and white interiors
ISBN 978-1-932664-07-2

wet moon
book 1: feeble wanderings
by ross campbell

BUZZ!

By Ananth Panagariya & Tessa Stone
176 pages, softcover, 2-color interiors
ISBN 978-1-62010-088-2

BUZZ!
ANANTH
TESSA

SHARKNIFE, VOLUME 1: STAGE FIRST

By Corey Lewis
144 pages, softcover, black and white interiors
ISBN 978-1-934964-64-4

COREY LEWIS
SHARKNIFE

SUPERPRO K.O., VOLUME ONE

By Jarrett Williams
256 pages, softcover, black and white interiors
ISBN 978-1-934964-41-5

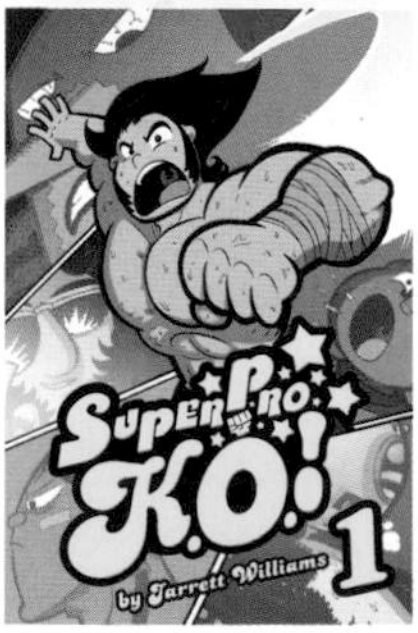

SuperPro K.O.!
by Jarrett Williams
1

COSTUME QUEST: INVASION OF THE CANDY SNATCHERS

By Zac Gorman
56 pages, hardcover, full color interiors
ISBN 978-1-62010-190-2

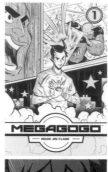

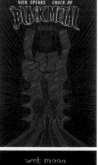

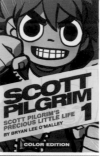

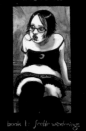

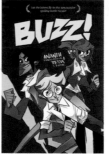

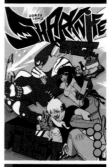

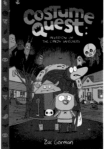

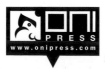

Costume Quest:
INVASION OF THE CANDY SNATCHERS
Zac Gorman

ONI PRESS
www.onipress.com

For more information on these and other fine Oni Press comic books and graphic novels, visit www.onipress.com.

To find a comic specialty store in your area, call 1-888-COMICBOOK or visit www.comicshops.us.